GETTING IT RIGHT

GETTING IT RIGHT

THE MANAGER'S GUIDE
TO BUSINESS COMMUNICATION

A. D. ADEY
&
M. G. ANDREW

1990
JUTA & CO, LTD

First published in 1990

Copyright © Juta & Co, Ltd
PO Box 14373, Kenwyn 7790

ISBN 0 7021 2453 2

Printed and bound by Creda Press, Solan Road, Cape Town.

FOREWORD

Management in South Africa faces many problems in the nineties and in the twenty-first century. One of the most crucial is the communication problem: in a multi-cultural society, interpersonal, cross-cultural, and group communication is one of the most important management skills.

This book, *Getting it Right*, is a much-needed text that concentrates on business communication skills. The target readership is managers at any level, management students, and those studying for diplomas or degrees in business-related subjects. The book covers the syllabuses of the diplomas of various professional institutes, and in particular the syllabus for the Communication course of the Diploma in Business Administration examined by the South African Institute of Management.

The book is not, however, intended to be only a textbook; it is rather a practical guide on how to communicate in business. The book starts with general communication theory before applying the theory to cross-cultural, group, and organizational communication. Then follow three chapters on language that attempt to capture the essence of correct English without being pedantic or technical; the chapters on time (tenses) and number (explaining the unique concept of number in the English language) should be of particular value to speakers of English as a second language. The last six chapters deal with the oral, written, and non-verbal modes. Besides a chapter on written skills in sales, marketing, advertising, and promotion, there is a chapter on non-verbal communication which includes a particularly valuable section on graphic presentation, which should be of assistance to those who have difficulty with economic, statistical, or mathematical diagrams.

In the end, this book is more like an introduction to business than a book about theoretical communication. Management, marketing, advertising, and industrial relations are approached from the perspective of business communication in such a way that readers will either be introduced to these aspects of business or will be reminded of their training in these disciplines.

Each chapter has a useful summary of the important concepts and terms dealt with in the chapter, as well as application of the principles in the form of case studies and questions that test the understanding of these principles. The authors plead for a case-study approach to learning rather than the limited 'Business English' approach to written communication, which is common in most examinations.

The authors are both involved in management, education, and communication. Professor David Adey is the Director of the Bureau for University Teaching at the University of South Africa and is a Member of the South African Institute of Management; he is a well-known author and editor. Mr

Mick Andrew is currently the National Chairman of the South African Institute of Management and is a Fellow of the Institute; he is the Director of Studies of the Damelin Education Group.

I recommend this book to students, trainee-managers, aspiring managers, and managers in South Africa with the hope that it will do much to improve managers' communication skills in our multi-cultural society.

M. COWLEY, F.S.A.I.M.
Executive Director
South African Institute of Management

April 1990

TABLE OF CONTENTS

Chapter 1
COMMUNICATION AT WORK 1
COMMUNICATION MODELS 2
TERMINOLOGY AND CONCEPTS 9
APPLICATION 10

Chapter 2
THE 4 A's OF COMMUNICATION 17
STEPS IN THE COMMUNICATION PROCESS 18
    Attention 18
    Apprehension 19
    Assimilation 20
    Action 20
TERMINOLOGY AND CONCEPTS 21
APPLICATION 21

Chapter 3
BARRIERS TO EFFECTIVE COMMUNICATION 25
THE BARRIERS 26
    Noise 26
    Differing Perceptions 27
    Language Problems 28
    Inconsistencies in Communication 29
    Differences in Status 30
    Distrust 31
    Emotional Communication 31
    Apathy 32
    Resistance to Change 32
OVERCOMING BARRIERS TO COMMUNICATION 33
THE IMPORTANCE OF LISTENING 34
TERMINOLOGY AND CONCEPTS 36
APPLICATION 37

Chapter 4
CROSS-CULTURAL COMMUNICATION 39
BASIC SOCIOLOGICAL CONCEPTS ABOUT CULTURE 40
CROSS-CULTURAL PROBLEMS 42

PROCEDURES FOUNDED ON VALUES ACCEPTABLE TO ONE
CULTURE ONLY 43

COMPLEXITIES AND PROBLEMS OCCURRING IN CROSS-
CULTURAL INTERACTION 44

BEHAVIOUR THAT CAUSES CROSS-CULTURAL
MISCOMMUNICATION 47

OVERCOMING BARRIERS TO CROSS-CULTURAL
COMMUNICATION 48

BRIDGING CULTURAL GAPS IN THE WORKPLACE 50

TERMINOLOGY AND CONCEPTS 50

APPLICATION .51

Chapter 5
GROUP COMMUNICATION 53

INTRODUCTION 54

SMALL INFORMAL GROUPS 54
    Family Groups 54
    Friendship Groups 55
    Work Groups .56

SMALL GROUP STRUCTURE 57
    Communication Networking 57
    Affective Relations Structures 61
    Power Structures 63
    Leadership Structures 65

THE LEADERSHIP GRID MIRROR 66

FORMAL GROUPS 67

TERMINOLOGY AND CONCEPTS 69

APPLICATION .70

Chapter 6
COMMUNICATION IN THE BUSINESS ORGANIZATION 75

INTRODUCTION 76

THE FORMAL ORGANIZATION 76
    Line Authority 80
    Staff Authority 83

COMMUNICATION SYSTEMS 85
    Vertical Communication 85
    Lateral or Horizontal Communication 86
    Diagonal Communication 87
    Contracting Communication Network 88
    Informal Communication 89
    External Communication 89

CONCLUSION .90

TERMINOLOGY AND CONCEPTS 90

APPLICATION 91

Chapter 7
THE CONCEPT OF TIME IN ENGLISH **93**

INTRODUCTION 94
TIME NOW AND THE PRESENT 94
    Exercise 1 95
    Exercise 2 97
TIME JUST BEFORE THE PRESENT 98
    Exercise 3 101
TIME THEN 103
TIME BEFORE THE PAST 104
THE PAST TENSES AND REPORTED OR INDIRECT SPEECH 105
    Exercise 4 105
FUTURE TIME 106
TIME JUST BEFORE THE FUTURE 108
THE FUTURE-IN-THE-PAST 109
    Exercise 5 109
CONDITIONAL AND UNREAL TIME 110
    Exercise 6 111
CONCLUSION: AUXILIARY VERBS 112
TERMINOLOGY AND CONCEPTS 114
APPLICATION 115

Chapter 8
THE CONCEPT OF NUMBER IN ENGLISH **117**

THE CONCEPT OF NUMBER 118
COUNTABLE AND UNCOUNTABLE NOUNS AND THE USE OF
THE INDEFINITE ARTICLE 118
THE CONCEPT OF NUMBER AND THE RULE OF CONCORD
BETWEEN THE SUBJECT AND THE VERB 125
OTHER WORDS THAT ILLUSTRATE THE CONCEPT OF NUMBER
IN ENGLISH 129
TERMINOLOGY AND CONCEPTS 131
APPLICATION 131

Chapter 9
THE CONCEPT OF CORRECTNESS **135**

INTRODUCTION 136
TEN RULES OF CORRECT ENGLISH 136
    The Correct Case of the Pronoun 136
    The Correct Use of the Noun in the Possessive Case 140
    The Correct Use of the Participial Phrase 141

The Correct Use of *and* 142
The Correct Use of the Comma 144
The Correct Use of the Colon 146
The Correct Positioning of Related Words 147
Correct Spelling 148
Correct Word Division 148
The Correct Use of the Passive Voice 149

CONCLUSION: AN ENGLISH USAGE ALPHABET 149

TERMINOLOGY AND CONCEPTS 158

APPLICATION 159

REFERENCES 161

Chapter 10
MODES (MEDIA SYSTEMS): PREPARATION 163

INTRODUCTION 164

AUDIENCE ANALYSIS 164
Demographic Profile 164
Family Life Cycle Profile 165
Social Class Profile 166
Lifestyle or Psychographic Profile 166
Consumer or Buyer Behaviour Profile 166

THE ORGANIZATION OF THE INFORMATION 167
Media Selection 167
Gathering Information 168
Drafting 168
Revising 169
Editing 170

FORMS OF COMMUNICATION 171
Friendly/Expressive 171
Polite and Courteous 171
Entertaining 171
Informative 172
Instructive 172
Complaining 172
Persuasive 172

CONCLUSION 175

CONCEPTS AND TERMINOLOGY 175

APPLICATION 176

Chapter 11
MODES (MEDIA SYSTEMS): ORAL COMMUNICATION 179

INTRODUCTION 180

FACE-TO-FACE CONVERSATIONS 180
Interviewing 180
Negotiating 189
Consulting 190

MEETINGS 193
    Preparation 193
    Different Types of Meetings 194
    Procedure at Meetings 196
    The Role of the Chairman 201
    The Role of the Secretary 202

PUBLIC SPEAKING AND SPEECHES 203
    Acting 203
    Delivery 204
    Entertainment 205
    Presentation 206
    Theme 207

TELEPHONE CONVERSATIONS 207

CONCEPTS AND TERMINOLOGY 210

APPLICATION 212

Chapter 12
MODES (MEDIA SYSTEMS): WRITTEN COMMUNICATION
READING SKILLS 215

INTRODUCTION 216

SCANNING 216

SKIMMING 217

COMPREHENSION 217

CRITICAL ANALYSIS 228

CONCLUSION 229

CONCEPTS AND TERMINOLOGY 230

APPLICATION 230

Chapter 13
MODES (MEDIA SYSTEMS): WRITTEN COMMUNICATION
GENERAL BUSINESS WRITING SKILLS 235

INTRODUCTION 236

PRÉCIS (SUMMARIES) 236

TELEGRAMS 240

TELEXES 241

FAX MESSAGES 241

EXPANSION OF NOTES INTO AN ACCEPTABLE WRITTEN
FORMAT 242

ESSAY WRITING 242
    Preliminaries 242
    Components of the Essay 243
    More about Paragraphing 253
    Concluding Remarks about Essay Writing 255

LETTER WRITING 257

    Layout 258
    Different Types of Letters 262
CURRICULA VITAE 290
    Personal Details 291
    Education 291
    Work Experience 291
    References 292
    Publications, Research, Public Addresses, etc. 292
    Present Salary 292

MEMORANDA AND NOTICES 292

REPORTS 293

NOTICES, INVITATIONS, AGENDAS AND MINUTES OF MEETINGS . 307
    Notices 307
    Invitations 308
    Agendas 309
    Minutes 310

FINAL COMMENTS ON WRITING 312

CONCEPTS AND TERMINOLOGY 312

APPLICATION 313

Chapter 14
MODES (MEDIA SYSTEMS): WRITTEN COMMUNICATION
SALES, MARKETING, ADVERTISING AND PROMOTION **318**

INTRODUCTION 318

SALES LETTERS AND PERSUASIVE WRITING 320

QUESTIONNAIRES AND SURVEYS 318

ADVERTISEMENTS 328
    Press 329
    Outdoor Advertising 332
    Direct Mail and Sales Letters 336
    Print at Point-of-Sale 338
    Other Forms of Copywriting and Creative Work 341
    Conclusion on Advertisement Writing 342

PRESS RELEASES 342

CONCEPTS AND TERMINOLOGY 346

APPLICATION 346

Chapter 15
MODES (MEDIA SYSTEMS): NON-VERBAL COMMUNICATION . . . **347**

INTRODUCTION 348

KINESICS 348

PROXEMICS 353

PARALINGUISTICS 359

GRAPHICS 360

Introduction 360
Shapes, Pictures, Symbols, Photographs 361
Examples and Illustrations 364
Figures, Charts and Diagrams 365
The Use of Graphics in Statistics and Economics 369
Graphical Representation 381
Graphic Presentation of Data 387
Special Graphic Representations of Statistical Data 394
THE USE OF AUDIO-VISUAL MEDIA 400
Concluding Remarks about Preparing Effective Visuals 403
TERMINOLOGY AND CONCEPTS 404
APPLICATION 405

REFERENCES **411**

1

COMMUNICATION
AT WORK

GOALS OF THE CHAPTER

If we are to get communication right or make it work, we need some theoretical knowledge of the communication process. By the end of this chapter you should be able to:

❑ understand the process of communication better
❑ develop models of communication
❑ know some of the terminology used in communication theory
❑ criticize and analyse communication at work

COMMUNICATION MODELS

To make communication work - to get it right, in other words - requires a **sender** (or a source of the communication) and a **receiver** (or a destination to which the communication is sent). The sender may direct his communication into the void, to an inanimate object, to God, or even to himself, but there is always a destination. This most basic form of communication is called *intra*personal communication and is very important. *Inter*personal communication involves other people, but intrapersonal communication is mainly concerned with communication for the benefit of the sender. It relieves his tensions, hurts, irritations, and anxieties and can be very important as a preparation for interpersonal communication. If a manager used intrapersonal communication more, he would select and sort his ideas more satisfactorily before transmitting messages to others. He would control his emotional responses and formulate his message with greater clarity. Intrapersonal communication is the essence of thought processes, meditation, and prayer, and its benefits have been recognized down the centuries. In the hustle and bustle of business, however, managers tend to ignore these benefits.

The most basic communication then, is:

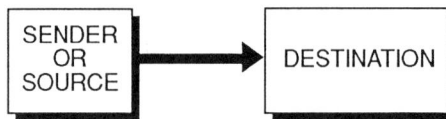

```
┌─────────┐              ┌──────────────┐
│ SENDER  │              │              │
│   OR    │─────────────▶│ DESTINATION  │
│ SOURCE  │              │              │
└─────────┘              └──────────────┘
```

Model 1

This kind of communication does not have to pay much attention to the type of language or the method of communication. It may be a grunt or a shout or a meaningless swearword. It is basic in that we are like an animal communicating without the need to be fully understood or like a person completely alone on a desert island talking to his surroundings or like a traveller in a foreign land talking a language that no-one else understands. Fortunately - or unfortunately, as we shall see later - this most basic form of communication, even if it is not fully intelligible, can be partly understood and is very important in understanding communication at work. (We shall study non-verbal communication and its importance later.)

Let us suppose that our communication is a little more advanced. We try to express our communication in a way that someone else will understand. There is likely to be more control of language and more effort on the part of the speaker or communicator. He thinks of *how* to communicate, *how* to put across his message. He may use a language or a series of signs intended to transmit his message to another. He **encodes** or makes use of a **code** (see next page).

```
┌──────────┐         ┌──────────┐         ┌──────────────┐
│  SENDER  │         │          │         │              │
│    OR    │────────▶│   CODE   │────────▶│ DESTINATION  │
│  SOURCE  │         │          │         │              │
└──────────┘         └──────────┘         └──────────────┘
```

Model 2

A traveller in Italy who knows no Italian but wants to order at a restaurant may use his hands to show he wants to eat what the person sitting at the next table is eating. He is encoding his message even though he uses no words. He realizes that, if he uses English, the waiter will not understand him and therefore he desperately attempts to encode his communication to his waiter by using signs.

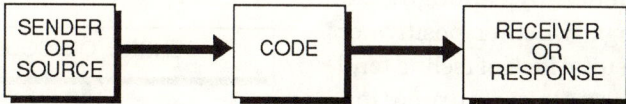

```
┌──────────┐         ┌──────────┐         ┌──────────────┐
│  SENDER  │         │          │         │   RECEIVER   │
│    OR    │────────▶│   CODE   │────────▶│      OR      │
│  SOURCE  │         │          │         │   RESPONSE   │
└──────────┘         └──────────┘         └──────────────┘
```

Model 3

Do we now understand what communication is all about? By no means. What happens if the sender's code has been misinterpreted? Perhaps he wanted a plate of spaghetti but the waiter brings him bread, because the person at the next table is eating both bread and spaghetti and the waiter has decoded his communication in a different way by bringing him the bread only. Has communication taken place? Yes, because there has been a sender, a code, and a receiver who has responded. But the communication has not been *successful* communication. It is faulty communication, but communication has nevertheless taken place because there has been a source, a code, a receiver, and a **response**. (This response has commonly been called feedback, but there is no reason to use jargon when we have a perfectly good word like response.)

To understand the process of communication better we need to expand our model further:

```
┌─────────┐   ┌──────────┐   ┌──────┐   ┌──────────┐   ┌──────────┐
│ SENDER  │   │ SENDER'S │   │      │   │RECEIVER'S│   │ RECEIVER │
│   OR    │──▶│ABILITY TO│──▶│ CODE │──▶│ABILITY TO│──▶│    OR    │
│ SOURCE  │   │  ENCODE  │   │      │   │  DECODE  │   │ RESPONSE │
└─────────┘   └──────────┘   └──────┘   └──────────┘   └──────────┘
```

Model 4

This may still give us faulty communication, but we have at least progressed to the realization that communication depends on the sender's ability to encode the message and also on the receiver's ability to decode the message. What are the requirements for good encoding and good decoding? Knowledge, past experiences, feelings or emotions, and attitudes all affect our ability to encode or decode successfully. **Knowledge** of another's language, knowledge of the subject-matter of the communication, general education, background - all these play their part. An experienced communicator will probably code or decode better than an inexperienced one, but **experience** involves more than experience of communication: we are thinking of experience of human relations, experience of life in its broadest sense. **Feelings or emotions** play their part because if the sender or the receiver is choked with feelings of hatred or pride or indignation he is unlikely to be able to code or decode successfully. Feelings need not, of course, be negative: feelings of love or sympathy may help the encoding or decoding. Generally, though, excessive feelings, whether positive or negative, or a total lack of feeling tend to distort good communication through too much excitement or through apathy. In all communication the control that **selecting and sorting** of one's ideas promotes is important when encoding or decoding. **Empathy** with the other person's background is vital: we shall deal with this in more detail under cross-cultural communication. **Attitudes** are the result of one's education and upbringing and culture, and these can cause barriers to communication if the sender's attitudes are completely different from the receiver's. Again awareness of differences, and selecting and sorting ideas before communicating can assist one's ability to encode or decode messages effectively.

We can therefore develop our model further (model 5).

There is, however, more to be said about the middle box CODE. So far we have discussed the sender's and the receiver's ability to encode or decode the message. Now we need to

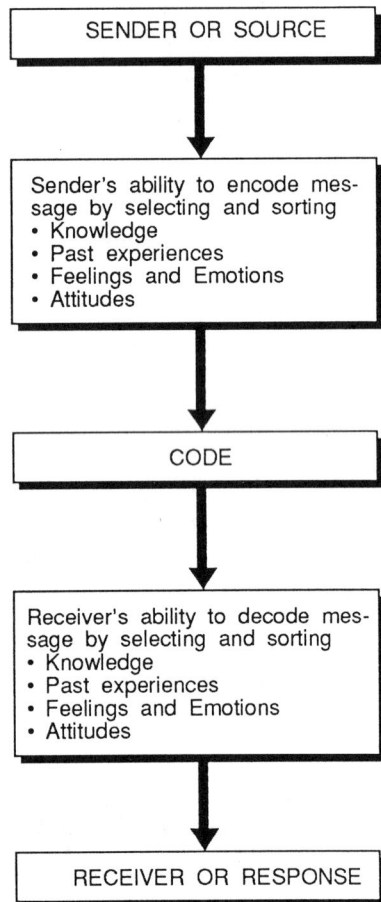

```
┌─────────────────────────────┐
│     SENDER OR SOURCE        │
└─────────────────────────────┘
              │
              ▼
┌─────────────────────────────┐
│ Sender's ability to encode  │
│ message by selecting and    │
│ sorting                     │
│ • Knowledge                 │
│ • Past experiences          │
│ • Feelings and Emotions     │
│ • Attitudes                 │
└─────────────────────────────┘
              │
              ▼
┌─────────────────────────────┐
│            CODE             │
└─────────────────────────────┘
              │
              ▼
┌─────────────────────────────┐
│ Receiver's ability to decode│
│ message by selecting and    │
│ sorting                     │
│ • Knowledge                 │
│ • Past experiences          │
│ • Feelings and Emotions     │
│ • Attitudes                 │
└─────────────────────────────┘
              │
              ▼
┌─────────────────────────────┐
│   RECEIVER OR RESPONSE      │
└─────────────────────────────┘
```

Model 5

think of the code itself. The sender of any communication has many choices to make when encoding a message. Will he use speech, writing, symbols, non-verbal signs? Will he arrange his words, whether spoken or written, or symbols or non-verbal signs in a particular way? Will he shout, speak quietly, sing, record, speak over an intercom system, use a microphone? Or will he use a letter, a memorandum, a report, an advertisement, a book, a poster, an audio-visual system like a video, or a graphic means? Will he adopt a particular body posture? Will he use his hands? Will he adopt a particular facial expression? These are some of the questions the sender can ask when encoding a message. We do not say that every sender of a message asks these questions or that it is necessary or advisable to ask them in a self-conscious way, but practice in asking these questions will allow him to make the right choices intuitively. Like a good sportsman or a good actor, a good communicator must practise skills so that they become natural and unconscious when he is called upon to act.

The **medium** of communication the sender chooses is his means of communication. Will he use verbal or non-verbal communication? If verbal, then will it be spoken or written? If spoken, will it be an interview, a meeting, a telephone message, a recording or a video? If an interview, what kind of interview? If a meeting, will it be formal or informal? If written, will it be a letter, a memorandum, a report, an advertisement, a poster with words, a graphic design with words? If non-verbal, will it be a picture, a poster without words, a chart, a film without words, or a piece of music? All these questions concern the choice of medium.

The **channel** of the communication is the route or direction in which the message is going to travel. Some experts on communication theory refer to the channel as the method of transmission and seem to treat medium and channel as a spoken message, as the voice, the radio, the television, or the telephone. They refer to the channel for a written message as paper, a telegram, a telex, or a fax. Some speak of the channel

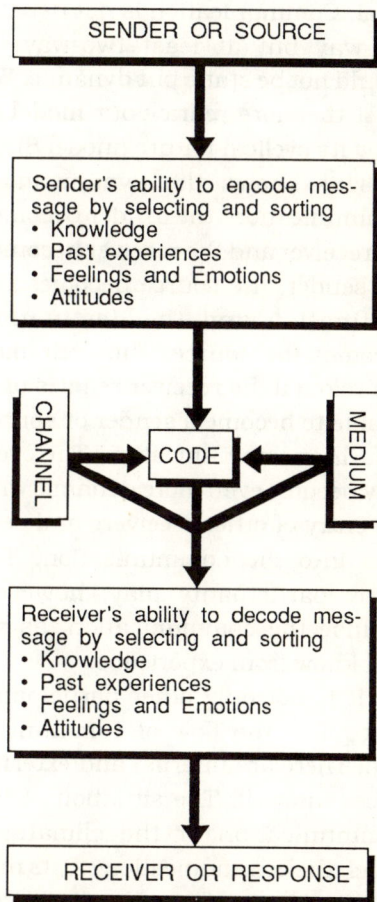

```
┌─────────────────────────────────────┐
│          SENDER OR SOURCE            │
└─────────────────────────────────────┘
                  │
                  ▼
┌─────────────────────────────────────┐
│  Sender's ability to encode mes-     │
│  sage by selecting and sorting       │
│  • Knowledge                         │
│  • Past experiences                  │
│  • Feelings and Emotions             │
│  • Attitudes                         │
└─────────────────────────────────────┘
                  │
   ┌────┐         ▼          ┌──────┐
   │CHANNEL│──▶ ┌──────┐ ◀──│MEDIUM│
   └────┘       │ CODE │     └──────┘
               └──────┘
                  │
                  ▼
┌─────────────────────────────────────┐
│  Receiver's ability to decode mes-   │
│  sage by selecting and sorting       │
│  • Knowledge                         │
│  • Past experiences                  │
│  • Feelings and Emotions             │
│  • Attitudes                         │
└─────────────────────────────────────┘
                  │
                  ▼
┌─────────────────────────────────────┐
│        RECEIVER OR RESPONSE          │
└─────────────────────────────────────┘
```

Model 6

of vision or sound. In business communication the channels of communication are usually divided into formal or informal channels. The formal channels are downward, horizontal, or upward directions of communication, while informal channels are gossip, the grapevine, brainstorming, suggestion schemes or some other form of communication that allows anonymity and makes disciplinary action against the people using these channels difficult.

Our model is becoming more complicated, but it is almost complete (model 6).

At either end of our linear model more information needs to be given. The communication process starts with a need to communicate. This impetus could be a **sensation** that impresses itself upon the sender and that causes him to respond to the **stimulus**. Similarly, when the message reaches the receiver, it is in the form of a sensation or stimulus to which he responds by way of interpretation or reconstruction of the idea he receives (model 7).

Our model of the communication process should not be linear but cyclical. Communication is not usually one-way but at least two-way. It should not be static but dynamic. We must therefore redraw our model to show its cyclical nature (model 8).

This shows the dynamism of communication: the sender becomes the receiver and the receiver becomes the sender; the source becomes the destination and the destination becomes the source. The cycle may be broken if the receiver refuses or is unable to become a sender or source of further communication. The cycle may become even more dynamic with the entry of other receivers and senders into the communication. Too many participants may, however, confuse the communication, as we well know from experience.

It is not only other participants that affect the flow of communication. There are internal and external forces, as well. The situation of the communication or the climate in which the communication exists may cause all sorts of complications that filter or distort the message. It may be that there is traffic noise that dis-

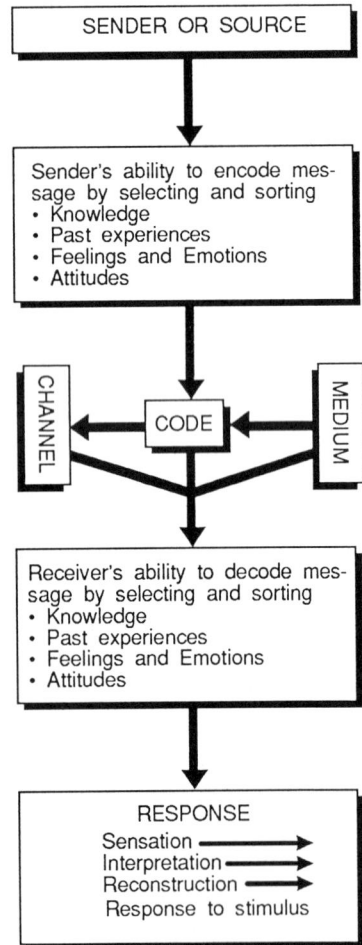

Model 7

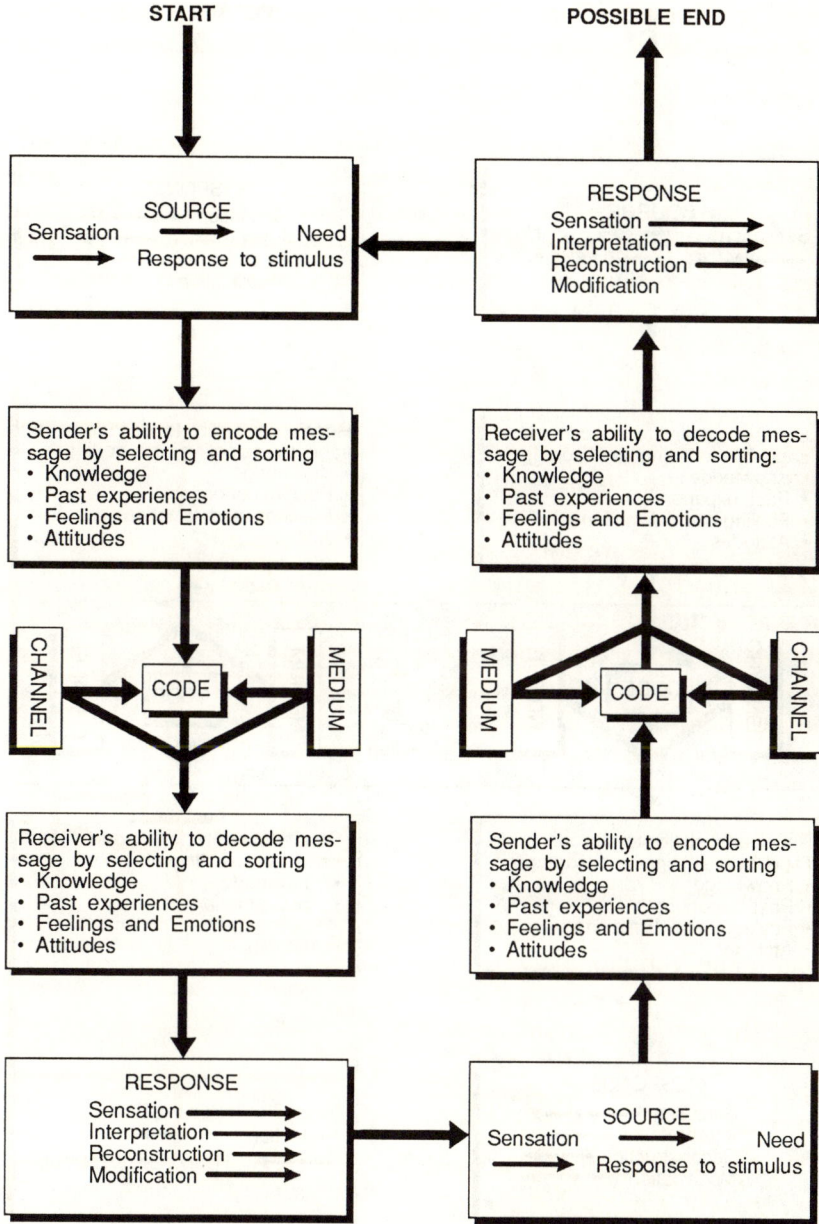

START   POSSIBLE END

```
SOURCE                          RESPONSE
Sensation ────▶ Need            Sensation ──────▶
────▶ Response to stimulus      Interpretation ──▶
                                Reconstruction ──▶
                                Modification
```

```
Sender's ability to encode mes-     Receiver's ability to decode mes-
sage by selecting and sorting       sage by selecting and sorting:
 • Knowledge                         • Knowledge
 • Past experiences                  • Past experiences
 • Feelings and Emotions             • Feelings and Emotions
 • Attitudes                         • Attitudes
```

```
CHANNEL ──▶ CODE ◀── MEDIUM        MEDIUM ──▶ CODE ◀── CHANNEL
```

```
Receiver's ability to decode mes-   Sender's ability to encode mes-
sage by selecting and sorting       sage by selecting and sorting
 • Knowledge                         • Knowledge
 • Past experiences                  • Past experiences
 • Feelings and Emotions             • Feelings and Emotions
 • Attitudes                         • Attitudes
```

```
RESPONSE                            SOURCE
Sensation ──────▶                   Sensation ────▶ Need
Interpretation ──▶                  ────▶ Response to stimulus
Reconstruction ──▶
Modification ────▶
```

Model 8

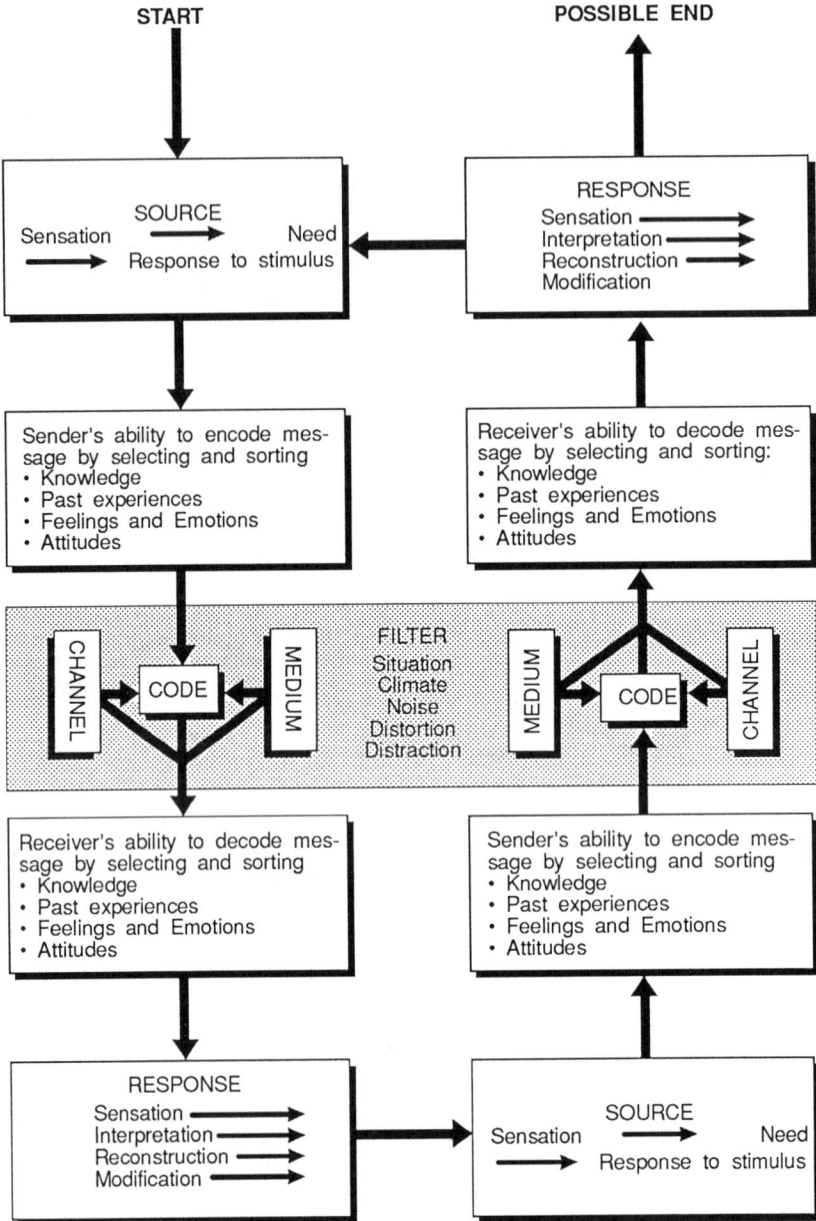

START   POSSIBLE END

SOURCE
Sensation → Need
→ Response to stimulus

RESPONSE
Sensation ———→
Interpretation ———→
Reconstruction ———→
Modification

Sender's ability to encode mes-
sage by selecting and sorting
• Knowledge
• Past experiences
• Feelings and Emotions
• Attitudes

Receiver's ability to decode mes-
sage by selecting and sorting:
• Knowledge
• Past experiences
• Feelings and Emotions
• Attitudes

CHANNEL   CODE   MEDIUM   FILTER
Situation
Climate
Noise
Distortion
Distraction
MEDIUM   CODE   CHANNEL

Receiver's ability to decode mes-
sage by selecting and sorting
• Knowledge
• Past experiences
• Feelings and Emotions
• Attitudes

Sender's ability to encode mes-
sage by selecting and sorting
• Knowledge
• Past experiences
• Feelings and Emotions
• Attitudes

RESPONSE
Sensation ———→
Interpretation ———→
Reconstruction ———→
Modification

SOURCE
Sensation → Need
→ Response to stimulus

Model 9

torts the message. Or a faulty telephone. It may be that one of the participants is anxious because he has an appointment that he is being prevented by the conversation from keeping. It may be that it is excessively cold or hot. It may be that one of the participants is ill. The status of one of the participants may be such that it affects the flow of the communication. The tone of voice of one of the participants may annoy the other: it may be angry or uninterested or boring. Perhaps one has a distracting characteristic, such as a twitch or a continual cough. Perhaps one has an embarrassing feature of dress, an undone button, a skew tie, an odd sock, or a plunging neckline. Perhaps the dress or the hairstyle is outrageous. All these cause 'noise' that affects the communication.

We must, therefore, place in the middle of our model the **filters** that distort the reception of the message (model 9).

TERMINOLOGY AND CONCEPTS

Make sure that you know what these terms and concepts mean. If you don't know, go back over the chapter and find them.

1. INTRAPERSONAL COMMUNICATION
2. INTERPERSONAL COMMUNICATION
3. MODEL
4. SENDER OR SOURCE
5. DESTINATION
6. CODE
7. RECEIVER OR RESPONSE (FEEDBACK)
8. ENCODING OR DECODING
9. KNOWLEDGE
10. PAST EXPERIENCES
11. FEELINGS OR EMOTIONS
12. ATTITUDES
13. SELECTING AND SORTING
14. MEDIUM
15. CHANNEL
16. SENSATION
17. NEED
18. STIMULUS
19. LINEAR
20. CYCLICAL
21. STATIC
22. DYNAMIC
23. 'NOISE'
24. FILTER
25. CLIMATE

APPLICATION

In order to apply what we have learnt we shall study two case-studies. The first we shall analyse, and the second can be used as an exercise.

CASE STUDY 1

The scene is the foyer of a marketing enterprise. The managing director, Mr Rumble, comes out of his office and goes towards the receptionist, Miss Maud Awesome, who is trying to answer calls and attend to customers.

Mr Rumble calls across the foyer, 'Maud, have the sales figures arrived yet?'

Maud is already flustered and is on the telephone, so she does not answer immediately.

Mr Rumble waits impatiently, tapping his fingers on the counter.

Maud finishes her call and goes on serving a customer. Mr Rumble, who has given specific instructions that customers always come first, cannot contain his irritation: 'Maud, have the sales figures arrived?'

'Which sales figures?' asks Maud.

'I told the sales director to tell the sales managers to let me have the sales figures by 10 this morning.'

'So why should *I* have them then?'

'Well, I haven't received them yet and I was wondering whether they had left them with you,' said Mr Rumble.

'Oh,' said Maud and went on serving the customers.

'Well, get a memo to each sales manager and tell them I need them immediately,' he said, walking off.

Now let us look at our Model 9 again and apply it to our case study:

QUESTION 1: What is the sensation or need that starts the flow of communication?
ANSWER: Mr Rumble needed the sales figures and felt anxious at not having them. He responded to this stimulus.

QUESTION 2: What knowledge, past experiences, feelings and emotions, and attitudes did Mr Rumble have to sort through in responding to the need to have the sales figures?

ANSWER: He knew that he needed the sales figures and that he had asked the sales director for them. From past experience he would have recognized whether his orders were usually carried out promptly or not. If they were, he would be surprised at not having the sales figures. If his orders were not usually carried out promptly, he would realize the need to insist on getting them. His feelings and emotions included annoyance at not having the sales figures, pique that his order had not been carried out, and concern that the lack of sales figures might cause a delay in providing vital management information. His attitudes stemmed from years of business culture: he was used to efficiency and he had demonstrated it in his own business life and that is why he was proud to have reached the top.

QUESTION 3: How well did Mr Rumble select and sort these ideas? Which should he have made clearer and which should he have omitted?
ANSWER: He did not do very well. He should have mentioned that he had asked the sales director to ask the sales managers to let him have the figures and that, since he had not received them, he was wondering whether the receptionist had perhaps received them. He should have expressed his concern but not his annoyance and pique (especially not in the hearing of the customers in the foyer). He did not think of his target audience, Miss Awesome, and he spoke as if she were responsible for the sales figures, not the sales managers and the sales director. He was too excited about his own affairs and unconcerned about Miss Awesome and the customers. He relied on his status as managing director to give him the right to interrupt.

QUESTION 4: How did he encode his message?
ANSWER: He used a common language, English. He used a question whereas he could have explained before asking a question.

QUESTION 5: What can be said about the destination of his message or the channel he used?
ANSWER: Mr Rumble should have directed his message to the sales director or to the sales managers, not to the receptionist. Earlier he had directed his message correctly when he asked the sales director to ask the sales managers for their figures, although he could possibly have gone direct to the sales managers.

QUESTION 6: What channel of business communication did Mr Rumble use?
ANSWER: He used downward communication, i.e. from top management to lower levels in the organization.

QUESTION 7: What medium of communication did Mr Rumble use to the sales director and to the receptionist?
ANSWER: He used face-to-face, spoken communication. This was a correct medium to use because the information was needed in a hurry. His last exasperated order to the receptionist to send a memorandum is faulty for two reasons: (1) it is not the receptionist's work to send a memorandum to the sales director and the sales managers; (2) it is a time-consuming business to send a memorandum. He should have used spoken communication for speed, possibly the internal telephone system.

QUESTION 8: Was Mr Rumble successful with his first attempt at communication?

ANSWER: No, Miss Awesome did not answer. It is not clear whether she had heard him but there was no visible response.

QUESTION 9: What is the situation or climate through which Mr Rumble's communication was filtered? Was there any 'noise', distortion, or distraction?
ANSWER: The situation was not conducive to good communication. Miss Awesome was very busy both on the telephone and with customers. That is why she did not reply immediately. She was obeying orders to attend to customers first. There was too much distraction for her to hear and respond.

QUESTION 10: How did Mr Rumble communicate his impatience?
ANSWER: He used non-verbal communication as he tapped his fingers on the counter.

QUESTION 11: Does Mr Rumble's second question to Maud improve his message in any way?
ANSWER: At least he is closer to Maud now, but his irritation has increased: he is not only irritated that the sales figures have not arrived but he is also unreasonably irritated with Maud. He repeats the same question and has not tried to improve his message in any way.

QUESTION 12: How did Maud try to decode Mr Rumble's message and encode her response?
ANSWER: She knew nothing about the sales figures. Her background and present position gave her no knowledge or past experience of sales figures. She was probably offended by Mr Rumble's calling across the foyer at her, his impatience, and his irritability. Her attitude was probably one of resentment that he had been so impolite to her and the customers. Nevertheless she controlled her resentment and asked a question for clarification of the message. She was a better communicator than Mr Rumble, but then it is easier to choose a medium and channel and code in response to a sender than it is to start a communication.

QUESTION 13: How did Mr Rumble decode Maud's question and encode his response?
ANSWER: Not as well as Maud did. He expressed his irritation at not having the figures, but again to the wrong person. His status did not allow him to apologize to Maud.

QUESTION 14: Does Maud's second question show she interpreted Mr Rumble's words wisely?
ANSWER: She could have become subservient because of her inferior status, her lower level of education and experience, and her fear. Instead she came to the point and forced Mr Rumble to say what he should have said at the beginning. She selected the pertinent question, 'So why should *I* have them then?' from all the other possibilities. Her response is fairly insolent and risked further annoyance on Mr Rumble's part.

QUESTION 15: How does Mr Rumble's third message improve on his previous two?
ANSWER: In his third message he came to the real point. If he had said this at the beginning, he would have been expressing his uncertainty and merely exploring a possibility. He would not have been excited and would have given due consideration to the person who was his audience. But he is obviously a person who relies on status and dignity and does not like losing face. His third communication is more controlled. He does lose some face, but this is his fault entirely. He has behaved badly.

QUESTION 16: How did Maud's last remark bring the communication to an end?
ANSWER: Her 'Oh' is significant. There was really nothing further she could do or say. It was obvious that she did not have the sales figures and that Mr Rumble should go elsewhere in his investigations. Her minimal response is a controlled way of saying this without becoming cheeky. She then returned to her work since there was no way she could help.

QUESTION 17: Comment on the effectiveness of Mr Rumble's last statement.
ANSWER: It appears this is a last-ditch attempt to regain his status. He threw out a nonsensical order, again in the wrong direction and using the wrong medium. He did not wait for a response and walked off.

QUESTION 18: Use diagrams to show the communication that takes place.
ANSWER: See next page.

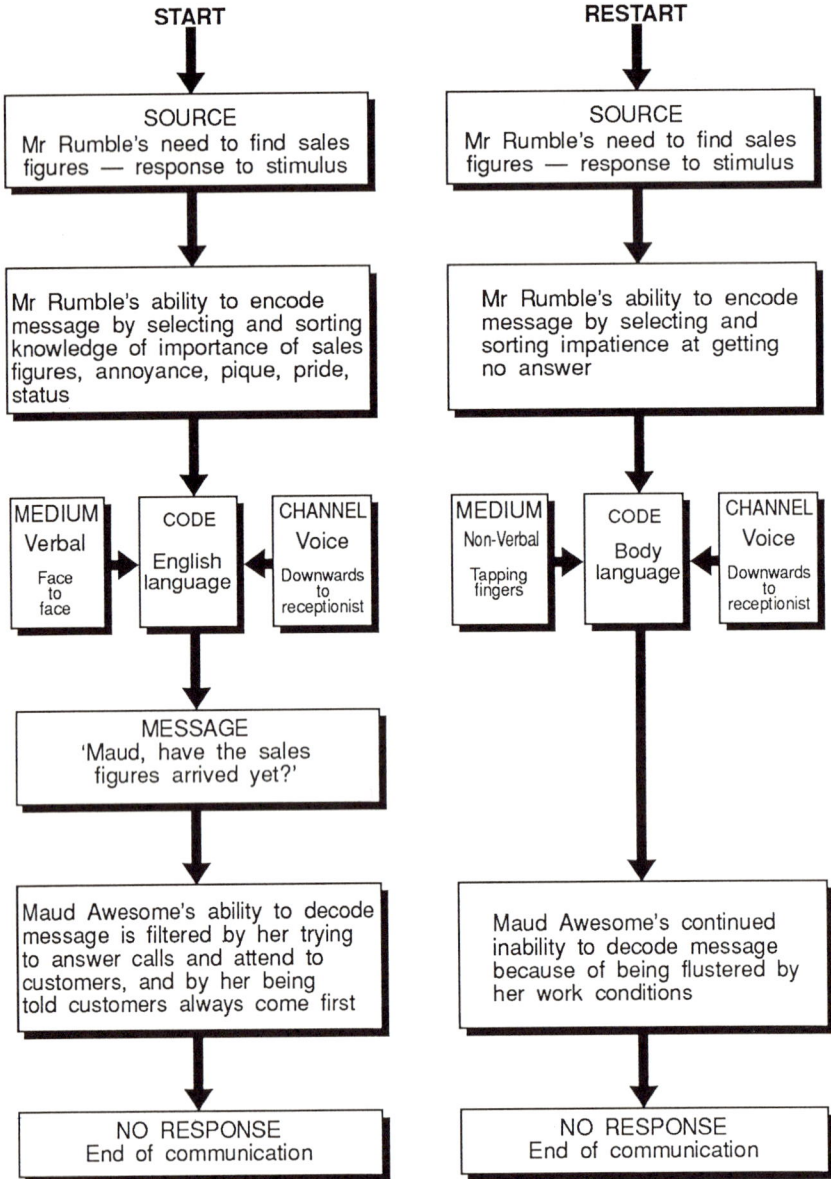

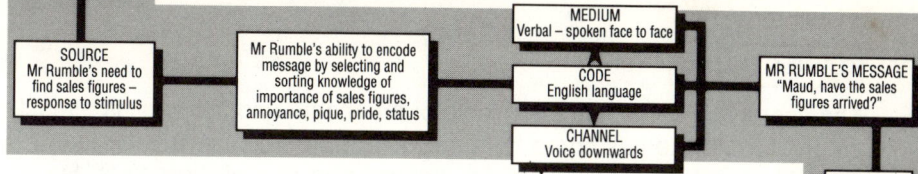

SOURCE
Mr Rumble's need to find sales figures – response to stimulus

→ Mr Rumble's ability to encode message by selecting and sorting knowledge of importance of sales figures, annoyance, pique, pride, status

MEDIUM
Verbal – spoken face to face

CODE
English language

CHANNEL
Voice downwards

MR RUMBLE'S MESSAGE
"Maud, have the sales figures arrived?"

Maud's ability to decode

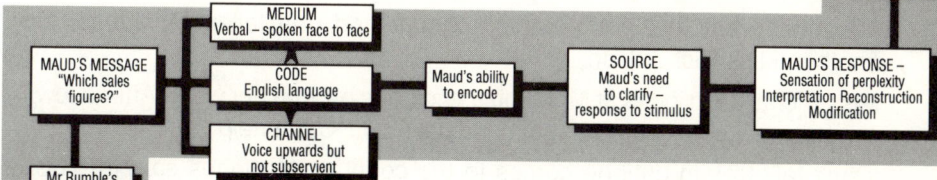

MAUD'S MESSAGE
"Which sales figures?"

MEDIUM
Verbal – spoken face to face

CODE
English language

CHANNEL
Voice upwards but not subservient

Maud's ability to encode

SOURCE
Maud's need to clarify – response to stimulus

MAUD'S RESPONSE –
Sensation of perplexity Interpretation Reconstruction Modification

Mr Rumble's ability to decode

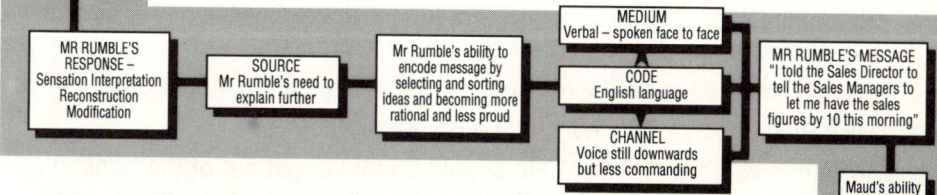

MR RUMBLE'S RESPONSE – Sensation Interpretation Reconstruction Modification

SOURCE
Mr Rumble's need to explain further

Mr Rumble's ability to encode message by selecting and sorting ideas and becoming more rational and less proud

MEDIUM
Verbal – spoken face to face

CODE
English language

CHANNEL
Voice still downwards but less commanding

MR RUMBLE'S MESSAGE
"I told the Sales Director to tell the Sales Managers to let me have the sales figures by 10 this morning"

Maud's ability to decode

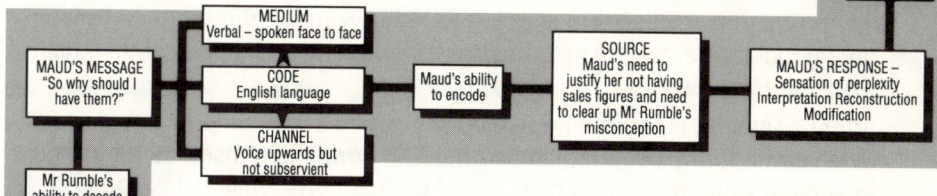

MAUD'S MESSAGE
"So why should I have them?"

MEDIUM
Verbal – spoken face to face

CODE
English language

CHANNEL
Voice upwards but not subservient

Maud's ability to encode

SOURCE
Maud's need to justify her not having sales figures and need to clear up Mr Rumble's misconception

MAUD'S RESPONSE –
Sensation of perplexity Interpretation Reconstruction Modification

Mr Rumble's ability to decode

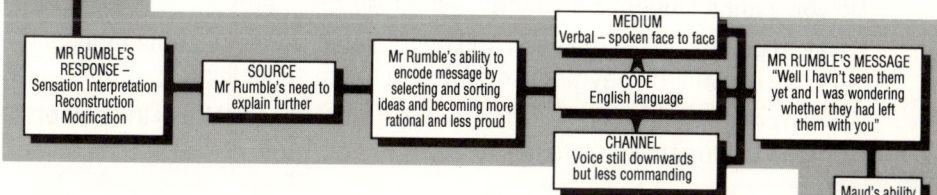

MR RUMBLE'S RESPONSE – Sensation Interpretation Reconstruction Modification

SOURCE
Mr Rumble's need to explain further

Mr Rumble's ability to encode message by selecting and sorting ideas and becoming more rational and less proud

MEDIUM
Verbal – spoken face to face

CODE
English language

CHANNEL
Voice still downwards but less commanding

MR RUMBLE'S MESSAGE
"Well I haven't seen them yet and I was wondering whether they had left them with you"

Maud's ability to decode

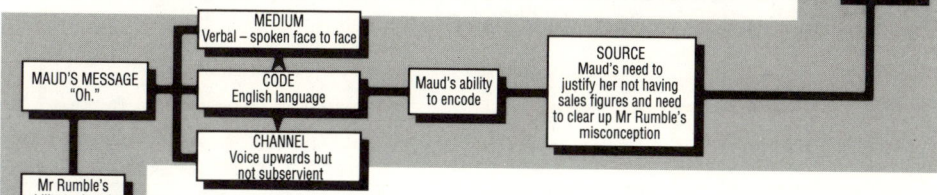

MAUD'S MESSAGE
"Oh."

MEDIUM
Verbal – spoken face to face

CODE
English language

CHANNEL
Voice upwards but not subservient

Maud's ability to encode

SOURCE
Maud's need to justify her not having sales figures and need to clear up Mr Rumble's misconception

Mr Rumble's ability to decode

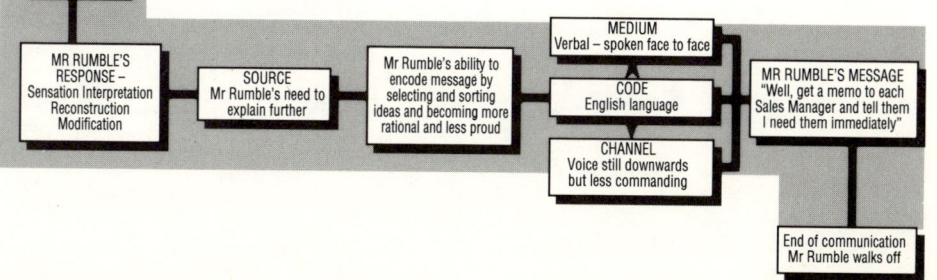

MR RUMBLE'S RESPONSE – Sensation Interpretation Reconstruction Modification

SOURCE
Mr Rumble's need to explain further

Mr Rumble's ability to encode message by selecting and sorting ideas and becoming more rational and less proud

MEDIUM
Verbal – spoken face to face

CODE
English language

CHANNEL
Voice still downwards but less commanding

MR RUMBLE'S MESSAGE
"Well, get a memo to each Sales Manager and tell them I need them immediately"

End of communication
Mr Rumble walks off

CASE STUDY 2

The scene is a bank. It is the middle of the month and the bank is almost empty. Mr Mkhize has come from a rural area to enquire about a loan to send his son to university. He sits patiently on one of the chairs. He is shabbily dressed.

'I wonder what that hobo wants,' commented one teller, Mr Jones, to another, Miss Richardson.

Miss Richardson looks at Mr Mkhize and goes on with her work. After a few minutes she looks his way again and calls out, 'Can I help you?'

'Don't talk to him until he comes to the counter,' Mr Jones said to Miss Richardson.

Mr Mkhize rises and walks to the counter. He speaks with a heavy accent. 'May I please speak to a somebody about my problem.'

'"A somebody!" He can't even speak properly,' muttered Mr Jones.

Miss Richardson asks kindly, 'What is your problem, sir?'

'How can you call him "Sir"? He should be told to get out of the bank, It's this kind of person who lowers the tone of this bank,' complained Mr Jones.

'My problem is my son. He is going to the university. But I am not having the financial wherewithal to subsidize his educational pursuits,' Mr Mkhize explained hesitantly.

'What pompous language he uses! Why can't he talk simply? I'm glad he didn't come to my counter,' commented Mr Jones to himself as he turned to serve a well-dressed client who had walked confidently to his counter.

'Do you want a student loan, then?' asked Miss Richardson.

'Can you be able to tell me each and every detail, because I am fearing if I can cope up with the payments on my own to the schooling?'

'We can certainly help you, sir. Please take a seat, and I shall ask the person in charge of student loans to talk to you.'

Using the questions and answers on Case Study 1 as your guide, analyse the communication at work in this Case Study 2.

2

THE 4 A's OF COMMUNICATION

GOALS OF THE CHAPTER

There are four steps in the communication process. By the end of this chapter you should be able to:

❑ describe the steps in the communication process
❑ apply these steps to any business communication
❑ criticize and analyse the communication process with reference to these steps

STEPS IN THE COMMUNICATION PROCESS

If a manager is to get it right when he communicates, he needs to realize that successful communication, though it may start with himself, is not a one-way process at all. Response or **reciprocity** is the essence of communication. Communication is reciprocal. A manager is not an oracle who pronounces the infallible truth. He is a human being involved with other human beings. He is not only a giver of information; he is also a person who has to understand the other person and who has to work hard to get the other person to understand him. Communication is as much a matter of human relations as it is a matter of conveying knowledge or information. Perhaps the contribution of human relations is more important in communication than the contribution of providing knowledge. We have grown up in an educational system that expects the teacher or lecturer to pronounce while the unfortunate students are expected to listen or take notes. It is natural, therefore, that when we become managers we tend to assume the role of knowledgeable teachers who require others to listen to us. Such natural or immature behaviour has little place in business, in the classroom, or in the lecture room.

If we use the four A's of communication we should be able to correct this immaturity in communication. These are the four steps in the communication process:
1. ATTENTION
2. APPREHENSION
3. APPRECIATION
4. ACTION

Attention

Some of us may be used to the army command, 'Attention!' The officer or sergeant realizes that the soldiers must come to attention before they can respond effectively. Of course, we are not here suggesting an authoritarian attitude in gaining the attention of the person with whom we are communicating. But gaining attention is vital. (Later when we come to persuasive communication we shall deal with the AIDA approach to persuasion: Attention, Interest, Desire, Action. This approach is similar to the 4 A's approach we are now discussing.)

To gain the attention of the person with whom we wish to communicate, we must respect his circumstances. Factors which prevent his giving us his attention may be the type of 'noise' we discussed in the previous chapter - traffic noises, a faulty telephone, anxiety, excessive heat or cold, status, an irritating tone of voice on our part, or distracting mannerisms or dress. Or it may be pressure of work or family problems. Part of gaining the attention of the receiver of any communication is the human greeting or the question about the other person's state of health or family or work circumstances. Too often, though, such introductions are so false and stereotyped that they have little or no purpose. Do we really want to know how the other person is?

Haven't we ourselves so often responded, 'Fine' to the question, 'How are you?' even though we have been ill? We know the other person is not really concerned and wouldn't want us to go into detail about how we are really feeling. How often is the patter so false that we don't even wait to hear the answer before we get on to what we see as the main purpose of the communication? If we are to gain attention, however, we need to identify with the person where he is now and how he is now so that he will be more inclined to identify with us where we are now and in our present need. In a very human sense this is what the Christian doctrine of the incarnation is all about: the need to identify and not merely to expect the other person to respond because of our higher status.

We must have the good grace not to interrupt but to involve ourselves in the other person's work or human condition and to involve him in our condition. Most downward communication from superior to subordinate does not include such involvement with the result that the superior often considers the subordinate stupid because he does not understand.

Of course, we must be realistic too and accept that much communication in business has to be of the downward kind and has to be brief because of its urgency. But, if the right human relationship has been developed in the past and the right tone of politeness and appreciation is used, attention can be secured even if we have to dispense with preliminaries and niceties because of an emergency.

Gaining the attention of the receiver requires preparation, whether that preparation is the result of years of experience and is largely unconscious or whether it is well thought out before the initial communication takes place. Gaining attention is not the brash salesman's ploy but is sensitivity to the other person and his circumstances.

Apprehension

What comes to our minds when we think of this word? Isn't it fear? Or an unhappy feeling about the future? But the word's primary meaning is understanding. The two meanings are very closely associated, and if we can bear in mind the connection and be sensitive to changing apprehension (fear) into apprehension (understanding), we shall be better aware of the psychology of communication. Sometimes we as managers are aware of the lack of understanding and we try to defend our inability to communicate by asking, 'Do you understand?' As we shall see when we come to interviewing skills in more detail, such a question is an unfair question. If there is any apprehension (fear) on the part of the receiver, he will not be honest and say, 'No.' He will say, 'Yes,' whether he understands or not.

This gaining the apprehension or understanding of the receiver is a difficult matter. But it is essential if communication is to be successful. Some managers will ask, '*What* do you understand?' rather than '*Do* you understand?' But even this very often creates the wrong kind of apprehension and becomes a threat. Apprehension is a very subtle part of the communication process.

If the relationship is right between the sender and the receiver, there should be indirect ways of ascertaining whether the apprehension is of the negative or the positive type. Discussion of *how* the message can be implemented (with a great deal of input from the 'receiver') would be the best way of ensuring that understanding has been achieved.

Assimilation

A person can understand a message but need not necessarily accept it or agree with it. He has not assimilated the idea into his own being.

Assimilation has three meanings: absorption into the body as with foods; becoming part of another social group or state; and becoming like someone else or another group. In communication all three apply. A receiver must assimilate the communication until it becomes part of himself. In this way the difference between different social groupings in business can be broken down. If a person assimilates an idea into himself he becomes one with the sender of the communication and this is the ideal result of communication. In business, participative management is often admired. Assimilation of an idea goes a long way towards ensuring participation among employees. The more real the communication that takes place, the more democratic does the business become.

The first, second and third steps in the communication process, Attention, Apprehension and Assimilation, show clearly how reciprocal a process communication is. The second and third steps involve the receiver of the communication in the message itself. Through the apprehension and assimilation steps the receiver has the chance to mould the message by questioning and clarifying and adapting the message until agreement is reached between the sender and the receiver about what the message actually is. It is through the reciprocal nature of communication that true learning takes place. Blind acceptance without participation leads to acceptance without conviction, similar to rote-learning in education. But the process of apprehension and assimilation allows for interpretation and discussion, which would easily lead to expansion and refinement of the original concept.

Action

The last step in the communication process is action. Unless communication results in some kind of action, it can easily remain abstract and theoretical. So many good ideas in business as well as elsewhere have resulted in sterile acceptance and agreement but have not been translated into action.

Once assimilation has taken place, there should be a natural desire on the part of the receiver to implement the idea, but again the manager needs to promote and encourage the required action and possibly to involve himself in the execution of the action plan. Support and facilitation are important aspects of the manager's involvement in this last stage of the communication process.

TERMINOLOGY AND CONCEPTS

1. RECIPROCITY
2. ATTENTION
3. IDENTIFICATION
4. APPREHENSION
5. UNDERSTANDING
6. ASSIMILATION
7. ACCEPTANCE
8. ACTION

APPLICATION

CASE STUDY 1

The manager, Mrs Brown, has decided that the working hours will be changed from 8.30 a.m.–5 p.m. to 8.00 a.m.–4.30 p.m. She therefore calls the foreman of the factory, Mr Jones, into her office. She is on the telephone when he arrives. It is an important telephone call and he hears her say, 'Yes, I will send the order immediately.' She puts the telephone down, but her mind is still on the order.

'Good morning, Mr Jones. How are you today? Please sit down. I want you to tell the workers in the factory that, as from the first of next month, the working hours will change. We shall start work at 8 and end at 4.30. Is this clear? Please tell all staff members concerned. Thank you. That will be all.'

Mr Jones, who has been trying to say something since she started speaking, leaves with a weak, 'Yes, Mrs Brown.'

CASE STUDY 2

The manager, Mrs Green, has considered changing the working hours from 8.30 a.m.–5 p.m. to 8.00 a.m.–4.30 p.m. She therefore calls the foreman of the factory, Mr Jackson, into her office. She is on the telephone when he arrives.

'Excuse me a moment,' she says to the person on the line. 'Mr Jackson, please take a seat. I won't be long.'

She finishes off her conversation.

'Thank you for waiting. That was rather an unexpected, urgent call about the Savilles order. Do you think it will be ready by this afternoon as promised?'

'Yes, I think so, Mrs Green. Everything's going according to plan.'

'That's good. I do appreciate your keeping to schedule. You know, the Savilles order is important to us.'

'Yes, I know. We've worked overtime to get it out on time.'

'Thanks again.... Mr Samuels told me your daughter is ill. How is she today?

'She's had to go to the doctor today. She may have to go to the hospital.'

'Oh, I am sorry. Please keep me informed and don't hesitate to take time off to see her.'

'Thank you, but we are very busy now.'

'Well, I'll get right down to the purpose of my asking you to come in to see me. What do you think of the idea of changing the working hours and starting and ending half an hour earlier each day?'

'I'm not sure. I haven't really thought about it before. Is there any reason for changing?'

'Well, I thought that finishing earlier would give everybody more time in the evening. I've noticed quite a few are very eager to go home earlier than 5 and there have been quite a few early leavers in the evening. The work rate seems to slow down considerably after 4.30.'

'Yes, I've noticed that too. But if we end at 4.30, don't you think it will slow down after 4?'

'Yes. That may be true. But do you think it's worth a try?'

'I know some people's transport won't get them here by 8.'

'What percentage would that be of the staff?'

'About half, I imagine.'

'Well, how would it be if half the staff started at 8 and finished at 4.30 and the other half started at 8.30 and finished at 5?'

'That might cause problems. Would you mind if I investigated the matter and reported back to you on Wednesday?'

'That's exactly what I was going to suggest to you. Perhaps you and I should draw up a questionnaire which we would ask the staff to answer.'

'Yes. That's a good idea. I'd also like to include some questions about our annual sports day.'

'All right.... As long as we keep the questionnaire short. Not more than ten questions. Let's meet together this afternoon, and we'll ask my assistant to take it down in shorthand.'

'If you don't mind, may we make it first thing tomorrow? There's the Savilles order....'

'Yes, of course. That's the most important thing at the moment. Tomorrow then at 8.30.'

'I'm usually in at 8. Could we make it then?'

'With pleasure. I'll see you at 8. Would you like to meet here?'

'Yes. Goodbye then. And thanks for the interest you show in my daughter's health.'

'I'm sure you'd do the same for me. Thank you. Goodbye.'

Compare and contrast the way each of these case studies uses the four steps in the communication process.

3

BARRIERS TO EFFECTIVE COMMUNICATION

GOALS OF THE CHAPTER

There are many barriers to effective communication. This chapter sets out to:

❑ analyse the barriers to effective communication
❑ overcome these barriers
❑ overcome bad listening habits
❑ encourage good listening skills

THE BARRIERS

In studying the communication process in Chapters 1 and 2 we have already been introduced to some of the barriers to effective communication. The most common barrier to effective communication is a cultural difference, a personality defect, or a physical defect in either the receiver or the sender of the message. Every person is different from any other. No one person has the same cultural, psychological, and biological components as another person. There are, of course, varying degrees of compatibility, but we can never assume that effective communication will automatically result: it would be better for us to assume that there are barriers and to try to work at overcoming them.

The main barriers are 'noise' (or interference or competition) during the communication process, differing perceptions, language problems, inconsistencies in communication, differences in status, distrust, emotional communication, apathy, and resistance to change. Let us deal with each one in turn.

Noise

We have already seen that 'noise' is any interference or disturbance that confuses the message or competes against communication. It may be literal noise: for instance, traffic noise, a faulty air-conditioning system, too much talking or heckling during a lecture or speech, an announcement on the intercom system, a blaring radio, a television set left on, a faulty line on the telephone, the continual crying of a child, continual coughing during an influenza epidemic, rustling of papers or sweet wrappings, or an interrupting telephone ring. These are easy enough to distinguish. Metaphorical noise would include competing demands upon a person's attention such as domestic problems an employee is experiencing, too many demands upon a person's time, feelings of insecurity, too much emotion or too little emotion, or distrust; in fact, any barrier can be considered noise in a figurative sense. A person's credibility may be suspect: if he is known to panic about almost every situation and sound the alarm on every occasion, soon the many false alarms will destroy his credibility and this will compete with the effective reception of his message of alarm. Sometimes subversive action is based upon this kind of dulling of reception: frequent bomb scares create either panic or indifference on the part of people hearing about these scares and after a series of false alarms people are totally unprepared when it is a real alarm. A manager who insists on every printing order being required ASAP (as soon as possible) and believes in management by crisis is an ineffective manager who should plan in a more efficient way: the printing department will eventually treat his orders as impossible to effect.

Differing Perceptions

As we have already said, each of us is unique: we see things differently from others. Speaking very literally, we can speak of differing standards of eyesight: a short-sighted person has different problems of vision from a far-sighted person or a normal-sighted person; blind or partially sighted people have their special problems. In the same way we can speak metaphorically of people seeing things differently. Look at the following drawings:

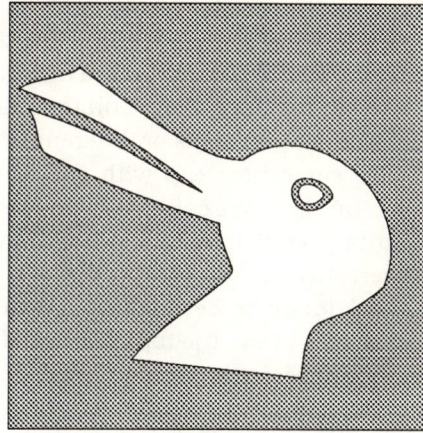

Figure 1

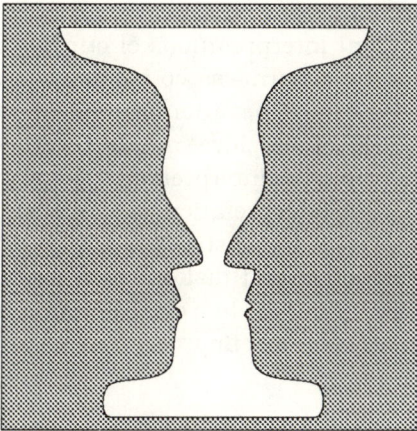

Figure 2

Figure 3

Figure 4

(From: D Krech, R. Crutelfield, and N Levison (1974), *Elements of Psychology*, Third Edition, New York, Alfred A. Kinorf)

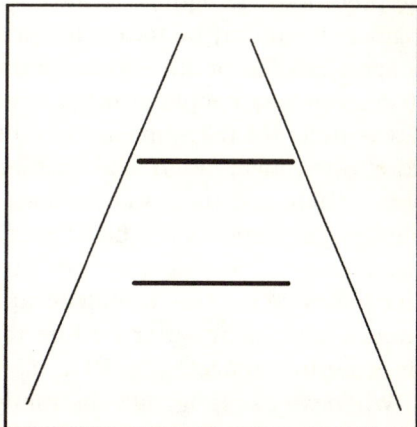

Figure 5

What do you see in figure 1? A bird or a rabbit or both? Or something different? What do you see in figure 2? A vase or two people looking at each other or both? What do you see in figure 3? The letter B or a 13 or both? What do you see in figure 4? A young woman or an old woman or both? Very often people of different ages or different backgrounds see these things differently.

The same happens with the way we interpret or see things with our understanding. We call this **interpretative perception**. Where there is only one interpretation of something and we can prove that there is only one answer, there is less of a problem.

Look for instance at figure 5. Which is the longer of the two parallel lines? Most of us will say the top one, but, if you take a ruler, you will see that they are equal in length. We can prove this and we speak of this as a verifiable fact. But not all perception can be proved right or wrong: it depends upon our interpretation. Knowing this will help us in our communication. We shall then try to convey our interpretation of reality accurately and to correct or understand interpretations different from our own.

In business we must be aware of different interpretations of our messages. What may appear to the speaker to be a harmless compliment to a woman employee may be regarded by her as an improper attempt at flirtation. What may appear to be harmless teasing of a fellow employee may be regarded by him as an insult. A deserved promotion may be interpreted by some as favouritism. The environment may alter the interpretation of behaviour: outspokenness or criticism may be interpreted as constructive in a buzz-group, but it may be interpreted as destructive and disloyal in a formal gathering. Certain jokes are acceptable and humorous in a closed group but may be inappropriate and in bad taste in an open meeting.

Language Problems

Most differences in perception are caused by differences in visual or spoken interpretations. Language is the basis of most communication. The type of language used may be totally misunderstood by people of different cultural backgrounds. In South Africa we use the phrase 'just now' to refer to the future, whereas people of other countries use it to mean what it actually states—*now*. If I tell someone to do something just now and I mean at the end of our conversation, the listener cannot be blamed for getting up and doing it there and then. Instructions that involve time can often be vague: a manager gives an order to be effected 'as soon as possible' or 'at your earliest convenience'; he is probably trying to be polite or unauthoritarian; but after three hours he may be fuming because his order has not yet been executed. It would have been better for him to say precisely what he wanted: 'I want this order to be effected by 10 a.m.'

When we use language abstractly there is much room for inference, i.e. for an assumption or interpretation on the part of the listener. **Abstraction** in language means that there is some area of vagueness, some lack of precision, some room for interpretation or inference on the part of the receiver. Obviously there are disadvantages and advantages in abstract language: managers who never allow interpretation and continually criticize others' inferences are dictatorial, whereas those who appreciate others' contributions are more tolerant. But there are some messages that need to be direct and precise and do not allow for interpretation. Such messages cannot be abstract and it would be a mistake on the part of the manager to be too tolerant of others' misinterpretation.

The use of **jargon** in communication often distorts a message. Users of jargon tend to assume that everyone understands the jargon, whereas this is seldom true. Doctors treating patients may use terms that patients do not understand but the patients are usually too polite or ignorant to ask what the terms mean. The use of jargon tends to blur communication and to make people feel excluded if they do not understand or to make people feel superior or included if they do understand. This leads to dishonesty on the part of listeners because they do not want to admit that they do not understand and that they are inferior or excluded. Salespeople often use jargon and this leads to misunderstanding on the part of buyers and dissatisfaction with the product they have bought.

The same applies to language that categorizes or **labels** people or things. Such words as *radical* or *reactionaries* and *conservatives* or *liberals* do not serve much purpose because they have widely different meanings according to their contexts. A person can be both radical and reactionary depending on the situation. The trouble with labels is that they tend to stick whether they are appropriate or not. The label *director* in a business context can be another confusing label: I can be a director of my own one-man business, but society equates the position of director with a large corporation and gives me a status that does not fit in with my limited business experience. Words that are used as labels, such as *intellectual* or *unintellectual*, confuse issues and are often meaningless.

Language may be deliberately misleading. Business policy includes the strategy of planned obsolescence, but it would be unwise to make this known to the buyer of a product. Salespeople deliberately avoid referring to this strategy of manufacturing. A buyer of an overhead projector or a photocopying machine is not warned on purchase that the machine cannot be used continuously during a working day: after the machine has been purchased and used for six months, the person servicing the machine explains that the machine has been overused and needs to be replaced. The owner of the machine then feels he has been misled and changes his supplier. All this arises from poor communication.

Inconsistencies in Communication

Such inconsistency in communication can also be involuntary. Often the spoken word conflicts with non-verbal behaviour or with the image that a communicator projects without his realizing it. Greetings can become so stereotyped that they become meaningless or offensive. We respond so mechanically that even though we are ill we may answer a person's 'How are you?' by saying 'Fine, thanks. And you?' without realizing what we are saying. We wonder how many doctors encounter this rather contradictory language from their patients.

In business the image projected by a careless receptionist or telephonist may distort the image the firm wishes to project. We need to see ourselves as others see us. This would make us more aware of our non-verbal behaviour and achieve consistency in our communication. It is all a matter of awareness and practice, as we shall see when we deal with non-verbal communication. We need to practise self-control and to become like actors who can play a role even if their personal circumstances are anything but ordered. This is difficult, of course, and probably accounts for the amount of stress in actors' lives, as well as in the lives of businessmen.

Differences in Status

Status has great importance in society. The regard a person is given by others affects the reception of his message. A minister of religion has a status of authority among his congregation; he may, however, be poorly regarded by people hostile to his religion. The status of a teacher may be high in developing countries but may be much lower in a developed country which may label him on the grounds that 'those who can, do; those who can't, teach'. In business, status tends to be based on the position to which a person has been elevated. Status does not depend, however, only on position; it also depends on the attributes a person demonstrates in his everyday dealings with others: if he acts in a way that is to be respected, he is shown respect and therefore has deserved his status. Most men can be called fathers and therefore in a sense have the status of fatherhood, but few fathers live up to the standards fatherhood requires and therefore do not deserve this status; consciously or unconsciously children may then diminish their regard and respect for their fathers.

There are therefore two types of status, the **nominal status** and the **real** or **deserved status**. Often the difference between the two is blurred. The father expects his status to be accepted even though he does not deserve it and the child may give token obedience even though he resents it. The same applies to the teacher. There is therefore a third type of status: the **perceived status** of the person, how a person is perceived by the other. This could at times be the nominal, at others the real status, and even a combination of the two.

This influences communication: the sender of a message is judged by the receiver, and this judgement affects the message itself. If the receiver respects the sender, he will be more inclined to accept the message. This can distort the message and become a barrier to effective communication, because it is no longer the actual message that is important but the perceived status of the sender. A manager who is perceived to be a manager only nominally may be judged to be hostile to the aspirations of the work force and to be speaking only on behalf of the owners of the enterprise; his communication may then be resisted even though the contents of the message are reasonable. The status of the receiver of a message is also important: if the manager perceives the receiver as a subordinate and not as a fellow worker who deserves respect, this perceived status will affect the way he communicates his message. If the receiver has a poor image of himself and sees his status as lowly, this will also affect his reception of the message: he may act resentfully or subserviently. This judgement of messages in terms of nominal or perceived status is a form of labelling or stereotyping and leads to problems in industrial relations.

Effective communication is promoted by real or deserved status being afforded to both the sender and the receiver of the message. What this means is recognition of each other's status as unique human beings and as participants in the communication process. This would involve empathy and not domination and would be based on mutual respect.

Distrust

Closely associated with status is distrust. Any signs of distrust in the communication process are barriers to communication. If either the receiver or the sender doubts the credibility of the other, suspicion will dominate the communication, and the contents of the message will be discounted. Two people who are constantly arguing will create a barrier of distrust. The same applies if there has been a history of broken promises. A person who has a string of degrees but is inefficient in his work or lacking in experience tends to be distrusted. Similarly, a person who shows no interest in the welfare of others is likely to be mistrusted. This barrier is closely linked with what we have described previously as inconsistency in communication. A record of inconsistent communication will lead to distrust.

Emotional Communication

We have already stated that emotions can be helpful or harmful in the communication where the emotions distort the message. We tend to react to the emotions, and the message is not communicated effectively. Typical reactions are aggressive or defensive responses. Too much emotion threatens people. This is particularly true in dealings between superiors and subordinates. Unless a background of acceptance has been established, a superior tends to be threatening and is inclined to be aggressive, and a subordinate tends to be threatened and defensive. Much of the confrontation between management and staff springs from emotional outbursts and lack of planning before the communication takes place.

We need to be realistic about excessive emotion in communication. The situation or context will determine whether the emotion is excessive or not. Great feelings of love on seeing a loved one for the first time in six months would not be excessive; in fact controlled emotions in this situation might be interpreted as lack of feeling. Sorrow at a funeral may be a similar case. In business there is often a situation where a great deal of emotion may be inevitable and warranted: if a customer or an employee continuously exceeds the bounds of reason and propriety, it may be necessary to meet his emotional behaviour with a high level of emotion. Sometimes this is the only level of communication possible. Often anger at the other person's unreasonable or improper behaviour may achieve a better result than calmness. The person involved in the communication needs to judge when a calm, rational approach needs to be replaced by an angry, emotional response. The initial result is often one of surprise on the part of the customer or the employee who thinks only he is entitled to display emotion, and the final result may be either further offence or - the desired result - a realization that he is being unreasonable. If further offence is caused, it is unlikely that the conversation would have ended differently anyway. Often a heated end to a conversation prompts an apology from the irate customer or employee at a later stage, and this gives the opportunity for more rational communication. Sometimes the angry response to anger or excessive emotion may lead to an immediate or speedy change for the better in the conversation. One has to be very experienced and sensitive to know when to change from an adult approach to a parent approach to the other person.

Apathy

Lack of any emotion is just as bad as too much emotion. Communication is promoted by controlled emotions such as enthusiasm, friendliness, concern and sympathy. It is distorted by indifference, unconcern and insensitivity. This barrier to business communication is often demonstrated by a lack of social responsibility on the part of a firm and an overriding obsession to achieve higher and higher profits for the owners.

Resistance to Change

There is so much change in twentieth-century society and there is likely to be even more in the twenty-first century. It is an unsettling factor to many, and an exciting one to others, but most of us fear change, and this applies particularly to older people or to insecure people. The advent of computerization has caused fear and distrust among many excellent staff members. This has led to reduced productivity and even resignation of staff who were once valuable assets to the firm. This can be attributed largely to poor communication of the changes and to lack of sympathy and training. It is a general rule for managers that change should be well planned: the greater the change, the longer should be the notice period before change is introduced. Sudden changes are disrupting and can cause chaos in the organization. A change of location may lead to resignations that cripple an enterprise. A transfer or the appointment of a new supervisor brings with it the need to adapt and often leads to resistance.

Besides careful planning and adequate notification of change, it will help to understand some of the negative reactions of people to change. Some people simply *avoid* change: they go on working or acting as if there has been no change. Others *reject* change: they do not take it seriously and see it as mere talk. Another approach is to *distort* or *subvert* the change: such people use subjective interpretations to try to ensure the change will be either minimized or maximized according to their own and not the firm's interpretations. All these reactions can cause friction in the workplace and need to be monitored very carefully. Sensitivity on the part of those administering the change is necessary, otherwise conflict will spread.

In South Africa changes in corporate culture will often lead to cross-cultural miscommunication and conflict among subcultures within the corporate structure. Resistance to a woman or to a black in a management position could have disastrous effects. Resistance to open canteens when for years they have been separated according to status or colour causes many problems. Resistance to a young person appointed to be in charge of more senior staff when in the past appointments have tended to be made on the grounds of seniority needs to be dealt with tactfully. The appointment of a member of an executive's family can be seen as unfair and resisted sullenly. Whereas management should carry out reforms as part of its social responsibility, it cannot be seen to be acting impetuously and insensitively.

OVERCOMING BARRIERS TO COMMUNICATION

We have already suggested ways of overcoming these barriers to communication, but here briefly are some more general ways of doing this:

1. *Use face-to-face communication* wherever possible and appropriate. People appreciate being communicated with on a one-to-one, face-to-face basis. There are opportunities for getting direct responses (or feedback) in a face-to-face situation, whereas written or group communication does not achieve this as easily.
2. *Be sensitive to the other person's background.* This requires a knowledge of and sympathy towards the other person's viewpoint, no matter how different it is to one's own.
3. *Use direct, unambiguous language.* The clearer and less abstract the message, the better it will be apprehended and accepted. Symbolic meanings of words must be carefully explained so that there is no confusion because of cultural differences.
4. *Use frequent repetitions.* Teaching requires frequent restatements and revision. Communication requires the same. Reinforcement of communication through written repetition of a face-to-face communication is useful. Follow-up is important to see that action follows apprehension and acceptance. (Sometimes repetition is referred to as redundancy;

because this sometimes has a negative connotation, we prefer the word 'reinforcement'.)

5. *Be supportive to counteract defensiveness.* Where it is clear that the message may not be totally appreciated or it may be resisted, continual support of the other in this difficult task would be helpful. A supportive approach should be adopted, rather than a judgemental approach. The more objective a description is and the less subjective or evaluative it is, the more supportive it will be. If communication is seen as controlling rather than problem-solving, a defensive reaction will result. Empathy rather than apathy or neutrality is important. Demonstration of the advantages of a particular course of action to the employees and not only to management may be necessary: in this way trust can be established. Communication that is based on equality rather than on superiority of the one over the other will help to overcome the barrier of defensiveness or status. Openness to suggestions from the other person will help to overcome the defensive attitude that one has all the answers and the other has just to shut up and listen.

6. *Be a good listener.* Two-way communication involves listening to and understanding the other person. This is so important that we need to give it more attention.

THE IMPORTANCE OF LISTENING

We have concentrated largely on the speaker and his words in communication. Listening is very important in face-to-face communication. The receiver of spoken communication has a responsibility to listen. How often does a person speak and we do not listen effectively? Listening is not passive, it is active. When a renowned scholar delivers a lecture, he expects his audience to listen actively. It is a demanding, sometimes painful, experience, but the more actively we listen, the more we shall benefit from the lecture. Many people become impatient with speech that requires effort: we are so used to mass communication that is aimed at the lowest common denominator that it is difficult for us to become creative listeners.

Listening to a lecture is, of course, part of learning. We subject ourselves to this type of communication, which is mostly one-way, because we have admitted we do not know enough about a subject or because we want to pass an examination or because we want mental stimulation. Sometimes we take notes when we are listening to a lecture, but this can be overdone: excessive note-taking becomes dictation-taking and does not involve our minds at work. This is why shorthand skills are not really an advantage in studying.

By listening to another we pay him a compliment; we show our respect; we make him feel that his contribution is appreciated. We all know how hurtful it is when we know people are not taking the trouble to listen to us. Listening is a matter of taking trouble. It is a learned skill, not one that comes easily. We have to overcome so many barriers in communication that we must learn skills of good listening and avoid bad habits that block communication.

Let us first deal with some of the bad habits of people who do not listen properly:

I They are *impatient* with speakers.

N They allow *noise*, literal or metaphorical, to make them lose their concentration.

A They do not make *allowances* for differences of perception, status, culture or personality.

P They *pretend* to listen but they are thinking of something else.

P They allow *peripheral* aspects such as a little mistake, a faulty projector or a speech defect to distort the communication.

L They are *lazy*.

I They are *impatient*, and *interrupt*.

C They do not listen to the *context* of the whole speech but only to facts that interest them.

A They become *anxious* about personal, selfish considerations.

B They are easily *bored*.

L They *lose* interest.

E They *end* the communication before it is finished.

As our acronym shows, these are INAPPLICABLE habits for good listening. We need to know about these bad habits not only so that we may avoid them but also so that we may be aware of them in other people and counteract them in our communication with bad listeners.

What then are good listening habits? We may summarize them in the one word SENSITIVE:

S We should be *sincere* towards the person to whom we are listening.

E We should *evaluate* the contents of the communication to prepare for a sensible, objective response.

N We need to pay attention to the speaker's *non-verbal behaviour* because it helps our understanding of the oral message.

S We should *summarize* in the form of a written or mental note to help us respond to the speaker.

I We should show active *interest* in the speaker's message.

T We should listen carefully to the *tone* of voice of the speaker because this helps us to understand better.

I We should *interact* with the speaker through supportive verbal or non-verbal responses.

V We need to show we *value* the speaker's contribution objectively and in an open-minded way.

E *Encouragement* is necessary so that the speaker feels appreciated.

If we are sensitive to what a speaker says, we are less likely to be subjective and self-centred and more likely to help a person express himself freely.

Interruptions, authoritative statements, and judgements tend to end communication, whereas encouragement and openness to alternative courses of action help a speaker to feel he is part of the decision-making process. Often speakers want their problems solved by someone else's decisions, but it is better for the person to be helped towards his own resolution of his problems. If a climate of sensitive openness exists, even silence becomes creative and unthreatening. When we are afraid of silences and abhor this vacuum, the climate is usually unfavourable for good communication.

TERMINOLOGY AND CONCEPTS

1. BARRIERS TO EFFECTIVE COMMUNICATION
2. NOISE (LITERAL AND METAPHORICAL)
3. DIFFERING PERCEPTIONS
4. INTERPRETATIVE PERCEPTIONS
5. LANGUAGE PROBLEMS
6. ABSTRACTION IN LANGUAGE
7. INTERPRETATION
8. INFERENCE
9. JARGON
10. LABELS
11. INCONSISTENCIES IN COMMUNICATION
12. IMAGE
13. STATUS
14. NOMINAL STATUS
15. REAL OR DESERVED STATUS
16. PERCEIVED STATUS
17. DISTRUST
18. EMOTIONAL COMMUNICATION
19. APATHY
20. RESISTANCE TO CHANGE
21. AVOIDANCE
22. REJECTION
23. DISTORTION OR SUBVERSION
24. FACE-TO-FACE COMMUNICATION
25. ONE-TO-ONE COMMUNICATION
26. REPETITION, RESTATEMENT, RE-INFORCEMENT, REDUNDANCY
27. SUPPORTIVE COMMUNICATION
28. DEFENSIVE COMMUNICATION
29. LISTENING
30. INAPPLICABLE HABITS
31. SENSITIVE SKILLS

APPLICATION

1. What are the barriers to good communication?
2. How do we overcome barriers to successful communication?
3. What are the listener's responsibilities in communication?
4. Discuss how bad listening habits prevent effective communication.
5. Write a case study that demonstrates any five barriers to effective communication and then comment on how these barriers could have been overcome.
6. Choose any one of the barriers to effective communication and expand what has been written in this chapter about it. Give examples from your business experience.

4

CROSS-CULTURAL COMMUNICATION

GOALS OF THE CHAPTER

Cross-cultural psychologists attempt to analyse the different forms of social behaviour in different cultural environments and to establish what is common across these cultures and what can be considered to be universals in our social behaviour.

By the end of this chapter you should be able to:

❑ use basic sociological terminology that explains the origin of cross-cultural problems
❑ understand what is meant by culture and subculture
❑ discuss cross-cultural problems
❑ analyse procedures founded on values acceptable to one culture only
❑ give examples of complexities and problems occurring in cross-cultural interaction
❑ be sensitive to behaviour that causes cross-cultural miscommunication
❑ have a basis for overcoming barriers to cross-cultural communication
❑ know how business attempts to bridge cultural gaps

BASIC SOCIOLOGICAL CONCEPTS ABOUT CULTURE

From earliest times each nation or group of people has had a distrust of those different from themselves. This distrust shows itself in diverse ways: the scornful names given to foreigners; the names given to themselves, for example, 'Bantu' or 'Navaho' meaning 'the people'; the special consideration in the form of social welfare given to local residents and not given to foreigners; the customs and rituals designed to keep themselves separate from others. This kind of difference is not only negative: it does not lead only to distrust of others; it may also lead to a pride in one's own ideas and beliefs that is demonstrated in a high code of morals and a high standard of civilization. Each nation rightly celebrates its historical achievements in the form of holidays, processions, and commemorative events. All these significant and coherent rituals form part of a people's **culture**, that system and pattern of behaviour that makes people belong and feel secure.

Culture is not a static concept, however. Like language, it is dynamic. In the last fifty years with all the technological progress in the world, we may know what is happening in any part of the world and we may witness other nations' behaviour and rituals in a way that our ancestors could not. Cultural barriers are breaking down and there is cross-cultural understanding that leads to changes in basic patterns of life. There are, of course, benefits and dangers in this process of change. Some deplore the lack of beliefs and value systems of the young, while others laud the spread of education and technology as progress. Such differences in attitudes are not new: we read of them as part of the thinking of the ancient Greeks, the people of the Bible, and the ancient Chinese, not only of modern nations.

We speak loosely of 'a culture' to mean the pattern of behaviour of one nation, or of a part of a nation such as a tribe, or of a social class, or even of a group of nations. We speak of western culture almost as often as we speak of American or African culture or the culture of Aborigines or the subculture of religion, race, age and sex.

David Hume writing in the eighteenth century stated:

> The vulgar are apt to carry all national characters to extremes; and, having once established it as a principle, that any people are knavish, or cowardly, or ignorant, they will admit of no exception, but comprehend every individual under the same censure. Men of sense condemn these undistinguishing judgements; though, at the same time, they allow that each nation has a peculiar set of manners, and that some particular qualities are more frequently to be met with among one people than among their neighbours. (*Of National Chambers*)

Hume here accepts that there is some truth in the concept of cultural differences though there is a danger in carrying them 'to extremes' and in becoming prejudiced. We should not stereotype individuals, nor should we be 'undistinguishing' in our judgements of them.

What then is culture? For our purposes we may say that culture is the complex pattern of behaviour that is common to members of a society; such behaviour is learned and handed down from one generation to another; it consists of norms, mores, beliefs, values, ideas, customs, attitudes and symbols which are shared to some extent by the members of that society. (We may say that culture is a way of life, whereas a society is a group of people who adopt a particular way of life.)

Norms are the recognized standards of behaviour within a society and they are translated into the **mores**, i.e. the manners and morals, of that society and into its customs and beliefs. When we speak of the **beliefs** of a society, we are not necessarily speaking of religious beliefs, which tend to be more conscious; ordinary beliefs are the broad statements that reflect people's assessments and awareness. Sometimes these vague beliefs become **values**, which guide people towards customs or acceptable behaviour within the society. Such values tend to be lasting and are not easily changed. They influence people's perceptions and attitudes.

Others' perceptions and attitudes are very important in business communication. We often try to influence others' perceptions and attitudes in persuading them to follow a certain line of thought or action. **Perception** is the way a person selects and sorts, arranges and processes, and interprets stimuli and information from his environment in order to synthesize them into what he considers to be a meaningful and structured approach to his world. An **attitude** is a tendency to respond towards or to react against any idea or object; it is a tendency that is learned and may be mental, emotional, or behavioural, or combinations of these three. Attitudes frequently start with perceptions, move into evaluations, and end in action. People's attitudes are expressed verbally as opinions or beliefs.

The members of a society use language and symbols that draw them in to a common culture. The use of a common language is probably the most distinguishing feature of culture. With certain languages like English, French and Spanish, however, language itself transcends cultural boundaries. They become *linguae francae*, i.e. languages adopted for local communication over an area in which several languages are spoken. In this case language may play an important role in cross-cultural communication. It is this use of English in South Africa that is so important.

Each culture has **symbols** of its own. A nation's flag is an important symbol that rallies people's emotions and allegiance. The symbols of religion are important to a member of a particular religion or denomination. Historical monuments are important to cultures and subcultures. The Voortrekker Monument has great meaning for the Afrikaner subculture but little for the other subcultures in South Africa. Symbolic dress or symbolic actions become important to certain subcultures: for instance, the 'New Look' in women's fashions in England after the Second World War had a symbolic significance that went far beyond dress as the Government began to refer to its 'New Look' policy. The burning of bras or the burning of passes was a symbolic act respectively for worldwide feminism and black liberation in South Africa. Such symbolic acts, which were probably regarded as stupid by people outside the subcultures of feminism and blacks, were of great significance to the people within the subcultures. Words have symbolic meanings that reverberate in a society: 'apartheid' is such a word in South Africa, and 'computerization' is another in the business world.

CROSS-CULTURAL PROBLEMS

From what we have said about culture it should be obvious that there will be cross-cultural problems. Whenever people of different cultures or subcultures meet, an understanding of their norms, mores, attitudes, and values is important for cross-cultural communication to take place.

Ethnocentricity is a tendency on the part of one culture or subculture to judge other cultures according to its own cultural norms or values. In western culture it is a norm for a person to look at another person when conversation is taking place; in other cultures, however, it may be regarded as impertinent for a stranger to look another person in the face. When a South African white manager judges a black employee to be shifty or unreliable or cheeky when the black does not look at him when they are speaking, we have an example of ethnocentric behaviour on the part of the white that causes cross-cultural problems.

Closely associated with this ethnocentricity is the habit of **cultural relativity**, in which judgements of what is 'good' or 'bad' according to one culture are applied to another culture. For example, what is considered respectable clothing in one society may not be considered respectable at all in another society. What may be called a good business ethic in a capitalistic country may be called bad in a communist country. Anthropologists, in order to avoid ethnocentricity and this negative type of cultural relativity, respond to the term more positively and refer to cultural relativism as the direct opposite of ethnocentricity. Relativism is the more enlightened approach that is prepared to judge behaviour according to the cultural context of the society in which the behaviour takes place. It is this kind of understanding and broad-minded attitude that we need to foster in cross-cultural communication.

We must understand that there will naturally be a resistance on the part of society to an attempt to change cultural norms, customs, attitudes, and values. We should be sympathetic and patient: at times it may not be necessary to change (it could be prejudice on our part to expect a change); at other times, where change may be necessary, guidance and training will have to be given. Merely to expect change to take place as a matter of course is the worst type of ethnocentricity. Fortunately for all of us, culture is dynamic and adaptive, especially with technological progress and speedy communication facilities, and we can therefore promote cultural adaptation as a distinct possibility. We should, however, accept that adaptation is easier among developed peoples than in subsistence or developing societies. The role of education in promoting cultural adaptation and acculturation (i.e. the learning of a different culture from the person's own) is important, and the best education systems promote acculturation. One of the major disadvantages of the Bantu Education system is that it set out to do just the opposite of acculturation, and South African blacks have suffered as a consequence. It will be a major task for management in the years ahead to overcome such disadvantages and to encourage cross-cultural communication and acculturation in business. In developing a corporate culture the diversity of subcultures within an organization must be taken into account, otherwise the corporate culture will merely demonstrate the ethnocentricity of top management and not be a *corporate* culture at all.

PROCEDURES FOUNDED ON VALUES ACCEPTABLE TO ONE CULTURE ONLY

In countries with various racial groups or with different subcultures there are often procedures established to suit the values of the majority or the dominant group or culture. In the Republic of Ireland, for instance, divorce and abortion are forbidden because of the strong Catholic values of the majority. This may not be acceptable to the Protestants in the country, but they have to live with these laws. In Malawi women's dresses must be below knee length, and visitors often have difficulty with what they consider to be a silly law. In South Africa whites are subject to army call-up despite the fact that the subculture of Jehovah Witnesses believe that it is wrong to take up arms.

It is not only laws that are founded on values acceptable to one culture only. Sometimes regulations or service conditions are based on values acceptable to some but not to others. In South Africa this is largely caused by a strong Calvinist subculture. For instance, until recently women in the teaching profession were not allowed to wear slacks. A different kind of procedure, not based on religious values, was that married women were not allowed to hold permanent posts as teachers. Similarly there are procedures of retirement — women at sixty years, men at sixty-five — that may be seen to be unacceptable to the subcultures of women or of the aged.

When we come to subcultures of race there are very often procedures that favour one subculture and not another. For instance, marriage customs differ and what is considered to be marriage in one society may not be acceptable to another. In South Africa we are passing through an era of discriminatory legislation which favoured one culture to the detriment of other cultures. Laws like the Group Areas Act, Job Reservation, and the Bantu Education Act were based on values acceptable to the white subculture only.

Business procedures are often founded on values acceptable to one culture only: compulsory pension and medical aid deductions are not always acceptable to poorer employees. Appointments to important positions may be influenced by criteria more favourable to one subculture that another. Even psychological testing of intelligence quotients may favour one subculture over another. On the international trading scene special trade concessions and penalties are introduced to favour one country's economy over another.

Such procedures founded on the values acceptable to one culture only have been in existence in all countries from time immemorial. Sometimes they have served a good purpose, at others they have been regarded as iniquitous. It is not the purpose of this book to pass judgement but to give examples that the reader will be able to complement from his own experience so that he will have a greater awareness of the background to cross-cultural interaction.

COMPLEXITIES AND PROBLEMS OCCURRING IN CROSS-CULTURAL INTERACTION

Language is probably the most complex problem in cross-cultural interaction. Where cultures meet, different languages cause problems. One's language is a precious possession and a society is not easily persuaded to give it up. The struggle for recognition of Afrikaans in South Africa is a telling example of this. But there are times when societies may object to being forced to use their mother-tongues. The struggle by blacks in South Africa to be taught through the medium of English rather than through the vernacular medium demonstrates the emotional complexity of language in a society.

Generally, however, we tend to have an ethnocentric attitude towards our own language. We expect that what works for our culture or subculture should work for another culture or subculture. But this is a mistake. Ernest Mchunu, a prominent black marketing and management consultant who used to market Coca Cola in South Africa, has pointed out how the popular advertising slogan 'Things go better with Coca Cola' was a thoughtless slogan when applied to blacks in South Africa at a time when things were definitely not going better for blacks! The history of multi-national marketing is riddled with examples of mistakes that arise from literal translations from the language of the marketers into the language of the consumers. When the Big John brand name was translated into French as *Gros Jos*, the marketers did not realize that this was a colloquial term in French for a big-breasted woman. Is it any wonder *Playboy* magazine awarded a 'Booby Boo Boo Award' to the marketers?

Even within one language there may be differences of interpretation from one society to another: in South Africa a rubber means an eraser whereas in the United States of America it means a contraceptive device. In South Africa a napkin means what Americans call a diaper, whereas in the United States a napkin is what we call a serviette. We certainly have to watch our language in cross-cultural interaction.

Likewise, a symbol may be important to one culture but anathema to another. The swastika is an example of this: before it became associated with Nazism, it had a respectable reputation. The Cadillac has developed into a symbol of luxury in the United States, but it may be regarded as typical of capitalist excesses in socialist countries. The owl may be a symbol of wisdom in many societies but of death in others. This should tell us that in cross-cultural interaction we have to be careful of symbolic associations.

In South Africa there are many complexities and problems in cross-cultural interaction. Because of our racial divisions whites tend to regard blacks as subordinate, and this assumption plagues all our cross-cultural interaction. No successful communication can take place when there is this master-servant attitude. (Until fairly recently our employment law was based on this master–servant concept.) Managers need to respect the individuality of each person and regard him as a person first and not as a subordinate. White culture has been based for a long time on the concept of racial superiority of whites and racial inferiority of blacks. This vitiates proper labour relations because blacks are seen as permanently subordinate, whereas in other societies a subordinate can be regarded as a person on the way up to managerial status and therefore deserving of consideration and respect. Our new labour policies are breaking down these superiority-inferiority barriers. If each person can be treated as a potential manager there is no room for domination and subservience.

There is often a reluctance on the part of blacks in cross-cultural interaction to assume leadership roles. This is understandable historically and culturally. Black society is based on a group identity whereas white society is much more individualistic. Whereas a white will be keen to get to the top in business and is filled with ambition, often with detrimental consequences, a black in a position of leadership — especially an older person — will hesitate to exercise a leadership role which may involve authority and discipline. This comes from a conviction that all people are equals and from a rejection of the historical white leadership role of the master. This attitude is often misunderstood as ineffectual leadership by white managers. This is a complex problem that needs to be treated with sympathy and tact.

There is a concept made popular by Brenda Fassie in one of her songs that includes the words, 'Umuntu ngumuntu ngabantu'. Roughly translated, this means, 'A person is a person through other people' and it epitomizes a concept which we may call **ubuntuism**. It is strongly opposed to individualism and is equally strongly in favour of the community. One's own position in society — one's humanity — is dependent upon one's attitudes to and relationships with others in the community. This is a commendable concept which could be valuable in business: it is opposed to racism and exclusivism and is more in keeping with Japanese principles of management than our traditional South African form of management. If we understand and learn from this concept, we may be able to solve some of the problems that have vexed our society. Such a concept is close to the concept of community that is found in the Afrikaner subculture; it is mainly the English subculture in South Africa that is based on invididualism, ambition, and superiority.

For historical reasons educational opportunities have not always been equal. This has led to differences in income, housing, and standards of living. The more educated one is, the more likely one will be able to cope with modern technology. An inability in a technological environment is not necessarily a deficiency in intelligence but may be caused by educational deprivation. Business therefore has a responsibility to understand and compensate for deficiencies in educational opportunities. There is a great need for ongoing training and informal and non-formal education, which should not be based on traditional and largely ineffective Western standards of formal academic education.

Because of poverty, certain subcultures develop standards of family living, space, and leisure different from those of more affluent subcultures. Because of cramped living conditions the luxuries of space and leisure as experienced by the rich are almost absent. Since they are always living in close proximity to others and since buses and trains are always crowded, we cannot expect them to have the same appreciation of our typically English reserve and standoffishness. Yet we so often *do* expect this: we object to being crowded in a queue; we expect the same standards of hygiene and behaviour as our own and do not realize that these come from our higher standard of living conferred on us by birth or by privilege.

People who live in large families very often see things differently from those who live in small families. This is a truism we all accept. Yet we frequently object to or do not understand concepts of family life which are different from our own and which frequently we have forced on others. How often does an employer make a remark about an employee who has asked for the umpteenth time to attend the funeral of a relative? We show no understanding of the extended family concept because we ourselves live in very close-knit family units. We comment on employees' low moral standards, but we show no understanding of the crowded living conditions. Business has a social responsibility towards employees that extends much wider than providing a decent living wage.

We could go on and on about the problems of transport, housing and other social conditions of the poor, but we have probably said enough to allow managers to become more aware in their interaction with members of cultures or subcultures different from their own. What we have said should also be applied to such subcultures as sex (for instance single-parent families) and age.

BEHAVIOUR THAT CAUSES CROSS-CULTURAL MISCOMMUNICATION

From what we have already said, it should be obvious that there is much behaviour that causes cross-cultural miscommunication. Ethnocentric behaviour which expects everyone to accept one's own values may have a place in a family or a religious community because it promotes and inculcates values, but it is insensitive when it comes to cross-cultural interaction. To expect the same standard of time-keeping from people with poor transport facilities as from people with company cars can lead to miscommunication. To expect the same standard of productivity from people who are well rewarded for their hard work as from people who are not adequately rewarded is just exploitation of cheap labour and leads to friction and miscommunication.

Of course we can lay all the blame on the part of management in its behaviour towards subordinates and overlook the natural personality defects that apply to all people, managers and subordinates. Cross-cultural miscommunication takes place between equals from different cultures and subcultures as well. It is not merely a business phenomenon; it is a matter of human relations and applies to employees as well as employers.

We can therefore say that in cross-cultural interaction we have to be particularly careful not to behave in ways that cause cross-cultural miscommunication. Behaviour that is condescending, critical, accusatory or proud does not promote good communication. Such behaviour often shows itself through a loud voice and a stern, domineering attitude. The manager tends to pride himself on not being too friendly and on being always controlled and correct. He frequently frowns and may point with his finger at the other person or tap with his finger or pencil on the desk while he is talking. Such impatient attitudes do nothing to assist communication.

Attitudes towards domestic servants often fall into this category. Besides the refusal to learn servants' real names or make the effort to pronounce them properly, employers often given them new names or call all servants by names such as John or Josephine. In the past housewives used to insist on being called 'Madam' and issued such inane commands as 'Madam would like some tea. Please bring it to the Madam in her room.' Communication with subordinates is often reduced to loud commands in absurdly pretentious language totally meaningless to the subordinate who decodes the message as 'He is angry again. I'd better keep out of his way.' Downward communication of this kind does not encourage exchange of views and treats subordinates as children, rather than equals. Paternalism or patronization is a common behavioural pattern. Is it any wonder then that subordinates behave like children in a subservient, self-conscious way and say what they think they are expected to say?

Members of a minority or an underprivileged subculture often show their uncertainty or insecurity by being excessively polite or flattering. This is then regarded as hypocrisy or as calculating behaviour, and the result is that they are not trusted or respected. If their language is incorrect, the listener forgets in his pride that they are speaking a foreign language and that he would have similar or perhaps greater difficulty if he were speaking in their language and consequently he regards them as stupid or uncivilized. On the other hand, if they speak confidently and correctly, they are regarded as upstarts showing impudence and arrogance. It is frequently a no-win situation.

Because of this, members of a subculture may be inclined to despise their own culture and adopt the culture of the majority or the privileged. This may cause just as many problems because they are frequently not accepted by either their own society or the society they have tried to join. Accepting an alien culture is often a denial of self, a kind of cultural suicide. It is sad to observe the disintegration of such people in real or metaphorical exile, especially since they are driven to it through the thoughtless behaviour of a dominant group.

Other results of cross-cultural frustration are hostility towards people of other cultures and withdrawal from cross-cultural interaction. Such behaviour leads to further distrust and to subversion and revolution.

OVERCOMING BARRIERS TO CROSS-CULTURAL COMMUNICATION

With all these procedures, complexities, problems and forms of behaviour militating against cross-cultural communication, should we just give up and admit failure? While there can be no doubt about the difficulties, there are certain universal principles that will help us to overcome the barriers in the way of cross-cultural interaction. No culture accepts that it is right to kill, physically injure, or steal. Every culture accepts certain family concepts such as the close relationship between mother and child, the right to be free from pain and the right to be healthy and beautiful. Every human being is capable of cognitive development and we all share certain emotions. There are many similarities despite our differences. That is why politicians try to develop bills of rights that lay down common or universal principles that are inviolable. There are basic **rights** that we should be able to afford to any culture or subculture:

❑ the right to freedom from discrimination;
❑ the right to work;
❑ the right to freedom of expression;
❑ the right to free association with whomever one chooses;
❑ the right to freedom of movement;
❑ the right to one's own religious and cultural traditions;
❑ the right to privacy;
❑ the right to meet together in a group (usually called the right to assembly);
❑ the right to justice;
❑ the right to education at least to high school level;

❑   the right to perform one's parental role;
❑   the right to participate in public issues;
❑   the right to being informed of world issues.

Then there are **values** that we can accept are fundamental to any culture:

❑   the wish to achieve and succeed;
❑   the wish to have material comforts;
❑   the wish to progress;
❑   the wish to be free;
❑   the wish to develop one's own individuality;
❑   the wish to be part of a community;
❑   the wish to be able to converse in one's own language;
❑   the wish to be treated with respect;
❑   the wish to be practically efficient.

Finally we all have **fundamentals** in common: we are all born; we all develop
to puberty; we all have physiological needs such as food, water, air, shelter,
sex, rest and self-preservation; we all have social needs of companionship,
love, affection, belonging and security; and we all have individual needs such
as respect, expression, accomplishment, possession of personal property,
and independence; and we all die.

Some of these are basic principles; others are controversial; but they are
common to all of us, whether we belong to one culture or another. If we could
remember these aspects of our common humanity, we should be able to
improve our cross-cultural communication.

More practically, we should be able to interact with others by being
sensitive to cultural differences. Instead of being condescending, critical,
accusatory, proud or patronizing, we should be relaxed and attentive in the
presence of a person of another culture. We should be at ease and put him
at ease through empathy with him. If he needs it, we should be supportive
of him in his difficulties. We should use simple language that he can
understand and, without pointing out any mistakes he may make with a
language that is not his own, we should encourage him to express himself
without being self-conscious. We need to learn about him and his culture
and to accept that his culture is to be respected, not looked down on merely
because it is different from our own. Where a person comes from a less
privileged, poorer society we must be on the lookout for social factors beyond
his control that may make his standards of behaviour different from our own.
We should avoid prejudices and stereotyping and show the right kind of
awareness and discernment by trying to make allowances for his difficulties.
By showing concern for his needs and emphasizing our common human
heritage, we shall adapt and encourage him to adapt. This cross-cultural
perspective will help not only him but ourselves because we shall gain new
insights and understanding from intercultural relationships that are ge-
nuinely creative and mutually rewarding.

BRIDGING CULTURAL GAPS IN THE WORKPLACE

In business it is often important that employees from different cultures or subcultures should adapt to the **corporate culture** of the business. This corporate culture may be quite different from the cultural background of any of the employees. Some, especially the educated, will adapt more easily than others. Acculturation in business is just as important as acculturation in the wider society — perhaps more so since outside working hours the employee can choose to keep to his own society, while at work he is compelled for the larger part of his day to fit in with the culture of his workplace. Cross-cultural relationships are inevitable, and management has a responsibility to train and educate their employees to be able to cope with such interaction. Social responsibility to employees and their families and communities is of increasing importance in business.

Personnel managers have a great responsibility in promoting the welfare of disadvantaged groups, such as women, members of racial minorities or the underprivileged, disabled people, and the aged. Intercultural relationships can be fostered, and all these groups may then feel they belong and have an important role to play. Communication channels that are kept open encourage participation. Industrial relations managers have an even greater role to play in promoting intercultural harmony and in settling conflicts that are very often caused by intercultural miscommunication.

It is in the three departments — training, personnel, and industrial relations — that the most can be achieved in promoting cross-cultural communication and in bridging cultural gaps among employees.

TERMINOLOGY AND CONCEPTS

1. CULTURE
2. SUBCULTURE
3. SOCIETY
4. NORMS
5. MORES
6. BELIEFS
7. VALUES
8. CUSTOMS
9. PERCEPTIONS
10. ATTITUDES
11. SYMBOLS
12. ETHNOCENTRICITY
13. CULTURAL RELATIVITY
14. CULTURAL RELATIVISM
15. ACCULTURATION

16. UBUNTUISM
17. UNIVERSALS
18. CORPORATE CULTURE

APPLICATION

1. Turn back to Case Study 2 in Chapter 1 and analyse this again as a case study on cross-cultural communication.
2. Write a case study based on *one* of these incidents:
    (*a*) a person from an underprivileged subculture is late for work for reasons beyond his control;
    (*b*) a person from a different subculture requests permission to go to a funeral;
    (*c*) a person from a different subculture has a different concept of leadership from that of his manager.
    In the case study give an example of each of
    (i) ethnocentricity;
    (ii) cultural relativity.

Read either *I heard the owl call my name* by Margaret Craven or *Things fall apart* by Chinua Achebe. The first of these two novels is about cross-cultural relationships in British Columbia while the second is about cross-cultural relationships in Nigeria.

5

GROUP COMMUNICATION

GOALS OF THE CHAPTER

This chapter sets out to:

- ❏ analyse group communication
- ❏ study small group communication both in informal and formal groups
- ❏ comment on small group structure
- ❏ consider various leadership styles
- ❏ apply them to formal group activity in business

INTRODUCTION

So far we have studied mainly one-to-one communication (sometimes called dyad communication). Much communication takes place in groups, and therefore we need to pay special attention to their structure and processes, the behaviour and roles of members in groups, and to leadership characteristics.

A study of a small group, which could include as few as three and as many as thirty-six people, yields valuable psychological insights, whereas a study of a large group does not yield as much interesting information. One of the reasons for this is that small groups tend to be more cohesive, whereas groups randomly assembled do not have the same sense of identity. A small group tends to function less formally, whereas a large group functions formally according to stricter laws and procedures. Although in business we deal mainly with formal groups, some insight into the functioning of small informal groups will be valuable.

SMALL INFORMAL GROUPS

Typical small informal groups are family groups, friendship groups, and work groups. Besides cohesiveness, these groups are characterized by sustained communication. They meet frequently without formal convening; they will have shared perceptions, goals and norms; and they will accept that certain members have roles or positions to uphold. We can expect that their relations with each other will not be neutral but will be affective, i.e. to do with liking or disliking each other; emotional behaviour is more likely to be accepted in small informal groups.

Family Groups

All of us have the opportunity of participating as members of a family. It is probably the most formative influence on how we communicate with others. If we have been raised in a rather autocratic environment where the parents', usually the father's, word is law, then our social behaviour will probably be either a respectful submission to authority or a rebellious reaction to it. If, on the other hand, we have been brought up in a democratic way, we are probably more inclined to treat others democratically. If we have lived in an environment of deprivation we are likely to have different values from a member of a privileged home environment.

Our perception of belonging to the family group will usually be strong, no matter what the circumstances of the family. Whether we like it or not, we are born into a particular family with certain genetic and environmental influences that set us apart from other people. This usually makes the family group the most cohesive of groups.

A family group will be more likely to share perceptions, goals, and norms than any other group. The family is a training and experimental group where its members, through discussion and example, work out their relations with one another and with the outside world, set their goals in life, and establish norms of behaviour for the family that may be quite different from those outside the family. While there may be a certain amount of 'keeping up with the Joneses' and conformity to the norms of the wider society, the family often creates its own different norms and values.

The roles of members of families are usually clearly defined: the father may be seen as the breadwinner and therefore the head of the household in terms of task-performance and ideas; the mother may be seen as the preparer of the food and the leader as far as social and emotional needs are concerned. Of course, roles are always dynamic and may change considerably according to situations and personalities. Similarly girls in the family may adopt certain roles whereas boys may adopt others, although these differences are not as great as they used to be. What we have said previously about status is very similar to what we now say about roles. Roles are not static and they depend on perceptions. Whereas a *position* as father or breadwinner may be very clear, the *role* of task leader could quite easily be assumed by the mother or the eldest child.

Family structures differ from society to society and according to the size of the family. The group dynamics of a family which includes grandparents, uncles, aunts and cousins, differs from the group dynamics of a family consisting only of parents and children. Similarly, a one-parent family structure changes roles and tasks. A family with a step-parent or step-children may create different roles, and a single-child family will be different from a family with two or more children. The large family of thirteen children that used to be quite common in the nineteenth century would obviously have required a different kind of management from the relaxed friendly relations of the family with a considerably smaller number of children such as is common today.

Friendship Groups

These groups may be groups formed during adolescence, or clubs, or associations such as Round Table or Rotary or Lions. The main difference between the family group and the friendship group is that the friendship group does not exist *per se*. The members have voluntarily associated themselves with the group. The task of maintaining the group's identity is therefore a greater need than in the family, and because of this the friendship group often resorts to some form of regulating behaviour such as a constitution, though it may not be clearly defined in the less formal friendship groups. The norms of what type of behaviour is appropriate and who is entitled to be a member of a friendship group may be undefined, never written down, and perhaps hardly spoken about, but they nevertheless exist in any friendship group.

In the friendship group there is no definite leadership role such as the mother or the father in a family group, and this leads to leadership roles that tend to change in the group. Sometimes the club will have a stipulated policy that no person may hold a position of office in the club for longer than a year or two; in the friendship group roles are more fluid and change frequently with or without stated policies or regulations. The primary goal of the friendship group is often merely to meet together to enjoy each other's company, but secondary goals may flow from this primary goal: for instance there may be fundraising drives, social service projects, sporting activities, and the organization of entertainment. As the goals become more numerous, the structure tends to change from informal to formal and committees are formed and members appointed to or elected to various positions of office. Very often what was a secondary goal for the group becomes a primary goal for the office-bearer. Again we must distinguish between position and role: the mere appointing or electing a member to a position does not mean that he is capable of fulfilling that role and often a person on his committee may exercise a better leadership role than the one appointed. This is inevitable where positions are rotated artificially among members.

Friendship groups are not as long lasting and do not have as permanent a membership structure as family groups: adolescents form stronger bonds with members of the opposite sex and form their own family groups which become more important than the friendship groups; members of clubs may no longer have the sporting ability, or the inclination, to continue their membership as they grow older and devote more time to their careers; some associations such as Round Table have a compulsory retirement age because one of the bases of the association is to keep it reserved for young people; a club for divorced or single people will exclude a member who marries or remarries. This ever-changing membership structure makes the group more dynamic and less predictable.

Work Groups

The third informal group is the group formed among fellow-workers. This may be a group that meets during tea-time or lunch-time or a social group that meets after work on a Friday for a drink. Or it may be an informal group that meets to discuss staff issues. We are speaking here of the informal work group, not the formal committee, social club, or staff association.

Despite their informality, work groups tend to be more task-orientated than family or friendship groups. It is the work environment that provides the cohesiveness of the group and therefore it is natural that work should be the main topic of communication. Status or position will play a larger role in the work group. Although affective relations may develop, the purpose of the group is not primarily to develop such relations.

These informal work groups are very important in business. The 'grapevine', as it is so often called, is ignored only by insensitive managers. Management needs to know what is being said in informal work groups and the only way, apart from the dishonest use of informers, is for management to involve itself in these informal work groups in a participative rather than a status role. This is, of course, difficult because a person from a hierarchical position may place restraints on the free flow of communication on which informal work groups thrive. If, however, management has the right attitude of relaxed interaction, it can very often gain valuable insights from informal groups.

SMALL GROUP STRUCTURE

From our introduction to small informal groups we can move on to look in general at small group structure. **Structure** refers to the relationships that exist among the various members of the group. Of course, structure is static in comparison to **process**, which is dynamic and refers to the changes in structure that take place during the life of the group. Since process is difficult to study, we shall keep to structure, but, whether we are talking about structure or process, there are four aspects that help one to analyse communication in the small group:

1. COMMUNICATION NETWORKING
2. AFFECTIVE RELATIONS STRUCTURES
3. POWER STRUCTURES
4. LEADERSHIP STRUCTURES

Communication Networking

There are different kinds of communication networks:

The **single strand** diagram depicts communication in which information is passed from one person to another who then passes it on to another and so on. This type of communication can be very ineffective because the information is filtered by each recipient's perception and it is likely that by the time the message reaches 4 it will have been greatly distorted. A game that illustrates this distortion is to whisper a message to one person in a class and then ask him without any questioning of the message to pass it on to the next person until the whole class has received the whispered message. It is highly likely that the message that reaches the last person will bear no resemblance to the original message at all. The single strand suggests upward communication, but it could also be used for downward communication.

In the **probability chain** the information is passed on without any plan at all. 1 tells 2 who tells 3 and 5, who do not pass on the message, whereas 8 tells 9, who happens to tell 10. In this random process 4, 6, 7, and 11 are simply excluded from receiving the message because nobody thought of telling them. Besides the filtering that must go on, as in the single strand, there is the possibility of hurt feelings on the part of those who have, probably quite unintentionally, been excluded.

In the **chain** we have the same kind of communication as in the single strand: although the message suffers from the same distortion and filtering, the different pattern suggests that it is no longer simply an upward communi-

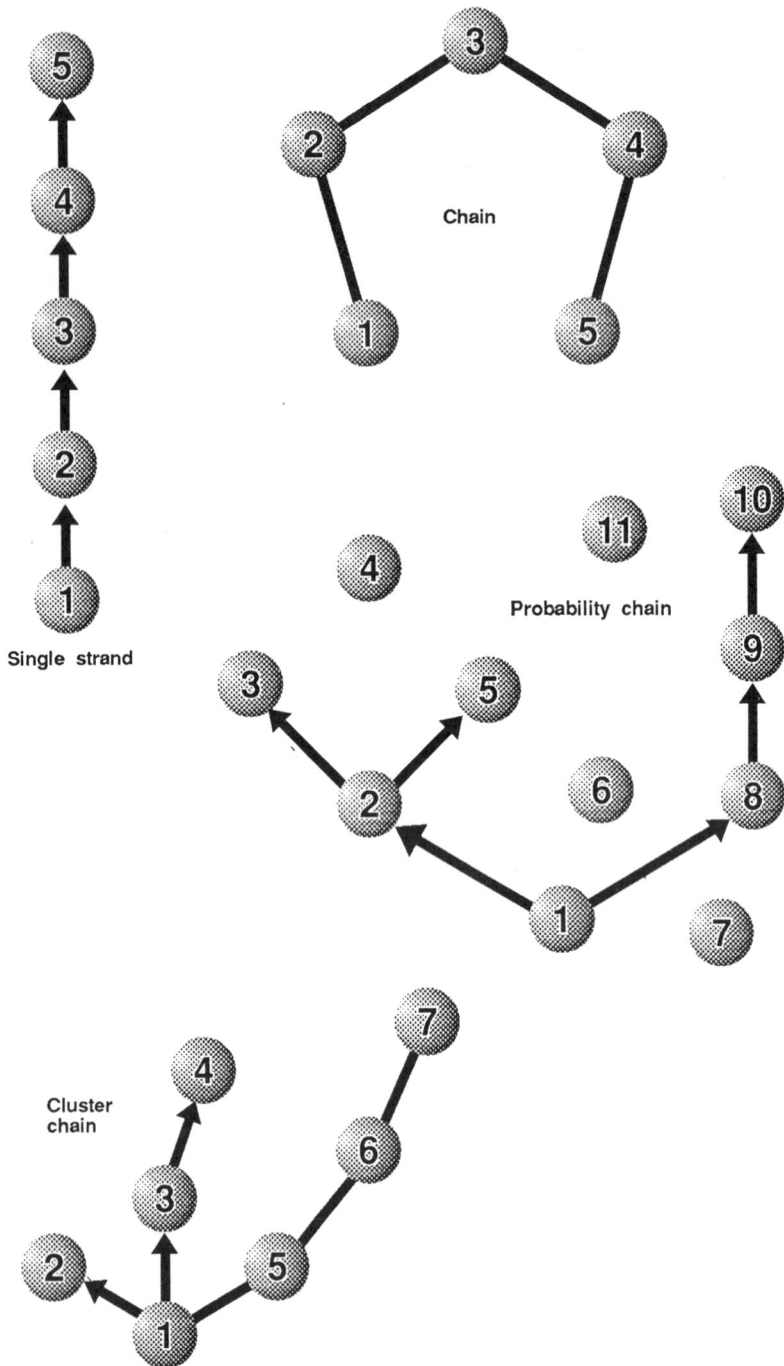

Single strand

Chain

Probability chain

Cluster chain

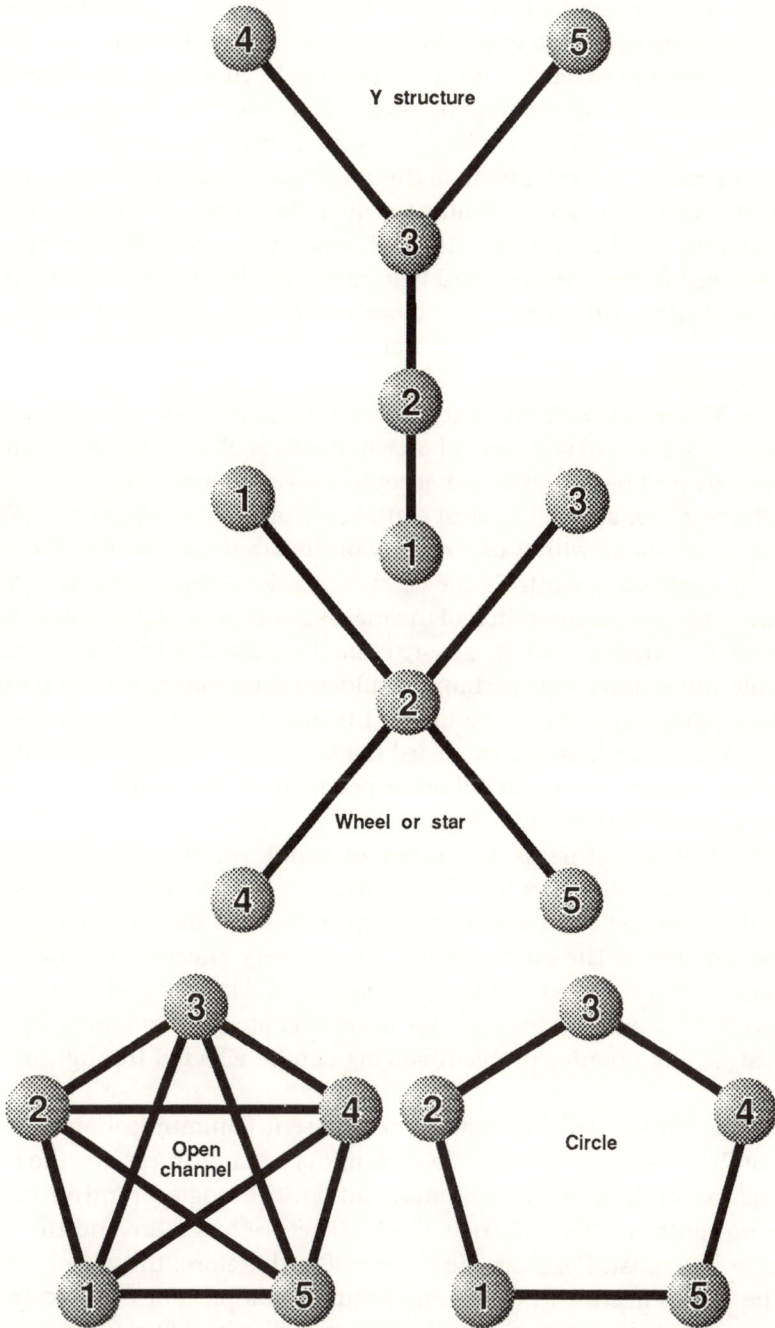

Y structure

Wheel or star

Open channel

Circle

cation as in the single strand but involves some upward and some downward communication.

In the **cluster chain** there is a more deliberate selectivity that takes place: 1 tells 2, 3, and 5; 3 tells 4; 5 tells 6 and 6 tells 7. This is more structured and may involve specific requests from 1 to 3 to tell 4 and to 5 to tell 6 who is then requested to tell 7. Because 1 is more in control of the dissemination of the information, there is more likelihood of effective communication, but the cluster chain still suffers from distortion through filtering.

The **circle** is a development of the single strand and the chain structures: it has the same pattern of 1 telling 2, who tells 3, who tells 4, who tells 5, but the difference is that 5 then tells 1, who may then judge the effectiveness of the communication process and who may then have to repeat the message more explicitly. Although 1 has more control and therefore there is more centralization, this network does not allow as much centralization as the Y and the wheel structures do.

The **Y structure** shows that 3 is the central pivot of the communication process: a great deal will depend on whether 3 is able to decode the message adequately and pass it on in an acceptable way to 4 and 5.

The **wheel** or **star** is the most centralized of all these structures. Whether the message starts with 2 or with any of the other members of the wheel, 2 is at the centre and controls the communication. There is likely to be more accuracy in the dissemination of the message because of 2's central position. This has also been called the gossip chain because 2 is seen as a gossip who tells all and sundry of a perhaps confidential message. We are all familiar with the situation when, for instance, 1 tells 2 of something he simply cannot keep to himself and asks 2 to regard the information as strictly confidential, but 2 is a gossip who must tell other people until the 'confidential' message becomes public knowledge.

The last structure is the **open channel** where any member of the communication structure has the opportunity of discussing the message with any other member. This is the least centralized and the most participative of all the channels. The open channel can be very effective in business. It is sometime referred to as the **buzz group**, in which everybody is encouraged to have his say and in which any ideas are accepted without judgement; often a great deal of creative problem-solving can be effected through this openness.

What can we deduce from these different communication structures? Research has shown that when a message is a simple message, the more the centralization the better the communication. The single strand and the chain have no centralization, whereas the Y structure has more and the wheel or the star has most. For a simple instruction, therefore, the wheel or the star will be most effective in disseminating information. For complicated problems, however, the open channel emerges as the best structure.

The centralized structures often cause dissatisfaction among members because they resent the control of the central figure. They feel that their contributions are not appreciated sufficiently. In the open channel, however, there is no dominant figure and members appreciate that everyone has an equal say. It is obviously the most democratic of the group structures.

It is the manager's task, therefore, to choose the best structure for the particular message. It will depend on whether the message is simple or complex and on whether the purpose is orientated towards task performance or orientated towards member-satisfaction.

Affective Relations Structures

When we speak of participation and member-satisfaction, we are already dealing with structures that affect relations within the group. It is important for managers to be aware of affective relations, i.e. the likes and dislikes of the members of a group. A disaffected member may cause much damage because he is resentful or is resented in a group. On the other hand a member who is more popular than any other member in the group can also cause problems: popularity can be both an asset and a liability in a group. Popularity tends to be a subjective matter, and a person may be afforded a status that is not warranted or that does not serve the task orientation of a group.

A psychiatrist, Jacob Moreno (1934), represented affective relations by means of a sociogram and measured ways in which people in a group expressed their likes and dislikes. By means of such sociometric data he could monitor the affective relations operating in a group. Study the following sociogram:

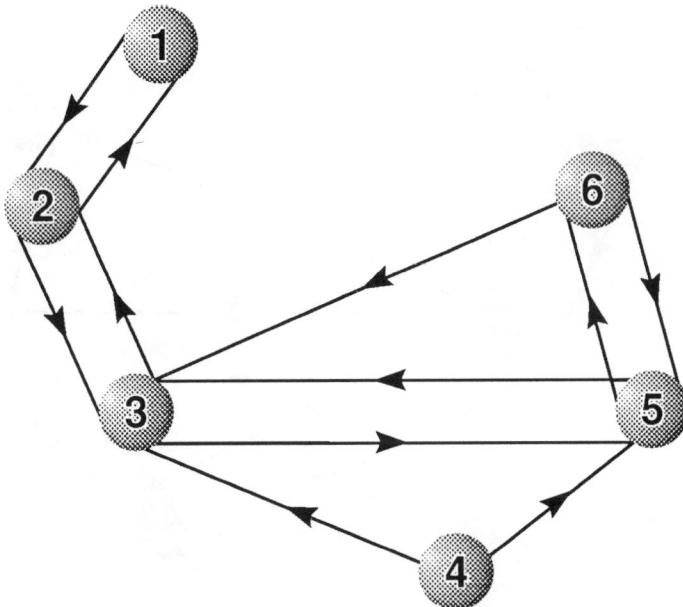

This represents a group of six persons and shows the positive affective relations in the group: 1 responds positively to 2, who reciprocates and responds positively to 3 as well; 3 reciprocates and responds positively to 5; 4, 5, and 6 all respond positively to 3; 4 responds to 5, but there is no reciprocal response to 4 at all; 5 responds to 6 as well as 3; and 6 responds to 5 as well as to 3. From this sociogram it is clear that 3 is the central focus of the positive affective relations: 2, 4, 5, and 6 like him. On the other hand 4 is excluded from receiving positive affective responses We could also speak of two smaller subgroups consisting of 1 and 2 and then 5 and 6. In such a group it could quite easily happen that 3 becomes the leader, that 1 and 2 could form a clique or that 5 and 6 could, and that 4 becomes disaffected and either drops out or works against the rest of the group. The task of a leader (3 perhaps) in such a group may well be to integrate 4 into the group by showing a special relationship towards 4 and encouraging others to do the same. Such sensitivity towards outsiders is important in group work and takes us beyond simple likes and dislikes: in the interest of group relations 4 should be integrated whether he is liked or not. 1 is also rather isolated and needs to be more integrated. The sociogram might then be reconstructed like this:

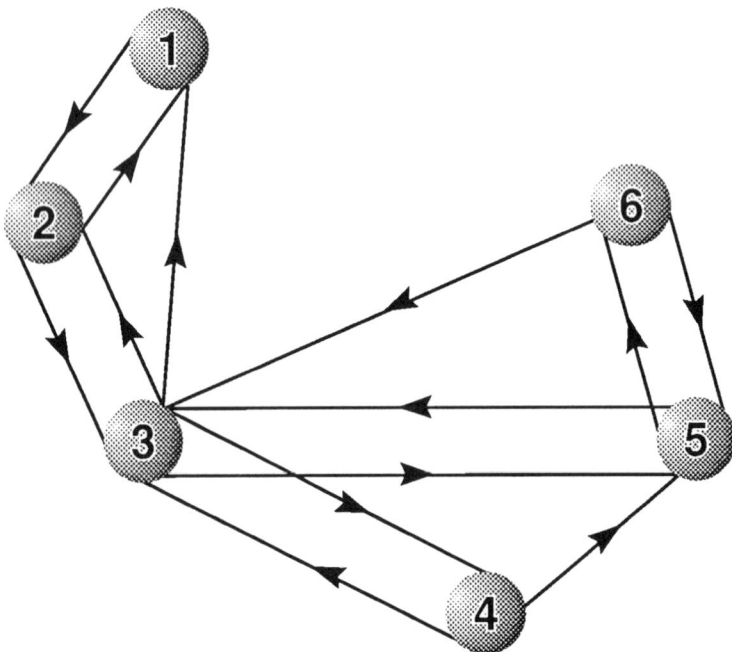

This shows much more integration but places a great burden on 3, who becomes even more of a central figure. With all the affective relations emanating from and being directed towards 3, he will find it difficult to bear all this responsibility and make a significant contribution to the performance of the task at hand. He would probably be better advised to suggest tactfully to another member of the group that he should try to integrate 4 and 1 more effectively. The sociogram might then look like this:

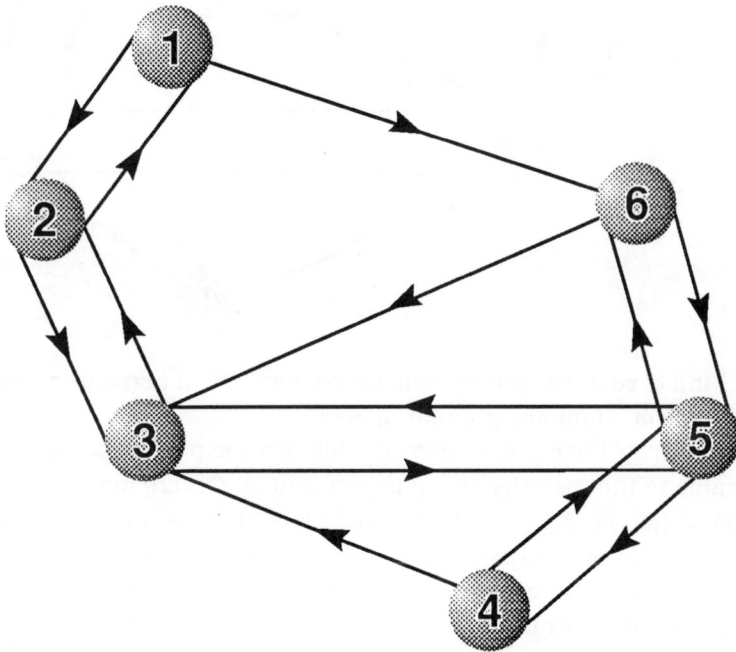

This shows more cohesion in the group, but creates other dynamic factors that may strain group relations almost to the point of friction. 6 could, for instance, feel he is giving more than he receives and he may become disaffected.

Such sociographics and sociomonitoring have a place not only in group relations but are also used in studies of advertising and consumer behaviour.

Power Structures

It should be evident that we are now moving into power structures within a group. In the original sociogram we studied 3 has influence over 2, 4, 5, and 6 and therefore is the most powerful member of the group.

There are, however, different types of power. 3 may gain power because of his popularity; 4 as an outcast may try to emulate 3 in some way because he wishes to identify with him as the most popular member of the group. This

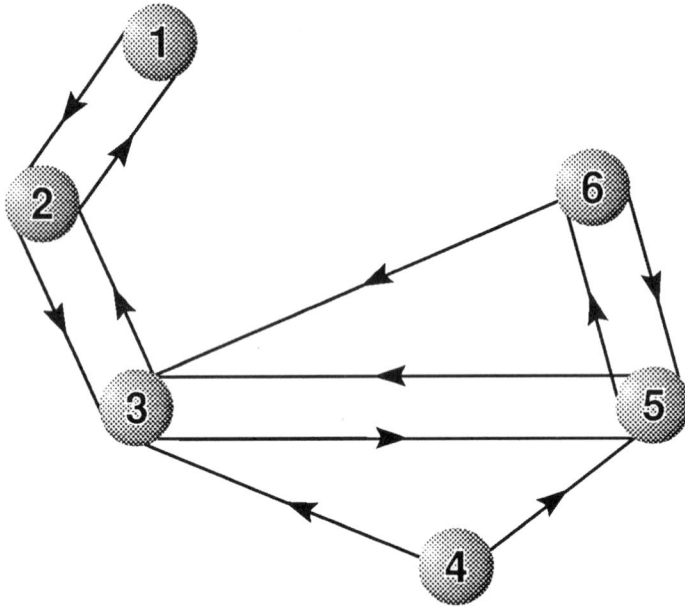

is the kind of **referent power** that advertisers use in persuading us to adopt the lifestyle of a famous, popular figure.

But 3 may have power because he is an expert in some field that is applicable to the task the group is performing. Others may respond to him because of his expertise, in which case he has what we may call **expert power**.

Closely related to expert power, is the power that comes from having more information than anyone else. 2, 4, 5, and 6 may defer to 3 because he has **information power** rather than because of any skill in human relations. He may be equipped with the type of information that is able to sway an argument and, whether the other members like 3 or not, they have to admit that 3's information is correct.

Both expert power and information power will put 3 into the position of a teacher over pupils. This kind of position may yield **coercive** or **reward power**. Other members of the group may perceive 3 as a kind of father figure who is able to exert the power to punish or to reward. In business this is frequently associated with the hierarchical structure of the organization: 3 may be the senior member in the group or the manager. This may then give him what may be called **legitimate power**, which will make others accept his rulings as if he were the only person who can legislate what is right or wrong.

As one moves into power structures one moves more and more into centralized structures and participation becomes minimal. Group dynamics requires us to be aware of power structures so that we may diffuse centralization when necessary and encourage a more relaxed participation.

Leadership Structures

In most groups a leader will emerge and then the group will be structured in some way round his leadership style. Usually a leader is a person who is equipped with above-average intelligence, has the ability to apply his knowledge to a particular problem, and is able to communicate well; he will be able to participate in a social context, will be prepared to co-operate, and will be popular among those with whom he associates; he will be self-motivated and prepared to show initiative and to persevere in doing what he has set out to do. These personality characteristics are, however, very general and there are as many different leadership styles as there are people.

In group dynamics leadership is not static: it moves from person to person according to the situation and the task at hand. Leadership is not a position but a natural, ever-changing response to situations within a group. There are two main functions of leadership that emerge in any group activity: task leadership and group maintenance leadership.

Task leadership has to do with initiative and purpose: the leader has a clear idea of what the task at hand is and guides the group towards this goal; he sees the group as an instrument to achieve the goal and through continual reminders and direction he will strive to bring the group back on its course. **Group maintenance leadership**, on the other hand, has to do with the welfare of the group, with the individual members in the group and with their being involved and feeling secure; the leader will be concerned about promoting positive affective relations in the group.

These two functions need not necessarily be found in one person. Often a group will have one person who is the task leader and another person who concerns himself about the emotional needs of the group. But everyone who exercises leadership should be aware of both functions and their respective values. If the task at hand is urgent and clear-cut, it is likely that the group will operate in a very disciplined way and that the task leader will be dominant. If, however, the task is less clearly defined and the purpose of the group is more social, then the task leader could be a hindrance; such a group needs to be more democratic and participative.

From this we can see that we may speak of leadership styles. Rensis Likert (1967) divides leadership styles into four types:

1. exploitive-authoritative
2. benevolent-authoritative
3. consultative-democratic
4. participative-democratic

The **exploitive-authoritative** style shows no regard for the members of the group and uses the group merely for dissemination of instructions. The group has no part in decision-making. The group is bullied into performing the tasks at hand and there is little trust within the group. The members are exploited for the purposes of the task and the leader adopts an authoritarian attitude.

The **benevolent-authoritative** style is more benevolent towards group members but is still autocratic. Instead of being threatening and exploitive, the leader is more patronizing and condescending. Although there is more trust among group members than there is with an exploitive-authoritative leader, the group members behave cautiously. There is more trust and more decision-making allowed in the group. Often, however, because of the benevolence of the autocratic leader, there is a measure of co-operation.

The **consultative-democratic** style of leadership allows practical decisions to be made within the group but major decisions are still taken by the leader. There is a greater degree of confidence within the group and there is opportunity for free discussion on the understanding that the contributions may be vetoed by the leader who still keeps control. Generally with this type of leader the group members show trust and there is little unco-operative behaviour.

The **participative-democratic** leader allows maximum participation from group members who together take decisions. The leader facilitates discussion and maintains the level of trust and confidence at the highest level. The socio-emotional level of friendship and co-operation is high. Although decision-making may take more time, motivation is high among members.

THE LEADERSHIP GRID MIRROR

We may summarize what we have said in this leadership grid mirror:

	1–3	4–6	7–9
7–9	1.9 PEOPLE ORIENTATED 'I am the friend of the group members. I want to understand each member and respond to his feelings and interests so that there is confidence and trust.'		9.9 PROBLEM-SOLVING ORIENTED 'I participate with the group in solving problems and accomplishing the task in an atmosphere of trust and respect. I want people to be committed and productive.'
4–6		5.5 BALANCED ATTITUDE 'I achieve adequate productivity through balancing task performance with maintenance of group members' morale at a satisfying level.'	
1–3	1.1 LAISSEZ-FAIRE ATTITUDE 'I don't really care either about the group or the task. The task is performed with the minimum of effort as and when circumstances allow.'		9.1 TASK-ORIENTATED 'With the minimum of human relations I organize work conditions so that the task is performed speedily and efficiently. I am in complete charge.'

Vertical axis: 1 2 3 4 5 6 7 8 9
Horizontal axis: 1 2 3 4 5 6 7 8 9

Applying the different leadership styles to this grid mirror we could say that 9.1 represents the exploitive-authoritative style, whereas 9.9 represents the participative-democratic style. We call 1.1 a **laissez-faire** leadership style: leadership abstains from interference with individual action; it abdicates its responsibility. The **people-orientated** position 1.9 is an extreme that may suit a friendship group without any task orientation but is seldom effective in business unless the purpose is merely to restore human relations that have been neglected. A good example of 1.9 would be a social occasion for an informal work group. The **balanced attitude** position of 5.5 is interesting. This is a type of compromise situation in which there is no urgency to achieve either high productivity or high morale. The quality of the product or of the human relations may suffer but not too much to be serious in the short term. It does not, however, lead to excellence in the long term.

We may conclude by saying that leadership must adapt to the situation. The 9.9 position is obviously the ideal, but, as we have said, at times this may be time-consuming because it leads to too much deliberation: the ideal product and ideal human relations may put a firm out of business. The more pragmatic positions of 5.5 or 9.1 may be what a particular situation requires. Even 1.9 has its place, though 1.1 would be rarely justified.

FORMAL GROUPS

In discussing small-group structure we have referred also to formal groups from time to time. We need then to discuss the different types of formal groups, with special reference to business. There are five main kinds of formal group:

1. command (or executive) groups;
2. democratic (or committee or task) groups;
3. consensus (or problem solving) groups;
4. buzz (brainstorming) groups;
5. information-sharing (or teaching) groups.

Command groups are composed of a superior and his subordinates. A manager may be the person in command of a group of his subordinates, but he may be a subordinate member of another command group which may be led by his managing director. The essence of a command group is therefore that there is a hierarchical position of executive leadership. This tends to make the leader more autocratic in his approach, and there is usually an expectation on the part of the members of the group that most of the communication will be downward communication.

Democratic groups are committees or task forces formed to co-ordinate the expertise of the different members of the group. A committee differs from a task force in that a committee usually has a longer life, is based on members' roles in the organization or on their hierarchical position, and is usually told what its function is. The task force, on the other hand, has a shorter life since its purpose ends when the task is completed, is more active and independent in fulfilling the task, and depends more on expertise than position. We may subdivide committees into standing or permanent committees, boards and commissions. Although there may be an appointed or elected leader of this type of group, his leadership role is more democratic than that of a leader of a command group. His task is more of a convener, co-ordinator, or facilitator. He tends to adopt the consultative-democratic style of leadership since the committee's or the task force's function is usually to make recommendations to the executive to which it is responsible.

Consensus groups are usually formed to solve problems. The function of a consensus group is to bring together the knowledge and information of its members, to allow free expression about various alternative solutions to the problem, to arrive at a solution by consensus, and to achieve understanding of and active commitment to the decision taken. Decision-making by consensus is a long-drawn-out process and difficult to achieve. The leader of such a group has to be skilled in the participative-democratic style of leadership. He must neither dominate the group discussion himself nor allow anyone else to do so. He has to guide the members to a decision that is neither prematurely arrived at nor half-heartedly accepted. The group as a whole must be committed to the decision and this often involves accepting fruitful compromises that do not allow any faction to think it has won or lost. Participation and encouragement are two important factors in consensus groups, whereas domination and persuasion often feature in command groups and even in democratic groups in which majority votes are often forced on the committees.

The **buzz group** (brainstorming group) has many of the characteristics of the consensus group: it is very creative, it allows free expression without judgement, and encourages participation The difference is that brainstorming does not aim at arriving at decisions: the buzz group does the preparatory work for the decision-making process. Brainstorming requires quick contributions without prior preparation and without any criticism. These buzz groups are usually very enjoyable and encourage creativity outside the group. Research has shown that in fact individuals working alone rather than in a buzz group develop more creative ideas, but the stimulation that buzz groups promote, as well as the morale-building that takes place, makes brainstorming a very effective method.

An **information-sharing group** is a teaching group. Here it is accepted that a person or a group of persons has information to share and therefore it is similar to a lecture session with questions and answers. The trouble with most formal groups that allow free expression is that so often people are pooling ignorance rather than learning. The trouble with information-sharing groups on the other hand is that frequently the people with whom the information is being shared are passive and uncommitted; they have not accepted the need to learn what the expert knows and their motivation is therefore lacking. The Biblical statement, 'no prophet is acceptable in his own country' (Luke 4:24), has unfortunately much relevance in the business world: because of professional jealousy, businessmen do not readily accept that they can learn from colleagues and they give their attention only to celebrities from outside their ranks.

Again we need to realize that no one method suits all situations, and elements of each of these formal groups should be used in any group discussion. Nevertheless there are characteristics in each that allow managers to choose what type of structure would suit a particular situation A manager's individual leadership style may make him favour one structure over another and this could lead to effective decision-making. We shall look at these formalities in more practical terms when discussing the various modes or media systems of communication.

TERMINOLOGY AND CONCEPTS

1. ONE-TO-ONE COMMUNICATION (DYAD COMMUNICATION)
2. SMALL INFORMAL GROUPS
3. FAMILY GROUPS
4. FRIENDSHIP GROUPS
5. WORK GROUPS
6. SMALL-GROUP STRUCTURE
7. COMMUNICATION NETWORKING
8. SINGLE STRAND
9. PROBABILITY CHAIN
10. CHAIN
11. CLUSTER CHAIN
12. CIRCLE
13. Y STRUCTURE
14. WHEEL OR STAR
15. OPEN CHANNEL
16. AFFECTIVE RELATIONS STRUCTURES
17. POWER STRUCTURES
18. REFERENT POWER
19. EXPERT POWER
20. INFORMATION POWER
21. COERCIVE OR REWARD POWER
22. LEGITIMATE POWER
23. LEADERSHIP STRUCTURES
24. TASK LEADERSHIP
25. GROUP MAINTENANCE LEADERSHIP
26. LEADERSHIP STYLES
27. EXPLOITIVE-AUTHORITATIVE LEADERSHIP STYLE

28. BENEVOLENT-AUTHORITATIVE LEADERSHIP STYLE
29. CONSULTATIVE-DEMOCRATIC LEADERSHIP STYLE
30. PARTICIPATIVE-DEMOCRATIC LEADERSHIP STYLE
31. LEADERSHIP GRID MIRROR
32. *LAISSEZ-FAIRE* LEADERSHIP STYLE
33. PEOPLE-ORIENTATED LEADERSHIP STYLE
34. BALANCED ATTITUDE LEADERSHIP STYLE
35. TASK-ORIENTATED LEADERSHIP STYLE
36. PROBLEM-SOLVING LEADERSHIP STYLE
37. FORMAL GROUPS
38. COMMAND (EXECUTIVE) GROUPS
39. DEMOCRATIC (COMMITTEE OR TASK) GROUPS
40. STANDING COMMITTEES
41. PERMANENT COMMITTEES
42. CONSENSUS GROUPS
43. BUZZ (BRAINSTORMING) GROUPS
44. INFORMATION-SHARING (TEACHING) GROUPS

APPLICATION

1. Which of the group structures and leadership styles would be most
    effective for the following:
    (a) A board meeting of a company?
    (b) A service club (e.g. Round Table, Lions, Rotary)?
    (c) A sports club?
    (d) A meeting to decide on an advertising campaign for a new product?
    (e) A disciplinary hearing?
    (f) New product development?
    (g) A parent-teachers meeting at a school?
    (h) A staff meeting to explain a new procedure?
    Give reasons for your selection of the most effective structure and style in
    each case.
2. What would you say are the problems of communication in groups
    and how are they solved?
3. Compare formal and informal groups.
4. What factors influence small-group structure? Comment on each.
5. Discuss the various leadership styles and the contribution each
    style can make.
6. What are the different types of formal groups? Discuss how each
    may have a function in business.

CASE STUDY 1

The employees of GRADEGRIND ENGINEERING were accustomed to meet every Friday after work in the bar before going home. This Friday was special, though: George Barnes had been dismissed that day.

'Hullo, James. Have you heard the news? George has been sacked,' Frans said.

'He had it coming to him,' James replied.

'Oh, I don't know,' Jan answered. 'Everybody takes a bit on the side.'

'But that wasn't what it was about. Did you hear him swearing at Venter? Nobody in authority can put up with that kind of backchat.'

'I still think he should have been given a chance, though, James,' said Themba. 'Why don't we send a deputation to Mr Wright?'

'Are we sure we have all the facts before us?' Frans asked. 'We don't want to appear foolish, now, do we?'

'I was there at the time,' said James. 'Venter asked him why there was so much copper wire missing, and George just lost his cool and started calling Venter by every name under the sun. Venter tried to calm him down, but he wouldn't stop.'

'But no-one can be fired just like that. Doesn't he at least deserve a hearing?' asked Themba. 'I still say we should form a deputation and go to Mr Wright. He always talks about his open-door policy.'

'Yes. He'll probably show us his open door and tell us all to go,' laughed James. 'But I agree with you. We can't just leave a friend of ours in the lurch. Who should go?'

'All of us. There are only four of us. We'll just have to keep our cool,' said Themba.

'Then you'd better not do the talking,' said Jan wryly. 'Let James talk. He's got the facts. Do you think old Wright'll still be there?'

'Yes. Come on. Let's go,' said Frans.

1. Identify what kind of group this is.
2. Which members of the group emerge as leaders during this meeting?
3. What affective relations are at work in this group?
4. What problem-solving techniques does the group use?

CASE-STUDY 2

Mr Mokoena is the manager of the printing department of a large commercial enterprise. He has a complaint against one of the departments which continually tries to pressurize his staff to do urgent work immediately. This disrupts his schedule and causes other departments to suffer. He has reported this to Mr Van der Vyver, the Managing Director, who has called a meeting of heads of departments.

'Lady and gentlemen, this meeting has been called to discuss printing,' Mr Van der Vyver announces. 'Mr Mokoena, will you outline the problem?'

'Well, sir. It's like this. We try to run a good ship in the printing room. We schedule work on a FIFO principle. We require at least a month's notice for all printing jobs. And we satisfy all departments that plan their orders well in advance. But Mr Robertson's department is always trying to jump the queue and when I put his orders in line he countermands my orders and gets somebody else to do his jobs.'

'Well, if the work's urgent, it has to be done. That's all. My department brings in the most revenue of all the departments and is the busiest,' says Mr Robertson heatedly. 'I can't wait a month for my work. Being the busiest, my department needs printing done urgently, otherwise we'll lose customers. Mr Mokoena is tying up work unnecessarily in the printing room because he doesn't want his department to work too hard and so that he has a sense of power over other departments.'

'Don't you think,' asks Miss Naidoo quietly, 'that with planning you could give Mr Mokoena more time? Not every job should be a crisis, and after all Mr Mokoena *is* in charge of all the other departments when it comes to printing. He has been appointed Printing Manager and it is his job to schedule printing so that no department suffers.'

'Yes. My department had a printing job scheduled for Friday and when I asked Mr Mokoena for it he said that the machines had been occupied on one of your rush jobs,' says Mr Williams to Mr Robertson. 'I have an irate customer because his work wasn't ready for him.'

'And it wasn't my fault, Mr Williams. I had given the instructions that your job was next, but then Mr Robertson came and told Peter to do his job first. Since Mr Robertson is senior to me, Peter obeyed him. I was very angry about it and have reported both Mr Robertson and Peter to Mr Van der Vyver.'

'Yes,' says Mr Van der Vyver. 'That's why we're meeting here today. Have you anything more to say, Brian?'

'Well, only that the financial results speak for themselves. My department brings in the most money to the firm. My style of management is different from others, and this must be taken into account,' says Mr Robertson.

'That's another issue, Brian,' comments Mr Van der Vyver. 'We're talking about your printing jobs and whether you should have countermanded Sipho's order. Sipho is in charge of printing. How would you like it if another head of department interfered with your department?'

'Yes, I suppose you're right. I'd be as mad as a snake. But the job warranted drastic action,' defends Robertson.

Sipho Mokoena moves to the overhead projector and projects his printing schedule for the last two weeks. 'You see, Mr Van der Vyver. Here's the work we have done over the last fortnight divided into departments. You'll see we've done roughly an equal amount of work for each department. With all departments except Mr Robertson's, adequate notice has been given and, with the exception of the job Mr Williams mentioned, all printing has been on time. Now here is a record of Mr Robertson's orders and the lead time he has given us. You will see that we have accommodated his rush jobs in the past and got them to him on time. I believe we deserve his thanks and consideration, not criticism about power and laziness.'

'Well, Brian,' says Mr Van der Vyver, 'it does seem that all your jobs have been rush jobs lately. Is there a problem about giving more lead time?'

'I suppose it's because we have expanded lately and need another staff-member. At the moment I'm doing the work of three people, and there just aren't working hours for me to do things differently. I don't see the problem: after all, Mr Mokoena has done rush jobs for me in the past. Surely systems of scheduling are secondary to the actual business of getting things out on time?'

'I have spare capacity at the moment,' volunteers Miss Naidoo. 'Couldn't you use a member of my staff until your crisis is over, Mr Robertson? Felicity is very good at co-ordinating my printing requirements. Perhaps she could assist you.'

'That's very kind of you, Miss Naidoo, but I think my department is function-ing well enough. I guess I'll just have to stay later and fit into Mr Mokoena's system, but I don't like being treated like a naughty schoolboy who has disobeyed the rules.'

'Oh, come, Brian. That's not what this is all about,' laughs Mr Van der Vyver. 'Why don't you accept Arthi's offer of help? You *did* complain of being understaffed. We'll have to discuss that some other time. We have ap-pointed a few extra people to your department lately. I'm not sure another is justified. But we do appreciate your contribution to the company, Brian. You know that.'

'Well, what's all the fuss about then?'

'You need to think about the company, Mr Robertson,' says Mr Williams, 'not just your own department. The printing department functions as a co-ordinating department in a way. Mr Mokoena is doing an excellent job. We've never had a better-run printing department in all the years I've been here. He deserves respect and thanks too, you know.'

'I can see you're all against me.'

'That's not true, Brian. Arthi has offered help, and Sipho has, as he said, accommodated you in the past, almost to a fault of generosity. That's what happens when favours are given and then they become expectations and then rights. Perhaps, Brian, you should accept Arthi's offer, and I'll sit down with you and we can see how we can sort out your printing problems. It's true that systems are needed, but it's also true that systems can be changed when there's a crisis. But we can't manage by crisis only, Brian. Mr Williams has been seriously inconvenienced by his late printing job, even though he planned it well in advance. I agree with him that Sipho is doing an excellent job, just as I believe you are, Brian. Well, I think we've aired all the problems, and the solution lies now with Brian and me. Is there anything else, Sipho?'

'No, thank you, sir. Thank you for this opportunity to discuss the matter.'

'Well, I think this has been a useful meeting. Brian, will you see me later today?'

'Yes, sir.'

1. Draw a sociogram showing the affective relations in this group. Then comment on this sociogram.
2. Discuss the leadership styles of the various managers. Refer to the leadership mirror grid.
3. What role does Mr Van der Vyver play in this group? How effective is he?
4. What kinds of power structure are at work here?
5. How would you describe this formal group?

6

COMMUNICATION IN THE BUSINESS ORGANIZATION

GOALS OF THE CHAPTER

By the end of this chapter you should be able to:

❏ understand and evaluate organizational structures, and

❏ relate communication systems to the business organization.

INTRODUCTION

In the business organization there are both formal and informal organizational structures. We have already looked at informal structures in our chapter on Group Communication and there will be a certain amount of overlapping between this chapter and that one. In this chapter we look primarily at formal organizational structures and see how they affect various communication systems.

THE FORMAL ORGANIZATION

The formal organization is structured in a particular way so that the objectives of the organization may be achieved. There is usually a clear description of what each person will do in the organization, and the person's authority, responsibility, the kinds of decisions he is empowered to make, and the span of his control are usually clearly defined. In a formal organization formal methods of decision-making, for example, meetings and committees, are usually adopted.

An important concept in organizational structuring is the concept of **span of control**. It is a basic rule that there should be the fewest possible management levels and the shortest possible chain of command. The ideal span is usually considered to be between three and six subordinates reporting to one superior. We speak of a narrow and a wide span of control in a business organization. A narrow span of control would have more managers with fewer subordinates reporting to each:

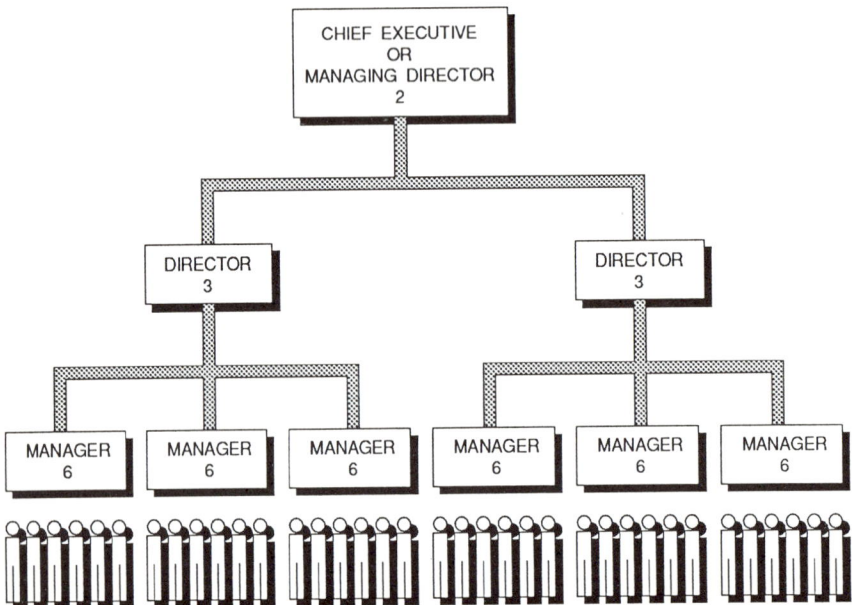

Figure 1
Narrow span of control

This diagram shows a chief executive or managing director with two directors in his span of control. You will see that each of these two directors has three managers in his span of control, while each of these managers has six subordinates in his span of control. There is in this organization a tall structure with a narrow span of control that allows each superior to control his staff fairly easily.

A wide span of control for an organization of roughly the same size would be represented in this diagram:

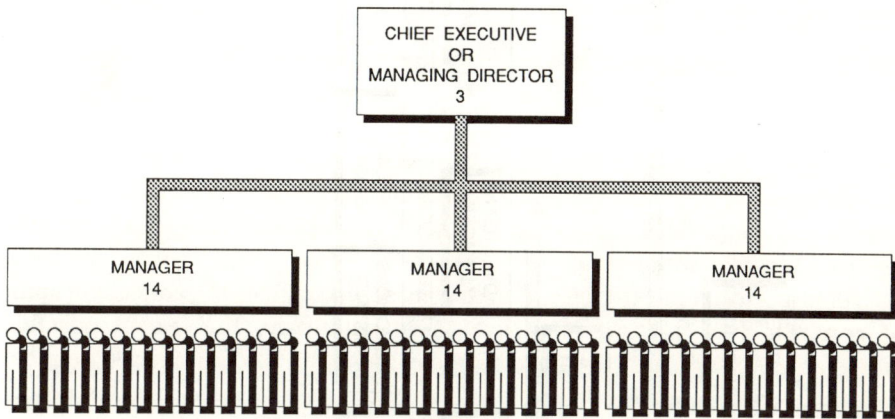

Figure 2
Wide span of control

The chief executive or managing director is responsible for three managers, each of whom is responsible for 14 subordinates. Although the control is not as tight as in the narrow span of control, this flatter structure allows more initiative on the part of the subordinates, and morale may be better because the subordinates do not feel that they are always under tight control.

When we speak of organizational structures, we speak of authority and status. In Chapter Three we have already discussed nominal status, real or deserved status, and perceived status. Similarly with authority, we can speak of four types of authority — the **formal hierarchical authority** that comes from nominal status given from the top; the **accepted authority** that is given by the subordinates at the bottom because of the status that is perceived by the subordinates; the **authority of knowledge** that comes from the expert power that the superior has because of his superior knowledge (real or deserved status); and the **authority of the situation** that may arise from time to time because of a particular situation, e.g. a crisis, when it really does not matter who is formally in control and when the situation thrusts authority upon whoever can assume it at the time.

In a formal organizational structure we often speak of **line authority** and **staff authority**.

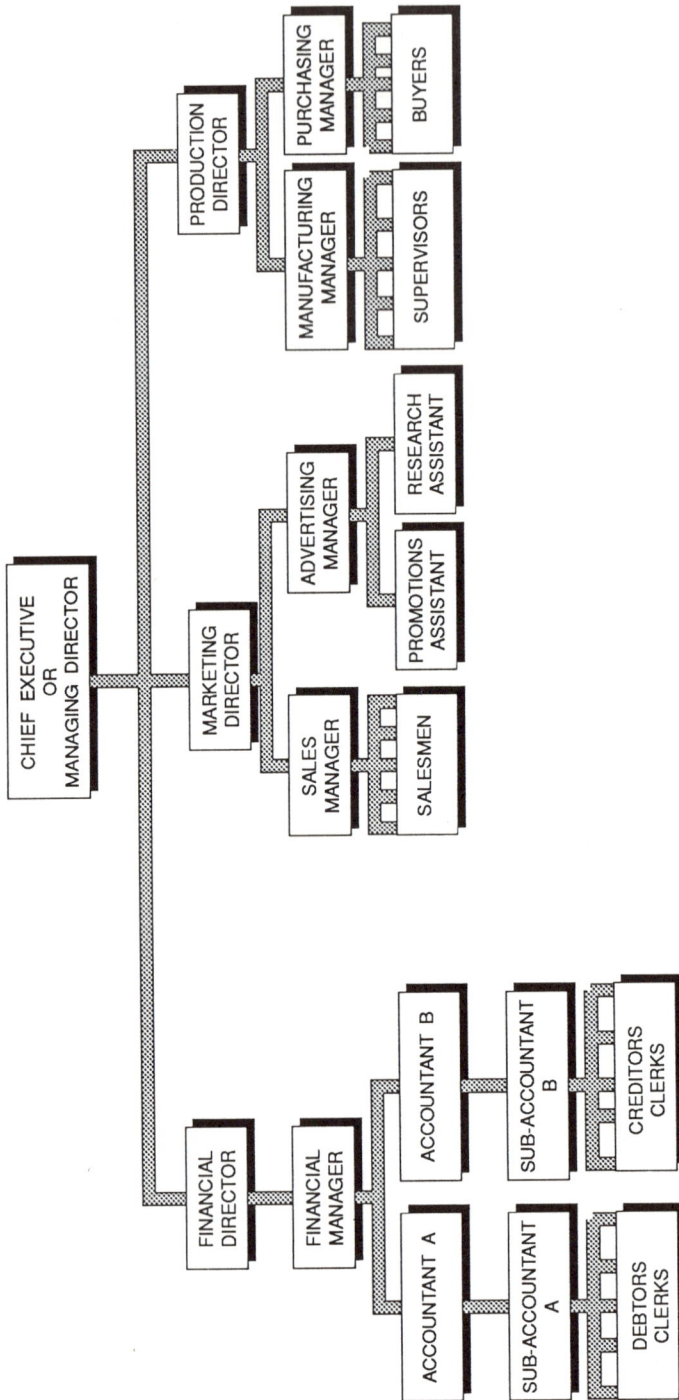

Figure 3
Functional line structure

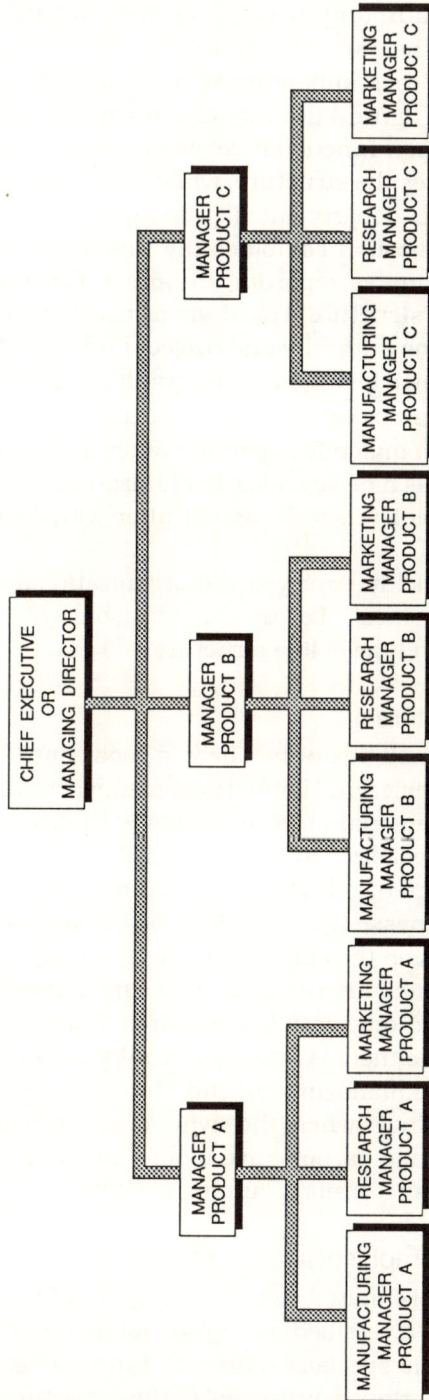

Figure 4
Product line structure

Line Authority

Managers have line authority because of their hierarchical positions over subordinates within their span of control. This is given to them by their own superiors in terms of their appointment or promotion to that position.

In the example in figure 4 (Funtional line structure) it is obvious that the structure is based upon functional departments of finance, marketing and production. Sometimes the structure, while still representing line authority, is based upon product departments (figure 5).

The matrix organization combines the functional and the product approach, with subordinates reporting to both a functional and a product manager. This type of structure is used when specific projects are undertaken which involve both line authority and project authority (figure 6).

Line structures can also be based on geographical considerations (figure 7).

Line structures can be centralized or decentralized. A centralized organization is one in which major decisions are taken at the highest level, usually at head office, whereas a decentralized organization allows decision-making to be delegated to lower levels of the organization with greater autonomy given to branches or plants.

We have now quickly surveyed the organizational structures that are most common in business. Let us consider some of the advantages and disadvantages of each type of line structure.

Functional line structure

This is suitable for small business. There is good control since each director or manager has a specified and limited area of expertise which he can develop. There are few interpersonal problems since each director or manager is in control of his own specialized area of responsibility.

There are, however, disadvantages. Functional line structures do not suit large or growing businesses because decision-making is slower. A great deal of responsibility rests on the chief executive or managing director to co-ordinate the different functions because each functional director or manager tends to be concerned only with his own area. This can create conflict and jealousy. Furthermore there is little opportunity for a breadth of experience for anyone except the managing director. The functional line structure is a relic of the small business where the owner or entrepreneur does everything and does not encourage participative management or breadth of responsibility. Consequently succession planning is limited.

Product line or geographical line structure

This structure is more suited to a large organization. Decision-making is speedier and is more diversified: each product manager has a wide range of experience both in his specialized area and in more general management. One of the most important advantages of this structure over the functional line structure is that each division is responsible for its own performance and business results.

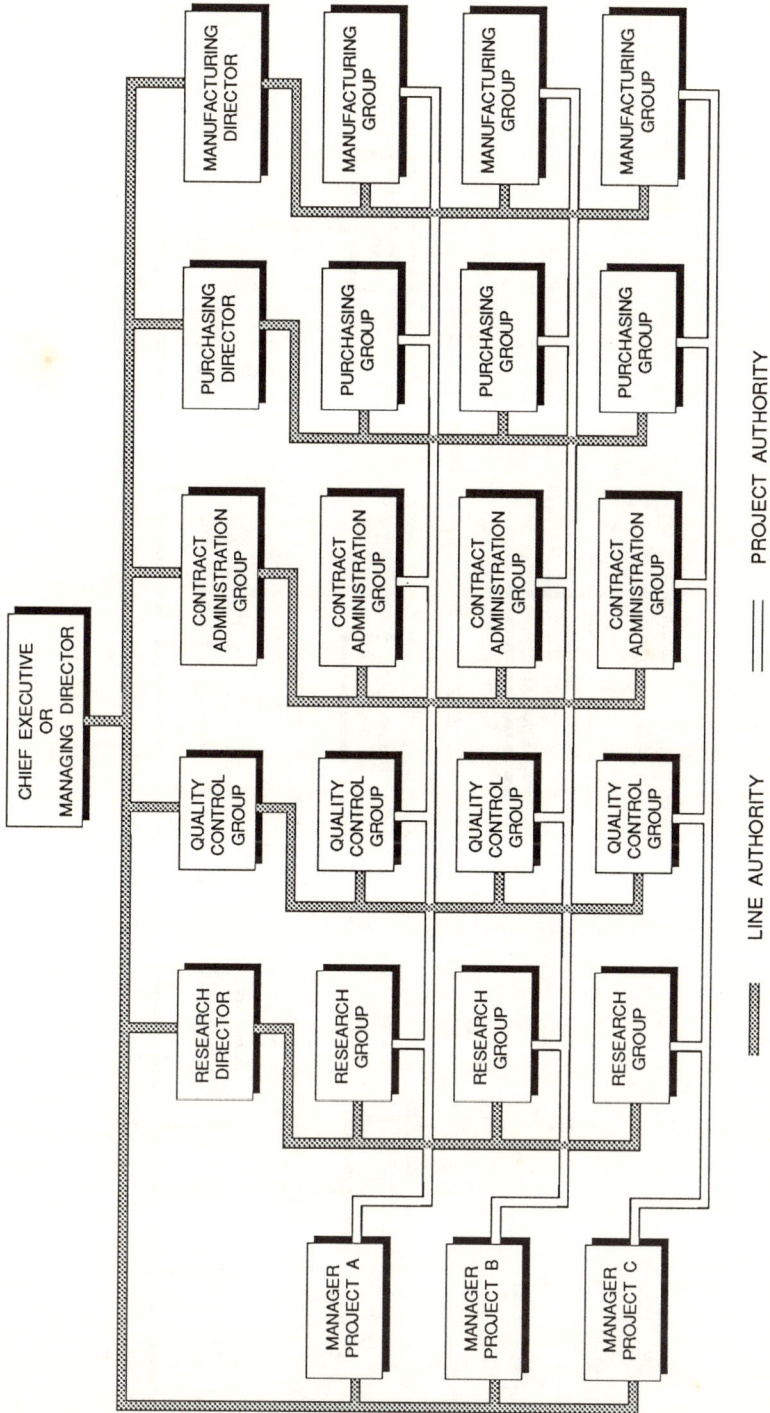

Figure 5
Matrix structure

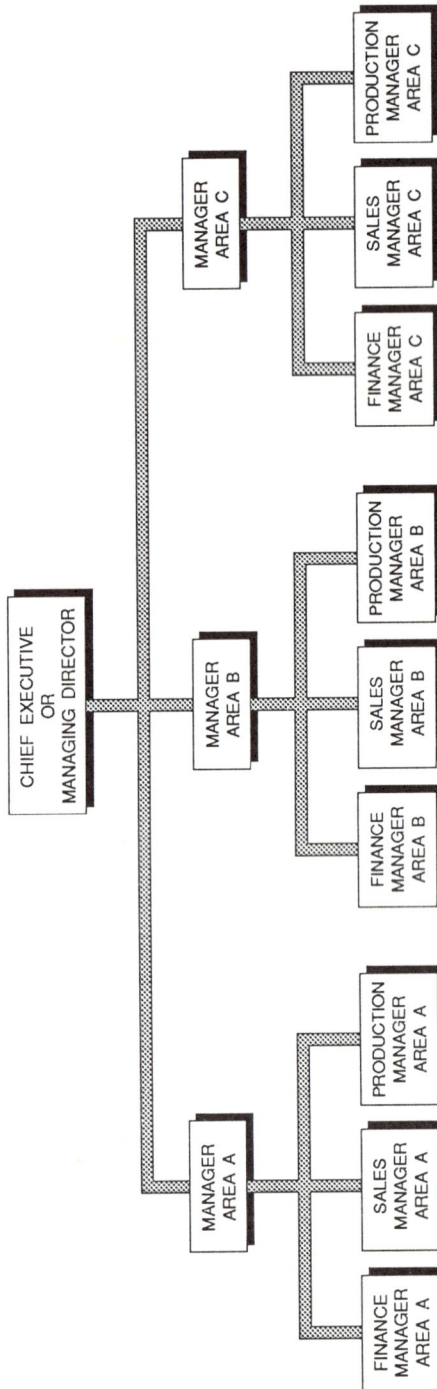

Figure 6
Geographical structure

A disadvantage is that duplication of effort may lead to unnecessary expense. Too much emphasis on results may lead to limited goals instead of overall objectives of the total organization.

Matrix structure

This structure allows for greater flexibility and involvement. Motivation is high, and employees are challenged to work together as a project team. There is greater flexibility in moving experts from one project to another as the project requires specific skills. This creates cost-effective employment of key personnel and obviates duplication of effort. Complex projects can be undertaken successfully through this type of project management.

A disadvantage is that there may be a feeling of being demotivated when a project team disbands and members have to regroup themselves for a different project. The feeling of let-down when the project comes to an end must be carefully handled and requires great maturity in terms of interpersonal relations. There is also a danger of too much flexibility: this could lead to the collapse of a project as a result of too much talk and not enough task performance. Since every person is responsible to a line authority and a project authority, divided loyalties could result.

Nevertheless the advantages of the matrix structure greatly outweigh the disadvantages, and there are few of the problems that arise from bureaucratic structures. As with a decentralized structure, top management can be freed to concentrate on strategic planning.

Staff Authority

Line authority is concerned directly with achieving the specific goals of the organization. Staff authority, on the other hand, provides advice and support to the line functions. A staff manager does not have the same legitimate power, reward power or coercive power; instead he concentrates on expert power. He must be a person who is sensitive to others and uses influence and persuasion rather than coercion. He must be skilled in presenting his views. Examples of staff functions are research, personnel, industrial relations, and quality control. We have already seen the difference between line authority and project authority, and therefore it should not be difficult to see the difference between line authority and staff authority.

Figure 7 should make this difference clearer; it shows that the distinctions between line and staff functions are often blurred: whereas a personnel manager exercises a staff function in the organization as a whole, he may also exercise a line function in being the formal head of his own department with legitimate power over the members of his department.

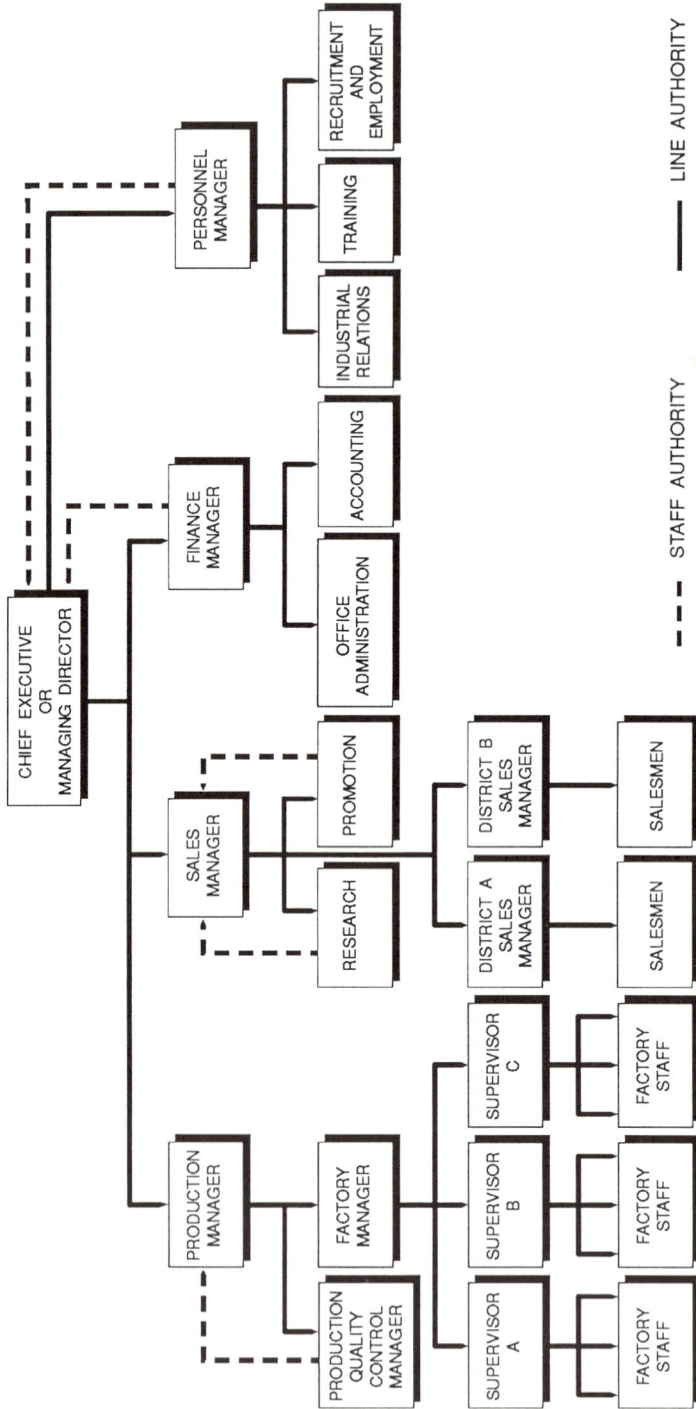

Figure 7

COMMUNICATION SYSTEMS

In the business organization there are different communication systems (or channels, as they are sometimes called). We shall discuss these forms:

1. VERTICAL COMMUNICATION (DOWNWARD AND UPWARD)
2. LATERAL (OR HORIZONTAL) COMMUNICATION
3. DIAGONAL COMMUNICATION
4. CONTRACTING COMMUNICATION NETWORK
5. INFORMAL COMMUNICATION
6. EXTERNAL COMMUNICATION

Much of what we say here will be similar to what we have already said in our chapter on GROUP COMMUNICATION, but in this chapter we look at communication specifically in the business organization.

Vertical Communication

Downward communication

In business much communication is of the downward form:

This communication from top to bottom goes down the various levels of the line structure from superior to subordinate and is used

❑ for giving instructions;
❑ for providing information about the policy of the organization;
❑ for providing information about the procedures of the organization;
❑ for providing performance appraisals to subordinates;
❑ for explaining the relationship of a specific task to the overall objectives of the organization.

Downward communication serves a useful purpose in co-ordinating and controlling the activities of the organization. Such communication may be through oral or written channels, by means of interviews, meetings, memoranda, reports, notice-boards, in-house newspapers, and induction manuals.

**Figure 8
Downward
communication**

There are, however, certain disadvantages associated with downward communication. It is essentially authoritative, and too much downward communication with too little upward communication will affect morale badly. If the communication is oral and the line of communication is long, the message will be filtered and distorted. In order to overcome this distortion

there must be opportunities for response from below, that is for upward communication, as well.

Upward communication

There is usually not enough upward communication in business. The main purpose of upward communication is to allow the upper levels of the hierarchical structure to know what is happening at the lower levels.

Upward communication is also through oral or written channels by means of interviews, meetings, suggestions, explanations, progress reports, and appeals for assistance to be given or decisions to be made. We should not omit the significant role that non-verbal communication can play in upward communication: because subordinates are often reluctant or ill-equipped to communicate freely with their superiors, non-verbal messages can often be more illuminating than oral or written messages.

The same distortion as occurs with downward communication occurs with upward communication: supervisors often filter messages from subordinates and managers do the same with messages from supervisors because they may feel threatened by the communication. As a result the message that arrives at top management may be severely reduced from the original message. Even so-called 'open door' policies do not always have the desired effect: subordinates do not feel confident or relaxed about discussing important matters with their superiors. Often this is the manager's fault because he cannot empathize with the circumstances of his subordinates. To a large extent this may be as a result of the appointment of managers who have not worked their way through the ranks or of managers who, having worked their way through the ranks, then take an unsympathetic attitude towards those whom they now consider to be inferior to them. A manager has to be very sensitive and open to subordinates' problems and to regard them as participants in the achieving of the objectives of the business organization rather than as mere tools.

Figure 9
Upward
communication

Lateral or Horizontal Communication

This form of communication takes place among people on the same hierarchical level of the business organization. This is very useful in co-ordinating and problem-solving and obviates wasteful communication with a common superior who then has to communicate with each of the people on the same level but in different departments. Lateral communication serves the further purpose of allowing peers to form good working and social relationships and so foster good team-work. People who have free communication with their peers also enjoy more work-satisfaction. Horizontal communication may be among members of the same project group or among members of different project groups or between line and staff employees. This communication helps to break down conflict rivalry and jealousy and to promote the objectives of the total organization. The only negative drawback is that people on the same hierarchical level could use lateral or horizontal communication to gang up on their common superior or superiors and form a power-block to defeat the wishes of top management, but this is where good industrial relations within the business organization are important. It is better to have good lateral communication than to prevent such democratic communication through autocratic management styles.

Figure 10 helps to explain exactly what horizontal or lateral communication is.

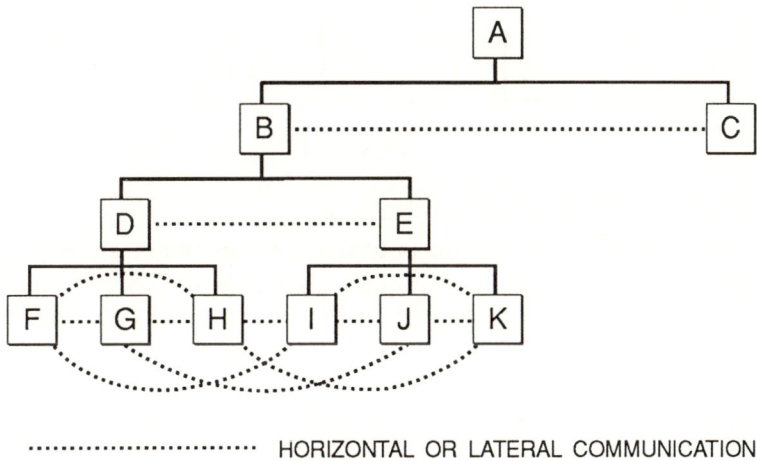

·························· HORIZONTAL OR LATERAL COMMUNICATION

Figure 10

The permutations of horizontal communication among F, G, H, I, J and K are, of course, many more than depicted in the diagram, but at least it helps to illustrate what lateral communication is.

Diagonal Communication

Communication between members who are not on the same hierarchical level is what we mean by diagonal communication. This is particularly common with line and staff departments and with projects when people on different levels of authority in different departments have the expertise needed for the successful outcome of the project. This may mean that those in higher positions have to liaise and work together with those in positions hierarchically lower, and sometimes those in higher positions have to submit to the expert knowledge of inferiors. Diagonal communication is potentially explosive unless employees are tactful and committed to the overall objectives of the organization.

Figure 11 illustrates a few examples of diagonal communication. One of the problems of diagonal communication is that the immediate line superior may feel left out or may consider that his authority is being snubbed in some way.

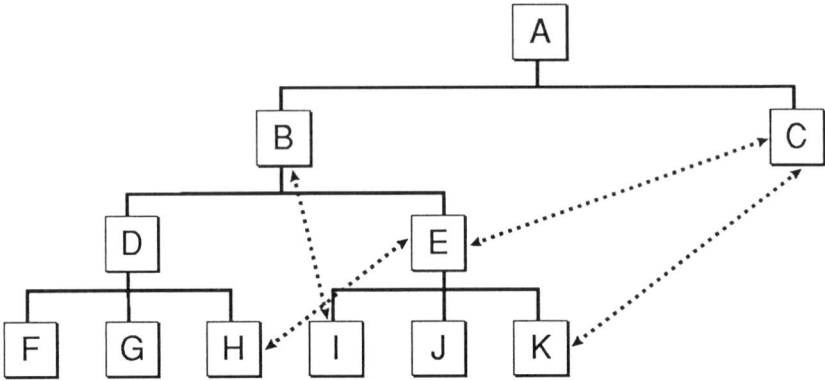

Figure 11

Contracting Communication Network

The word 'contract' as a noun is well known in business; it is a binding agreement between persons or groups. As a verb 'to contract' may mean to make or become smaller or shorter. As a communication network, a contracting network therefore implies that the communication channel starts as a large all-channel network (figure 12):

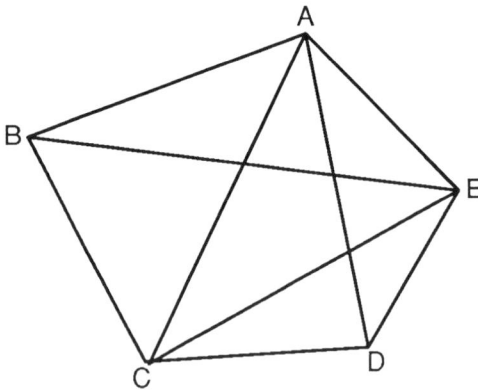

Figure 12

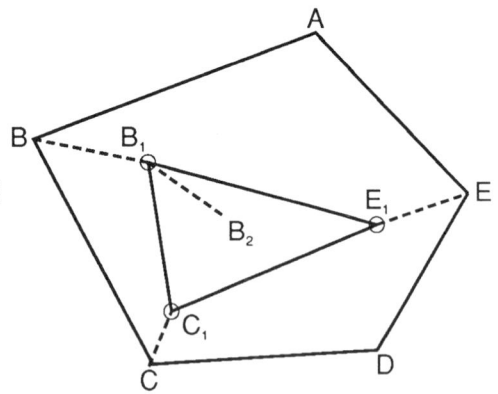

Figure 13

Here there is free expression among all the parties concerned. It is somewhat like brainstorming in that everyone has a say and is involved in the initial communication. From this all-channel network ideas crystallize and become clearer: the channel becomes shorter as two or three people (B, C, E) become the crystallizers or clarifiers. Eventually one person (B2) emerges as the definer or contractor of the policy or plan (figure 13).

B may or may not be the person at the top of the organizational hierarchy. If one person always emerges as the definer or contractor, it is just another example of hierarchical authority being forced upon subordinates. In ideal contracting networks, however, any member of the communication network can emerge as the definer or contractor according to his initiative or expertise in the particular problem under consideration. The best contraction is one which has the approval of all concerned: it becomes a contract binding on all the members because they have been involved democratically in the communication process. It is a contracting movement not only in the sense that the participants become fewer and fewer but also in the sense that the message becomes clearer and more defined. The best types of negotiations and agreements are examples of contracting communication networks.

Informal Communication

In the chapter on Group Communication we have already mentioned the most common informal communication networks such as the grapevine and social groupings within any business organization. In this chapter we merely re-emphasize the importance of informal communication in the business organization. No business organization can function statically according to a formal organization chart. There are informal relations that operate despite formal structures and that tend to reconstruct the business organization according to the affective relations that exist among people. The informal communication networks make the organization dynamic and exciting. A manager who insists on structural formalities and does not take into account the personalities involved in the business stunts the development of the organization. The head of the department who treats his staff patiently and in a relaxed way will get more out of his employees. The manager of a department who is on friendly terms with his production foreman will have a better chance to have his product available when he needs it than another manager who treats the production foreman merely like a machine. Such cross-departmental communication is close to what we have described as diagonal communication but it is not formalized in any way: it is not planned, nor is it controlled in any way. The formal communication channels must be adapted to the informal communication that takes place, not *vice versa*. In this way informal communication must be taken into account in setting formal objectives.

External Communication

An important part of business communication is the communication between the public and the organization. Here we immediately think of public relations and advertising, but every employee who communicates with the public, in the form of customers, shareholders or the media, is involved with public relations and advertising. And we must recognize that such external communication is not just one-way from the organization to the public; it must be two-way through careful listening and responding to customers' complaints, requests, and behaviour. In this regard surveys and market research play an important role in external communication.

CONCLUSION

We have now dealt with the social psychology of communication. We have studied communication theory, cross-cultural communication, group communication, and communication in the business organization. After three chapters on English usage that will help us to get our language right, we shall move on to modes of communication or what is also called media systems.

TERMINOLOGY AND CONCEPTS

1. THE FORMAL ORGANIZATION
2. ORGANIZATIONAL STRUCTURE
3. SPAN OF CONTROL
4. CHAIN OF COMMAND
5. NARROW SPAN OF CONTROL
6. TALL ORGANIZATIONAL STRUCTURE
7. WIDE SPAN OF CONTROL
8. FLAT ORGANIZATIONAL STRUCTURE
9. FORMAL, HIERARCHICAL AUTHORITY
10. ACCEPTED AUTHORITY
11. AUTHORITY OF KNOWLEDGE
12. AUTHORITY OF THE SITUATION
13. LINE AUTHORITY
14. STAFF AUTHORITY
15. FUNCTIONAL LINE STRUCTURE
16. PRODUCT LINE STRUCTURE
17. MATRIX STRUCTURE
18. GEOGRAPHICAL STRUCTURE
19. COMMUNICATION SYSTEMS (OR CHANNELS)
20. VERTICAL COMMUNICATION
21. DOWNWARD COMMUNICATION
22. UPWARD COMMUNICATION
23. LATERAL (OR HORIZONTAL) COMMUNICATION
24. DIAGONAL COMMUNICATION
25. CONTRACTING COMMUNICATION NETWORK
26. INFORMAL COMMUNICATION

27. EXTERNAL COMMUNICATION

APPLICATION

1. Draw an organizational chart of your own business organization and evaluate it according to the criteria mentioned in this chapter.
2. What do we mean by the following terms:
    (a) span of control;
    (b) line authority;
    (c) staff authority?

CASE STUDY 1

TOYJOY is a successful business organization that has developed considerably over the last few years. Its business is to make and sell toys and games. So far it has been organized according to a functional line structure as follows:

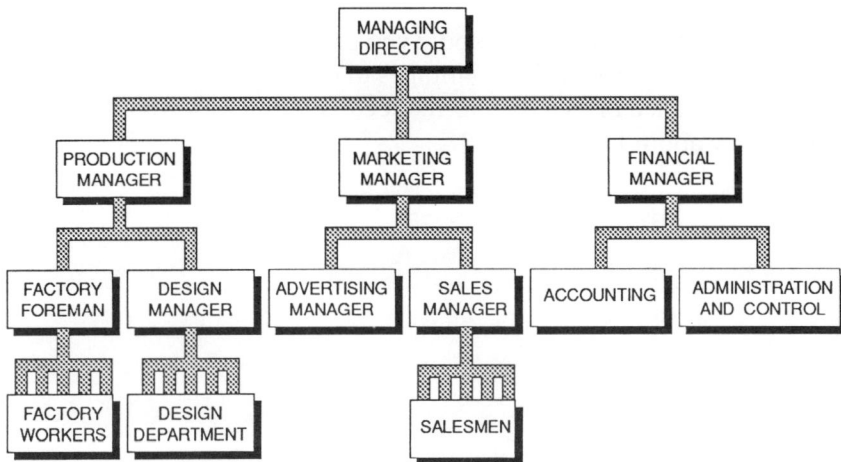

Figure 14

With increasing sales the Managing Director has decided to re-organize TOYJOY and has asked his top managers to propose what kind of organizational structure they think would be suitable. The MD favours a product line structure and wants to introduce three different product departments: children's toys, computer games, and adult games. At the moment children's toys comprise 60 % of sales, computer games only 15 %, and adult games 25%, but there is rapid growth in computer games and adult games.

1. Suppose you are one of the top managers and need to advise the MD. Which structure would you propose? Draw a new organization chart and write a report on the advantages of the new structure over the existing functional line structure.
2. What effect will your proposed new structure have on staff relations and on communication within TOYJOY?

CASE STUDY 2

INSTANT PRINT is a small business organization that specializes in printing. Mr Turvey started the business twenty-five years ago and is the owner-manager. He has just appointed a new foreman with supervision of twenty printers. Mr Turvey believes printers should get on with their job and that they need to be strictly controlled. The new foreman, Mr Fandeso, believes in giving praise and reward for good productivity and in keeping communication channels open, whereas Mr Turvey has always run the business on downward authoritative communication.

Mr Fandeso needs to persuade Mr Turvey of the value of changes in the communication systems.

1. If you were Mr Fandeso, how would you go about persuading Mr Turvey?
2. What are the dangers and advantages in each approach?
3. If you were called in as a management consultant, how would you advise Mr Turvey about his business?

7

THE CONCEPT OF TIME IN ENGLISH

GOALS OF THE CHAPTER

In this chapter we shall try to understand

❑ time now and the present
❑ time just before the present
❑ time then
❑ time before the past
❑ future time
❑ the future-in-the-past
❑ conditional and unreal time

and to use these concepts of time correctly in English

INTRODUCTION

The English have a different idea of time from most other people. Time is important to the traditional Englishman. He is precise about time and does not like to be late or to be kept waiting. Perhaps this comes from a rather exact tense structure of the verb in the English language, a structure that can be confusing to a person who speaks English as a second language. Of course, not every native English-speaker uses tenses correctly: there is an amusing story about an English girl who was in a class being taught the use of the past tense of the verb 'put' instead of 'putting' and who indignantly called out to the teacher, 'Johnny's puttin' *puttin'* where he shoulda puttin' *put.*' It is all very well to know the correct tense structure of English, but it is not always easy to use this structure correctly in everyday English. Elementary mathematics teaching often uses a number line to explain the number system:

$$\xleftarrow{\qquad} \begin{array}{ccccccccccc} -5 & -4 & -3 & -2 & -1 & 0 & 1 & 2 & 3 & 4 & 5 \end{array} \xrightarrow{\qquad}$$

This helps to teach negative and positive numbers. We shall use what we may call a time line to explain the English tense structure.

$$\xleftarrow{\qquad\qquad} \text{PAST} \qquad\qquad \text{PRESENT} \qquad\qquad \text{FUTURE} \xrightarrow{\qquad\qquad}$$

Although some scholars have said that there are really only two tenses, present and past, in English, we shall use the three basic tenses — past, present, and future — and then discuss conditional or unreal time.

TIME NOW AND THE PRESENT

The present tense, e.g. I *speak*, seldom refers to **time now**. We use the form, '*I am speaking*', to refer to time now. This is not the present tense, or the simple present as it is sometimes called; it is the **present continuous tense**. Confusion is caused by the names we give to tenses and by the way we are usually taught the tenses in English. Usually we start with the simple present tense and we naturally think that the present tense refers to the present, that is to *time now*, but it does not always. The present continuous, used to refer to an action now being performed, refers to *time now* or to the very immediate future, and it is with the present continuous that we should start our study of the concept of time in English.

The concept of **time now** is almost impossible to grasp. *Now* is unable to be captured at all in speech. Before you can say it, *time now* has gone, or else *time now* started some time in the past and is still continuing into the future. In a sense then time now is either a fleeting instant or a continuing experience hovering around present time.

NOW

PAST   PRESENT   FUTURE

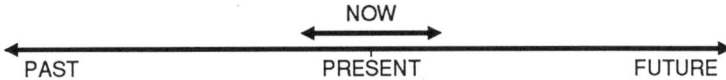

There is therefore a very close relationship between what is called the **present perfect tense** and the present continuous tense: we express this relationship very often by the use of the two adverbs *just* and *now*. Perhaps the close relationship between these two words causes the confusion among speakers of English when they use the two words together. Does *just now* mean present time or past time or future time?

It can be all three:

❑ I am *just now* drinking my third cup of tea. (Present)
❑ I have *just now* drunk my third cup of tea. (Past?)
❑ I shall *just now* drink my third cup of tea. (Future?)

In South Africa the expression 'just now' usually refers to future time, whereas in England and the United States it usually refers to present time, as we have already discussed.

  Time now is expressed by the use of the present continuous form: *He is now studying*. How do we use the so-called present tense or simple present tense then? The **simple present tense** is used in English for general truths or actions of habit, and not necessarily for *time now*.

❑ It rains in summer in most of South Africa.
❑ He brushes his teeth every morning after breakfast.

The present tense does not refer to the present at all but in a sense to all time:

PAST   PRESENT   FUTURE

Let us look at a few examples:

Exercise 1

Supply the correct present tense of the verb in brackets:

1. She (ride) to school each morning.

2. We now (study) the concept of time in English.

PAST   PRESENT   FUTURE

3. I now (sit) on a chair and (study).

PAST   PRESENT   FUTURE

4. He always (wake) up before six o'clock.

$\longleftarrow\hspace{8cm}\longrightarrow$

5. He usually (eat) cereal for breakfast, but today he (eat) porridge.

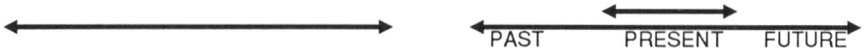

$\longleftarrow\hspace{4cm}\longrightarrow$ $\longleftrightarrow$

PAST   PRESENT   FUTURE

6. Dictionaries (explain) the meanings of words.

$\longleftarrow\hspace{8cm}\longrightarrow$

7. The man, who (run) across the road, (live) on the corner.

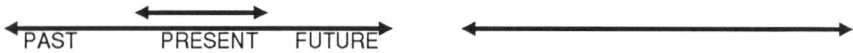

$\longleftrightarrow$ $\hspace{2cm}\longleftarrow\hspace{4cm}\longrightarrow$

PAST   PRESENT   FUTURE

8. A sponge (absorb) water.

$\longleftarrow\hspace{8cm}\longrightarrow$

9. Where you (go) for your holiday each year?

$\longleftarrow\hspace{8cm}\longrightarrow$

10. Where you (go) for your holiday this year?

$\longleftarrow\hspace{4cm}\longleftrightarrow\hspace{4cm}\longrightarrow$

PAST   PRESENT   FUTURE

Answers

1. She rides to school each morning.
2. We are now studying the concept of time in English.
3. I am now sitting in a chair and studying.
4. He always wakes up before six o'clock.
5. He usually eats cereal for breakfast, but today he is eating porridge.
6. Dictionaries explain the meanings of words.
7. The man, who is running across the road, lives on the corner.
8. A sponge absorbs water.
9. Where do you go for your holiday each year?
10. Where are you going for your holiday this year?

Sentences 1, 4, 5, 6, 7, 8, and 9 use the simple present to refer to habitual actions (1, 4, 5, 7, 9) or general truths (6, 8). Sentences 2, 3, 5, and 7 refer to *time now*. What about sentence 10? This does not refer to *time now* but to **time soon**. We use the present continuous tense for the immediate future (*time soon*) as well as for *time now*. So far, so good. But there are certain verbs in English that do not usually take the continuous tense, e.g. want, wish, love, like, hate, dislike, care, know, understand, have, own, possess, see, hear, recognize, accept, notice, believe, feel, think, mean, remember, forget, forgive, refuse, suppose, be, seem, belong to, contain, consist of, matter. We do not usually say, *I am wanting, I am loving, I am liking*; instead, **even if it is time now**, we say *I now want, I love her, I like this.*

Exercise 2

Supply the correct present tense of the verb in brackets:

1. I now (hate) to go to town on Saturday.

PAST   PRESENT   FUTURE

2. He now (own) two cars.

PAST   PRESENT   FUTURE

3. They now (seem) quite happy.

PAST   PRESENT   FUTURE

4. She now (know) how to sew.

PAST   PRESENT   FUTURE

5. He now (remember) her name.

PAST   PRESENT   FUTURE

Answers

1. I now hate to go to town on Saturday.
2. He now owns two cars.
3. They now seem quite happy.
4. She now knows how to sew.
5. He now remembers her name.

There are, however, verbs that sometimes take the present continuous and at other times do not. For example, the verb *appear* when it means *seem* does not take the present continuous, but, when it means something different, can take the continuous form:

❑ He *appears* quite happy at the moment.
❑ She is *appearing* in a new play on Broadway.

The verb *gather* does not take the continuous form when it means *understand* but does when it means *collect*:

❑ I gather that he is an alcoholic.
❑ I am gathering my papers together.

Furthermore, even those verbs that do not usually take the present continuous form may do so when we wish to give special emphasis to their relation to *time now* or to *time soon*. They are used idiomatically with words like *always* or *forever*. Here are a few examples:

❑ He is thinking of leaving.
❑ You're just being naughty now.

❏ You're forgetting something, aren't you?
❏ I'm thinking of the time when you made a fool of yourself.
❏ You're *always* hearing strange noises.
❏ You're *forever* seeing the worst side of him.
❏ You're *forever* having delusions of grandeur.

In the last three sentences the words *always* and *forever* mean *all the time* but there is a strong relation to *time now* as well.

TIME JUST BEFORE THE PRESENT

On our time line we have a point just before the present:

```
 ◄──────────────────────
◄────────────────────────────────────────────────────────►
   PAST                  PRESENT              FUTURE
```

To express time just before the present we use the **present perfect tense**. This represents an action that has stopped just before the present:

❏ I have just spoken to my mother.
❏ I have just drunk my third cup of tea.
❏ I have just heard some good news.

Besides the adverb *just* we also use the words *since* and *for* to express *time till now* or *time starting in the past up to now.*

❏ She has been absent *since* Friday.
❏ It has rained *for* five days.

The important feature of the present perfect tense is that the action is complete or 'perfect' just before the present. It is very closely related to *time now* because the action was finished just before *time now*. The present perfect tense is very often used in English, probably more than in any other language, and this causes difficulty to many speakers of English as a second or third language. It is used when we are thinking of an indefinite time in the past in its very definite relationship to time now. It should never be used in relationship to a definite time in the past. We never say, *He has paid his account yesterday.* Because we refer to a definite time in the past, we have to say, *He paid his account yesterday;* here we use the past tense. But we can say, *He has paid his accounts promptly for the last five months;* here we are referring to past time in relation to time now, and it is this definite relationship to the present that makes the present perfect tense a present tense rather than a past tense. This tense has sometimes been referred to as the *before-present tense.*

Besides the words *just, for,* and *since,* common words that are used with the present perfect tense are *already, ever, never,* and *not yet:*

❏ I have *never* seen her before.

❑   He has *not yet* completed his diploma.
❑   She has *already* drunk three cups of tea.
❑   Have they *ever* won a match?

Often the present perfect tense is used with negatives as in the previous examples, *I have never seen her before* and *He has not yet completed his diploma.* Other examples are:

❑   I haven't seen you for ages.
❑   He hasn't spoken to me since Christmas.

The important principle to understand about the present perfect tense is that it is more closely related to *time now* (the present) than *time then* (the past) because we are referring to an action that has finished just before *time now.*

But again we have difficulty in grasping or capturing *time now.* Therefore we often resort to a **continuous** form of the present perfect to show that although the action started in a time past it may continue through time now into the future. What, for instance, is the difference between *It has rained for five days* and *It has been raining for five days?* Strictly speaking, the difference is that the sentence *It has rained for five days* means it is no longer raining, whereas the sentence *It has been raining for five days* means that it is still raining. We may demonstrate it on the time line like this:

❑   It has rained for five days.

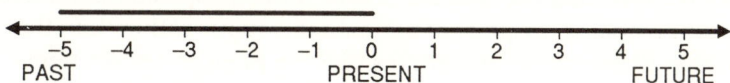

```
    ◄──┬────┬────┬────┬────┬────┬────┬────┬────┬────┬──►
      −5   −4   −3   −2   −1    0    1    2    3    4    5
     PAST                   PRESENT              FUTURE
```

❑   It has been raining for five days.

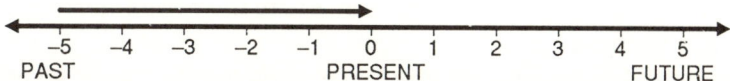

```
    ◄──┬────┬────┬────┬────┬────┬────┬────┬────┬────┬──►
      −5   −4   −3   −2   −1    0    1    2    3    4    5
     PAST                   PRESENT              FUTURE
```

Here are some sentences to show the difference between the present perfect continuous tense and the present continuous or the present perfect tense:

❑   I have been working here since 1977.

```
    ◄──────┬──────────┬───────────┬─────────────────┬──►
         PAST       1977        PRESENT            FUTURE
```

❑   I have worked here since 1977.

```
    ◄──────┬──────────┬───────────┬─────────────────┬──►
         PAST       1977        PRESENT            FUTURE
```

❑   I am working here now.

```
    ◄──────┬──────────────────────┬─────────────────┬──►
         PAST                   PRESENT            FUTURE
```

The relationship between the present perfect continuous and the present perfect tenses is very close and is often blurred. We say, for instance,

❑   Have you been waiting long for me?

```
          ┌──────────────────►
◄─────────┴─────────────────┬──────────────────────►
    PAST                 PRESENT               FUTURE
```

even though it would be more correct to say,

❑   Have you waited long for me?

```
          ┌─────────────────┐
◄─────────┴─────────────────┴──────────────────────►
    PAST                 PRESENT               FUTURE
```

One assumes the question is asked when a person arrives to keep an appointment and therefore strictly speaking the waiting is over (completed). We sometimes use the present perfect continuous tense in this way when we wish to make the point of a relatively long period that has passed without interruption:

❑   I've been waiting for you for half an hour.

```
          ┌──────────────────►
◄─────────┴─────────────────┬──────────────────────►
    PAST                 PRESENT               FUTURE
```

Again strictly speaking the waiting is over, but the speaker emphasizes the length of time by using the present perfect continuous rather than the present perfect tense. Similarly we sometimes use the present perfect tense when a period of time mentioned is obviously not yet over: *I haven't played tennis this year.* Even though the year may not have finished, the negative fact (not playing) has been completed. The reference is to the period starting from the beginning of the year up to the present (time now). Similarly we can say, *I haven't seen him today;* here we mean *from early morning to the present* even though the day is not over. Of course we must remember that the verbs that do not usually take the continuous tense add to this confusion between the present perfect and the present perfect continuous. We would say, *I have owned a motorbike for a year;* this could refer to a completed action starting a year ago and now ended

```
          ┌─────────────────┐
◄─────────┴─────────────────┴──────────────────────►
    PAST                 PRESENT               FUTURE
```

or it could refer to an uncompleted action starting a year ago and still continuing.

```
          ┌──────────────────►
◄─────────┴─────────────────┬──────────────────────►
    PAST                 PRESENT               FUTURE
```

We must never say, *I have been owning a motorbike for a year.* Similarly we should never say

- ❑ He has been having a cold for five days.
- ❑ He has been loving her for ten years.
- ❑ They have been knowing each other since their school days.

We say rather

- ❑ He has had a cold for five days.
- ❑ He has loved her for ten years.
- ❑ They have known each other since their school days.

The distinction between whether the action is completed or continues is not possible with these verbs.

Exercise 3

Give the correct tense of the verbs in brackets:

1. I (learn) Economics for the last six months, but I (understand) it yet.
2. I (work) here since October last year, but I just (decide) to leave.
3. He already (write) three letters since I (sit) here.
4. He (be) away from work all day because he (be) ill.
5. She (wash) her hair every day.
6. They (not see) each other since they had an argument.
7. He (lose) his spectacles. He (search) for them for three days, but he (not find) them yet.
8. Everything (go) up in price since the petrol increase.
9. He (talk) on the telephone now.
10. 'You (live) here long?' 'No, I just (move) here.'

Answers

1. I have been learning Economics for the last six months,

PAST   PRESENT   FUTURE

but I have not understood it yet [or I do not understand it yet].

PAST   PRESENT   FUTURE

2. I have been working since October last year,

PAST   PRESENT   FUTURE

but I have just decided to leave.

PAST   PRESENT   FUTURE

3. He has already written three letters

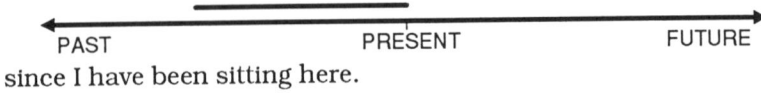

PAST — PRESENT — FUTURE

since I have been sitting here.

PAST — PRESENT — FUTURE

4. He has been away from work all day

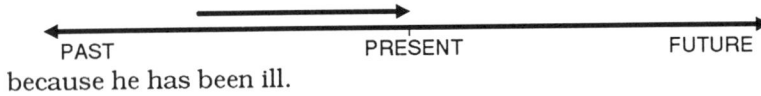

PAST — PRESENT — FUTURE

because he has been ill.

PAST — PRESENT — FUTURE

5. She washes her hair every day.

PAST — PRESENT — FUTURE

6. They have not seen each other since they had an argument.

PAST — PRESENT — FUTURE

7. He has lost his spectacles.

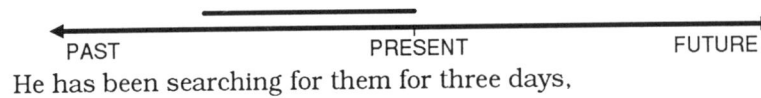

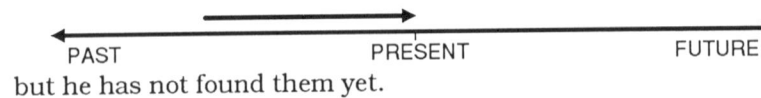

PAST — PRESENT — FUTURE

He has been searching for them for three days,

PAST — PRESENT — FUTURE

but he has not found them yet.

PAST — PRESENT — FUTURE

8. Everything has gone up in price since the petrol increase.

PAST — PRESENT — FUTURE

9. He is talking on the telephone now.

PAST — PRESENT — FUTURE

10. 'Have you been living here long?'

PAST — PRESENT — FUTURE

'No, I have just moved here.'

PAST — PRESENT — FUTURE

TIME THEN

The **past tense** is easy to understand and appears in most languages. What makes the English past tense difficult for foreigners is that there are different ways of forming the past tense of English verbs. With what we call *weak verbs*, the past tense is formed with -*d* or -*t*: *played, kicked, burnt*. With other verbs, which we call *strong verbs*, there is no -*d* or -*t* ending but only a vowel change or pronunciation change: *broke, chose, sang, read, led*. With *mixed verbs* there is both a vowel change and -*d* or -*t* ending: *brought, taught, swept, told*. The only way to master these forms is by continual practice and observation.

Time then refers to a time in the past when the action took place. Just as in the simple present tense there are two ways of expressing the present (e.g. *he plays* and *he does play*), so in the simple past there are two forms (e.g. *he played* and *he did play*). The second of these forms is used for emphasis, negatives, or questions:

❏ He *did* play.
❏ He *did not* play.
❏ *Did* he play?

A word frequently used with the past tense is ago: *He started working here a month ago.* This refers to a definite time before the present:

```
◄─────────────┬──────────────────────────────────►
          1 MONTH      PRESENT
```

Whenever an adverb or adverbial phrase refers to a definite time in the past, the past tense must be used:

❏ He started working here *last June.*
❏ He started working here *yesterday.*
❏ He came here *on Tuesday.*

All this is, as we have said, easy to understand. A common construction in English is a sentence which uses the past continuous tense:

❏ When I saw him last year, he *was working* in Johannesburg. The first tense *saw* refers to a definite time in the past(*last year*):

```
                SAW
◄───────────────┬───────────────────────────────►
          LAST YEAR      PRESENT
```

The second verb refers to a continuous action starting some time in the past and continuing for an indefinite period of time that may or may not have ended:

```
              WAS WORKING
              ◄─────────►
◄─────────────┬──────────────────────────────────►
          LAST YEAR      PRESENT
```

There may be two continuous actions going on at the same time:

❏   He was playing the piano while I was reading.

This refers to two actions continuing at the same time, and the beginning and the ending of the respective actions are not specified:

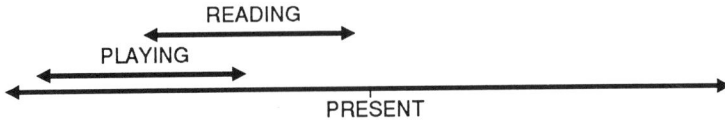

The **past continuous tense** is used for past actions that are often repeated:

❏   He was always complaining.
❏   He was forever making mistakes.

The words *always* and *forever* are often used in these constructions. If we were to represent such actions on our time line, they would be represented something like this:

The individual actions together make up a continual action and therefore we use the past continuous tense.

TIME BEFORE THE PAST

Just as the present perfect tense refers to a time before the present, so the **past perfect tense** refers to a time before a definite time in the past.

❏   When I saw him, he had just graduated.

The action of graduating had been completed by the time I saw him. Besides the conjunction *when*, the conjunctions *before* and *after* are often used in sentences with the past perfect tense.

❏   *After* they had finished eating they went to work.
❏   *Before* they went to work, they had finished eating.

Although the **past perfect continuous tense** is not very often used, we should know how it is formed. Just like the present perfect continuous tense (have + been + (verb) -ing), the past perfect continuous tense is formed by had + been + (verb) -ing, e.g. *I had been considering resigning for many months.*

THE PAST TENSES AND REPORTED OR INDIRECT SPEECH

A very common use of the past tenses is in reported or indirect speech. **Direct speech** quotes the actual words spoken:

❑ He said, 'I have had enough.'

Indirect speech does not use quotation marks (or inverted commas) and changes the tense of the verb(s) in the direct speech into the appropriate past tense.

❑ He said that he had had enough.

Here the present perfect *have had* changes into the past perfect *had had*. Similarly the simple present will change into the simple past; the present continuous will change into the past continuous; and the present perfect continuous will change into the past perfect continuous. It is important to note that this applies only if the verb of saying is in the past tense; in our example *said* is the verb of saying and is in the past tense. If the verb is not in the past tense the indirect or reported speech verb does not change its tense.

❑ He has reported, 'We made a great success of the project.'
❑ He has reported that they made a great success of the project.
But
❑ He reported, 'We made a great success of the project.'
❑ He reported that they had made a great success of the project.

We notice that the past of a simple past tense is the past perfect in the same way as the past of a present perfect tense is the past perfect. This is logical because in each case the action of the verb in the direct speech preceded the action of saying.

Exercise 4

Supply the correct tenses of the verbs in brackets:
1. They (go) to the conference last year.
2. He (sort) the papers when the manager (walk) into his office yesterday.
3. You (not receive) an increase since you (join) the staff a year ago.
4. She (tell) me yesterday that she already (finish) her work.
5. I am sorry that I (not realize) that you (lost) your father when I (see) you last week.
6. When I (go) to see him yesterday, he (listen) to the broadcast of the budget; he (say) that he (listen) since eleven o'clock.
7. After he (leave) school, he (go) to university for three years, then (start) work in Durban, where he now (live).
8. He (try) a long time before he finally (succeed) in solving the problem.
9. The personnel manager asked him what positions he previously (hold).
10. She told me what his name (be) after he (leave).

Answers:
1. They went to the conference last year.
    EITHER:
    (a) He had sorted the papers when the manager walked into his office yesterday.
    OR
    (b) He was sorting the papers when the manager walked into his office yesterday.
3. You have not received an increase since you joined the staff a year ago.
4. She told me yesterday that she had already finished her work.
5. I am sorry that I did not realize that you had lost your father when I saw you last week.
6. When I went to see him yesterday, he was listening to the broadcast of the budget; he said that he had been listening since eleven o'clock.
7. After he had left school, he went to university for three years, then started work in Durban, where he is now living.
8. EITHER:
    (a) He had tried a long time before he finally succeeded in solving the problem.
    OR:
    (b) He had been trying a long time before he finally succeeded in solving the problem.
    (The answer (b) suggests continual repeated attempts leading to frustration.)
9. The personnel manager asked him what positions he had previously held.
10. She told me what his name was after he had left.

FUTURE TIME

The **future tense** is perhaps the easiest tense in the English language. Originally there was no separate tense for the future in English. (This gives weight to the statement referred to previously that there are only two tenses in English — the present and the past.) We still use various **present forms** to **express future time:**

❏   The concert starts at 8 o'clock. (Simple present tense?)

8.00
PRESENT

❏   I'm going to the concert. (Present continuous tense?)

CONCERT
PRESENT

❏   She is singing tonight. (Present continuous tense?)

TONIGHT
PRESENT

❑   She is going to sing tonight. (Present continuous tense?)

All these sentences express future time, and yet what we usually call the future tense (the shall/will form) is not used. There are many other substitutes for the future. All these express future time in some way or other:

❑   He is to arrive at eight.
❑   He is about to resign.
❑   Do you wish to leave now?
❑   Do you want to leave?
❑   He intends to resign.
❑   They mean to go overseas next year.
❑   They hope to go overseas next year.

All these can be expressed with the future auxiliary *will:*

❑   He will arrive at eight.
❑   Will you leave now?
❑   He will resign.
❑   They will go overseas next year.

Although the meanings are not exactly the same, there is sufficient similarity to understand that the future tense with *shall* and *will* is not as necessary in English as the present and past tenses are.

Nevertheless the future with *shall* and *will* is used, and we need to say something about it. Traditionally *shall* is used with the first person (*I* and *we*) to express the future and with the other persons (*you, he, she, it, they*) to express definite intention or compulsion. Similarly *will* is used with the first person to express definite intention or compulsion and with other persons to express the future.

❑   I shall see you tomorrow. (Future)
❑   You shall do your assignment now. (Compulsion)
❑   He will meet you at five o'clock. (Future)
❑   I will do my best.(Definite intention)

But these traditional distinctions are disappearing. We tend to use *will* with all persons to express the future:

❑   I will do it for you tomorrow.
❑   He will do it for you tomorrow.

It is hardly wrong to use *will* with the first person any longer to express the future, but, as we have said, the form *going to* is used more frequently:

❑   I am going to do it for you tomorrow.
❑   He is going to do it for you tomorrow.

The **future continuous tense** (*will be (verb) -ing*) is also common. It expresses the same idea of continuity as the present continuous and the past continuous tenses do: *When I see you again, I'll be wearing my new suit.* The time referred to in *I'll be wearing* may be shown on the time line:

PRESENT   FUTURE

The future continuous tense is often used in questions:

❑   Will you be working tomorrow?

Notice the subtle difference between this and

❑   Will you work tomorrow?

The first (*Will you be working tomorrow?*) is a query about the person's activities the next day, whereas the second (*Will you work tomorrow?*) is a request (often used with the word *please*) for the person to work the next day.

Let us return to the sentence *When I see you again, I'll be wearing my new suit.* This time we pay attention to the temporal or time clause *When I see you again*: it is interesting that, although the verb *see* obviously refers to a future time, it is in the present tense. Temporal clauses with main clauses in the future take the present, not the future:

❑   When you come tomorrow, I'll be waiting for you.
❑   He will come when you are ready.
❑   He will be angry when you do that.

TIME JUST BEFORE THE FUTURE

The **future perfect tense** refers to a time just before the future.
❑   By next year the house will have been built.

PRESENT   NEXT YEAR

This is what we expect of perfect tenses: the present perfect refers to a time just before the present, and the past perfect refers to a time just before the past; it is therefore to be expected that the future perfect refers to a time just before a stated future time. It refers to an action that we foresee will have been completed before a certain projected future time.

The **future perfect continuous tense** is occasionally used:

❑   By July next year he will have been living in this house for six years.

This means that he is expected to continue living in the house after July:

PRESENT   SIX YEARS

With temporal clauses we do not, however, use the future perfect tense when we are referring to future time. We use rather the present perfect tense:

❏ We shall leave when we have had our breakfast.

We do not say *when we shall have had our breakfast* even though we are referring to a time just before a projected future occasion.

We can now compare these two sentences:

❏ We'll not leave till the post arrives.
❏ We'll not leave till the post has arrived.

The meaning is almost identical, but the first sentence implies that at the moment the post arrives we shall leave, whereas the second implies a certain delay — perhaps to read the post that has arrived.

THE FUTURE-IN-THE-PAST

There are certain occasions when we need to use the future-in-the-past. The most common is in reported or indirect speech:

❏ The man said, 'I shall see you tomorrow.'
❏ The man said that he would see me the next day.

The future-in-the-past uses *would* or *should* in the same way as the future tense uses *will* or *shall*.

The other use of the future-in-the-past is in conditional tenses. We shall come to them in the next section.

Exercise 5

Supply the correct tenses of the verbs in brackets:

1. The auditors (come) to inspect the firm's accounts next week.
2. I never (forget) what my managing director just (tell) me.
3. The financial statements (be completed) before the next meeting.
4. We (discuss) the matter tomorrow after you (finish) your report.
5. In a few hours' time, when he (make) his decision, we (know) whether we (waste) our time.
6. When they (come) here again, we (move) into our new office.
7. I (wait) for him when we (arrive) at the airport.
8. We not (take) a decision till we (hear) from our lawyers.
9. The chairman announced that there (be) another meeting in two days' time.
10. We (be asked) yesterday to forecast what our profits (be) by the end of the year.

Answers

1. The auditors will come to inspect the firm's accounts next week.
    OR:
    The auditors are coming to inspect the firm's accounts next week.
    OR:
    The auditors will be coming to inspect the firm's accounts next week.
2. I shall never forget what my managing director has just told me.
3. EITHER:
    The financial statements will have been completed before the next meeting.
    OR:
    The financial statements will be completed before the next meeting.
4. We shall discuss the matter tomorrow after you have finished your report.
5. EITHER:
    In a few hours' time, when he makes his decision, we shall know whether we have been wasting our time.
    OR:
    In a few hours' time, when he has made his decision, we shall know whether we have wasted our time.
6. EITHER:
    When they come here again, we shall have moved into our new offices.
    OR:
    When they come here again, we shall be moving into our new offices.
7. I'll be waiting for him when he arrives at the airport.
8. EITHER:
    We shall not take a decision till we hear from our lawyers.
    OR:
    We shall not take a decision till we have heard from our lawyers.
9. The chairman announced that there would be another meeting in two days' time.
10. We were asked yesterday to forecast what our profit would be by the end of the year.

(As we see from these answers, there are many different answers possible.)

CONDITIONAL AND UNREAL TIME

The future-in-the-past used to be used in English to express wishes: *Would that I had succeeded!* This rather old-fashioned construction means *I wish that I had succeeded*. The use of the future-in-the-past in this way used to be called the optative mood of the verb. Wishes express unreal time: in the previous examples it is obvious that *I* did not succeed and therefore *I* wish that something that did not happen had actually happened. It is impossible to express conditional or unreal time on the time line we used for past, present and future time.

Conditional sentences use this idea of unreal time:

❑   The firm would have better results if productivity were improved.
❑   The firm would have had better results if productivity had been improved.

The first of these two sentences refers to a probable result if an imaginary event took place. The second sentence refers to an impossible result because we know that productivity was not improved.

There are really three ways of expressing imaginary events:

1.   If he comes, we will see him.
2.   If he came, we would see him.
3.   If he had come, we would have seen him.

No 1 expresses a likely or probable imaginary result if a certain condition is fulfilled. The conditional clause verb is in the present (*comes*) and the main clause verb is in the future (*will see*). (Sometimes, if we wish to express a polite request, we use the future (*will*) or the future-in-the-past (*would*) with conditional sentences: *If you will/would take a seat, I'll attend to the matter.*)

No 2 expresses an unlikely or improbable imaginary result if a certain condition, which we imagine but which we know is not happening now, were to happen. (This is sometimes called the **subjunctive** in English to explain why we say *If he **were** to come, we would see him* instead of *If he **was** to come, we should see him.* It includes all the unreal conditions we often use: *If I were you, I'd resign; If I were a bird, I'd fly away; If he were President, he would make many changes; If she were married, she would drive her husband crazy.*) Apart from these subjunctive forms, we can say that the conditional clause is in the past tense (*came*) and the main clause in the future-in-the-past (*would see*).

No 3 expresses an impossible result that we imagine would have happened if a certain condition, which we know did not happen, had been fulfilled. We use the past perfect tense (*had come*) in the conditional clause and the perfect of the future-in-the-past (*would have seen*) in the main clause.

Exercise 6

Supply the correct forms of the verbs in brackets:
1.   If he had known that, he not (make) that mistake.
2.   If he arrives, she (take) him to see the new plans.
3.   If he came, I (know) nothing about it.
4.   He would improve if he (pay) more attention to his work.
5.   He will be promoted if he (continue) to work so well.
6.   He would have arrived if he (catch) the morning flight.
7.   If she were a man, she (get) the job.
8.   If he (be) more reliable, he would inspire more confidence.
9.   Unless he (hurry), he will be late for the meeting.

Answers

1. If he had known that, he would not have made that mistake. (No 3)
2. If he arrives, she will take him to see the new plans. (No 1)
3. If he came, I knew nothing about it. (No 2)
4. He would improve if he paid more attention to his work. (No 2)
5. He will be promoted if he continues to work so well. (No 1)
6. He would have arrived if he had caught the morning flight. (No 3)
7. If she were a man, she would get the job. (No 2)
8. If he were more reliable, he would inspire more confidence. (No 2)
9. Unless he hurries, he will be late for the meeting. (No 1)

The same conditional tenses are sometimes used without the conjunction (*if* or *unless*) with No 2 and 3 sentences:

❑ Had he known that, he would not have made that mistake. (cf. 1)
❑ Were she a man, she would get the job. (cf. 7)

Other constructions are possible with conditional or unreal time:

❑ But for that setback, he would have become famous.
(This means the same as: *If it had not been for that setback, he would have become famous* (No 3).)

The words *providing that* and *supposing* are also used:

❑ You can take leave *providing that* you fill in a leave form.
(Compare this with *You can take leave if you fill in a leave form* (No 1).)
❑ What would happen *supposing* he died?
(Compare this with *What would happen if he died?* (No 2).)

Finally the expression *If only* is used to express wishes or hopes:

❑ *If only* he were to take more interest in his work, he would be promoted. (No 2)

Sometimes we leave the main clause out and it becomes a wish or a hope on its own:

❑ *If only it stops raining!* (I hope it will stop raining.) (No 1)
❑ *If only it would stop raining!* (I don't really expect it to.) (No 2)
❑ *If only it had stopped raining!* (I know it didn't stop raining.) (No 3)

CONCLUSION: AUXILIARY VERBS

We have now looked at various concepts of time in the English language. Some of these concepts are the same for all languages while others are peculiar to English or differ from some other languages and therefore cause confusion. The English language affords many possibilities of expressing different concepts of time and these assist precise communication.

We have not referred directly to **auxiliary verbs** in this chapter, except where they are used to form tenses. We have referred in passing to the use of *be* in forming continuous tenses, to the use of *do* and *did* in forming alternative forms of the present and past, to the use of *have* in forming the perfect tenses, and to the use of *shall* and *will* in the formation of future tenses. There are, of course, other auxiliaries to which we have not referred: *may, can, must , need, ought, dare,* and *used.* These auxiliary verbs do not refer so much to time as to what classical languages tend to call moods: *may* is close to the subjunctive mood and *must* to the imperative mood, for example.

Auxiliary verbs are used in many different idiomatic ways. These idiomatic uses do not fall within the scope of this book, but one mistake needs to be mentioned:

❑   He can be able to come.

This mistake may arise from the fact that *can* means the same as *is able to* and therefore they are mistakenly used together rather than as alternatives: either *He can come* or *He is able to attend.* It interesting to note that there is not, however, the same confusion between *must* and *have to*: we have never heard anyone say, for example, *I must have to work late tonight.* A more plausible reason for this mistake with *can* and *be able to* is the confusion between *can* and *may*: whereas we can say *He may be able to come* we should not say, *He can be able to come.*

An interesting idiomatic usage of auxiliary verbs with the perfect infinitive is directly connected with the concept of time in English. The auxiliary verb **may** is used with the perfect infinitive form to express a speculation or doubt about a past action:

❑   He may have done the work.
❑   He might have done the work.

The difference between these two sentences is slight: *might* emphasizes the doubt even more than *may*; both sentences mean, *It is possible that he did the work*, but *might* expresses a stronger doubt.

The auxiliary verb **could** is used with the perfect infinitive form to express a past ability that was not, however, used:

❑   He could have told us the answer.

This means he knew the answer but he did not tell us. An interesting comparison is with *can* and the perfect infinitive form:

❑   Can he possibly have known the answer?
❑   He cannot possibly have known the answer.

The use of *can* instead of *could* in this interrogative or negative form throws a great deal of doubt into the sentence. The auxiliary verb **must**, on the other hand, is used with the perfect infinitive form to express strong conviction about something that is nevertheless uncertain; the conviction comes from a present deduction about any action that is past:

❏   He must have known the answer.

The negative form of the auxiliary verb **need** is used with the perfect infinitive form to express the lack of obligation to perform an action, which was nevertheless performed:

❏   He needn't have spent so much time on that work.

The auxiliary verbs **should** and **ought** are used with the perfect infinitive to express the past neglect of a certain action that is seen at the time of speaking as an unfulfilled responsibility:

❏   He should have spent more time on that work.
❏   He ought to have spent more time on that work.

From these few remarks about auxiliary verbs we see again how expressive a language English is in dealing with the concept of time.

TERMINOLOGY AND CONCEPTS

1.   TIME NOW
2.   PRESENT CONTINUOUS
3.   SIMPLE PRESENT
4.   HABITUAL ACTION
5.   GENERAL TRUTHS
6.   TIME JUST BEFORE THE PRESENT
7.   PRESENT PERFECT
8.   PRESENT PERFECT CONTINUOUS
9.   TIME THEN
10. PAST
11. PAST CONTINUOUS
12. TIME BEFORE THE PAST
13. PAST PERFECT
14. REPORTED OR INDIRECT SPEECH
15. DIRECT SPEECH
16. FUTURE TIME
17. TIME JUST BEFORE THE FUTURE
18. FUTURE PERFECT
19. THE FUTURE-IN-THE-PAST
20. CONDITIONAL AND UNREAL TIME
21. LIKELY OR PROBABLE CONDITIONS
22. IMPROBABLE CONDITIONS

23. SUBJUNCTIVE USE OF 'WERE'
24. IMPOSSIBLE CONDITIONS
25. AUXILIARY VERBS
26. AUXILIARY VERBS + PERFECT INFINITIVE

APPLICATION

Supply the correct tenses of the verbs in brackets:
1. This is the third time you (stay) away from work in two months; you (stay) away last Tuesday. If you (be) absent again this year, I (dismiss) you.
2. In five minutes' time, when the meeting (begin), I (sit) in this room for the last three hours.
3. I apologize that you (be) not met at the station. If I (know) you (come), I meet you.
4. Mr Jones just (go) to the bank. You (see) him if you just (walk) along that road. (Three possibilities for the second sentence.)
5. He (be) the prize-winner if he not (offend) the judges with his arrogant behaviour last week.
6. I (see) him yesterday when he (eat) his lunch. (Two possibilities for *eat*.)
7. By this time next week I (be) in New York. I (travel) half-way round the world by then. After I (make) the same trip last year, I (be) exhausted.
8. I (work) in this position for the last ten years. I (look) for a better position soon. (At least three possibilities for the verb *look*.)
9. Whenever she (say) that to me, I (feel) insulted.
10. He ought to (do) the work on the car more carefully. Then he (can) to sell the car for a much higher price, but now he (must be) satisfied with a price that (cover) his costs only.
11. What you (do) now? You should (finish) that job two hours ago. Unless you (finish) it by lunch time, I (ask) someone else to do it.
12. You needn't (write) to him because we (go) to see him tomorrow.
13. If I (be) you, I (apologize) to him. What you (do) to him is not right. Anyone else (be) angry if you (do) it to him.
14. I hear you just (graduate). Where the graduation ceremony (take) place?
15. You (wait) here long? Who you (wait) for? You (be) sure you (make) the appointment for seven o'clock and not seven-thirty?

(For other excellent exercises on the correct use of tenses, see W. Stannard Allen's book, *Living English Structure* (Longmans, first published in 1947).)

8

THE CONCEPT OF NUMBER IN ENGLISH

GOALS OF THE CHAPTER

The English language uses a concept of number that causes problems for speakers of English as a second or a third language. First-language speakers of English have little or no problem with this concept, not necessarily because they understand it but because they have grown up with the concept and because practice has allowed them to assimilate it in their youth. By the end of this chapter you should be able to:

❑ understand the concept of number in English
❑ understand the difference between countable and uncountable nouns
❑ use the indefinite article correctly
❑ distinguish between words that are sometimes countable and sometimes uncountable according to their contexts
❑ observe the rule of concord between the subject and the verb
❑ use correctly words that illustrate the concept of number in English
❑ use pronouns correctly according to their number in their contexts
❑ correct sentences that abuse the concept of number

THE CONCEPT OF NUMBER

Traditionally English language teaching has begun with the study of the various parts of speech — noun, verb, adjective, adverb, pronoun, preposition, conjunction, article, interjection. And in this traditional approach the noun is divided into four types, Proper, Common, Collective, and Abstract. W. Stannard Allen in his *Living English Structure — A Practice Book for Foreign Students,* first published in 1947, begins with a section on countable and uncountable nouns. The division of nouns into countable and uncountable nouns has more significance than the traditional categories of nouns. Because English uses the indefinite article, *a* or *an,* in front of a countable noun in the singular, because certain of the English tenses require the verb to take different forms with singular and plural subjects, and because certain other words depend on the concept of number for their correct usage, it is useful to understand this concept. As we have already seen, speakers of English as a first language will have used the indefinite article correctly and unconsciously from their childhood days, but it will be interesting for them to learn the concept and it will be helpful for them as managers to understand the problems that speakers of English as a foreign language have with the concept. For those in South Africa who have to use English in business when it is not their home language, a study of the concept of number in English may help them to improve their English usage.

COUNTABLE AND UNCOUNTABLE NOUNS AND THE USE OF THE INDEFINITE ARTICLE

A noun is **countable** if it has a plural form. An **uncountable** noun usually has no plural form and does not normally take an indefinite article (*a* or *an*) in front of it when it is used in the singular. A countable noun on the other hand can have an indefinite article in front of it. In the sentence, *A cow gives milk,* the noun *cow* is countable and in its singular form can be preceded by the indefinite article *a,* whereas *milk* is uncountable. We cannot therefore say *a milk.* Since African languages do not have the indefinite article, many black South Africans become confused by the use of the indefinite article in English. The Afrikaans language uses the indefinite article but often a noun that is uncountable in English may take the indefinite article in Afrikaans and therefore there is confusion when an Afrikaner speaks English. For example an Afrikaner may say *a bread* because in Afrikaans he may ask for *'n brood* when he orders a loaf of bread at a shop. Typical uncountable nouns in English are foodstuffs:
❑   butter, cheese, milk, bread, coffee, jam, mutton, garlic, celery, mint, sugar, tea, meat, flour, food, marmalade, rhubarb, beer, wine, bacon, venison, pork.

So-called **abstract nouns**, which are the names of concepts or states of mind and which refer to ideas that cannot be felt, tasted, heard, smelt or seen as separate objects, are usually uncountable:

❑ courage, friendship, stupidity, truth, fear, love, hope, misery, despair, delight, sleep, health.

We do not therefore speak normally of *a courage* or *a despair* except in unusual circumstances to which we shall refer later. Another group of words that are usually uncountable are words that refer to the weather in general terms:

❑ darkness, cold, warmth, daytime, sunshine, rain, weather

Names of academic disciplines are usually uncountable:

❑ literature, philosophy, geology, geography, biology, algebra

Names of sporting pursuits are uncountable:

❑ football, soccer, rugby, cricket, hockey

Names of materials are also uncountable:

❑ glass, iron, wood, paper, cloth, stone

Names from agriculture fall into this category as well:

❑ grass, corn, wheat, maize

Some nouns, although they are always in a plural form, have a singular meaning and, of course, they are therefore classed as uncountable nouns:

❑ news, politics, economics, physics, mathematics, measles.

Other commonly used words that are uncountable are:

❑ money, advice, information, stationery, gambling, baggage, luggage, dirt

These lists are not comprehensive and merely help to illustrate the concept of uncountable nouns. The linking of countable nouns to the **indefinite article** when they are used in the singular is a feature of English that causes difficulty. A few comments about the use of the indefinite article would not therefore be out of place. Generally speaking, the indefinite article is used before a countable noun in the singular when the noun is referred to for the first time and when it refers to no particular person, place, or thing.

❑ I saw *a man* running across the street.

The use of the indefinite article before *man* tells us that it is the first time I saw him and I could not distinguish which particular man he was. The next time I refer to this man I will use the definite article (*the*) in referring to him because he has become a definite or particular person (he has already been mentioned before):

❑ *The man* was wearing a brown jacket.

This is the most common usage of the indefinite article then: when it refers to a noun mentioned for the first time and representing no particular person, place, or thing. There are, however, other uses of the indefinite article.

1. The indefinite article is used to show that the countable noun in the singular is used to represent all things of that kind.
    When we say *A dog has ears*, we mean *all* dogs have ears; *every* or *any* dog has ears.
2. The indefinite article is used with a noun that is a complement of a verb:
    He is a manager.
    This very often includes a name of a profession:
    He is a doctor.
    Mr Smith is an engineer.
    But it could also include a description of some kind of characteristic or quality:
    Chief Luthuli was a great man.
    He became a good businessman.
3. An indefinite article often has the meaning of *one*:
    I have a son.
    This means I have one son.
    Do you have a car?
    The answer to this question could be *Yes, I have a car* or *Yes, I have two cars.*
4. An interesting use of the indefinite article is with two things that usually go together, such as *a cup and saucer, a knife and fork.* Notice we do not repeat the indefinite article.
5. Certain exclamations use the indefinite article:
    What a hot day it is!
    Such a pity you cannot attend the meeting!
    What a mistake that was!
    What a good meal this is!
    In these exclamations the indefinite article is used with countable nouns in the singular. For uncountable nouns and for countable nouns in the plural the indefinite article is not used:
    What good meals this restaurant serves!
    What bad news this is!
    What good advice he gives!
    What courage he showed!
6. The indefinite article is used with the words *few* and *little*. When the indefinite article is used before *few*, i.e. *a few*, it must be followed by a countable noun in the plural:
    I have a few papers on my desk.
    When the indefinite article is used before *little*, i.e. *a little*, it must be followed by an uncountable noun (obviously in the singular since uncountable nouns have no plurals):
    I have a little money.

The expression *a few* means a small number: *I have a few papers on my desk* means *I have a small number of papers on my desk*. But *few* without the article means something different: *I have few papers on my desk* denotes scarcity or lack: it means *I don't have many papers on my desk and I don't have much work to do*. The distinction between *a few* and *few* is an important one that speakers of English as a foreign language often find difficult. *I have a few friends* may mean that the speaker, without boasting, is expressing a certain satisfaction about the number of friends he has. But if he says, *I have few friends*, he is definitely stating that he lacks friends and he probably regrets that he does not have more.

Similarly the difference between *a little* and *little* expresses a fine distinction. *I have a little money* denotes that the speaker does not have much money but he may have enough for a modest purchase: to buy a newspaper or to lend to another person. But if the speaker says, *I have little money*, he expresses regret that he does not have more. If someone is asking him for a loan and he answers *I have a little money*, the obvious implication is that he may lend him some money; but if the answer is *I have little money*, the implication is that he cannot lend him any money and probably needs a loan himself.

7. The indefinite article may be used before some numerical expressions: a dozen (12), a score (20), a century (100), a hundred, a thousand, a million. Sometimes the word *half* precedes the numerical expression: half a dozen (6), half an hour, half a year. There are certain expressions like *a lot of, a great many* and *a great deal of* that use the indefinite article:
   I have a lot of money.
   I have a great many papers on my desk.
   I have a great deal of work to do.
   Notice that *a lot of* and *a great deal of* are followed by uncountable nouns, whereas *a great many* is followed by a countable noun in the plural. Similarly *an amount of* is followed by an uncountable noun, whereas *a number of* is followed by a countable noun in the plural:
   An amount of money was missing.
   A number of letters was (or were) missing.

8. The indefinite article is used in expressions of price or speed or in expressions or ratios to show that it is used distributively to mean *each* or *every*:
   R10 an hour
   sixty kilometres an hour
   twice a year
   60 c a metre.

9. The indefinite article is used with a person's name and title to imply that the person is a stranger:
   I met a Mr Jones at the party.
   There is a Mrs Green to see you.
   There was a Professor Smith at the meeting.

These sentences tell us that, although the speakers knew the names of the people, they did not know them personally.

10. The indefinite article is used with possessives in the following way:

He is a friend of my brother's.

This means the same as *He is one of my brother's friends.* Other examples are

I borrowed a pen of Tony's.

I read a magazine of John's.

11. The indefinite article is sometimes used to mean the same as *like* when used with a proper noun:

He is a Pele.

This means *He is like Pele*, i.e. a good soccer player. Another example is:

'A Daniel come to judgement.'

Here Shylock in Shakespeare's play *Merchant of Venice* was praising Portia as being as wise as Daniel.

12. The indefinite article is used with a countable noun when it occurs after an adjective preceded by adverbs such as *too, how, so* and *as*:

She is not as good a typist as that.

She is as quick a typist as you are likely to find.

It's too sensitive a matter to discuss with the staff.

We did not realize how important a decision it was.

13. Sometimes the indefinite article has the meaning of *the same* in idiomatic expressions:

Birds of a feather flock together.

This means *Birds of the same feather or the same sort.* Another example is:

They're all of a size.

14. A difficult idiomatic usage includes the indefinite article even with uncountable nouns:

He shows a wisdom beyond his years.

This means the same as *He showed a type of wisdom that we should expect of a person much older.* This idiomatic usage of the indefinite article even with an uncountable noun should convince us of the truth of the statement that there are no hard-and-fast rules of English: there is an exception for every rule. But it does not mean that we should forget about learning the rules. When we know the rules we shall more easily learn the exceptions. The **general rule** that we have learnt is that the indefinite article precedes a countable noun in the singular but not an uncountable noun. The characteristic of the **exception** to this general rule is that an uncountable noun may be preceded by the indefinite article if there is a qualifying phrase or clause after the uncountable noun. In the example *He showed a wisdom beyond his years*, the qualifying phrase is *beyond his years*. In the example *There is a happiness that is close to sorrow*, the qualifying clause is *that is close to sorrow*. The last example could mean *There is a type of happiness that is close to sorrow*, i.e. that causes tears.

In both the examples we have explained the exception to the general rule by inserting the words *type of* between the indefinite article and the uncountable noun and we could therefore explain away the exception by saying that it is an idiomatic ellipsis, in which the words *type of* or *sort of* have been omitted.

Our difficulties with countable and uncountable nouns are not over yet. There are some uncountable nouns which, in different contexts, are countable. The word *air* is usually uncountable:

❑   The *air* we breathe in cities is usually polluted.

But the word *air* can be countable when it means a melody or in the idiomatic expressions *to put on airs* or *airs and graces*. The sentence *He has an air of importance* may be another example of the exception to the rule which we mentioned above. Here the word *air* means *appearance* or *manner*. The word *paper* when used to refer to the substance manufactured from wood is uncountable (*a noun of mass* as J. Y. T. Greig calls an uncountable noun):

❑   Sappi produces paper from wood.

But when it means a newspaper or an examination paper or documents it is a countable noun (or a *noun of multitude* as Greig calls it):

❑   I bought a paper today.
❑   It was a difficult paper we wrote today.
❑   There were a few papers on his desk.

Other examples of words that can be either countable or uncountable according to their contexts are *iron, drink, dress, stone, rock* and *glass*. To sum up then, countable nouns (or nouns of multitude) are generally preceded by the indefinite article when they are used in the singular, while some nouns are either countable or uncountable (or nouns of mass). In the rare case of uncountable nouns being qualified, uncountable nouns may be preceded by the indefinite article.

We have so far dealt with examples of when the indefinite article *is* used. Perhaps some remarks on when the indefinite article is *not* used would help round off this discussion.

1. The indefinite article is not used before countable nouns in the plural:
    Dogs are animals.
2. The indefinite article is not generally used before uncountable nouns:
    He offered me advice on how to do the job.
    (Some often make the mistake of saying *an advice* or using *advice* in the plural.) If we wish to indicate a certain quality of an uncountable noun, we use the adjective *some:*
    He offered me *some* advice on how to do the job.
    He gave me *some* bread.
    There is *some* truth in what he said.

We shall end this section with some advice about **the definite article and when to use *a* or *an***. Although this is not about the concept of number, it is a good time to make these points now.

1. The definite article *the* is used to identify the noun it precedes as a definite or special example. The first reference to the noun may be preceded by an indefinite article, but, once the noun has been identified as a known example, it will be preceded by *the*:

    I saw *a* man walking down the road. *A* dog attacked *the* man, who kicked *the* dog.

2. The definite article is used before nouns of which there is usually only one of its kind, e.g. *the* sun, *the* moon, *the* sky, *the* station.

3. There is sometimes an important difference in meaning between certain nouns preceded by the definite article and those nouns used without the article:

    He went to the prison.

    He went to prison.

    The first sentence means something different from the second sentence. It does not imply that he is a prisoner whereas the second does. Compare these other examples:

    He's at school.

    He went to the school to see his son's teacher.

    He's in hospital.

    He went to the hospital to see a patient.

    The ship's at sea.

    We went to the sea to have a swim.

    You have probably noticed that there is a strong sense of place attached to these words. When they are used without the article, there is a close association with the special function of these nouns:

    He went to university.

    This means he went to study. But if the noun is used with the article there is a different sense:

    He went to the university to pick up his son.

    Here there is only a sense of place and no sense of his going to study. Other words that have differences in meaning when used with and without the article are *bed, port, dock, deck, church, train* and *canvas*.

4. Finally, there is some confusion between when to use *a* and when to use *an*. The rule is that *a* is used before consonants and *an* before vowels. The only exception is that *an* is used before *h* which is silent , e.g. *an honest man*. Some people still insist on saying *an historic occasion* or *an hotel* , but these are wrong. We should say *a historic occasion* and *a hotel*.

THE CONCEPT OF NUMBER AND THE RULE OF CONCORD BETWEEN THE SUBJECT AND THE VERB

The English language requires certain different forms of the verb when the subject is singular or plural.

- ❏ He *is* a good manager.
- ❏ They *are* good managers.
- ❏ He *has* a flair for statistics.
- ❏ They *have* a flair for statistics.
- ❏ He *was* a good administrator.
- ❏ They *were* good administrators.
- ❏ He *stands* to gain from the transaction.
- ❏ They *stand* to gain from the transaction.

This is simple enough. But, because English has these different forms of the verb for singular and plural and because other languages like Afrikaans and African languages do not have different forms for singular and plural, mistakes do occur. Speakers of English as a foreign language need to take note of these differences and to try to adapt to the English usage.

However, even speakers of English as a first language make mistakes and do not obey the rule of concord. Here are a few examples of typical mistakes and their correct forms.

1. Some nouns, as we have already seen, appear to be plural but are usually used in the singular:
   athletics, politics, economics, statistics, mathematics, news, measles, mumps.
   We say, *Mathematics is difficult,* not *Mathematics are difficult; The news is at eight o'clock,* not *The news are at eight o'clock; Measles has broken out,* not *Measles have broken out.*
2. Some nouns may appear to be singular but are usually used in the plural; *people, acoustics, heroics, hysterics.* It is correct to say:
   People *are* living there.
   The accoustics of the room *are* poor.
   Heroics *have* no place in business.
   Hysterics *have* no place in business.
3. Unfortunately, however, there are some words which can be either singular or plural. Although *people* is usually plural, we can nevertheless speak of *a people* or *peoples:*
   The English *are* a strange people.
   There *are* many different peoples who inhabit South Africa.
   The difference is between *people* meaning *persons in general* and *a people* meaning *a race or a tribe or a nation.*
   Similarly the word *ethics* is singular when it is used as the name of a science or a field of study:
   Ethics *is* a course of study in philosophy.

But it is plural when it means *rules of conduct:*
The ethics of that business firm *leave* a lot to be desired.

4. Often the subject of the verb (i.e. the noun or the pronoun that is usually the doer of the verb's action) is separated from the verb by many words. The number of the verb (whether it is a singular or a plural verb) is taken from the subject even though there are many words intervening:
The teacher, as well as her pupils, *leaves* school at three o'clock.
The intervening words *as well as her pupils* do not make the verb plural (*leave*) because it is *The teacher* who is the subject of the verb, *leaves.* Words like *as well as* . . . , *together with* . . . , *in addition to* . . . , *with* . . . , *except* . . . , and *no less than* do not affect the number of the verb; only the subject does.
The teacher, together with her son, *was* involved in an accident.
The Managing Director, in addition to the rest of the Board, *was* dismissed.
The Manager, with his Secretary, *has* to attend the meeting
The committee, except two of its members, *needs* to be re-elected.
The whole Board, no less than twelve members, *was* found guilty.

5. Often when the singular subject is followed by the preposition *of* with a plural noun we make the mistake of making the verb plural:
The decision of the two men were proved to be wrong.
It is the decision (singular) that was proved wrong. Sometimes a plural subject is followed by *of* with a singular noun and this causes difficulty:
The decisions of the managing director was always wise.
Of course the verb should be *were.*
Similarly subjects that begin with *one of* must be in the singular despite what follows the word *of:*
One of the many decisions *was* to promote Jones to foreman.
Surprisingly though, *none of* is so often followed by a plural verb that it has become accepted:
None of us *were* at the meeting.
Despite the fact that the verb should obviously be *was,* common usage has forced the incorrect *were* to be accepted. This is in keeping with the principle that a language is a living language and depends upon usage rather than hard-and-fast rules. The word *was* in the above sentence would obviously also be accepted as correct and is still to be preferred.

6. The words *one of* . . . are frequently followed by a relative clause and this causes further problems: which of these two is correct?
   ❑ Churchill is one of the best leaders who *has* led their countries in war.
   ❑ Churchill is one of the best leaders who *have* led their countries in war.
The first is wrong and the second is right. The sentence could be rephrased:
One of the best leaders who *have* led their countries in war is Churchill.

Many people become so confused by the issues of number in this sentence that they would either say or write:

One of the best leaders who *has* led their countries in war *is* Churchill.

or

One of the best leaders who *have* led their countries in war *are* Churchill.

Such mistakes come from a failure to realize that the subject of the verb *have led* is *leaders* whereas the subject of the verb *is* is *one*.

7. A singular verb is used with *each, every, everyone, everybody, nobody, someone,* or *something:*

Everybody thinks he has all the answers.

8. *Neither . . . nor* and *either. . . or* are not clear-cut examples. In the sentence,

Neither my brother nor my sister *was* able to attend my wedding

,the verb must obviously be singular. But in the sentence,

Neither my brother nor my sisters *were* able to attend my wedding,

the verb is correctly plural. The rule is that the verb takes its number from the subject nearest to it. Thus the sentence,

Neither my sisters nor my brother *was* able to attend my wedding,

is correct.

This applies to *or* and *nor* as well:

Mother or children *are* not to blame.

Was the teacher or the students to blame for the poor results?

But, if the sentence becomes too awkward, it should be rephrased:

Was the teacher to blame for the poor results, or *were* the students?

When *either* is used without *or* and when *neither* is used without *nor*, the subject is singular:

Both parties *were* prepared to accept the blame, but neither *was* really responsible.

9. Where there is a compound subject, the verb is usually plural:

Father and son *were* killed.

But if the subject consists of two concepts that are used so often together that they are inseparable, a singular verb is used:

Bread and butter *is* all we have.

Bacon and eggs *was* served for breakfast.

If the word *and* joins two nouns that refer to one person, then the verb is singular:

My guardian and benefactor *was* anxious to see me.

This means that my guardian and my benefactor was one and the same person.

Even if the subject is obviously a compound subject, it is treated as singular when the word *each* or *every* precedes the compound subject:

Each husband and wife has to sign the passport papers.

10. There are certain **idioms** in English that defy all the rules, however.

More than one order *has* been issued.

Lots of paper *has* been wasted.

A number of papers *have* been lost.

'Many a flower *is* born to blush unseen' (Gray's *Elegy*).

All these aberrations seem to be based on the verb taking its number from the subject nearest to it.

Other vagaries are expression such as:

The United States of America *opposes* terrorism.

That twelve months in the army *was* the best time of my life.

Another ten rands *is* needed.

Whereas we can accept (1) as the name of one country, it is difficult to justify (2) and (3). *That twelve months . . . was* can probably be justified by regarding it as an ellipsis for *That (period of) twelve months . . .* and (3) can similarly be justified as an ellipsis for *Another (amount of) ten rands. . . .*

11. Difficulty is sometimes experienced with the relative pronoun *what*. Since it can mean either *that which* or *those which* the verb with a relative clause beginning with *what* as its subject could be either singular or plural. The best advice is to judge according to context and, if there is a complement, as there often is, according to the number of the complement:

     What I mean to say *is* this.

     What I consider relevant *are* certain decisions taken at recent Board meetings.

12. Sometimes the verb precedes the subject. In speech it is often difficult to know in advance whether one will refer to the delayed subject as singular or plural, but in writing it is always advisable to correct the verb to suit the number of the subject:

     There *are* a diningroom and three bedrooms in the house.

13. Finally there are certain *nouns of multitude* as Fowler calls them in his *Modern English Usage*. (These *nouns of multitude* mean something different from Greig's *nouns of multitude*. Fowler uses the term to refer to nouns that represent a group of people and can be regarded as an entity or as the individual people in the group.) Such nouns can take either a singular or a plural verb depending on whether the speaker or writer wishes them to be regarded as a whole or as individuals. Examples of such words are *staff, team, crowd, company, management, army, government, majority, minority, number, party*.

     The government *were* in danger of losing the election.

     This suggests the members of the government were not a cohesive whole.

     The team *is* confident of victory.

     This suggests that the team is a unity.

OTHER WORDS THAT ILLUSTRATE THE CONCEPT OF NUMBER IN ENGLISH

We have already referred to the following expressions and their relation to countable and uncountable nouns:

- ❑ *a few* and *a little*
- ❑ *few* and *little*
- ❑ *a great many* and *a lot of* or *a great deal of*
- ❑ *a number of* and *an amount of*

In each case the expression on the left of *and* is followed by countable nouns while the expression on the right of *and* is followed by uncountable nouns. The same applies to the words *fewer* and *less*:

- ❑ Fewer *students* enrolled this year than last year.
- ❑ Less *income* was received this year than last year.

Similarly words like *several* and *some* indicate number or a certain quantity. The word *several* is used only with countable nouns in the plural to represent the same idea as *quite a few* (i.e. more than some but still not being specific about the number):

- ❑ There were several mistakes in the book.

The word *some* can be used with either countable nouns in the plural or with uncountable nouns to represent a certain number without specifying exactly how many:

- ❑ There were some mistakes in the books.
- ❑ Please may I have some wine?

The word *some* here represents a smaller number than *several*.

Other expressions that are used with countable nouns are a *variety of* or *various:*

- ❑ There was a variety of opinions expressed.
- ❑ There were various opinions expressed.

The English language uses a rather complicated concept of number and speakers of English as a second language have to learn the **different ways of forming the plurals of words:**

chair	chairs
hero	heroes
piano	pianos
donkey	donkeys
body	bodies
calf	calves
roof	roofs
tooth	teeth
foot	feet

house	houses
mouse	mice
child	children
ox	oxen
phenomenon	phenomena
criterion	criteria
innings	innings
sheep	sheep
formula	formulas or formulae
syllabus	syllabi or syllabuses
genius	geniuses
genie	genies or genii
radius	radii
hippopotamus	hippopotamuses
bureau	bureaux
portmanteau	portmanteaus or portmanteaux

Sometimes there are two plurals with each having a different meaning:

index	indexes, indices
appendix	appendices, appendixes
brother	brothers, brethren

English **pronouns and personal adjectives** have different forms for singular and plural depending on their case:

I — we	it — them
me — us	my — our
he — they	mine — ours
him — them	his — theirs, their
she — they	her — their
her — them	hers — theirs
it — they	its — theirs

The only exception is *you* which has the same form for singular and plural, but the verb always takes the plural form whether the subject is singular or plural:

❑ You *are* a good student.
❑ You *are* good students.
❑ That book *is* yours.
❑ That *is* your book.

The pronouns and adjectives *this* and *that* have plural forms *these* and *those* respectively:

❑ This business is a close corporation.
❑ These businesses are companies.
❑ That instruction has to be obeyed.
❑ Those instructions have to obeyed.

Some users have difficulty in distinguishing the pronunciation of *this* and *these* and therefore tend to confuse them.

The correct number of the pronouns used is important, and many people use pronouns wrongly:

❑ *Everyone* is confident *they* will pass the examination.

This is wrong if *everyone*, which is singular, refers to the same person as *they* (plural) is supposed to. It should be:

❑ *Everyone* is confident *he* will pass the examination.

The feminist movement would prefer *he or she* but this becomes too cumbersome and for purposes of simplicity either *he* or *she*, but not both, should be used. Traditionally the pronoun *he* has served to refer to either sex.

Often *nouns of multitude*, i.e. nouns that can be regarded as either singular or plural, cause problems with pronouns:

❑ The Government *are* in danger of losing *its* power.
This sentence is wrong. It can be corrected in two ways:
1. The Government *are* in danger of losing *their* power.
2. The Government *is* in danger of losing *its* power.
Either the Government is seen as an entity as in (2) or as individuals as in (1). We must not mix up the concept of number by using a plural verb and then a singular pronoun.

TERMINOLOGY AND CONCEPTS
1. COUNTABLE AND UNCOUNTABLE NOUNS
2. INDEFINITE AND DEFINITE ARTICLES
3. NOUN OF MASS
4. NOUN OF MULTITUDE
5. CONCORD
6. SUBJECT
7. COMPOUND SUBJECT
8. CONCEPT OF NUMBER

APPLICATION

Exercise 1
Add *a* or *an* where necessary:
1. . . . door is made of . . . wood.
2. . . . lemon has . . . sour taste.
3. I prefer . . . mutton to . . . pork.
4. . . . student may choose . . . literature and . . . philosophy.

5. ... sportsman must be . . .. good athlete.
6. Boys often choose . . . soccer or . . . rugby as . . . sport, whereas girls choose . . . tennis or . . . hockey.
7. What . . . good advice he gave me!
8. I have . . . little money, so I can't lend you any.
9. I have . . . few books on . . . economics but I should like to get some more.
10. I have . . . few books on . . . economics and therefore I should like to get some more.

Exercise 2

Add *a*, *an*, *some*, or *the*, where necessary:
1. Mr Jones was sent to . . . prison for embezzling funds. . . . manager went to . . . prison to visit him and take him . . . books.
2. My brother is at . . . school. If you go to . . . station at three o'clock, you will be just in time to meet him because he comes home by . . . train.
3. Let's get . . . wine for . . . dinner.
4. Waiter, there's . . . fly in . . . soup! Please get me . . . more.
5. Next year he will go to . . . university to study . . . economics. Then he plans to work in . . . tax department of our firm where he will gain . . . practical experience in applying . . . knowledge he has obtained.

Exercise 3

Choose the correct alternative from the pair of alternatives in brackets in each of these sentences:
1. There are (fewer/less) people at the concert than (were/was) expected.
2. His hysterics (is/are) a source of annoyance.
3. We shall need more money. Fifty rands (is/are) not enough.
4. His hair as well as his beard (has/have) turned grey.
5. Not one of the employees got back to (his/their) work on time after the Christmas lunch.
6. Everybody said (he/they) (was/were) pleased with (his/their) performance at work.
7. There is a small (number/amount) of money available for the great (number/amount) of projects that (have/has) been undertaken.
8. He is one of the best statesmen that (has/have) served (his/their) country.
9. What confused them (was/were) the different conclusions arrived at by the researchers.
10. More than one of us (has/have) expressed surprise at the low profits which (were/was) declared.

Exercise 4

Correct the following sentences:
1. Everyone should be trained to look after their own financial affairs.

2. I have received important advices about how to be more productive in my work.
3. Neither my father nor his relations was prepared to comment on politics.
4. There were a great amount of people at the conference.
5. One of the greatest tragedies that has ever occurred was the earthquake that caused the losses of a great deal of lives.
6. Less people attended than were expected.
7. Another fifty rands were needed to make up the deposit.
8. Many a mistake on the part of managers have resulted in a business failure.
9. Every boy and girl at the school have to wear the proper uniform.
10. The acoustics in the lecture theatre has to be improved.

9

THE CONCEPT OF
CORRECTNESS

THE GOALS OF THIS CHAPTER

In this chapter we study

❏ ten rules of correct English
❏ an English Usage Alphabet

INTRODUCTION

The English have traditionally been people who pride themselves on correctness. There is a correct way of holding a knife and fork; there is the correct side of the road for a gentleman to walk on when walking down the street with a lady; it is correct to allow a woman to precede a man through a doorway; there are many correct forms of behaviour that are passed on from one generation to another. As we have seen in our chapter on cross-cultural communication, the norms for one society may differ from those of another society, but few people would doubt that correctness plays an important part in English culture. Such correctness often leads to stiffness and lack of spontaneity — the 'stiff upper lip' caricature of the English who find it hard to express their feelings, for instance — but those who wish to communicate through the medium of the English language should be aware of some of the conventions of correctness in the language.

In the first chapter of *The Elements of Style* by William Strunk Jr. and E. B. White, the writers give eleven rules of correct English usage. Since we have discussed two other concepts of correctness in the two previous chapters — 'The Concept of Number' and 'The Concept of Time' — we are going to try to emulate Strunk and White by giving ten rules of correct English usage in this chapter.

TEN RULES OF CORRECT ENGLISH

1. The Correct Case of the Pronoun

The pronoun in English has three cases and often three different forms of the pronoun:

1. **subject** of a verb: 'He went to the office';
2. **object** of the verb or after the preposition: 'He gave *her* a present'; 'She accepted a present from *him*';
3. **possessive**: 'This book is *mine*'.

The correct cases may be placed in a table:

SUBJECT (or nominative case)	I	you	he	she	it	we	they	who
OBJECT (or accusative case)	me	you	him	her	it	us	them	whom
POSSESSIVE (or genitive case)	mine	yours	his	hers	its	ours	theirs	whose

There is another case called the **reflexive case** (*myself, yourself, herself, itself, themselves*) used with certain reflexive verbs (*hurt, pride, kill,* etc.),but this case is seldom used. It is, however, a common mistake to use the reflexive case instead of the other cases:

❑   Tom and myself accepted the invitation. (CORRECT: Tom and I....)
❑   I invited Tom and himself. (CORRECT: Tom and him)

The personal pronouns have **adjectival forms** as well: *my, your, his, her, its, our, their.* These are forms used in front of nouns:

❑   This is my (your, his, her, its, our, their) food.
❑   We can therefore expand our table:

SUBJECT	I	you	he	she	it	we	they	who
OBJECT	me	you	him	her	it	us	them	whom
POSSESSIVE	mine	yours	his	hers	its	ours	theirs	whose
ADJECTIVAL	my	your	his	her	its	our	their	—

Because of these different forms we often make **mistakes of case**:
❑   Tom and me have decided to go to the conference.
❑   He gave Jane and I a lift.
❑   This is a matter between you and I.
❑   The man who we met yesterday is my managing director.

All these sentences contain mistakes of case. They should be written correctly as follows:

❑   Tom and *I* have decided to go to the conference. (I = subject of the verb 'have decided')
❑   He gave Jane and *me* a lift. (me = object after the verb 'gave')
❑   This is a matter between you and *me.* (me = object after the preposition 'between')
❑   The man *whom* we met yesterday is my managing director. (whom = object of the verb 'met')

These are comparatively easy mistakes to detect. What about the following?
1.   You can give this present to whoever you like.
2.   Mr Botha is the person whom we think will be elected.
3.   Mr Botha is the person whom we hope to elect.
4.   He writes better than me.
5.   He likes Tom better than me.
6.   Us workers preferred to start at eight o'clock.
7.   A group of us workers preferred to start at eight o'clock.
8.   Do you mind me coming too?

Sentences 1, 2, 4 and 6 contain mistakes of case. Sentences 3 and 7 are correct. Sentences 5 and 8 may be correct or incorrect, depending on the meaning of the sentence. Let us look at each one in turn.
1.   You can give this present to whoever you like.

This is wrong because *whoever* should be *whomever* since it is the object after the preposition *to*. It should be:
You can give this present to *whomever* you like.

The second sentence is more difficult, especially when we compare it with the third sentence:
2. Mr Botha is the person whom we think will be elected.
3. Mr Botha is the person whom we hope to elect.

In sentence 2 the pronoun *whom* should be *who* because it is the subject of the verb *will be elected*:
2. Mr Botha is the person *who* we think will be elected.

The mistake is caused by the words *we think* that are added by the way (in parenthesis) but do not affect the case of the pronoun. Sentence 3, on the other hand, is correct because the pronoun *whom* is the object of the verb *hope to elect*: 'We hope to elect Mr Botha'.

Let's look at sentence 4:
4. He writes better than me.

The pronoun should be *I* because what we mean is 'He writes better than I write'; The verb *write* is understood to be the verb of the subject *I*. In such sentences it is better to supply the understood verb and then the case is obvious: 'He works faster than I do.'

Sentence 5 we said is either correct or incorrect, depending on the meaning of the sentence: do we mean (*a*) 'He likes Tom better than he likes me' or do we mean (*b*) 'He likes Tom better than I like Tom'? If we mean (*a*) then sentence 5 is correct; if we mean (*b*) then sentence 5 is incorrect. It is likely we mean (*a*) and therefore the sentence is likely to be correct.

Sentence 6 is incorrect because *We workers* is the subject of the verb *preferred to start*.

Sentence 7, however, is correct because *us workers* is the object after the preposition *of*.

Sentence 8, like sentence 5, may be correct or incorrect, depending on the meaning of the sentence. As it stands,
8. Do you mind *me* coming too?

it means 'Do you mind if I too come?' It may also be correct if it is changed to read,
8 (*b*) Do you mind *my* coming too?

But now the meaning is 'Do you mind my coming as well as my doing something else'. The difference is that sentence 8 uses *coming* as a participle referring to *me* (the object of *mind*), whereas 8(b) refers to a verbal noun (or gerund) as the object of the verb *mind*. This is a very subtle difference, but there are other sentences where it would be wrong to use *me* instead of *my* or the object form instead of the adjectival form:

❑   Me failing surprised the teachers.
❑   You wanting to resign has put a new light on the matter.
❑   I announced him winning the race.

All these should use the adjectival form:

❑   *My* failing surprised the teachers.
❑   *Your* wanting to resign has put a new light on the matter.
❑   I announced *his* winning the race.

Although correct, these sentences are rather awkward, and it is usually advisable to reconstruct the sentences to avoid the awkwardness:

❑   The teachers were surprised that I had failed.
❑   That you want to resign has put a new light on the matter.
❑   I announced that he had won the race.

Awkward syntax is probably the biggest problem with the correct case of the pronoun. We can know all the rules and we can correct the case of the pronoun and still we can be left with a very awkwardly constructed sentence. Take this sentence, for instance:

❑   I saw a young girl whom I correctly guessed to be she who I had been told would be there.

If you have followed what we have said about the correct case of the pronoun, you would have been able to correct the sentence as follows:

❑   I saw a young girl whom I correctly guessed to be her who I had been told would be there.

But this sentence hasn't really been improved, has it? It is just as awkward as before. We may have corrected the grammatical mistakes, but the syntax is still very awkward. What we need to do is reconstruct the sentence:

❑   I saw a young girl and correctly guessed that she was the one I had been told would be there.

Often pronouns are awkward and are best avoided.

Before we leave this section on the correct case of the pronoun, we have to admit that, although the verb *to be* is supposed to take the same case after it as before it, the expression *It is I* is hardly ever used and *It is me* has become accepted English even though it is strictly speaking wrong. Similarly *It's him* instead of *It's he*, and *These are them* instead of *These are they*. (Perhaps the English aren't really as correct as we think . . . !)

2. The Correct Use of the Noun in the Possessive Case

We have already seen that the pronoun has a possessive (or genitive) form and also an adjectival form closely associated with the possessive form. We form the possessive of a **singular noun** by adding 's (sometimes called the apostrophe s). This will always be accepted as correct no matter what the final consonant is. There is nothing wrong with *Charles's book* or *Keats's poems*. There are, however, problems of pronunciation with too many *s* sounds together: we find it difficult to say *Jesus' sayings, for conscience' sake, for righteousness' sake* or *Moses' statutes*, or else we rephrase the statements, *the sayings of Jesus, for the sake of conscience, for the sake of righteousness,* or *the statutes of Moses*. It is a good idea not to use the apostrophe s for words that are difficult to pronounce because of the added *s* syllable: e.g. *rhinoceros's* would be better written *of a rhinoceros*.

We need to be reminded that pronouns do not use the apostrophe: *mine, yours, his, hers, its, ours, theirs*. Mistakes usually only occur with *its*. This is probably because of the confusion between the two completely different forms *its* and *it's*. As a possessive pronoun or adjective *its* never takes the apostrophe, whereas *it's* (meaning *it is*) always takes the apostrophe because it is a contracted form of *it is*.

The apostrophe is always used for this contracted form: originally all nouns had their possessive singular forms with an added syllable *es* at the end: *Godes gift*, for instance. As the language became simplified the *e* was dropped, and therefore the apostrophe is placed before the *s*. The pronouns on the other hand, had their different forms (*mine, yours, his, hers, its, ours* and *theirs*) and they have retained these forms without contraction; therefore no apostrophe is needed.

Before we move on to plural nouns in their possessive form, let us note that the possessive of *somebody else* is *somebody else's*:

That is somebody else's book. On the other hand, *who else* has as its possessive *whose else*, despite the colloquial use, *who else's*.

Plural nouns do not cause much bother in their possessive form. The rules are quite simple: if the noun ends with an *s* in the plural, then we merely add an apostrophe to the final *s*; if the noun ends in any other letter, we add 's as with the singular noun:

❏   the boys' books
❏   the kings' laws
❏   the children's toys
❏   the geese's food.

There is every likelihood that in time the apostrophe will disappear from the English language. So few people use it properly that common English usage will probably bring about its disappearance. Nevertheless a manager should, without too much trouble, get it right and so maintain the tradition of correctness befitting a true English gentleman!

3. The Correct Use of the Participial Phrase

Traditionally the participial phrase at the beginning of a sentence should refer to the subject of the verb in the sentence.

1. Walking down the street, he saw his brother.

This sentence has a participial phrase *Walking down the street*, the participle *walking*, the subject *he* and the verb *saw*. The subject *he* is the one who is doing the *walking* and the one who *saw his brother*. The participle *walking* therefore refers (or is related or attached) to the subject. There is no doubt about to whom *walking* refers.

2. On arriving at the office, his friends met him.

Here there is doubt about who was *arriving at the office*. It is more likely *he* was *arriving at the office* and therefore the sentence should be: On arriving at the office, he was met by his friends.

3. While running for the bus, it passed me by at great speed.

Here there is no doubt that the sentence is incorrectly constructed: who was *running*? was it *the bus*? or was it *me*? The sentence could be changed in this way:

❑   While running for the bus, I was passed by the bus going at great speed.

However, this is rather awkward. The sentence could be better reconstructed as follows:

❑   While I was running for the bus, it passed me by at great speed.

Many sentences with unattached participles need to be reconstructed in this way by changing the participial phrase into a clause with a definite subject that allows no doubt about who the participle refers to. There are, however, certain participial phrases that have become idiomatically correct.

❑   Seeing that he is ill, the meeting has been cancelled.

The participle *seeing* joined with *that* has come to have the same meaning as *because* and, although strictly speaking we should say, *Seeing that he is ill, we have cancelled the meeting*, such an unattached participial phrase has been accepted. There is no reason, however, why we should not get the sentence right by attaching the participial phrase to the subject of the sentence as we have done. Another commonly used participial phrase is one beginning with *Allowing for*:

❑   Allowing for good weather, the cricket match should end soon.

Who is *Allowing for good weather*? Obviously not *the cricket match*, which is inanimate and cannot *allow for* anything. One could reconstruct the sentence as follows:

❑   Allowing for good weather, we forecast that the cricket match will end soon.

Alternatively, we could regard the words *Allowing for good weather* as parenthetical in their effect and not bother. The more correctly we construct sentences, however, the better we shall communicate. Perhaps the best way to make such a statement is:

❑   If the weather is good, the cricket match will end soon.

There are many illogically used participial phrases that do not bother us much. For example:

❑   Not counting all his mistakes, his work is of a satisfactory standard.

Who is not counting his mistakes? His work? Obviously not. We could reconstruct the sentence as follows:

❑   Not counting all his mistakes, we may say that his work is of a satisfactory standard.

Or we could say:

❑   If we do not count all his mistakes, his work is of a satisfactory standard.

Obviously we must not be pedantic about every word that looks like a participle. The word *notwithstanding* obviously has its origin as a participle, but we should not find anything wrong with this sentence:

❑   Notwithstanding his faults, his promotion is deserved.

The word *Notwithstanding* has come to be a preposition meaning *in spite of* or an adverb meaning *nevertheless*. Notwithstanding the above, we rather like the humour of the next sentence, which comes from a sensitive awareness of language:

❑   He wore out his trousers, notwithstanding.

4. The Correct Use of *and*

Modern teachers of adult students are frequently asked, 'Is it wrong to start a sentence with the word *and*?' Such students were taught at school that it was wrong. Some of the best writers, however, start sentences with *and*. Of course the indiscriminate use of *and* at the beginning of a sentence or anywhere else in the sentence leads to poor communication. A sentence beginning with *and* can be very effective when a telling addition is made or a clinching conclusion is reached. And that is probably all we need to say about this problem!

The biggest problem with *and* is that it is used to link words that are essentially different. In the sentence

❑   He works hard, stays late, and never takes a holiday.

we have three actions that are correctly linked by commas and the conjunction *and*. But in the sentence

❑   He works hard, plays golf and squash.

the mistake is that the *and* is intended to link three ideas: (1) working hard, (2) playing golf, and (3) playing squash. There is confusion that there are three actions, whereas there are only two: (1) working hard, and (2) playing golf and squash. The sentence should be:

❑ He works hard, and plays golf and squash.

In this way the two actions are joined by the first *and* whereas the two sports that are the object of *plays* are joined by the second *and*. The mistake probably arises because we are taught not to use *and* unnecessarily, but here the two uses of *and* are necessary. We need to see the sentence syntactically, i.e. how it is constructed as a combination of elements. In this sentence we have two, not three, clauses:

❑ He works hard. He plays golf and squash.

We join those two clauses with the conjunction *and: He works hard, and (he) plays golf and squash.* Depending on the emphasis we wish to make, we could, of course, have used a different conjunction:

❑ He works hard, **but** he plays golf and squash.

If we had been taught this next use of *and* we probably would not have made that mistake: where there are lists of three or more terms with *and* before the last term, a comma should be used after every term except the last:

❑ He works hard, stays late, and never takes a holiday.

There are three terms being joined: (1) He works hard, (2) stays late, and (3) never takes a holiday. In the other sentence, however, there are only two terms: (1) He works hard, and (2) plays golf and squash. The *and* joining the two terms is necessary to make the syntactical connection. If there had been three terms, the sentence would have to be punctuated as follows:

❑ He works hard, plays golf, and squash.

This is obviously the wrong grouping of the terms. Another way to correct the sentence could be: (1) *He works hard,* (2) *plays golf,* and (3) *excels at squash.*

Now we have three terms, each separated by a comma from the next. It is not only clauses that obey the rule that where there are lists of three or more terms with *and* before the last term, a comma should be used after every term except the last. The rule of *the serial comma* applies also to single words and phrases:

❑ Tom, Peter, and John work together. (3 Nouns)
❑ They ran out of the house, across the road, and into the shop. (3 Phrases)

Many writers omit the second comma because they have been taught that you do not use a comma before *and.* Such teaching has led to the confusion we have already mentioned.

Where there are *two* terms joined by *and*, the comma is not necessarily used:

❑ Tom and Peter work together. (2 Nouns)

❑   They ran out of the house and across the road. (2 Phrases)

If we have two clauses joined by *and*, we do not use a comma to separate them unless some change or emphasis is needed:

❑   They went out of the house and ran across the road.
❑   They ran across the road, and a car hit them.

The reason for the comma in the second sentence is that the subject has changed: the pronoun *They* is the subject of the verb *ran*, whereas the next subject *car* is the subject of the verb *hit*. Compare this with the previous sentence where there is a close connection between the two clauses because the subject of *went* and *ran* is the same word, *They*. Coming back to our offending sentence *He works hard, and plays golf and squash*, we see that our correction, *He works hard, and plays golf and squash* requires the separating comma before *and* because, despite the identical subject *he*, the difference between working and playing needs to be emphasized. Edward Davis wrote, 'If you can use *and* well, you are an accomplished writer.' This is written in a very useful booklet *Introduction to Modern English Usage* (Cape Town: Oxford University Press, 1958), which is probably out of print by now.

5. The Correct Use of the Comma

We have already discussed the use of the comma with *and*, but there is more to be said about the use of the comma.

5.1 A comma is used before a conjunction introducing an independent clause.

We have already discussed this in relation to the conjunction *and*, but it applies to other conjunctions as well. If the connection between the two clauses is not very close, then a comma is placed before the conjunction.
❑   He was adamant that I should stay, but I had work to do.
❑   He was not convinced, nor was he co-operative.

If, however, the connection between two clauses is one of main clause and subordinate clause and their connection is close, no comma is needed to separate them.
❑   He did not come because he was ill.
❑   He saw him when he was crossing the road.

When the subordinate clause precedes the main clause, there is more cause for a comma separating the two clauses.
❑   Because he was ill, he did not come.
❑   When he was crossing the road, he saw him.

5.2 A comma is used before and after a non-restrictive relative clause and not before and after restrictive clauses.

A non-restrictive (or non-defining) relative clause is an independent thought introduced not to define the noun to which it refers but to give independent information.

❑ The firm, which had previously been one of the biggest in South Africa, was liquidated last month.

A restrictive (or defining) relative clause is a clause that defines the noun to which it refers.

❑ The man who won the prize was very happy.

5.3 Words used in parenthesis or in apposition are placed between commas.

Whenever there is an aside or something that is said by the way without too much of a break in meaning, these words are placed between commas.

❑ Mr Jones, my managing director, won a marketing award recently.
❑ His wife, the famous actress, died suddenly.
❑ Five employees, namely Jones, Naidoo, Mkhize, Van Rensburg, and Mitchell, were dismissed.
❑ John Samuels, Ph.D., was elected chairman.
❑ My uncle, having drunk too much, had to take a taxi home.
❑ Certain diseases, e.g. tuberculosis, can be cured.
❑ You will, however, experience a certain discomfort.
❑ You will have, by the way, a chance to win a prize.
❑ There is, as you are no doubt aware, a deposit to be paid.
❑ I am, Mr Jones, delighted to meet you.

Where the words in apposition are restrictive (or defining) in any way, no comma is used:

❑ Sinbad the Sailor was a favourite of young people many years ago.
❑ The playwright Shakespeare has no equal.
❑ Pompey the Great has never received adequate recognition.

The same applies to participial phrases that are restrictive or defining:

❑ The men working on the road were perspiring from their exertions.

If the parenthetical statement is more in the nature of an abrupt interruption to the flow of the sentence, then a **dash** is used before and after the statement instead of a comma.

❑ Tomorrow — and the next day if you fail tomorrow, and for each successive day till you succeed — you will work without a break.

A dash is used for emphasis when every other punctuation mark seems ineffective for the drastic purpose envisaged.

5.4 A comma should not be used to separate sentences without conjunctions.

Sentences without conjunctions are separated by semicolons or full stops (also called periods), not by commas.

❑   It was already dark; we had no chance of arriving before dinner.
❑   It was already dark. We had no chance of arriving before dinner.

If, however, we use a conjunction to link the two sentences, a comma is used to separate the two independent statements.

❑   It was already dark, and we had no chance of arriving before dinner.

Sometimes we mistakenly use adverbs as if they were conjunctions. Adverbs, like *accordingly, therefore, thus, then, besides,* and *however,* are adverbs, not conjunctions; therefore they must not be used with a comma to join sentences.

❑   It was already dark; therefore we had no chance of arriving before dinner.

There is one exception to rule 5.4: when the sentences are very short and very closely related, they may be separated by commas:

❑   I came, I saw, I conquered.
❑   I wake, I wash, I go to work.
❑   Man proposes, God disposes.

6. The Correct Use of the Colon

A colon is used after an explanatory statement to show that the following statement expands on or completes the explanatory statement.

❑   There are nine punctuation marks: the comma, the semi-colon, the full stop, the exclamation mark, the question mark, quotation marks, brackets, and the dash.

The colon usually follows a numerical statement either directly stated as in the previous example or as in the following:

❑   There was a major drawback: he had no passport.

A colon is often used to precede direct speech or a quotation:

❑   The Prime Minister said: 'I categorically deny such accusations.'
❑   There is a famous saying: 'Neither a borrower nor a lender be.'

It may also be used in certain technical ways:

❑   He was reading *A Vision of Reality: Metaphor and Metaphysics in the Poetry of W. B. Yeats.*
❑   He took as his text John 3:16.

7. The Correct Positioning of Related Words

People who are related to each other like to keep as close as possible to each other. Words that are related to each other need to be kept together in order to avoid misunderstanding. The rule is to keep together any words that are closely related to each other and to proofread sentences to make sure that confusion of interpretation may not take place. We have already seen the confusion caused by unattached participles; now let us look at the confusion caused by detached clauses that should have been related clauses.

❑ Some of my papers were in my office, which I had to take to the conference.

As this sentence stands, I had to take my office to the conference! Obviously the relative clause, *which I had to take to the conference*, refers to papers, and the sentence has to be reconstructed.

❑ Some of my papers, which I had to take to the conference, were in my office.

Here is another example:

❑ The book was lying on the table, which I thought had disappeared.

This rather amusing sentence can be corrected by placing the relative clause next to its proper antecedent:

❑ The book, which I thought had been lost, was lying on the table.

Unless we believe in books disappearing into thin air, the more precise statement is to be preferred. Often advertisements create this kind of humorous confusion:

❑ A country cottage required by young couple about to be married for six months to a year.

As it stands the words, *for six months to a year*, relate to the words *about to be married*, whereas we hope that they should apply to the word *required*:

❑ A country cottage required for six months to a year by a young couple about to be married.

The word *only* is often misplaced:

❑ He only worked for two months.

This means that only he worked for two months; no one else did. What the writer probably meant was

❑ He worked for two months only.

We should become aware of the differences in meaning caused by different positioning of words:

❑ I met him only last month.
❑ Only I met him last month.
❑ Last month I met only him.

The only way to achieve the correct positioning of related words is to be on guard for ambiguities and to proofread, edit, and revise any written work before it is in its final form. The best managers draft and redraft their work many times before it is acceptable. This often means that typists are given rather untidy manuscripts with many changes and corrections, but if the end result is a better piece of work because of all the redrafting, it can only be in the best interests of good business communication.

8. Correct Spelling

Correctness in spelling is very important in written communication, especially in business. Nothing makes a worse impression than careless spelling. The English language is notorious for its illogical spelling of words, but dictionaries should always be available for managers to make sure they have the correct spelling of a difficult word. The more often one looks up a word in a dictionary, the more likely it is that the correct spelling will be learnt. We could give a list of spelling rules, but there would be too many exceptions to each rule. If we know that we, like many great people, are poor spellers, we need to use a dictionary or have a good assistant or proofreader who will correct our poor spelling. But there is no excuse for wrong spelling in formal written English communication.

9. Correct Word Division

How to divide words at the end of a line is important to any manager who is concerned about correctness in written English. Each typist, secretary, word processor, proofreader, or editor needs to be given a few simple rules about word division (or syllabication, as it is also called). Then the manager needs to know these rules to ensure that they are carried out in written communication. There are four simple rules that usually apply when dividing words:
1. A single letter should not be left on its own at the end of a line or at the beginning of a line; e.g. one should not divide *a-dult* or *stor-y* in these ways.
2. Words may be divided after a vowel and before a single consonant, e.g. *me-lo-dy, de-li-ver, to-tal*; but see the last rule below.
3. Words may usually be divided between two consonants, e.g. *ad-minis-ter, es-cape, rub-ber, lad-der, at-tack*; but see the last rule below.
4. When a suffix is added to an existing word, the division comes before the suffix, e.g. *tell-ing, consider-ate, sell-er*.
    With these four simple rules we should have no difficulty with syllabication. Again a good dictionary should be able to clear up any doubts about how to divide a word into its correct syllables.

10. The Correct Use of the Passive Voice

In English we have an active voice and a passive voice. In the active voice the subject is the doer of the action. In the passive voice the subject is the sufferer of an action done by another party.

ACTIVE: The dog bit the boy.
PASSIVE: The boy was bitten by the dog.

It is a general rule in English to use the active voice in preference to the passive voice because the active voice is more direct and leads to a more vigorous style. There are, however, times when the passive voice changes the emphasis of a sentence to a more definite subject than a vague subject in the active voice can.

ACTIVE: People always praise his work.
PASSIVE: His work is always praised.

ACTIVE: They criticized me for being too cautious.
PASSIVE: I was criticized for being too cautious.

ACTIVE: Somebody will ask you a few questions.
PASSIVE: You will be asked a few questions.

In each of these sentences in the active voice the vague subject, *People, They, or Somebody,* makes the sentence dull and weak, whereas the passive voice starting with the more definite subject places the right emphasis at the beginning of the sentence. It is a pity that formal language teaching at school concentrates on changing sentences from the active voice to the passive voice when it should rather concentrate on the correct use of the passive voice for emphasis and clarity of thought. The way we have been taught to use the passive voice usually includes the awkward ablative of agent: 'His work is always praised *by people.*' We should always try to avoid this awkward construction. In the three previous sentences it is precisely to avoid the indefinite agent that we changed the active to the passive voice. The *by...* construction should be avoided as much as possible: usually its inclusion means that we should have rather kept the sentence in the active voice.

CONCLUSION: AN ENGLISH USAGE ALPHABET

We have now given our ten rules of correct English. Before we end this chapter, let us look at an alphabet of English usage.

A. Among/Between

The word *among* is used for more than two; *between* for two usually.

❑   A male teacher is a man among boys and a boy among men.
❑   The side table stood between the two chairs.

There is, however, a tendency to use *between* for more than two:

❑   I have to choose between the three people nominated.
❑   There was agreement between the four.

We prefer to use *among* in each of these examples.

B. Beside/Besides

The word *beside* is a preposition meaning *by the side of*:

❑   He sat down beside her.

It can also mean *to one side of* or *away from*:

❑   That is beside the question, i.e. it has nothing to do with the question.

The word *besides* is either (1) an adverb meaning *also* or (2) a preposition meaning *in addition to* or *except*:

(1) There is nothing more to say; besides the decision has already been taken.
(2) Besides Tom, there are five others who want to go.

C. Cope

This verb always takes the preposition *with*. It should not be used without the preposition: *I can't cope*. It should certainly not be used with the two prepositions *up with*:

❑   He could not cope up with the work.

This latter usage is common among many South Africans, but is incorrect in English usage.

D. Different From

The preposition that is always correct with the word *different* is *from*. Sometimes *to* is correct, but, despite American usage, *than* is wrong. It is advisable therefore to use *different from*.

E. Economic/Economical

The word *economic* is the adjective that describes economics, the social science that concerns itself with the preservation, production and distribution of resources of value. An *economic* decision is therefore one based upon these principles of economics. The word *economical* means much the same as *thrifty*:

❑   That was an economical purchase.

F. First

The word *first* is both an adjective and an adverb. It is like the other very similar sounding word *fast*. No one would dream of saying *fastly*, but more and more people are using *firstly*, whereas it should be *first*. The same applies to other numbers like *second*, *third*, and *fourth*.

G. Get

There is nothing wrong with the verb *get*, despite what our teachers may have told us. But there is no reason to use *have got* instead of *have:*

❏ He has not got any money *should be* He has no money.

And it is even worse to say:

❏ He has not gotten any money.

The past participle of *get* is *got*, not *gotten.*

H. However

The word *however* is more of an adverb than a conjunction. It is like the words *accordingly, besides, then, therefore,* and *thus.* When *however* means *nevertheless*, its most common meaning, it should not be used to start a sentence but should appear later in the sentence:

❏ He was, however, unable to attend.

If, however, it is used in a different sense, it may begin the sentence:

❏ However hard he tries, he will not succeed.

I. Interesting/Interested/Disinterested/Uninterested

The words *interesting* and *funny* are very often used unnecessarily:

❏ I heard an interesting (or funny) story yesterday.

Usually what follows is not very interesting or not very funny, and even if it turns out to be interesting or funny, some of the point is lost by labelling it as interesting or funny. The negative of *interested* is *uninterested*, not *disinterested.* The word *uninterested* means *not interested*; the word *disinterested* means *impartial, not taking sides one way or another, unbiased, with an open mind.*

J. Jargon/Journalese/Circumlocution/Tautology

Jargon is language that is difficult to understand because it uses technical language not understood by the audience or it uses foreign words or multi-syllabled words that confuse. Journalese is the jargon used by newspaper writers to try to create an impression of cleverness; often it is just the opposite, merely absurd. Circumlocution is a roundabout way of saying things; it is sometimes used to create the same impression of cleverness: calling something *a terminological inexactitude* when you mean *a lie* may be funny the first time you hear it but it becomes absurd when you hear it so often that it becomes boring. There is no excuse for using such circumlocution as *each and every one, at this point in time,* and *in this day and age.*

Tautology is saying the same thing as has already been said, e.g. *lord and master, interesting matters of interest, circumstances surrounding the event, a new innovation.*

K. Kindly Requested

In business communication we often come across the statement
❏   You are kindly requested to . . . .

If we look carefully at this, it means that the person who is making the request is telling us he is being kind. Probably what is meant is
❏   You are requested to be so kind as to . . . .

Even this is rather circumlocutory and could be more simply stated:
❏   Please . . . .

L. Like

This word should not be used as a conjunction in the same way as the conjunction *as:*
❏   Tell it like it is *should be* Tell it as it is.

Like is a preposition and is followed by a noun or pronoun:
❏   *He is just like his father.*

But we say,
❏   He acts *as* his father did when he was young, *not* He acts *like* his father did when he was young.

M. Mutual/Common/Reciprocal

The word *mutual* means *two-way:* two people may have mutual feelings. The word *common* refers to two or more things or people: thus two people may have *common interests.* The difference is that, whereas you can use *common* for two or three or more, you can use *mutual* only for two. The word *reciprocal* means *in return* and means almost the same as *mutual,* except that it refers to something done in return. We may summarize as illustrated on the next page.

N. Numbers

When using numbers in written English, the numbers up to 100 are usually written out in words. Dates are written out partly in numbers and partly in words, e.g. *28 March 1989.* As the date when a letter is written (not as a date mentioned in the body of the letter) the numbers *1989-03-28* may be used. The year is always written out in numbers without spaces, *1989,* but the century is written out in words, the *twenty-first century.* With thousands there must always (except for dates) be a space between the digit representing

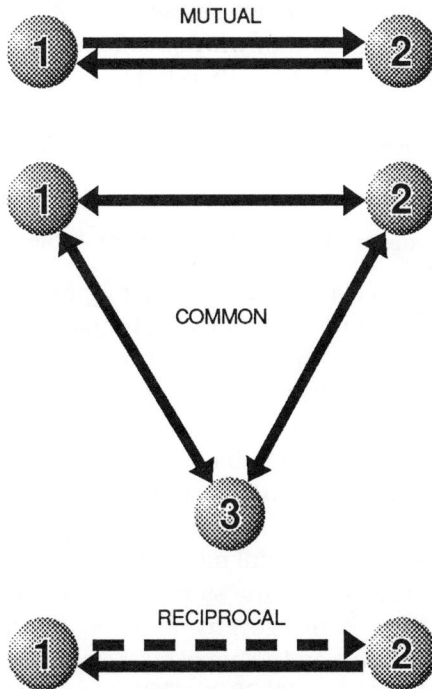

thousands and the digit representing hundreds: *6 000*. There is also a space between the number and any metric symbol, e.g. *58 c, 5 g, 68 %*. The word *per* is sometimes replaced by the oblique symbol, e.g. *80 km/h* (80 kilometres per hour), *6 %/a* (6 % per annum). Note that there is no full stop after metric symbols (they are symbols, not abbreviations).

O. One

This word is often used to mean *a person*, but its use leads to many errors, e.g. *One must clean his teeth*, instead of *One must clean one's teeth*. Although the indefinite word *one* can be useful, it can lead to awkward constructions; wherever possible, such awkward constructions should be avoided.

P. Prepositions

There is a mistaken idea that it is always wrong to end a sentence with a preposition. This is another of those 'rules' that we are taught at school. When Winston Churchill was criticized for ending sentences with prepositions, he pointed out in his humorous way the absurdity of this 'rule' by writing to his editor, 'This is something up with which I shall not put!' The rule is that of clarity and fluency: if a sentence can be clearer or less awkward by placing the preposition elsewhere than at the end of the sentence, then we should change its position, but we must be careful not to make it even more awkward by changing its position. It would be absurd to ask *For what are you searching?* instead of *What are you searching for?*

It is idiomatic in English that with questions the preposition goes at the end of the question. Similarly with relative pronouns, we do not say in idiomatic English

❑ The book for which you are looking is on the table.

We say rather

The book that you are looking for is on the table.

There are, however, certain usages with prepositions that are definitely wrong. The South African colloquialism, *Are you coming with?* is one such mistake. There is no reason for this (except the direct translation from Afrikaans *Kom jy saam?* where *saam* is not a preposition but an adverb). In English a preposition governs a noun or noun substitute, and therefore we need to have the noun or noun substitute: *Are you coming with me?*

Often what we call a preposition is really an **adverbial particle** that goes along with the verb, e.g. *get up, look out, go into.* These verbs depend on the adverbial particles for their special meanings. Such verbs are called phrasal verbs. The adverb particles are the same words as the prepositions, e.g. *up, out,* and *into;* but they do not govern nouns or noun substitutes. There is therefore a difference between *I get up at six o'clock* (up = ADVERB PARTICLE) and *Get up the ladder!* (up = PREPOSITION governing 'the ladder').

There is a much worse practice involving prepositions, and it is a mistake that businessmen are prone to make. Possibly because of the Afrikaans influence on English in South Africa we often come across words like *thereby, therein, therefor* (usually misspelt *therefore,* which means something quite different), *hereby, herewith, wherefor, whereby,* and *wherewith.* Such words are particularly favoured by members of the legal profession. They should be avoided as far as possible — the words that is, not the members of the legal profession, although perhaps they too!

Q. Quotations

Quotation marks are used at the start and at the end of a quotation. Modern practice is to use single quotation marks rather than double and to keep double quotation marks for quotations within quotations:

❑ He said, 'I am reading "Ode on a Grecian Urn" again.'

Notice the positions of the comma after *said* and the full stop after *again*: the comma outside the quotation marks and the full stop inside. Where a quotation is not a full sentence, the full stop would go outside the quotation marks:

❑ He referred to tea as 'the cup that cheers but does not inebriate'.

When quotations are long, it is better to indent them, and then quotation marks are not necessary. Sources of quotations should always be stated in proper detail and according to the particular convention used, e.g. as a footnote or endnotes as at the end of a chapter or a book. (Where not many quotations are used, it is permissible to place the source details in brackets after the quotation.)

R. Reference/Regard/Respect

These words are used in different combinations to act as introductory phrases. They must not be used as sentences on their own, and we should retain their position at the beginning of sentences as far as possible. The words *with reference to* are used to introduce a sentence 'with reference to' a previous letter or transaction or arrangement:

❑   With reference to our conversation of Tuesday, I now wish to offer you further details.

The words *with(out) regard to* and *in regard to* use *regard* in the singular, but the words *as regards* use *regard* in the plural. They are usually used at the beginning of a sentence to introduce the main statement. When used in the middle of a sentence these phrases should be replaced by a simple preposition: *I want to enquire as regards the next meeting;* should be *I want to enquire about the next meeting.* Sometimes the word *regarding* is used as a preposition: *I want to say something regarding this matter.* Again *about* is better.

The word *respect* is used in the phrases *with respect to* and *in respect of.* The same criterion applies to these phrases: the use of *about* is preferable. The word *respecting* is used in the same idiomatic way as *regarding.*

Of course both *regards* and *respects* are used in idiomatic English as greetings: *Send my regards to your parents* or *Pay my respects to Mr. Smith.* If we are going to use the words *With regards* at the end of a letter, it should be used only in friendly informal letters, not formal business letters. Another overused word is *respective* or *respectively.* Although they do have a precise purpose in specifying relationships, they are usually not necessary and often cause confusion. *I gave my assistant and my typist a letter and a report respectively.* This means *I gave my assistant a letter and my typist a report* and there is no need to use *respectively* at all.

S. Syntax

This word means the arrangement of the words in a sentence in order that they may relate to each other both grammatically and logically. The basic requirements of a **simple sentence** are that it should have a subject and a finite verb and that it should make sense. More **complex sentences** have a definite relationship between the main clause and its subordinate clause or clauses. (A clause is a group of words which contain a subject and a finite verb.) Then there are **compound sentences** with two at more independent (or main) clauses with or without subordinate clauses relating to one or more of the main clauses. These relationships between the various parts of the sentence used to be taught by the analysis of sentences into their respective grammatical parts, but this tended to be rather dull and exclusively grammatical. What is needed is a feel for what makes an acceptable sentence both in the grammatical relationship of its elements and in the logical ordering of its thoughts. An awareness of clarity of thinking comes from the study of the syntax or structure of a sentence in both these ways, which really cannot be separated.

T. Try to

We try *to* do something. We cannot try *and* do something. The words *try and do something* would mean we try and we do it. What we mean is that we try to do something and our attempt may be successful or unsuccessful, but at least we will have tried to do it. It is true that *try and* has become a colloquial idiom of English, but if we believe in the value of syntactical English, we should try to use *try to* correctly.

U. Unique

This word means *one and only* or *without equal*. We cannot therefore logically say that something is *very unique* or *most unique*. We cannot qualify the word in these ways: *very, more, most, rather, somewhat;* we can qualify the word *unique* with *quite, nearly, almost, really, surely* and *perhaps.* The word should not, however, be used as often as it is: there are very few unique things in this world, and by using the word too much we debase its value.

V. Verbal/Verbiage/Verbosity

The word *verbal* means concerned with words, usually in an oral rather than a written sense. A *verbal contract*, for instance, is one that is not written down. Non-verbal communication is communication that does not use words. The word *verbiage* means the use of too many words and is now used to refer mainly to written words. The word *verbosity* means almost the same as *verbiage* but is now used to refer mainly to spoken communication rather than written. The adjective from *verbosity* is *verbose*.

W. Word Confusion

There are certain words confused with others.

Because they look the same

affect	effect
alternate	alternative
comprise	consist of
consequent	consequential
contemptible	contemptuous
continual	continuous

definite	definitive
deprecate	depreciate
distinct	distinctive
eligible	illegible
expedient	expeditious
imperial	imperious
inflammable	inflammatory
ingenuous	ingenious
judicial	judicious
laudable	laudatory
luxuriant	luxurious
masterful	masterly
observance	observation
passed	past
reverend	reverent

Because as different parts of speech they require different spellings

NOUN	VERB
advice	advise
device	devise
practice	practise
prophecy	prophesy

We need to learn the difference between the words in each of these pairs.

XYZ

These last three letters are difficult, but boys have a good interpretation of them: 'Examine your zip.' This is said to someone whose zip is unfastened. We need metaphorically to examine our zips to make sure we don't get caught with our pants down because of our faulty English usage! Nevertheless, let us try to find useful hints for each of the X, Y, Z.

X. Excellence

We need to strive for excellence through planning, drafting, revising, and editing our work. We should not, however, use *very, rather, more, most, somewhat* to qualify the adjective *excellent* in our speaking or writing. Again we should be careful not too over-use this word: not everything we come across is excellent.

Y. Yester/Yon/Yore

These words are archaic or obsolete words. Apart from *yesterday* all the other combinations with *yester* (*yester* itself, *yestereve, yesterevening, yestermorn, yestermorning, yestern, yesternight, yesteryear, yestreen*) are archaic. The words *yon* and *yonder* and *yore* are also archaic or obsolete. Avoid them.

Z. Zero Defect

This has become a cliché in business. Nevertheless, the more we strive for *zero defect* in our English usage, the more likely we shall succeed.

TERMINOLOGY AND CONCEPTS

1. CASE
2. SUBJECT
3. NOMINATIVE
4. OBJECT
5. ACCUSATIVE
6. POSSESSIVE
7. GENITIVE
8. APOSTROPHE
9. PARTICIPLE
10. CONJUNCTION
11. INDEPENDENT CLAUSE
12. MAIN CLAUSE
13. SUBORDINATE CLAUSE
14. NON-RESTRICTIVE RELATIVE CLAUSE
15. RESTRICTIVE RELATIVE CLAUSE
16. PARENTHESIS
17. APPOSITION
18. SEMI-COLON
19. FULL STOP
20. PERIOD
21. COLON
22. WORD DIVISION
23. ACTIVE VOICE
24. PASSIVE VOICE
25. JARGON
26. JOURNALESE
27. CIRCUMLOCUTION
28. TAUTOLOGY
29. PREPOSITIONS
30. ADVERBIAL PARTICLES
31. PHRASAL VERBS
32. QUOTATION MARKS
33. SYNTAX
34. VERBAL
35. NON-VERBAL
36. VERBIAGE
37. VERBOSITY
38. WORD CONFUSION

39. ARCHAIC
40. OBSOLETE
41. CLICHÉ

APPLICATION

1. The correct case of the pronoun
Correct the following sentences where necessary:

1. We ought to help people who we consider poor.
2. We ought to help people whom we consider are poor.
3. The man who I saw yesterday is a famous businessman.
4. The man who you said you saw yesterday is a famous businessman.
5. You should talk to whomever will listen.
6. Has Smith or me been elected?
7. Let's you and I talk it over.
8. The manager and myself attended the conference.
9. The foreman objected to them coming late.
10. Is this your book or mine?
11. He gave the book to John and I.
12. He is as good as me.
13. Him arriving late every day led to his dismissal.
14. Whom did you hear had been promoted?
15. Was it she whom you had been told had been promoted?

2. The correct use of the noun in the possessive case
Supply the apostrophe where necessary in these sentences:

1. This is somebody elses book.
2. This is not Toms book; it is yours.
3. He refused to undergo military training for conscience sake.
4. Its Toms book; whose else could it be?
5. The dog has hurt its leg.
6. We visited the heroes graves.
7. The donkeys face was contorted with pain.
8. The womens meeting was disrupted.
9. The womans duty is often to care for her childrens needs.
10. Blessed are they who hunger and thirst for righteousness sake.

3. The correct use of the participial phrase
Correct the following sentences where necessary:

1. Seeing that it is late, dinner had better be served.
2. Running for the bus, it collided with a car.
3. Knowing all the details, it was a simple matter to write the report.
4. He met his friend, accompanied by her children, going down the street.
5. Being young and inexperienced, the work was too difficult for me.

4. The correct use of 'and'

Correct the following sentences where necessary:

1. They interned every man woman and child.
2. We come to work have tea and start our day's programme.
3. He is managing director, is in charge of marketing and of sales.
4. They worked hard and the work was soon finished.
5. There was no hope for us, we had to return without success.

5. The correct use of the comma

Correct the following sentences where necessary:

1. The man whose suitcase I had mistakenly taken was very angry.
2. Mr Jones whose son played cricket for South Africa works with me.
3. He was ill but he came nevertheless.
4. I think Mr Smith you are wrong.
5. There were only five people present, this was however a quorum.

6. The correct positioning of related words

Correct these sentences where necessary:

1. Some of the employees were already at the station, who did not know the trip was cancelled.
2. The announcement was in today's newspaper, which shocked us greatly.
3. We only had an hour to get ready.
4. Orphaned at five years of age, his uncle was his only means of support.
5. ACCOMMODATION: A house of a professional gentleman with many attractive features going overseas for R1 500 per month.

7. English usage

Correct the following sentences where necessary:

1. He shared the money between the three children.
2. There is nothing we can give, beside money.
3. I simply cannot cope up with all the work.
4. This is quite different than that.
5. He based his findings on recent economical studies.
6. Firstly you should read the prescribed texts. Secondly you should do the assignment.
7. The poor man has gotten no money.
8. He should have arrived at five o'clock. However, his car broke down.
9. I was surprised at his disinterested attitude. I was expecting him to show more interest, but he showed no interest whatsoever.
10. The reason that I did not arrive was because I was delayed at work.
11. The three of them had a mutual friend.
12. The appointment was for 1989-05-06.
13. One should be more careful about his children's safety.
14. May I ask for whom you are looking for?

15. He said, 'I shall see you tomorrow'.
16. He had nothing to say with regards to that matter.
17. You should try and see that film.
18. That was rather a unique occasion.
19. You should practice your piano playing more often.
20. He would not accept his friend's council and decided to do it anyway.
21. You have done very excellent work.
22. I saw him yesterevening.
23. People should not ask such questions.
24. At this point in time we should all save more.
25. He went right passed me.

REFERENCES

Here are some useful books that will serve as reference books in your quest for correctness:

Fowler: *Modern English Usage* (Oxford)
Strunk & White: *The Elements of Style* (Macmillan)
Partridge: *Usage and Abuse* (Penguin)
Treble & Vallins: *A.B.C. of English Usage* (Oxford)
Vallins: *Perfect your English* (Ward, Lock, & Co. Ltd)
Davis: *Introduction to Modern English Usage* (Oxford)
Adey: *Word Power (Ad. Donker)*

10

MODES (MEDIA SYSTEMS): PREPARATION

GOALS OF THE CHAPTER

By the end of this chapter you should be able to:
❏ analyse your target audience
❏ organize your information through its various stages of
    media selection
    gathering information
    drafting
    revising
    editing
❏ understanding the various uses or purposes of communication as
    friendly/expressive
    polite and courteous
    entertaining
    informative
    instructive
    complaining
    persuasive

INTRODUCTION

The most effective message uses the most suitable medium, that which will relate to the needs of its specific audience. The available media are oral, written, and non-verbal systems. We shall discuss each of these in detail in successive chapters; here we will first examine the importance of audience analysis, then look at the organization of information through its various stages, and then discuss the various uses or purposes of communication — informative, instructive, and persuasive.

AUDIENCE ANALYSIS

Whether we are speaking to one person, a small group, or a large audience, we have to be aware of our audience. In business it is important to analyse our audience in as detailed a way as possible. In marketing and advertising it is important to obtain a profile of our target audience or target market.

Audience analysis is an important part of communication, especially of persuasive communication. The content of the communication will change according to the type of communication — informative, instructive, and persuasive — and the targets of communication. Audience analysis is essentially an exercise in segmentation, that is in analysing the audience according to demographic, psychographic, domestic, and social factors.

Demographic factors include age, income, sex, education, race, nationality, religion, and location. **Psychographic factors** refer to life-style, personality traits, attitudes, motivation, and self-image. The audience can be further segmented by referring to various stages of the family life cycle or by referring to the social class of the audience.

Mass communication is often directed at young people in our society. Such communication takes a different form and uses different content from the communication directed at specialist groups such as housewives. In addition, in mass communication like advertising, we need to be able to link the psychographics of mass-media users to the psychographics of the users of products and services. This is what is called the *Socio Monitor*.

Audience analysis is a formidable task in South Africa because of the multi-racial structure of our society, but this makes the task of audience analysis or targeting all the more important.

Here is a typical audience profile that could be used in South Africa:

1. Demographic Profile

1.1 Sex
Male
Female

1.2 Age
Under 16
16–24
25–34
35–49
Over 50

1.3 Language
English
Afrikaans
African Language: Specify
Other: Specify

1.4 Race
White
Coloured
Indian
Black: Specify
Other: Specify

1.5 Income
A
B
C
D
E
(These letters refer to different levels of income. With differing rates of inflation it would be unwise to give current levels because they would soon be out of date. It is enough to say that A is the highest income and E the lowest.)

1.6 Location
City
Town
Village
Rural

1.7 Education
Under Standard 8
Standard 8–10
Post-matriculation: Specify

2. Family Life Cycle Profile
1. Bachelorhood or Spinsterhood — the single person living alone
2. Newly Married Couple with No Children
3. Young Married Couple with Children under 6

4. Young Married Couple with Children over 6
5. Older Married Couple (over 45) with Children
6. Older Married Couple with Children who have left home
7. The Solitary Survivor — the one left after the other dies

3. Social Class Profile

1. Upper Upper
2. Lower Upper
3. Upper Middle
4. Lower Middle
5. Upper Lower
6. Lower Lower

4. Lifestyle or Psychographic Profile

1. *Open*: positive, enterprising, nonconformist (OPEN)
2. *Conscientious*: careful, controlled, conformist (4C)
3. *Uninvolved*: negative, apathetic, indifferent, dispassionate (UNAID)
4. *Relaxed*: indulgent, permissive (RIP)
5. *Satisfied*: amiable, thrifty, introspective, status-conscious (SATIS)
6. *Closed*: limited, obstinate, suspicious, egocentric, disquieted (CLOSED)

(Obviously, as with so much psychological categorization, these are gener-
alized qualities, but some sort of psychographic evaluation of the target
audience is valuable.)

5. Consumer or Buyer Behaviour Profile

Marketing studies give us five categories of consumers that may be linked
with the psychographic categories:

1. Innovators (2,5 %) — adventurous riskers
2. Early adopters (13,5 %) — opinion leaders
3. Early majority (34 %) — deliberate adopters
4. Late majority (34 %) — followers
5. Laggards (16 %) — stubbornly resistant to change

(This classification was developed by Everett M. Rogers in his book *Diffusion
of Innovators* (New York: The Free Press, 1964) and has been consistently
used in business analyses of target audiences.)

Audience analysis is an awareness of the other person or persons in the
communication process and is an important phase in the preparation of the
most effective message to be communicated.

THE ORGANIZATION OF THE INFORMATION

Once we have analysed our target audience we can move on to the organization of our material. This involves various stages:

1. Media Selection
2. Gathering Information
3. Drafting
4. Revising
5. Editing

1. Media Selection

There are many media from which to select when we wish to communicate. Here are some of the possibilities.

1.1 Speech

1. Own speech
2. Someone else's speech, e.g. diplomatic messages
3. One-to-one communication by speaking, e.g. interviews, open-door policy
4. Informal group meetings, e.g. grapevine
5. Formal group meetings, e.g. committees, departmental meetings, inter-departmental meetings, briefing groups, meetings of representatives
6. Mass meetings, e.g. political meetings
7. Lectures, e.g. information-giving, formal presentations, sermons
8. Conferences, congresses
9. Telephone

1.2 Written communication

1. Letters
2. Memoranda
3. Reports
4. Telegrams, telexes, fax messages
5. Advertisements
6. Press releases
7. Newsletters
8. Curricula vitae
9. Pamphlets, handbills, posters, notice-boards
10. Brochures, information bulletins, manuals
11. Magazines, newspapers
12. Books
13. Suggestion schemes
14. Attitude surveys, questionnaires

1.3 Non-verbal communication

1. Kinesics (body language), facial expressions, gestures

2. Graphics, charts, diagrams, posters, flip charts, flannel boards, chalk-boards
3. Photographs, slides, overhead transparencies
4. Microscopes, telescopes
5. Demonstrations, models, samples
6. Paintings, sculptures

1.4 Audio-visual communication

1. Tape-slides
2. Films
3. Television, videos
4. Radio
5. Audio tapes
6. Records

1.5 Electronic communication

1. Electronic mail
2. Electronic typewriter, word processor, computer communication
3. Telephone, telex, fax messages
4. Viewdata (teletext), Beltel communication
5. Microfilm

2. Gathering Information

Before we can communicate with our audience through a particular medium we have to prepare what we wish to communicate. Ideas come to us as we work, sit, talk, read, listen, day-dream, dream — through life itself. The best communicators use note-taking, sketching, diaries and journals to record their thoughts. Brainstorming is useful, either on one's own or with others; this is spontaneous, free association of ideas without judgement or censure. From this can come some organization in the form of clustering of ideas or mind-mapping or diagrammatic representation. A heuristic approach is often useful: this is asking oneself or others basic questions about the topic and seeing whether useful ideas flow from these basic questions. It is similar to brainstorming in that there is no judgement or censure of ideas.

3. Drafting

This is a further stage in the organization of our material. Here more selection and rejection take place. We choose a title and we establish our purpose. We develop an outline in which a pattern or arrangement begins to emerge. This gives us our paragraphing for an essay or the topics for chapters of a book. We then write our first draft. If we have decided to use film as our medium, it may be the first draft of the film-script. If it is a poster, it may be our first sketch.

4. Revising

Most of us end our communication at the stage of drafting, and we think our first draft is the end-product. This is why much of our work is shoddy and incomplete. Unless we subject our communication to strict revision, it will be unsuccessful. We need to revise for style, logical arrangement of ideas, clarity, elimination of errors, and elimination of unworthy ideas.

4.1 Style

Your style of communication will depend on your language and your sentence structure. Perhaps you have used too much repetition that jars. Perhaps your sentences are too long or too boring. You need to consider different words that will make your statements clearer. You need to have a variety of sentence-length and type of sentence.

4.2 Logical arrangement of ideas

Paragraphing helps us to arrange our ideas. In our outline we have stated the main idea of each paragraph. This should have been expanded into a **topic sentence** that expresses the topic of each paragraph. Such a topic sentence can sometimes be at the start of the paragraph, in the middle, or at the end. There should be a variety in the positioning of the topic sentence. If each paragraph starts with the topic sentence, the paragraphs could be boring.

Have we supported the topic sentence with examples, expansion, discussion? If there is no such substantiation, the idea could be superficially treated. Have we looked at possible objections to our statements and dealt with them honestly?

Have we used **linked words** that help the flow of our communication? Sometimes numbering of the points we are making helps. At other times words like *therefore*, or *on the other hand* will help the reader or audience to understand better the logic of our message.

4.3 Clarity

Often what we think is very clear is not at all clear to our readers or audience. It is very difficult to put ourselves into someone else's mind-frame and to test whether we are likely to communicate. Fortunately there is an index that can help us. It is called the **Clarity Index** or the **Fog Index**. It is easily applied and has even been made into a computer program that can test the clarity of any communication that is run through the program. The index works in this way:

1. Choose a random section of about 200 words
   Count the number of words: a
2. Count the number of full stops, question marks, colons, and exclamation marks: b
3. Divide a by b. This gives the average number of words in a sentence: $\dfrac{a}{b}$

4. Count the words of more than two syllables. Exclude proper names and three-syllable words ending in *es*, or *ed*: c

5. Divide c by a and multiply by 100: $\frac{c}{a} \times 100$

   This gives the percentage of words of more than two syllables.

6. Add the average number of words per sentence ($\frac{a}{b}$) to the percentage of words of more than two syllables: $\frac{c}{a} \times \frac{100}{1}$. This is the Clarity or Fog Index: $\frac{a}{b} + \left(\frac{c}{a} \times \frac{100}{1} \right)$

7. Multiply your answer by 0,4 or $\frac{4}{10}$: $\frac{a}{b} + \left(\frac{c}{a} \times \frac{100}{1} \right) \times \frac{4}{10}$

This appears to be rather complicated, but it isn't really. The purpose of the final multiplication by $\frac{4}{10}$ is to bring the index into line with the number of years of schooling the reader may have had. If the answer to the penultimate stage — i.e. $\frac{a}{b} + \left(\frac{c}{a} \times \frac{100}{1} \right)$ — is 25, then multiplying by $\frac{4}{10}$ would give the answer ten. If a person has had ten years of schooling, he would have passed Standard 8 in the South African system of education. A business report can be expected to have a higher index: the answer to the penultimate stage — $\frac{a}{b} + \left(\frac{c}{a} \times \frac{100}{1} \right)$ — is likely to be about 35 and multiplying it by $\frac{4}{10}$ would give 14, i.e. a clarity index level that would suit a person with two years' schooling after Standard 10.

The formula does not tell you how good your writing is; it does not deal with style or grammar; it tells you only how clear or uncomplicated the writing is. The lower the index is, the easier it is to understand the writing. It is a very valuable index for a manager to use, especially in the multilingual society of South Africa.

4.4 Elimination of errors
This is where the concept of correctness, which we have already mentioned, applies. Mistakes in grammar, spelling, typing, and layout must be checked and corrected. The skill of a proofreader is needed.

4.5 Elimination of unworthy ideas
Before we can say a piece of work has been properly revised, we need to check whether each idea is necessary and serves a useful purpose. Often whole paragraphs or sentences can be eliminated or be rewritten.

5. Editing
When we think of editing, we think of the editor of a newspaper, but editing is part of every manager's work. Unless we carefully edit every communication

that goes out from our business enterprise, we shall be liable for the poor impression that our communication makes upon our readers. Editing is essentially a task connected with written communication. We need to edit with particular reference to punctuation, spelling, number, tenses, and other grammatical errors. To do this properly we need to be familiar with our three concepts of number, time, and correctness, which we discussed earlier.

Editing is not such an unfamiliar task for a manager: whenever we check the typing or word-setting of a letter, a memorandum, a report, or an advertisement, we are in effect editing the work. It is like the final revision or the final proofreading before the publication of the document.

FORMS OF COMMUNICATION

Communication can take various forms and the content of the communication will vary according to the different target audiences at which the communication is directed. The uses or purposes of communication are:

1. friendly/expressive
2. polite and courteous
3. entertaining
4. informative
5. instructive
6. complaining
7. persuasive

1. Friendly/Expressive

Friendly communication is designed to keep friendship and harmony between the communicator and the receiver of the communication. An informal personal tone is used, and normally the communication is between equals without any sense of superiority or inferiority. Precision of language is not required and the language is not usually technical or factual. The friendly or expressive communicator often uses emotive or poetic language to express his feelings, and a subjective attitude is acceptable.

2. Polite and Courteous

This type of communication is more formal and is usually addressed to someone who is older, of a higher status, or deserving of respect.

3. Entertaining

Entertaining communication attempts primarily to interest. The emphasis is not on educating but rather on giving pleasure. Humour, suspense, and a lively use of language are characteristics of entertaining communication. Literature, the theatre, and the cinema are obvious examples of this type of communication. Such communication skills are becoming more and more important in advertising. The creative copywriter needs to be at least partly an entertainer.

4. Informative

Informative communication does what the word suggests: it informs the receiver of something. It is usually objective, that is without subjective or personal emotion. It tends to be factual, precise, and technical. Such communication is frequently used in business when information needs to be passed from one person to another. For best results it should be simple and straightforward without any barriers such as emotion or status entering into the communication.

5. Instructive

This type of communication is didactic, that is, it intends to teach, and the assumption is that the instructor is more knowledgeable than the receiver. The tone is more imperative or commanding. Often technical language or jargon is used, and the instructor assumes that the audience will understand such language. In other words, more demands are made on the audience than in informative communication.

6. Complaining

Here the sender of the communication has become aggrieved in some way and is attempting to redress the wrong. The tone is usually that of a person on the defensive, and the words may therefore give offence to the receiver. Customer complaints are very relevant in business communication, and the better we, as consumers, know how to complain validly, and the better we, as businessmen, know how to respond correctly to customers' complaints, the better equipped we shall be in the business environment.

7. Persuasive

Persuasive communication may be defined as communication that intends to change the receiver's behaviour and attitudes in a way that the sender of the communication has previously determined. Persuasion is a subtle pro-cess that succeeds through manipulation of spoken, written, visual, or audio-visual symbols to achieve the predetermined purpose. This is the form of communication that advertisers use most often. (This does not mean that advertisers should not be friendly, polite and courteous, entertaining, or informative as well. From time to time there may be a place in advertising even for the instructive and the complaining forms of communication, but these would be few and far between.)

There are different types of persuasive communication, and since our business communication is so often of the persuasive kind, let us give more attention to these types. We shall see that the persuasive communication of business frequently draws also upon the other forms we have mentioned.

7.1 Hard-sell persuasion

As the name implies, this calls to mind the brash salesman whose main aim is to sell at any cost and who rides rough-shod over the sensitivities of his audience. Closing the sale is the most important part of the communication to him and he rushes to this point. Such persuasive communication is rightly condemned since it has given salesmen, advertisers, and business in general a bad name. Most businessmen today use more subtle and more dignified methods.

7.2 Soft-sell persuasion

Here, although the main aim is always to persuade the listener to buy the product or service, more account is taken of the receiver's personality and of his rights to make up his own mind. Advertising communication can never be really hard-sell since closing the sale is not part of the advertiser's task. Most advertising is therefore soft-sell persuasion. If we were to use hard-sell and soft-sell to describe advertising communication, these would be relative terms: hard-sell would have more hard-sell characteristics than usual, and soft-sell would be more subtle and sensitive. Hard-sell would be directed to a more dependent, less educated audience, and soft-sell to a more independent and more educated audience.

7.3 Prestige persuasion

Here the aim is to make the listener feel that he will gain prestige or status from owning the product that is being advertised. The tone is like the form of communication that we called polite and courteous. Flattery is often used in this form of persuasive communication, and the temptation is to play upon the listener's human frailty in this way. The advertiser must guard against insincerity and condescension. There is nothing wrong with giving a person self-esteem and encouraging him to be motivated towards goals of success, self-expression, and self-achievement, but this type of persuasion needs to be carefully and sensitively used.

7.4 Humorous persuasion

Witty or clever persuasion has an undoubted appeal, but it can be very unsuccessful too. Speakers or writers need to have a feel for what is entertaining or humorous. Very few advertisements that try to be funny succeed, and that is why we should be careful of using humour in persuasive communication.

7.5 Charity appeals

David Ogilvy calls this 'advertising for good causes' (*Ogilvy on Advertising*, Pan, 1983, p. 150). At most, advertising makes the public more sensitive to good causes so that, when approached personally, people will respond. This type of advertising is similar to the type of communication we have called informative (see 4 above). In South Africa petrol companies often inform the public about their involvement in wild life conservation schemes or educational schemes in order to give the public a better image of their companies and their products.

7.6 Competitions

We can try to persuade people to be better informed by offering them a chance to win something through a competition. The possible benefit to the audience in responding to the competition makes the persuasive communication more likely to succeed. Since obtaining some kind of response is one of the main aims of persuasive communication, this form of advertising can be very successful if the competition is directly linked to the product being advertised.

7.7 Reminder campaigns

These are also called 'advertising specialties' or 'reminder advertising'. Usually they take the form of giving away calendars, novelties, match-books, or other gifts to existing and prospective customers. The free gifts are intended to create goodwill and to remind the recipient to do business with the firms that have sent the gifts. There must be no obligation on the recipient, and the gifts should never be seen as bribes. This kind of persuasive communication is closely associated with direct-mail advertising.

7.8 Sample campaigns

A persuasive letter accompanied by a free sample is closely associated with reminder campaigns. The purpose is to introduce the public to new products.

7.9 Premiums

These are offers of a free gift available to anyone who purchases the product advertised. Such offers are useful when a product is being launched. They induce customers to buy the product and to respond to the advertisement, but research has shown that the customer who responds in this way is not necessarily going to become a long-term purchaser of the product.

7.10 Introductory offers

Closely linked with premiums are various kinds of introductory offers, e.g. introductory discounts, price-deals, 'cents-off' coupons, and limited-time offers. These are useful when introducing a new product or when trying to accelerate the sales of a product already in circulation. Again the object is to induce an immediate response.

7.11 Positive persuasion

Positive appeals portray comfort and satisfaction to be gained from using a product. They usually dramatize the benefit to be gained — sometimes exaggerating it absurdly. This kind of persuasion links up with the 'I'm OK' psychology of transactional analysis made popular by Thomas Harris in his book, *I'm OK — You're OK*.

7.12 Negative persuasion

This type of appeal often arouses fear in the consumer and links up with the 'I'm not OK' psychology. Again the negative appeals use dramatic means to show the danger to be avoided by using the advertised product. Feelings of insecurity, imminent danger, and the fear of ill-health or death are aroused as negative motivating forces.

CONCLUSION

This chapter has introduced us to communication media — oral, written, and non-verbal systems — and then considered the need for audience analysis, the organization of material, and the various forms of communication. In the next three chapters we shall deal with oral communication, written communication, and non-verbal communication respectively.

CONCEPTS AND TERMINOLOGY

1. MEDIA SYSTEMS
2. ORAL
3. WRITTEN
4. NON-VERBAL
5. AUDIENCE ANALYSIS
6. AUDIENCE PROFILE
7. DEMOGRAPHIC PROFILE
8. FAMILY LIFE CYCLE PROFILE
9. SOCIAL CLASS PROFILE
10. LIFE STYLE OR PSYCHOGRAPHIC PROFILE
11. CONSUMER OR BUYER BEHAVIOUR PROFILE
12. ORGANIZATION OF INFORMATION
13. MEDIA SELECTION
14. SPEECH
15. WRITTEN COMMUNICATION
16. NON-VERBAL COMMUNICATION
17. AUDIO-VISUAL COMMUNICATION
18. ELECTRONIC COMMUNICATION
19. GATHERING INFORMATION
20. DRAFTING
21. REVISING
22. STYLE
23. LOGICAL ARRANGEMENT OF IDEAS
24. CLARITY

25. CLARITY OR FOG INDEX
26. ELIMINATION OF ERRORS
27. ELIMINATION OF UNWORTHY IDEAS
28. EDITING
29. FORMS OF COMMUNICATION
30. FRIENDLY/EXPRESSIVE
31. POLITE AND COURTEOUS
32. ENTERTAINING
33. INFORMATIVE
34. INSTRUCTIVE
35. COMPLAINING
36. PERSUASIVE
37. HARD-SELL PERSUASION
38. SOFT-SELL PERSUASION
39. PRESTIGE PERSUASION
40. HUMOROUS PERSUASION
41. CHARITY APPEALS
42. COMPETITIONS
43. REMINDER CAMPAIGNS
44. SAMPLE CAMPAIGNS
45. PREMIUMS
46. INTRODUCTORY OFFERS
47. POSITIVE PERSUASION
48. NEGATIVE PERSUASION

APPLICATION

1. Choose a person in your organization with whom you often communicate. Write an audience profile of this person.
2. Choose a group of people with whom you do business. Construct an audience profile of this group.
3. Here are a number of typical opportunities for business communication:
   - ❑ Notification of a board-meeting;
   - ❑ Information about a new appointment;
   - ❑ Change of company policy about lunch times;
   - ❑ Security arrangements;
   - ❑ A staff party;
   - ❑ A new product launch;
   - ❑ A staff vacancy;
   - ❑ End-of-year financial results;
   - ❑ An urgent departmental meeting;
   - ❑ The death of a prominent member of staff;
   - ❑ A bursary scheme for employee's children;
   - ❑ A department's record-breaking productivity;

    ❑ A new photocopying machine has been installed;
    ❑ The retirement of one of the directors;
    ❑ Customer dissatisfaction.
    Choose the appropriate medium or media for each of these and give reasons for its or their appropriateness.

4. You have been asked by your managing director to write a report on the best photocopier to be purchased. Go through the various stages of:
    ❑ gathering information;
    ❑ drafting the report;
    ❑ revising the report;
    ❑ testing the clarity of your report;
    ❑ editing the report.

5. Give examples of each of the following forms of communication:
    ❑ friendly/expressive
    ❑ polite and courteous
    ❑ entertaining
    ❑ informative
    ❑ instructive
    ❑ complaining
    Write out at least one in full.

6. 'Persuasive communication is a form of manipulation.'
    Discuss this statement.

7. Choose one of these forms of persuasive communication:
    ❑ a charity appeal;
    ❑ a competition;
    ❑ a reminder campaign;
    ❑ a sample campaign;
    ❑ a premium campaign;
    ❑ an introductory offer.
    Compose the final copy for the form you have chosen.

8. Choose any passage of about 100 words of continuous prose from this book and work out the clarity index for this passage. Comment on the degree of clarity for a book of this kind designed to help managers in a multi-cultural society to improve their communication.

9. Choose any company report intended for shareholders. (Often these are published in newspapers.) Calculate the clarity index for this report and comment on its degree of clarity in relation to its expected readership.

10. Test the clarity of the final edited report you wrote in answer to 4 above. In other words work out the clarity index of your own writing.

11

MODES (MEDIA SYSTEMS): ORAL COMMUNICATION

GOALS OF THE CHAPTER

In this chapter we shall deal with oral communication. By the end of the chapter we shall have discussed:

- ❏ face-to-face conversations
- ❏ interviewing
- ❏ negotiating
- ❏ consulting
- ❏ meetings
- ❏ public speaking and speeches
- ❏ telephone conversations

INTRODUCTION

Oral communication is the most effective mode of communication when communication is urgent and immediate response is needed. It is less formal than written communication and can achieve better understanding because oral communication can combine with non-verbal communication to provide total interaction. The principles we have discussed in the first four chapters of this book are of the utmost importance in oral communication. The most common forms of oral communication are:

❏   face-to-face conversations (sometimes called one-to-one);
❏   meetings;
❏   public speaking and speeches; and
❏   telephone conversations.

FACE-TO-FACE CONVERSATIONS

Face-to-face conversation is the most effective form of oral communication because it is likely that concentration and attention will be at the maximum, and interruptions and barriers can be kept to the minimum. There is ample opportunity for open response if the level of trust is high, and problems of disagreement, distrust and tension can be worked through more easily than in other forms of oral communication.

Face-to-face communication can take the form of interviewing, negotiating, or consulting.

1. Interviewing

When we think of interviewing, we usually think of selection or recruiting interviewing or going to an interview for employment, but there are different kinds of interviews. We may think of an interview with the press or on television, an induction interview, a goal-setting interview, a performance-appraisal interview, a disciplinary interview, an exit interview, interviewing in consultancy, and the informal interview. Any face-to-face conversation is an interview, and it has been suggested that the word 'interview' should be dropped altogether because it has such foreboding connotations. Let us look at some general characteristics of a face-to-face conversation before we discuss particular types of interviews.

First the **setting** for the conversation must be conducive to a relaxed relationship: a conversation across a desk is often threatening; it is better for an office to have a corner where at least two people can sit in comfortable circumstances facing each other without a desk between them. Even if this is not possible, at least a desk should have two or three chairs next to each other so that the person who works at the desk may move to the other side of the desk and sit next to the person he is interviewing. Such a move on the part of the 'interviewer' is a gesture of goodwill on his part to set the 'interviewee' at ease. It is very important to create this type of friendly atmosphere. It is better, for instance for the 'interviewer' to get up and go to meet the 'interviewee' and accompany him into his office rather than expect the person to walk (often a long way) to the door of the room where 'the great Man' (the interviewer) is sitting at his desk.

We have used the words 'interviewer' and 'interviewee' in inverted commas because these very names suggest that one person is doing the interviewing and the other person is the passive recipient of the interviewing procedure. This suggests that the one has a dominant status and the other an inferior status. As we have clearly seen, **status** can be a barrier to good communication. Therefore the 'interviewer' must try to normalize the unequal relationship as much as he can. Even though in many types of interviews it is unavoidable that one person has the dominant status, he must try to restore balance to the relationship if he is to achieve the relaxed environment that allows for openness and honesty. With these reservations about calling the one person the 'interviewer' and the other the 'interviewee', we shall proceed for practical reasons to refer to them as interviewer and interviewee without the inverted commas.

As part of the preparation for the interview it is important that neither party keeps the other waiting. It is an insult to do this, and if it is unavoidable that one keeps the other waiting, apologies should be made unreservedly. It is better, however, to ensure that both parties are available before the stipulated time. The interviewer should ensure also that interruptions are not allowed during the interview, except for emergencies when again due apologies should be given. The interviewer and the interviewee should be well prepared, with all the necessary documentation at hand. It is not a good idea, however, to be constantly referring to the documentation during the interview because this can be very distracting. The same applies to writing notes during the interview: it can be distracting and threatening. If the interviewee thinks that his words are being recorded either in writing or on tape, he may consider it is more like a police interview than a relaxed meeting. There are obvious advantages to the interviewer in making notes, but he should be able to remember enough to make the necessary notes immediately after the interview. It is important, therefore, to allow time after the interview for this purpose.

Many interviewers talk too much; the interviewee should be given the opportunity to express his views freely. Although questions may elicit responses from the interviewee, the interview should not consist of a series of questions and answers. This would again be too much like interrogation. Questions should not be of the closed type that can be answered with either a 'Yes' or a 'No'. Questions should not be threatening: for instance, the question, 'Why did you stay in that position only three months?' suggests negative thoughts on the part of the interviewer. Questions should not allow the respondent to answer in a way that he thinks the questioner expects to be answered: there's hardly anyone who is likely to answer negatively to a question like 'Do you think you performed well in that position?' If a person is called upon to answer a series of questions that may make him nervous, he will give a great deal of thought to the answers and not be spontaneous and relaxed. In such a tense interview it is unlikely that genuine feelings or opinions will emerge. In every face-to-face conversation sincerity should be the main aim: it is only then that both people will feel comfortable and express their real views. If questions are asked, they should be about objective facts and should not imply a judgemental attitude; questions about facts may elicit the respondent's attitudes and opinions, but these will be spontaneously given because there has been no suggestion that they are demanded. Open questions that pose alternatives or that ask not only for answers but also reasons are probably the best questions to ask. On the matter of questions, we should also allow the interviewee to ask questions; it is not the interviewer's prerogative.

There is a very real sense in which the interviewer is also on trial in an interview: he represents his company and he is therefore involved in a public relations exercise to present the company in the best possible light. If the interviewee, whether he be an applicant for employment, an employee, a customer, or a client, feels that he is not being treated fairly or courteously in the interview, the company will suffer. Lack of preparation, a flippant attitude, anger, or lack of consideration give the interviewee a bad impression. At the end of the interview there must be a feeling of satisfaction that the interviewee has had a chance to express his views and that they have been heard and understood. Of course, no interviewee should leave with false hopes of success: far too many applicants leave feeling so confident of success that they feel insulted when they are informed that they have been unsuccessful. It is much better to make it clear that there are other matters to be considered before a decision can be made.

Now let us look at different types of interviews.

1.1 Selection interview

When interviewing a person for a position in a company, the interviewer should consider the following:

❏   physical appearance (dress, neatness)
❏   health and history of illness
❏   speech (clarity and coherence)
❏   confidence (shy? arrogant? submissive? self-assured?)
❏   attainments (experience and qualifications)
❏   aspirations (motivation and ambitions)
❏   interests (hobbies and social pursuits)
❏   family and living circumstances (including financial stability)
❏   personality (maturity, initiative, stability)
❏   citizenship

The interviewer should be wary of what is called the 'halo effect'. This is a labelling of the applicant as a particular type and such labelling then affects the interviewer's judgement. It is often caused by the first impression given by the applicant's appearance and is strengthened by the interviewer's pride in the fact that he summed up the applicant at first sight. Like love at first sight, summing up an applicant at first sight can be a dangerous mistake.

In a selection interview the applicant should have a clear understanding of:

- ❑ the job he has applied for
- ❑ the company and something of its history, philosophy, and culture
- ❑ why there is a vacancy
- ❑ his work conditions if offered the position
- ❑ possibilities of advancement in the company
- ❑ benefits (leave, pension, medical aid)
- ❑ whether he would like to work in this position.

A selection interview is notorious for being an unreliable gauge of a person's suitability for a position. It may be better to have a trial period of a few months when both the newly appointed person and the business organization can test their decision further. It is usually a good idea to give a serious contender for a position a second interview. This would be a more in-depth interview, perhaps with a panel of interviewers and with more stress on the applicant to see whether he can handle difficult problems. In this interview deliberate probing, in the form of opposing points of view and quick changes of subjects, may reveal something that did not happen in the first interview.

1.2 Induction interviews

Once a person has been appointed, a series of induction interviews with the new employee is important. His letter of appointment may be discussed. His line manager needs to introduce him to his particular duties. The staff manager needs to clarify his benefits and the social opportunities the company offers. The new employee needs to be introduced to his fellow employees. The methods of goal-setting and performance-appraisal need to be discussed. Whereas the selection interview has to include a certain amount of critical scrutiny of the applicant, there should be no judgement of the new employee in the induction interview. The communication should be purely informative, and the attitude of the interviewer should be friendly and helpful, without any criticism.

1.3 Goal-setting interviews

It is important, once a person has been appointed to work in a business organization, that he has clear goals set for him to achieve. Such interviews should be conducted regularly so that his performance may be fairly appraised. So often employees are expected to achieve goals, but the goals are not clearly explained to them. Employers know where they are going in their work if goals are set. Motivation is higher and it is more likely that the objectives of the organization will be met.

Here are some of the characteristics of good goal-setting:

❑ the goals must be realistic and able to be achieved;
❑ they must be challenging and satisfying, both for the employee and the organization;
❑ they must be measurable;
❑ they must be understood by the employee;
❑ the participation of the employee in setting the goals is important because he then feels more committed.

When setting goals, the interviewer should set the goals in a quantifiable way by:

❑ setting deadlines;
❑ stating the goals in clearly defined quantities, e.g. so many units per week;
❑ stating the desired quality of the work;
❑ stating the cost parameters.

The interview should also

❑ show how the goal fits into the broader objectives of the organization;
❑ specify and allocate the resources needed;
❑ clarify areas of responsibility and authority;
❑ summarize and obtain feedback from the employee;
❑ follow up and assist with problems.

Again we must realize that the goal-setting interview should not involve any judgemental opinions or behaviour. It is an exercise in participation and is essentially an opportunity for agreeing on targets to be met. Such as are agreed upon should be recorded and a copy should be given to the employee.

1.4 Performance-appraisal interviews

Once goals have been set and the employee has been given a chance to achieve these goals, an interview must be carefully planned and must not be too judgemental or subjective. It is appraisal, not a disciplinary hearing. Essentially the performance-appraisal should deal with facts that are clearly recorded and be as objective as possible. The purpose of the interview is to motivate the employee and to identify the problem areas so that more realistic goals may be set and help may be given. Discipline is exercised only if the employee consistently fails to achieve the goals he has accepted as reasonable.

The interview should start with a restatement of the goals and an appraisal of how far these were achieved. The employee should be asked to make this appraisal himself. He will usually begin with that part that has been successfully performed and the interviewer should give credit where it is due. Throughout this interview the interviewer should be specific, factual, calm, and concise, and the employee should in this way be encouraged to be the same. The emphasis is always on performance, not on the person, but where the employee admits there were problems, the interviewer should respond with empathy and re-enforcement rather than criticism. Blame should be avoided. In this way the interview can move on to new goal-setting and to a follow-up meeting with specific details such as deadlines and quantifiable standards. The interviewer should keep a record of the interview.

1.5 Reward interviews

If goal-setting and performance appraisals take place regularly, they will lead to reward interviews or disciplinary interviews. The reward interview is usually held once a year when increments or bonuses are given. It is usually a pleasant task, but sometimes the employee is not satisfied with his reward, and this should be freely discussed so that by the end of the interview he has talked through his dissatisfaction and has accepted that the extent of the reward is justified. Unfortunately it is not always possible to satisfy the employee's expectations, but the interviewer should be prepared to listen and to discuss any problems openly.

1.6 Disciplinary interviews or reprimands

These should never be impatient outbursts but should be designed to improve performance and to help the employee not to repeat mistakes. Often such reprimands are made necessary because the safety of the employee and his fellow-workers has been affected. The interview should concentrate on facts and should not be allowed to develop into an argument. Nevertheless the employee should be given the opportunity to state how he viewed the circumstances leading to the offence and he should be asked to suggest ways of improvement for the future. If an offence is a serious one, a letter to the employee may be necessary. A copy, signed by the employee to show that he has read it on a particular date, should then be kept in his file.

1.7 Counselling interviews

Sometimes employees have problems that are not caused by their work but may affect their work performance. The problems may be domestic, financial, or health-related. It is a manager's responsibility to listen and to counsel, and if the problem is beyond the manager's capabilities, to refer the employee to someone more qualified to help. Although ultimately it will be to the benefit of the business organization as a whole if the problem is solved, the manager has as his primary responsibility the well-being of the person with the problem, and the manager's sympathetic handling of the interview will play a large part in helping the employee not only with his problem but in improving their working relationship. A counselling interview is a major opportunity to form bonds of commitment and loyalty to each other and to the business organization. One of the main techniques in such counselling is that the manager should not offer prescriptive advice but should rather guide the employee towards finding the solution that will best suit his particular circumstances. Offering advice is often not solving a problem at all but making the employee dependent and even more helpless. If, furthermore, the advice offered does not work, the employee feels let down and may even blame the manager for making his problem worse.

1.8 Grievance interviews

It is not only the manager that has the right to reprimand an employee; an employee has the right to express a grievance against a fellow-employee, a senior, or even against the business organization as a whole. Since this can be a highly sensitive matter, it is a good idea for the organization to lay down grievance procedures, otherwise such occasions may become very emotional and destructive. If there are adequate grievance procedures, the manager will have time to prepare his response to the grievance, but often the employee feels so annoyed or frustrated that he wishes to discuss the matter immediately without going through any procedures. At such times the manager has to bear the brunt of the outburst and to allow the employee to state his case. His main responsibilities are to listen carefully and to try to calm down the employee. Then the two can work together, almost in the same way as in a disciplinary interview, trying to work out the best approach to improve the unsatisfactory working relationship that has resulted. The manager has to be careful that he is not seen as taking sides either for or against the aggrieved employee. He has to be objective, but he has to try to allow the person with the grievance to feel that he has had his say, that he has been heard, and that something — not always what he wanted when he stormed in with his grievance — will be done about his grievance.

1.9 Resignation interviews

This is an **exit interview** where the person leaves of his own accord. Often a resignation interview is unexpected. There are two possible situations: either the manager wants the person to leave, or the manager does not want him to leave.

When you want the person to leave, the interview is basically a public relations exercise: you want him to leave with the minimum of ill-feeling and the maximum of goodwill towards the business organization. It is important that there should be a relaxed attitude and that the person resigning should be put at ease, for often this is a very difficult decision for the employee and he is feeling awkward. Perhaps he has found a better position elsewhere and he may feel he is letting you down by resigning; in such a situation you need to congratulate him and wish him well. You could praise him for any positive contribution he has made and show an interest in where he is going and what his plans are. You could learn from him why he has made the decision to leave and you could perhaps put this information to some good use within the firm. Above all there should be empathy with him, and an invitation to keep in touch would help him to leave with a positive attitude to the organization. After all, he may become an important customer or client in the future.

When you do not want the person to leave, it may be necessary to establish whether the employee's decision is irrevocable and to ask for time for him to reconsider and you to consult further with the personnel department and to see whether his opportunities in his new position will match what your organization has in mind for him. This is essentially an excercise in negotiating. Of course, if his decision is irrevocable, there is nothing to do but to accept the resignation and then it becomes a similar public relations excercise as with the person whom you want to leave. If, however, there is a chance that he will change his mind, it is important that his resignation should not be accepted immediately and that another appointment be made to discuss the matter further. His exact reasons for leaving should be established at the first interview. If it is merely a matter of more money offered in the new position, it is dangerous to offer him more money because then a dangerous precedent has been established and the news will soon get around that all an employee has to do is threaten to leave in order to obtain an increase. It is better to compare the short-term gain with the long-term opportunities in his present position; the question of whether his long-term benefits, such as his pension, have been considered is relevant. It is important to express that the company will regret his departure and to see whether any difficulties in working relationships can be overcome. A positive attitude is needed on the part of the manager, and you should be careful not to make promises that cannot be kept and to make sure that any follow-up is speedily carried out. If the employee cannot, however, be persuaded to stay, he should leave without acrimony and with the best wishes of the organization.

1.10 Dismissal interviews

This is an **exit interview** where the employee does *not* leave of his own accord. Before conducting any dismissal interview, the manager has to make sure that the various steps before dismissal have been taken according to the law. The law requires that, except in exceptional cases such as desertion, where summary dismissal is allowed, the employee must be given a verbal warning, two written warnings, a final written warning (in which dismissal may be mentioned for the first time), and then a hearing before he can be dismissed. The employee must be given the opportunity to improve his work performance before he can be dismissed for performance deficiency. At the hearing he is allowed to be represented by a person of his own choice and he must be given the chance to hear the charges against him, to state his case, and to hear the findings of the hearing. The onus of proof is on the employer to prove that the employee has caused damage to the employer, that the offence has been committed frequently despite warnings, and that the dismissal is substantively fair. Unless these procedures have been followed, the employee could sue his employer for unfair dismissal, and the finances and the reputation of the business could suffer as a consequence.

The purpose of the labour relations laws is to prevent unfair dismissal of an employee, to protect the relationship between the employer and the employee, and to prevent unfair disturbance of the business. The required procedures protect the employee against impulsive actions on the part of the employer and they demand objectivity as the basis of the interviews and the hearing. Although some managers may consider these procedures to be troublesome, they are essentially fair and promote good employer-employee relations.

In any case of dismissal the manager must consider it as a business decision and be sure of the wisdom of such drastic action: is it worth it to the business to go to the expense of re-advertising the post and training someone else? Is it worth it to cause disruption to the business and to create possible tension among the other employees?

If due procedures are followed and the manager has given careful thought to the matter, it is unlikely that dismissal interviews will go wrong, but they are always unpleasant decisions for managers to have to take and can cause many sleepless nights and much soul-searching.

1.11 Retrenchment interviews

In larger business organizations especially, retrenchment is sometimes necessary. Obviously a manager should always try to avoid retrenchment. If it has to be done and a trade union is involved, due notice to the union has to be given. The employees must be advised, preferably in separate interviews. Efforts to secure other work opportunities for the employees to be retrenched should be made. One cannot use retrenchment as an excuse for getting rid of an employee for poor work-performance. Performance appraisals cannot be used as reasons for retrenchment. The criteria for retrenchment must be seen as fair: for instance, the last employees to be engaged by the firm should be the first to be retrenched, no matter how good they were at their work. Severance pay must be given according to the number of years' service to the organization, and a guarantee of re-employment if the business improves should be given. A manager must not allow selective re-employment, otherwise he and the organization will fall foul of the unions and labour law. In a way, retrenchment interviews are easier than disciplinary or exit interviews because the cause is business failure rather than the failure of the employee.

1.12 Press, radio, and television interviews

Often a manager is called upon to give a public interview on the radio or television or for the press. This can be intimidating, but is good for publicity and it should therefore be regarded as a business opportunity. Preparation, confidence, knowledge of the subject, and sincerity are the important requirements. Clarity of speech and courtesy to the interviewer, even when he is trying to 'rattle' you, help greatly. When it is a panel interview, you will need to make your contribution without dominating the discussion. With 'off-the-cuff' contributions, care must be exercised not to give away confidential information or to be caught off-guard. 'Live' interviews are the best as far as the audience is concerned, but they are the most dangerous for the inexperienced interviewee: hesitation, distracting mannerisms, too excited a voice, and indiscretions can ruin a manager's and his organization's reputation. This is why the kind of practice that an actor finds invaluable must be part of the manager's training.

2. Negotiating

Negotiation is a process of trying to reach an agreement between two or more parties, each of whom is in control of resources sought after by the other party or parties. The purpose of the negotiation is to agree on the resources that each can exchange to the benefit of the other party and to its own benefit also. The whole idea of negotiation is to concentrate on interests that are common and to reduce the differences the parties have; in other words to build on areas of co-operation and to work through areas of conflict. There must be fruitful compromise from both sides: if either side is not prepared to compromise,negotiation cannot take place. There must be willingness on both sides to give and to take.

An experienced negotiator demonstrates the following characteristics:

- ❑ he will initiate co-operation by emphasizing common ground before moving on to differences;
- ❑ he will consider problems as opportunities for problem-solving that will benefit both sides;
- ❑ he will be open-minded and creative rather than inflexible;
- ❑ he will deal with concrete, practical details rather than abstract principles;
- ❑ he will have available as much relevant information as possible and share it frankly;
- ❑ he will not form hasty judgements, nor will he allow hasty disagreements;
- ❑ he will draw attention to previous successes, previous agreements, previous relationships;
- ❑ he will clear minor disagreements before moving on to major ones;
- ❑ he will discuss differences rationally and without emotion;
- ❑ he will deal patiently with others' emotional outbursts;
- ❑ he will, without condescension, try to guide and educate less experienced negotiators;
- ❑ he will give praise to the other side whenever possible;
- ❑ he will work hard not to allow the other party to feel that it has lost face;
- ❑ he will use threats only as a last resort and then he must make sure that they are not empty threats.

One of the most difficult issues for managers in a negotiation experience is that of their holding different values from those held by the other party. Managers tend to regard management as a right that they have earned, whereas those who are not managers tend to regard management as a job that should be subjected to standards of performance appraisal, evaluation by those subordinate to them, and accountability. In negotiation managers have to behave as though the power of the two negotiating parties is equal, otherwise the barriers of status will destroy the negotiation. Other differences in values arise from different political or cultural values. Our chapter on cross-cultural communication is relevant in this respect.

It is important to agree on an **agenda** for the negotiating process and to establish the **roles** of the various negotiators. Negotiating is not brainstorming, and a definite negotiation structure helps. There should be an objective chairman; usually someone from management will chair the meeting. This means that he will have to put aside his partiality to the management cause and give all his attention to the free and fair exchange of views between the two parties. Each party usually has a chief spokesman who will act as an advocate for his party's case and who will cross-examine the other party when they present their case. There are times when the chairman and spokesman for management is the same person; this is most unwise, and is as absurd as the referee trying to play goal-keeper while he is refereeing. In some negotiations, specialists are required to give expert opinions. Although these specialists may be called in by one side, they should not take sides and should state their expert opinions as factually as possible. Then there may be observers on either side; often observers who do not participate in the actual negotiating process may be able to guide the spokesman more rationally than those who are involved emotionally and competitively. Negotiation experts regard three or four members on each side as the best number for effective negotiation and they consider that the setting should be neutral, with the sides facing each other and the chairman and specialists not aligned with either side.

The negotiation itself strives for common ground in issues, relationships, and decision-making. After an agreement is reached, it should be restated to avoid misunderstanding and then be reduced to writing so that commitment from either side may be obtained. Such commitment often comes only after the negotiators have reported back to meetings of the parties they represent.

3. Consulting

Consultants are often university staff members who use their academic expertise to advise others in practice and, in so doing, are able to augment their university incomes. The problem for them is that they may become removed from practice in their academic posts, and therefore they use consultancy to keep in touch. Others become consultants after years of partially successful business experience. There is a danger that a new adage may prove true: 'Those that can, do. Those that can't, consult.'

PARTICIPANTS

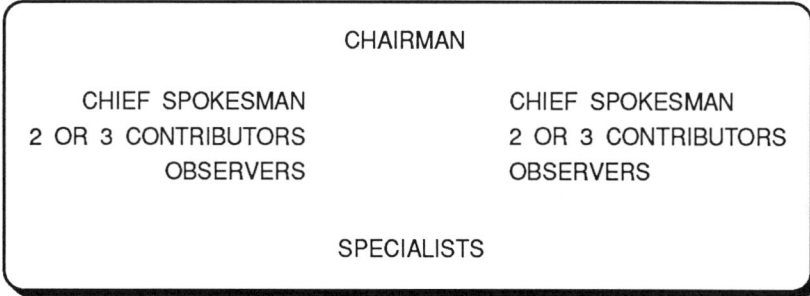

CHAIRMAN

CHIEF SPOKESMAN	CHIEF SPOKESMAN
2 OR 3 CONTRIBUTORS	2 OR 3 CONTRIBUTORS
OBSERVERS	OBSERVERS

SPECIALISTS

PRELIMINARIES

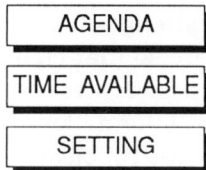

AGENDA

TIME AVAILABLE

SETTING

NEGOTIATION

DIFFERENCES	**COMMON GROUND**	**DIFFERENCES**
CONFLICT	ISSUES	CONFLICT
POWER	RELATIONSHIPS	POWER
CHALLENGE	AGREEMENT	CHALLENGE
THRUST	RECAPITULATION	THRUST
DEFIANCE	WRITTEN STATEMENT	DEFIANCE
PARRY		PARRY

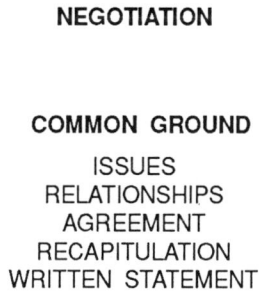

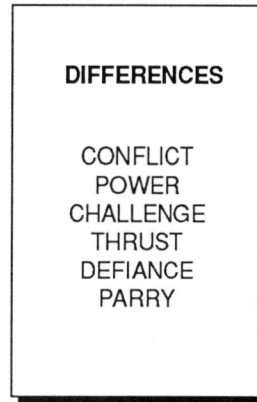

| CO-OPERATION | CO-OPERATION |
| GIVING COMMITMENT | GIVING COMMITMENT |

Nevertheless, consultancy is a part of business, and we need to know as managers how to consult and when to call in consultants. Consultants are used for a variety of reasons:

❑ when the business organization does not have expertise in a particular area;
❑ when an objective, independent opinion is needed;
❑ when decisions that are likely to be unpopular need justification;
❑ when extra help is needed temporarily and the organization does not need extra help permanently;
❑ when it will be useful to have a catalyst to bring a project to fulfilment.

There are various approaches to consulting. Consulting is similar to counselling, and many of the approaches in consulting are similar to those in psychological counselling. (1) One approach is to listen, to act as a supportive influence, and not to judge at all. This we may call the **psycho-therapeutic** approach. (2) Diametrically opposed to this is the **prescriptive** approach, which requires some very specialized skills on the part of the consultant for him to be confident enough to tell the client what to do. (3) Similar to this approach is the one which **challenges** the client's way of doing things and deliberately creates disharmony so that changes may take place. (4) Then there is the **catalyst** approach: here the consultant does not prescribe or confront, but tactfully provides information, interprets current procedures, and offers a diagnosis of what the problems may be so that the client may then solve his problem. (5) The last approach is the **instructive** approach, which offers teaching on problem-solving theories so that the client will be able to solve problems independently when he has the knowledge.

As with most business practice, there is no one correct approach to consulting. The consultant has to study the circumstances and adopt the approach most suited to the client's situation.

A consultant needs to be:

❑ a good listener and able to be quiet when necessary;
❑ courteous and polite;
❑ able to identify what the problems are;
❑ methodical and systematic;
❑ a good questioner;
❑ discriminating and able to distinguish reality from appearance;
❑ able to summarize well;
❑ able to speak and write well, especially persuasively;
❑ confident;
❑ a facilitator of decision-making and confidence in the client.

MEETINGS

We have already paid some attention to this aspect of communication in our chapter on Group Communication and later we shall look at written documents such as notices, agendas, and minutes in our chapter on Written Communication. In this section of Chapter 11 we study the procedural aspects of meetings and the role of the chairman and the secretary in conducting meetings.

Preparation

Before any meeting is held there should be adequate preparation. Any meeting should be properly convened, constituted, and be conducted in accordance with the constitution, i.e. the rules governing the objects of the association whether it be a business organization or a club. A meeting is properly convened if due, reasonable notice is given. Such notice need not be in writing, but it is more professional to supply written notice. A meeting is properly constituted if a quorum is present. (The word 'quorum' is a Latin word meaning 'of whom'; we could expand the Latin to mean 'the number of those who are required to constitute a valid meeting'.) Normally the constitution stipulates what a quorum shall be; if, however, the constitution does not stipulate the number, then a majority of members constitute a quorum for a full meeting. If no quorum is stipulated for a committee meeting, then all members have to be present. From this we can see that it is advisable to have a quorum clearly stipulated in the constitution, otherwise meetings will not be valid. We shall consider the constitutional procedure of meetings later.

Before the meeting takes place, we have therefore to prepare. We need to consider:

❑   the purpose of the meeting;
❑   who should be invited to attend;
❑   who the chairman will be;
❑   who the secretary will be;
❑   when the meeting will take place;
❑   where it will take place;
❑   the seating of the people at the meeting;
❑   what materials will be required, e.g. registers, minutes, documents, flip charts;
❑   what catering arrangements are needed;
❑   whether arrangements can be made to prevent interruptions;
❑   what members need to do in advance of the meeting.

Most of these duties of preparation are the secretary's responsibilities, though the chairman should make sure that they have been performed. Many of these duties are included in the written preparation of the notice, the agenda, and the minutes.

Different Types of Meetings

There are different types of meetings. Meetings may be private or public, formal or informal, open or *in-camera*. There are inaugural meetings, annual general meetings (AGMs), general meetings, extraordinary or special meetings, committee meetings, congresses, and conferences. These different types need little or no explanation: a dictionary will explain their main characteristics. A business organization usually uses these kinds of meetings: brainstorming; problem-solving; briefing; and consulting.

1. Brainstorming

We have already referred to brainstorming as a useful business tool. A brainstorming meeting involves participants from different levels of the organization and all are regarded as equals, each with a contribution to make. Ideas are called for on a particular topic without any prior preparation and all ideas are recorded, usually on a flip chart, without evaluation or judgement. Free, creative thinking is encouraged, and many useful business ideas are generated in this way. A brainstorming meeting is usually regarded as fun, and it helps to build morale among the participants and to encourage communication. At least some of the ideas generated will attract attention from other members and may be the basis for practical business implementation.

2. Problem-solving

This is less creative than brainstorming, but it is more conclusive. Participants are asked to evaluate and to take decisions. To begin with, an analysis of past and present strategies and successes and failures and of future objectives will be helpful. This kind of evaluation of strengths and weaknesses and of opportunities and threats — often called 'SWOT analysis' — is very useful and is similar to what has been called 'force-field analysis'. Put simply, **force-field analysis** asks four questions:

❑   Where are we at present?
❑   Where do we want to be in the future?
❑   What forces will help us to get where we want to be?
❑   What forces will prevent us getting where we want to be?

From this kind of preparatory analysis we choose areas on which to focus our attention. We then give our attention to each in turn, possibly at different meetings. We might use as a further stage participants' individual responses on each area; these are formulated on paper without consulting together. These responses are then shared in small groups where the responses are sorted and evaluated. Someone from each group then presents the main responses from the group to the whole meeting, and individuals are then asked to rate them in order of importance, e.g. 1 as most important, 2 as secondary, 3 as of least importance. From this, general acceptance of the most valuable responses is obtained.

The third stage is to try to solve the particular problems relating to each area of focus. Useful questions to ask are:

❑ What is our main concern or problem?
❑ What has caused it to be an area of concern or a problem?
❑ What can we do to improve?
❑ What resources are needed to do this?
❑ What follow-up is needed?
❑ Who will do what?

In order to solve the problem we need general commitment on the part of all the participants to the action to be taken even if specific people have been delegated to perform the specific tasks.

3. Briefing

Often meetings need to take place to brief people about work to be done. Sometimes the people to do the work will be people inside the organization and at other times they will be people who are outside, such as advertising agency representatives. It is important that such briefs should be in writing, preferably prepared before the briefing meeting, although the meeting may bring about certain changes in the brief and it may have to be reformulated. At the start of the meeting the brief should be presented by handing out copies of the written brief. Then it should be presented verbally and discussed. Repetition and clarification are important. Although what follows may appear rather dictatorial, it is useful to

❑ tell the group what the brief is about;
❑ tell the group what the brief is;
❑ summarize what the main points of the brief are;
❑ ask the group to repeat what the brief is about, what it is, and what the main points are;
❑ agree on changes to the brief;
❑ send the group another copy or the revised copy of the brief to expedite action.

Briefing must be precise and leave no doubt on either side about what is to be expected. It is very similar to the interview in which goals are set: one can appraise performance only if goals are clearly set and understood; one can insist on performance of the brief only if the brief is clearly formulated and understood.

4. Consulting

Although consulting meetings can take place within the organization, we prefer to refer to these meetings as the initial parts of the problem-solving meeting. What we mean by consulting meetings is the meeting between representatives of the organization and representatives of the consulting body. Here it is the task of the client to allow the consultants to understand the problem which has prompted the organization to hire their services. It is, in a way, similar at the start to a briefing meeting: the initiative is with the organization. As the meeting continues, the initiative must be assumed by the consultants, and they must be given access to relevant information. The client must be prepared to listen carefully to new ideas, criticism, and proposals and to co-operate. Often consulting meetings fail because management merely wants approval for its own course of action and is on the defensive. There is no need for a consulting meeting if management is not prepared to accept new ideas. As we have said about the consulting interview, it is, however, necessary for the consultant body to be sensitive and courteous.

Procedure at Meetings

The chairman should open the meeting punctually with a welcome to members present and a call for **apologies** from the floor. Usually the secretary has received apologies and will announce these. A person who apologizes for not being able to attend a meeting does not form part of a quorum. At formal meetings the chairman may ask the secretary to read the **notice** of the meeting or may ask for it to be taken as read. If a member objects to not having received notice or due notice of the meeting, the secretary must be able to prove that the proper notice was given.

Sometimes the constitution calls for a certain period of 'clear days' notice' having to be given: this means that the date on which the notice was date-stamped by the Post Office and the date of the meeting must not be included; for instance, if fourteen clear days' notice is required and the notice of the meeting was date-stamped 1 May, then the meeting cannot be held on 15 May; a meeting on 16 May or later would comply with the requirement of fourteen clear days' notice. The period of notice can be shortened or waived provided that all members are present at the meeting and that all members agree to this.

The **agenda** of the meeting usually goes out with the notice. (The word 'agenda' means 'those things that have to be done'; it is therefore strictly a plural noun, but we do speak of 'an agenda' nevertheless.) If no written agenda is available the chairman may ask the meeting to agree on an oral list of items to be discussed at the meeting; there must be agreement on such an agenda, and a majority of people present must agree if any change is made to the agenda previously accepted. The meeting may agree to leave out certain items on the agenda; normally this is because of pressure of time, and the item may be discussed at the next meeting.

Often, in addition to the normal agenda, the secretary prepares a chairman's agenda. This is the normal agenda with additional notes that guide the chairman about who will report on certain items or what to remember in connection with items. This is a most useful service to the chairman. If the secretary has not prepared such a chairman's agenda, it is advisable for the chairman himself to annotate his copy of the agenda in this way.

Normally the chairman then calls for the secretary to read the **minutes** of the previous meeting or for the meeting to agree to take the minutes as read. Once the meeting has decided the minutes are a correct record, the chairman usually signs the minutes. His next duty is to discuss **matters arising** from the minutes and not dealt with specifically in the agenda for this particular meeting. This is to guarantee that a report-back may be given on points discussed at the previous meeting and requiring action since that meeting. Usually the secretary will nominate in the agenda which matters arising need such a report-back. Only matters not finalized at the previous meeting may be raised under 'Matters arising from the previous minutes'; it is not an opportunity to start discussion again on matters that were previously decided.

It is now time to move on to the main part of the agenda — what is sometimes called 'New Business'. This would include such matters as correspondence, motions, reports, elections, appointment of auditors, and fees.

We probably need to say something about **motions** since there are definite procedures for motions, amendments, riders, and resolutions. Any member may propose a motion to the meeting. The meeting may then discuss it and take a decision on such a motion. Some meetings are bound by their constitutions to have a seconder for any proposed motion. Whereas the proposer is usually expected to introduce his motion, the seconder merely seconds the motion and may not speak on the motion before he seconds it. If the constitution requires a seconder and no-one wishes to second a proposed motion, the chairman should ask the proposer to withdraw his motion. If he does not do this, the chairman could then second the motion and immediately put it to the vote; under such circumstances it is likely to be defeated.

The motion that is proposed must be a positive statement (not in the negative) and must be clear and unambiguous. It must also be within the purpose of the meeting as expressed in the notice and the agenda.

As soon as a motion has been proposed (and, if necessary, seconded), a **counter motion** may be put to the meeting. The purpose of such a counter motion is to replace the motion and to defeat it. As soon as the counter motion is proposed (and seconded, if necessary), it is then debated and voted upon. An example of a counter motion is the **no-confidence** debate in parliament.

A motion may be amended in various ways:

❏ words may be deleted from the motion;
❏ words may be added; or
❏ the wording may be re-organized.

Any person who has not yet spoken in the debate may propose an **amendment**. If the constitution requires a seconder for an amendment, such a seconder must be found or else the amendment falls away. If the amendment is accepted by the meeting, the amended motion then becomes the **substantive motion**, which is then debated and voted upon. Unlike a counter motion, an amendment may not be a negation of the original motion. An amendment cannot change the nature of the original motion, as we shall see in the following example. There may be more than one amendment, and there may be addenda and riders as well. If there is more than one amendment, the last amendment will be voted on first, the second last second, and so on. **Addenda** and **riders** can be introduced after the motion or the substantive motion has been voted on and become the resolution, whereas amendments cannot.

The following example demonstrates what we have said about motions, amendments, addenda, riders, and resolutions:

Original motion
That there shall be an increase of 5 % on present salaries to all staff.
(Proposed and seconded — accepted)

Discussion

Proposed amendment 1
That there shall *not* be an increase of 5 % on present salaries to all staff.
(Not accepted — an amendment may not *negate* a proposal)

Proposed amendment 2
That there shall be an increase of *three days' leave* to all staff.
(Not accepted — an amendment may not *change the nature* of a proposal)

Amendment 1
That there shall be an increase of *4* % on present salaries to all staff.
(Proposed and seconded — accepted)

Discussion

Amendment 2
That there shall be an increase of 5 % on all present salaries *and wages* to all staff.
(Proposed and seconded — accepted)

Discussion

Amendment 3
That there shall be an increase of 5 % on present *monthly pay to all salaried staff.*
(Proposed and seconded — accepted)

Discussion
Amendment 3

Voting
Carried

Discussion
Amendment 2

Voting
Defeated

Discussion
Amendment 1

Voting
Carried

Substantive motion 1
That there shall be an increase of 4 % on present monthly pay to all salaried staff.

Discussion

Addendum
That there shall be an increase of 4 % on present monthly pay to all salaried staff *who have completed one year's service.*
(Proposed and seconded — accepted)

Discussion

Voting
Carried

Resolution
That there shall be an increase of 4 % on present monthly pay to all salaried staff who have completed one year's service.

Rider
That there shall be an increase of 4 % on the monthly pay to all salaried staff who have completed one year's service. *The increase will take effect on the next monthly pay day.*
(Proposed and seconded — accepted)

Discussion

Voting
Carried

Final resolution
That there shall be an increase of 4 % on the monthly pay to all salaried staff who have completed one year's service. The increase will take effect on the next monthly pay day.

It will be seen from this example that the correct procedure at a meeting, although at times it may seem long drawn out, helps the meeting to achieve clarity about its decisions. Without correct procedures, this kind of discussion could lead to chaotic decision-making.

From this example it can be seen that a motion or a substantive motion becomes a **resolution** when a decision has been taken on the motion or substantive motion. A special resolution is a decision which involves a change in the constitution. Normally the constitution specifies different requirements for special resolutions, e.g. a larger than usual quorum, more than an ordinary majority of votes, and a longer notice period.

There are **special rules of debate** for meetings. Although these may not always be observed at meetings, it is important to know them because a chairman may demand that these rules of debate be followed and ignorance of them could cause embarrassment. Rules that should be observed at all times are that the chairman's authority should be respected and only one person should speak at a time, with the permission of the chairman, and in a courteous manner. Other rules, which tend, however, not to be observed, are that speakers should not repeat themselves, should not address fellow-members directly but only indirectly through the chair, should rise when speaking, should stop speaking when the chairman rises, and should speak only once on any motion or amendment. The proposer of a motion does, however, have the right of reply before the vote on his motion takes place; this does not apply to the proposer of an amendment. When the proposer of a motion exercises his right of reply, he must be careful not to introduce new arguments; all he is allowed to do is to summarize the debate. In the rules of debate there are certain formal motions that may be put without a seconder; these are usually to bring about voting because the discussion has gone on too long or to reject a motion or to adjourn the meeting. These motions are very formal and are often not used in business meetings.

Although the chairman's authority must always be respected, a member may raise **a point of order** at any time during a meeting. Raising a point of order is a way of drawing to the chairman's attention some departure from proper procedure. Examples are:

❑   no quorum or any other unconstitutional matter;
❑   no due notice of a motion;

- ❏ no seconder of a motion (when a seconder is required by the constitution);
- ❏ no clear motion before the meeting;
- ❏ disrespectful language;
- ❏ a speaker digressing from the motion being discussed, or, as it is sometimes termed, the question before the meeting;
- ❏ the rules of debate not being followed.

There is a danger that a member may abuse points of order to obstruct free expression, but the chairman can always overrule on a point of order if he thinks this is the intention of the member who raises a point of order, especially if he persists in doing so.

Voting may take place in a variety of ways:

- ❏ by acclamation,
- ❏ by show of hands,
- ❏ by division (as in parliament),
- ❏ by ballot, or
- ❏ by poll.

Of these ways the ballot is the most satisfactory, whereas a show of hands is often the simplest. The difference between a poll and a ballot is that the poll is conducted only once: if no clear decision emerges, the issue cannot be raised again soon. Company meetings often use polls and scrutineers because of the serious nature of the decision being taken, the different weights given to shareholders' votes, and the necessity to confirm the eligibility of the voters.

A constitution sometimes allows voting by proxy. A **proxy** is a person who is appointed by a member to vote on his behalf. Special proxy forms are usually used to entitle the proxy to vote. His rights are usually carefully defined in the constitution. Proxies are often used at meetings of shareholders.

When the formal business of the meeting has been conducted, the chairman usually allows time for **general matters** to be discussed. These matters under general should not be matters of great importance because due notice should be given of such matters. The item 'General' of the agenda can be very useful to deal quickly with minor matters or to raise matters that can be discussed fully at subsequent meetings.

Finally the chairman needs to establish the date, place, and time of the next meeting and to bring the meeting to a formal end.

The Role of the Chairman

A chairman is elected, usually at an annual general meeting, to preside at meetings. If the chairman is unable to be at a meeting, his vice-chairman usually presides, but if neither is available, the meeting may elect a chairman for that meeting. The function of the chairman is to make sure that meetings proceed according to constitutional and legal stipulation and to ensure that meetings are properly convened and constituted.

His other duties and powers are:

- ❏ to draw up an agenda to promote orderliness at the meeting;
- ❏ to decide on the order of speakers and to allow all members the opportunity to express themselves;
- ❏ to accept or to reject motions put before the meeting;
- ❏ to rule on points of order;
- ❏ to control the members to allow only one person to speak at a time;
- ❏ to decide when a motion or a question before the meeting has been sufficiently discussed and may be brought to a vote;
- ❏ to adjourn meetings when necessary;
- ❏ to sign minutes as a correct record of the previous meeting and to see that they are properly filed;
- ❏ to guide discussion and not to dominate;
- ❏ to sum up when necessary;
- ❏ to see to it that a proper plan of action is drawn up for any resolutions made at meetings and to follow up to see that this plan is carried out;
- ❏ to close a meeting either when the time available has expired or when the business of the negotiation has been conducted;
- ❏ to ensure proper succession when he is unable to attend or when his term of office expires.

There is no doubt that the chairman is meant to be the leader, and therefore much of what has already been written about leadership applies to the chairman. He needs to be respected and enthusiastic, patient, sensitive, firm, unbiased, fluent and flexible. He must have a sense of purpose and be able to keep the meeting moving through the agenda, and at the same time he has to encourage participation from the members so that they enjoy attending meetings. Essentially his role is that of a dynamic facilitator.

The Role of the Secretary

The secretary is probably the most important executive at any meeting. He does not need the charismatic personality of the chairman, but he is the one who has to implement the decisions of the meeting and in this sense he is truly an executive. Not many people appreciate sufficiently the role of the secretary, possibly because in business the secretary tends to spend much time on typing and filing and reception work. The company secretary is one of the most important executives in the company, and the secretary of a meeting should have similar prestige.

His duties are:

- ❏ to prepare the notice, agenda, register of members, and the venue before the meeting;

❏ to take minutes and to be the chief assistant to the chairman during the meeting; and

❏ to attend to all correspondence, administrative work, and legal aspects in between meetings.

He is frequently called upon to attend to financial matters, particularly if there is no treasurer. In all his work he has to be very well informed, articulate in written English, and meticulous in his work.

PUBLIC SPEAKING AND SPEECHES

Managers are often invited to address the public,and their positions require them to make speeches within their own organization and to other organizations of professional associations. Few are effective speakers, however. In Chapter Ten we discussed the importance of audience analysis and other forms of preparation for communication. To make an effective speech a speaker has to become ADEPT.

A ACTING
D DELIVERY
E ENTERTAINMENT
P PRESENTATION
T THEME

Acting

Education does not give enough attention to this most important aspect: every person should be trained and given the opportunity to act. It is not for the chosen few or for the few who choose to act. Practice in acting helps to give a person confidence, to project his voice, and to be aware of an audience. Cricketers used to be encouraged to practise their batting in front of a mirror. Actors do the same when they are practising expressions. A manager about to deliver a speech should practise in front of a mirror too, even if the mirror is a group of people who can reflect his mannerisms and help him to improve his ability. No one should be so naive or arrogant as to think he can stand up and act without practice. The same applies to speech-making. Fortunately, with both acting and speaking, practice and experience do help the person to improve.

Acting ability helps the speaker to be relaxed, audible and expressive. It may also help the speaker to learn his lines so that he is not bound to his script. He will be able to control his movements so that movements add to, and do not detract from, what he is saying. The good actor is so aware of the meaning of each movement he makes that he controls those careless movements that often give away an inexperienced speaker, and he deliberately uses each gesture or facial expression for his purpose of communicating with his audience. Of course, to the audience everything appears so natural. This is the art of good acting: to have practised and practised until what has been so carefully studied appears quite natural to the onlooker. It is also the art of the good advocate and the good speaker.

Delivery

Closely associated with acting ability is the delivery of the speaker. How are you going to deliver your speech? Will you stand at a lectern reading your speech? Or will you deliver it impromptu while seated? Will your delivery be rushed and excited? Or slow and deliberate? Or a mixture? Will you be rigid or will you move freely in a relaxed way and involve your audience through eye contact and change of style?

There is difference of opinion about whether a speech should be written out and read to the audience, or written out and memorized, or reduced to notes and spoken extemporaneously, or given impromptu. Most people are impressed with good impromptu speaking; we often hear the remark, 'What a speech! He didn't refer to his notes once!' It is only an experienced speaker who can talk impromptu and give a good speech. Often people are more impressed by *how* a person speaks than by *what* he says. Some speakers actually trade on this and try to make a merit out of it: they say they can speak about nothing well and entertain their audiences, and there is some truth in this. Radio games and debating competitions, in which competitors have no time to prepare, are tests of speakers' ingenuity and are often amusing. More mature audiences require substance in a speech and can see through beautifully delivered speeches that have little or no content.

At the other extreme, a speech that is read as a 'paper' has limited appeal; this is accepted practice at conferences on academic or technical themes, but even here the speakers should vary their approaches so that their speeches are not delivered in a dull way and so that they, the speakers, are not bound to their 'papers'. One must admire the professor giving his inaugural lecture at the University of South Africa: he stood up to speak and dropped his papers so that they scattered on the floor; he then delivered a flawless inaugural lecture without referring to his papers at all. The moral of that story is that anyone should be so well prepared that he could do just what the professor did if something went wrong. So often lecturers or teachers complain that the overhead projector, the slide projector, or the film projector didn't work, and how could they teach when their whole lecture or lesson was based on the use of that medium? The answer is, of course, that one should be so prepared that such a mishap should not affect one's teaching.

Memorizing a speech requires the skill of an actor and relies on many rehearsals; very few speakers, especially businessmen, have the time for this amount of rehearsing and, consequently, they forget parts of their speech with disastrous hesitations and non-sequiturs.

Probably the most convenient method of delivering a speech is with notes. These notes should not be too conspicuous; small cards that can be easily held in the palm of the hand and shuffled are best. Such notes help to maintain logical sequence in the speech and allow the speaker to deliver his speech extemporaneously, i.e. making up the syntax of his sentences as he goes along. Such speeches are most likely to maintain the interest of audiences and to appear fresh and enthusiastic. Again, as we have said so often in this book, there is no one correct way: each method has its advantages and disadvantages, and the requirements of the situation must be carefully considered when deciding which method of delivery to use.

Perhaps a word about that most professional group of public speakers, those who deliver sermons, would not be out of place here. Even though they do not fall into our category of business communication, we can learn something from them. Some preachers deliver sermons from pulpits high above the congregation; others walk among the congregation as they preach. The latter preach as the Spirit moves them, for it is difficult for them to preach from the prepared script while they are moving about unless they have memorized it. Some congregations prefer their preacher to preach extempore; others find that this type of preaching becomes monotonous after many sermons from the same preacher and they prefer the thoughtful preparation of the scholar-preacher. Some preachers preach from a scriptural text — often one from the set of lessons of the religious calendar; others do not use a text, and preach on topics of their own choosing. All this is a matter of audience analysis and preparation: if the congregation needs a particular approach, it would be wrong to give it another; and a too carefully prepared and structured sermon may not suit a particular congregation used to an informal, chatty type of sermon. A preacher who continues to preach against his congregation's needs will soon be looking for another appointment. Some preachers are 'Bible-thumpers' and become excited when they preach; others are quiet-spoken and dignified. Both these types could have problems: the former may give offence; the latter may have members of the congregation snoring. There is a story about a preacher who used to write instructions to himself in the margin of his carefully written sermons; next to one section was an instruction: 'Shout this because the argument is weak.' Whether we should admire his honesty or disapprove of his dishonesty is debatable, but at least he knew something about the importance of delivery.

Entertainment

Every speaker — even a preacher — needs to be aware of the importance of entertainment in speaking. Those who think entertainment is not part of their business need to think again. There is no reason why lecturers or preachers should not put across their ideas in an entertaining way; it is an essential part of their training as actors that they are not there merely to instruct but also to keep their audiences awake and interested through entertaining ways of expressing themselves. We do not mean this in the narrow sense of making people laugh by telling jokes. We mean interesting illustrations, unusual ways of communication, use of audio-visual media — in short, consideration for their audiences' powers of concentration. There are different ways of doing this: an interesting illustration, directly related to a particular point the speaker is making, may expand on the understanding of that particular point. During a long speech it may be that after every twenty minutes — commonly thought to be the limit that an audience can concentrate without a break — the audience may be relaxed by an anecdote that may bear little or no relation to the topic. A well-known Archbishop in South Africa used to employ this technique very successfully. The entertainment of one's audience is not a cheap trick if judiciously used; it is a valuable technique that one can learn.

Presentation

Every speech is a presentation to an audience. In business we are used to sales presentations. A speech has as its aim to win a particular response from the listeners. In this sense it is persuasive communication. Speakers should take a lesson from a well-known preacher: he became tired of his congregation saying 'Thank you' when he shook their hands at the door after the service, so one day he responded to their 'Thank you' by saying, 'Yes, but what happened?' At the beginning of our preparation of a speech we should have a clear purpose in mind and at the end of our speech we should ask ourselves — even though we may not ask our audience directly — 'What happened?' In business we are used to evaluating business results, especially financial results; in giving a speech we should be similarly concerned about results. If we are, we shall care about our presentation.

In thinking about presentation we need to pay attention to the timing of each section of the speech. In dividing a speech into sections we are giving attention to preparation and logical development. It is a good idea to have at least one visual presentation for each section so that the audience's interest does not lag. It is important to keep your presentation within the time-limit prescribed.

Even if you have decided to write out your speech, it is a good idea to have it summarized on cards as well. Often familiarity with different types of delivery of your speech will help you to adapt in case something goes wrong at the last moment and it becomes impossible to present your speech as you had planned. Even if you have decided to speak from notes, a copy of your speech would be very useful if somebody approaches you afterwards for a copy and for permission to publish the speech or to quote from it.

Every speaker in delivering a speech is presenting himself and perhaps his business organization to his audience. Dress appropriate to the occasion, a correct tone of voice for the occasion, and avoidance of an arrogant or pedantic attitude help to achieve a favourable impression. An audience is easily distracted by something it considers inappropriate in the personality that it sees presented to it.

In considering first impressions we should remember that the start of a speech is very important. The first words must capture the audience's attention. As we saw earlier in Chapter Two, this is the first of the A's of communication. The start and the ending of the speech are very important and therefore it is inappropriate to start and to end with conventional statements or clichés, such as 'It is an honour and a privilege' and 'Thank you'. The first and last impressions should be carefully planned, and these parts of the speech should be rehearsed because of their crucial importance in the presentation.

Theme

It is probably considered surprising that we have spoken so much about acting, delivery, entertainment, and presentation, and only now we come to theme or content. We have disputed the claim that it is how a person speaks and not what he says that is important, but we cannot dispute the statement that, unless a person knows how to speak, what he says is unimportant. Content, without proper presentation of the content, is a waste of time, but content is nevertheless very important. A speaker has a duty to talk sense and to know what he is talking about. His primary concern is to communicate something that the members of the audience will find of value to them in their personal or business lives.

We use the word **theme** to refer to the unified thread of sense or intelligent thought that should run throughout a speech. Sometimes we are asked to speak on a topic, and this then becomes our theme. In preparing the speech we must make sure that everything we are going to say is connected with this theme or topic. Anything that cannot be related to the theme should be discarded. The title, topic, or theme helps us therefore to order our thoughts and to eliminate irrelevant thoughts.

What the speaker speaks about must be correct. There is no place in a speech for unethical distortions of the truth through half-truths, bias, or lies. Many politicians and businessmen may dispute this in private, but every speaker has a moral responsibility to tell the truth as it is and not to distort the truth to agree with the theme he is advocating. One way in which a speaker fails in this responsibility is to speak emotively or bombastically to sway certain sections of the population, usually the uneducated, to his point of view. He deliberately and craftily clouds his meaning behind emotion and vague, but high-sounding terms. Such cunning is so often successful that every manager must be aware of this kind of unethical communication and oppose it in the strongest terms. We come across this mainly in politics, in bargaining, and in advertising. Practice in seeing through unethical speeches to the real intention of the speaker should be part of every manager's training.

TELEPHONE CONVERSATIONS

We have probably covered the main points about telephone conversations in what we have already said about oral communication, for talking on the telephone is like any other interview except that we do not have the advantage of seeing the other person's non-verbal expressions and movements. Nevertheless there are certain points that are relevant only to telephone conversations, and we should give some time to these.

How do you greet the person on the other end of the line? If it is an incoming call, you could say 'Hello' and then give the name of your firm or you own name. This should always be a sentence, 'This is Thompson Brothers' or 'This is Miller speaking'; otherwise it sounds strange to say 'Hello — Thompson Brothers' or 'Hello — Miller'. It may sound as if there is a crossed line and someone wants to speak to Thompson Brothers or Miller. If you are unfortunate to have a surname that is also a first name — as one of the writers of this book has — you have a dilemma: if you say, 'Hello. This is Andrew speaking', the person on the other end may think this is an invitation to first-name familiarity and answer, 'This is Joan' or 'This is Bob' and this causes awkwardness. If on the other hand, you try to avoid this confusion by saying, 'Hello. This is Mr Andrew', you are going against a convention of correctness in English, for no-one should give himself the title of Mr — or any other title for that matter: to insist on being called Dr or Professor is just as incorrect. The best solution is to say 'Hello. This is Michael Andrew.' This makes it very clear that Andrew is the surname. The convention is, however, different for women: it is considered correct for a woman to introduce herself as Miss or Mrs. The reason for this is that, if a woman introduces herself as Cynthia van der Merwe, it is very difficult for the person on the other end of the line to address her except as Cynthia, for he does not know whether she is Miss van der Merwe of Mrs van der Merwe. There is a modern tendency in business to use first names, and the business organization has to decide whether it is its policy to be informal and use first names or to be more formal and use surnames. The former encourages familiarity, and the latter may cause embarrassment to women.

There is nothing more infuriating than to have to wait a long time before getting through to the person to whom you want to speak. Businesses should guard against causing this kind of annoyance. A manager should, from time to time, carry out an investigation into how well the organization copes with incoming calls by phoning himself or getting someone else to, and in this way monitor the effectiveness of his organization's telephone service. If a person is not available because he is talking to someone else, it is better to take the name and number of the person making the incoming call and the name of the business and then to ring him back than to keep him waiting. Of course, the prior enquiry should be made whether anyone else could help him. If the person on the other end insists on waiting, he should be continuously assured that you have not forgotten him and that the person he wants to speak to is still busy speaking to someone else. There should be a definite system for taking messages, and the manager should insist that messages are taken according to this system. There should be a message pad with the necessary details on it, and people taking messages should read the messages back to the incoming caller to make sure the number, the time, and other important details are correct.

TELEPHONE MESSAGE

TO: _____

FROM: _____

TIME RECEIVED: _____DATE: _____

TAKEN BY: _____

MESSAGE: _____

_____

_____

_____

_____

Example of a Telephone Message Pad

Another cause for annoyance is that the person you are speaking to is trying to conduct two calls at the same time or is engaged in some other business while you are talking to him. Such a person should either stop his other business or take the name and number and phone back. If there is an unavoidable interruption, an apology is needed.

A common failing on the telephone is to use slang. Many people are in the habit of saying 'Okay' continuously during a telephone conversation; this can be used almost as a sign of impatience that you want the other person to stop talking and it can sound very discourteous. Although telephone conversations should be kept as short as possible, the speaker should never sound abrupt.

Courtesy on the telephone is very important, as is discretion. Telephone conversations can be very private or confidential, and people should respect the confidential nature of calls. Personal calls during office hours should be discouraged, especially during busy periods, but due allowance should be made for the staff's personal needs, such as calls that can be made only during office hours and are necessary. Again a company policy about personal calls should be made known.

If you need to transfer an incoming call, you should introduce to each other the incoming caller and the person to whom you are transferring the call, wait a moment to make sure they are connected, and then put your phone down — depending, of course, on the particular procedure that applies for transferring calls.

Telephone selling has become an important part of business, and it has become necessary to train staff in effective telephone-selling skills. Employees are taught to guide the telephone conversation in order to obtain relevant information and to gain the customer's commitment. Skill in dealing with customer's objections leads to few rejections, and telephone sales can become a cost-effective way of doing business.

Telephones are becoming increasingly adaptable to business needs: there are opportunities for three-way conversations, for conference facilities, and for seeing the person you are speaking to. Although some of us dislike the telephone and may feel like the poet Ted Hughes, who wrote, 'Do not pick up the telephone. There is death in the telephone', few businessmen could conduct their business effectively without it.

CONCEPTS AND TERMINOLOGY

1. ORAL COMMUNICATION
2. FACE-TO-FACE (ONE-TO-ONE) COMMUNICATION
3. INTERVIEWING
4. INTERVIEWER
5. INTERVIEWEE
6. CLOSED QUESTIONS
7. OPEN QUESTIONS
8. SELECTION INTERVIEW
9. 'HALO EFFECTS'
10. PANEL INTERVIEW
11. INDUCTION INTERVIEW
12. GOAL-SETTING INTERVIEW
13. PERFORMANCE-APPRAISAL INTERVIEW
14. REWARD INTERVIEW
15. DISCIPLINARY INTERVIEW (REPRIMAND)
16. COUNSELLING INTERVIEW
17. GRIEVANCE INTERVIEW
18. EXIT INTERVIEW
19. RESIGNATION INTERVIEW
20. DISMISSAL INTERVIEW
21. RETRENCHMENT INTERVIEW
22. PRESS, RADIO, TV INTERVIEW
23. NEGOTIATING

24. CONSULTING
25. MEETINGS
26. PROPERLY CONVENED
27. NOTICE
28. PROPERLY CONSTITUTED
29. QUORUM
30. BRAINSTORMING
31. PROBLEM-SOLVING
32. BRIEFING
33. CONSULTING
34. CONSTITUTIONAL PROCEDURE
35. PROCEDURE AT MEETINGS
36. CLEAR DAYS' NOTICE
37. AGENDA
38. CHAIRMAN'S AGENDA
39. MINUTES
40. MOTION
41. AMENDMENT
42. PROPOSER
43. SECONDER
44. SUBSTANTIVE MOTION
45. ADDENDUM
46. RIDER
47. RESOLUTION
48. RULES OF DEBATE
49. RIGHT OF REPLY
50. POINT OF ORDER
51. VOTING BY ACCLAMATION
52. VOTING BY SHOW OF HANDS
53. VOTING BY A DIVISION
54. VOTING BY A BALLOT
55. VOTING BY A POLL
56. PROXY
57. CHAIRMAN
58. SECRETARY
59. PUBLIC SPEAKING AND SPEECHES
60. ACTING
61. DELIVERY
62. ENTERTAINMENT
63. PRESENTATION
64. THEME (CONTENT, TOPIC)
65. TELEPHONE CONVERSATIONS
66. MESSAGE PAD
67. TELEPHONE SELLING

APPLICATION

1. There are good video tapes on the various forms of oral communication we have discussed in this chapter. The films on business topics made by John Cleese are humorous and instructive and they usually come with booklets that suggest ways of encouraging discussion after the short films.
2. What are the principles of good interviewing?
3. What are the characteristics of
    - ❏   a good chairman;
    - ❏   a good secretary?
4. What are the benefits of speaking
    - ❏   from notes;
    - ❏   without notes;
    - ❏   from memory;
    - ❏   verbatim from a prepared text?
5. Organizations should employ telephone operators who are proficient in telephone techniques. Your organization has just employed a new telephone operator, and your managing director has asked you to prepare *ten* hints for the new telephone operator. Write these ten hints in an attractive, readable way, using the memorandum form of writing.
6. Make up your own case studies of typical business situations where oral communication occurs. Then evaluate the success of the communication that takes place.
7. Read the case study below and then answer the questions that follow.

COMMUNICATION PROBLEM

Mr Jones has sent for his secretary, Mrs Mary Stewart. She is well qualified, but she has never been taught to listen well, though she is certainly not deaf. Just as she is settling down to work one morning, one of the salesmen puts his head round the door and says, 'The boss wants you.' She has much work to do and she is slightly irritated to be interrupted. Nevertheless she goes to Mr Jones's office. He is busy pouring himself a cup of coffee and has his back to her as she enters.

'Good morning, Mr Jones.'

'Mary, I need a file,' he says with his back still to her.

'That reminds me. Bill asked me to buy him a file from the hardware shop,' thinks Mrs Stewart.

'It's the Peterson file,' he mumbles into the coffee pot.

'I want to see how many letters we've sent him about his overdue account.'

'Lettuce,' thought Mary to herself. 'I need to buy some lettuce.'

Mrs Stewart walked out without greeting Mr Jones, who did not know she was gone.

By the time she returned, he was on the telephone on a confidential business call and waved her away. She returned to her desk and started to do her work. Some minutes later she was interrupted by an angry Mr Jones on the internal telephone.

'Mary, where is that file I asked for?'

'Coming, Mr Jones.'

She walked into his office, but he was on another call. He waved impatiently to her to put the file on his desk. She left his office and went on with her work. No sooner had she started than Mr Jones came storming in.

'I wanted S. J. Peterson's file, not M. B. Peterson's.'

'Sorry, Mr Jones. I'll get it for you.'

'Please hurry. It's urgent.'

With the correct file Mrs Stewart returned. Mr Jones was out of his office, and so she left it on his desk. As she went out, one of his partners came in and placed some other documents on top of it. When Mr Jones returned, he went straight to his secretary's desk.

'Have you done what I asked you to? How much does Peterson owe?'

'I put the file on your desk.'

'Didn't you check the payments?'

'I mustn't forget to put my cheque in the bank today,' she thought. 'Hooray for pay day.'

'Er, no. You didn't ask me to,' she said mystified.

'I need the balance right away.'

'Yes,' thought Mary, spitefully, 'you are rather unbalanced, you old fogey.'

'Let's go and look it up in your office, shall we?' said Mrs Stewart aloud.

'In future, please do what I tell you to do. It will save a great deal of time. And, by the way, you're making too many mistakes with your typing; you'll have to concentrate harder.'

'Oh, Mr Jones, I'm not feeling too good today. I have a splitting headache. Can I go home early today?'

'Very well, then. But first let's find what I asked you for half an hour ago.'

'Good. I'll be able to deposit my cheque and do my shopping before I go home,' she thought maliciously.

❏ There are certain words called *trigger words* that trigger off other thoughts in Mrs Stewart's mind. Give four examples of these words and compare the different thoughts in her mind with those in Mr Jones's mind.

❏ Who is the more to blame in this case study? Mr Jones or Mrs Stewart? Give reasons for your answer.

❏ How do you think working relationships between the two could be improved?

12

MODES (MEDIA SYSTEMS): WRITTEN COMMUNICATION
Reading Skills

GOALS OF THE CHAPTER

The goals of this chapter are to improve reading skills as they affect business communication. By the end of the chapter you should be able to:

❑ scan a passage
❑ skim a passage
❑ read a passage for comprehension
❑ analyse and evaluate a passage

INTRODUCTION

There are four kinds of reading:

1. SCANNING
2. SKIMMING
3. COMPREHENSION
4. CRITICAL ANALYSIS

We have already discussed the importance of **audience analysis** in communication: when we wish to communicate with someone, we must know who our target audience is and what form of communication we wish to use. We are essentially considering the **purpose** of our communication with someone else. When we read, we are the writer's audience and we have to see ourselves as the receivers of the communication. As with listening, reading is not a passive experience; unless we actively engage in the reading process we shall not read properly. Our first step is to decide what our purpose is when we are going to read something.

SCANNING

If we are reading a newspaper we often merely scan the headlines until we find something that interests us. Suppose we want to buy a second-hand car: we scan the pages until we come to the classified advertisements; we continue to scan until we come to the type of car we want to buy; and then we stop scanning and we give our full attention to the advertisements that tell us about the kind of car we want to buy.

Scanning is a way of reading that is very quick and superficial as we look for a particular piece of information. In other words we must know first what it is we are looking for and we scan the pages until we come to that page where we shall find the information. We use an index in this way or a contents page. Suppose we want to find those pages that deal with a particular topic: we may first look at the contents page, and there may be a whole chapter on the topic; we then turn to that chapter and read it attentively. Often, however, there is not a specific chapter on the topic we want, and then we use the index and look up the various references to our particular topic. The index-reading is scanning as we go through the alphabetical list of words till we find our topic.

We scan a dictionary or a telephone directory or a card index system. We glance at the pages quickly but not very thoroughly until we find what we are looking for. Scanning implies that you are looking for something and that you have a specific purpose before you start.

SKIMMING

Skimming, on the other hand, does not necessarily have a prior particular purpose. Our purpose is more general; it is the kind of question, 'I wonder whether there's anything interesting here?' and we read the book, newspaper, magazine, or journal quickly.

Newspaper editors know that this is how people tend to read newspapers and they tend to fit in with people's reading habits. Have you noticed how often you read only the headlines or the first paragraph of a newspaper article and how seldom you read the whole article? Newspaper reporters are taught for this reason to put the most important material early and the less important material or detail at the end. They know that when people read newspapers they usually do not have much time — that they skim in fact rather than read. There is a difference between a daily morning newspaper and an evening newspaper because people generally have more time in the evening than in the morning to read, and there is a difference between a daily and a weekend newspaper because a weekend edition is usually read at a more leisurely pace. Then there is a difference between a monthly magazine and a weekend newspaper. Businesses need to be aware of people's reading habits because they affect advertising in the different print media: there is no point in having an advertisement that requires much reading or concentration in a morning newspaper because the reader does not have the time to give to it, and the advertiser will be wasting his money.

When we are sitting in a waiting room before we go in for an appointment, we tend to skim through a magazine to try to find something interesting. When we are interested in a particular subject, we may skim journals to see if they have anything of interest to say to us. We may first scan the contents page and then focus on a particular article. We turn to the article, but we are not yet sure that it is exactly relevant to our interest, so we skim the first few paragraphs to get the general idea and to see whether we should read the article more carefully. As soon as we take the decision to read more carefully, we change from skimming to reading attentively and we should really go back over that part we have merely skimmed.

So what is skimming then? It is reading quickly and noting only the main points or the general idea of what we are reading. It is more careful reading than scanning but it is not as careful as reading for comprehension or full understanding. It is a useful preliminary to study, but is not studying. When we skim, our mind moves quickly over the words and we tend not to read every word, only the ones that strike us as important.

COMPREHENSION

Most of us are familiar with this word from school. We have all done 'comprehension exercises'. These usually consist of set passages with questions to test the students' understanding of the passages. When we read for comprehension, we are doing just that: we want to understand or comprehend what we are reading. This is not easy and may take two or three readings. It may be necessary to make notes while we are reading or to draw diagrams to allow us to understand better what we are reading. We shall certainly have to give more time to our reading for comprehension than we give to our scanning or skimming. Sometimes our first reading will be skimming, and our second reading will be for greater comprehension. A good method of reading for comprehension is to underline or to highlight key words as we read the passage for the second time. This is what reading for comprehension is all about: to find the main ideas and to be able to express them in our own words so that we may demonstrate to ourselves and to others that we have understood what we have read. If we can do this, we have studied the passage well. Anyone can regurgitate or memorize, but studying is comprehension.

Reading for comprehension improves vocabulary. We learn how to use words in different contexts. Sometimes we come across words we do not know, but from their contexts we can work out their meanings or their approximate meanings. Of course, we could refer to a dictionary every time we come across a word we do not know, but this is time-consuming and sometimes puzzling because the dictionary may give different possible meanings that depend on the contexts in which the word can be used. If the **context** really gives us the meaning of the word anyway, it is better to look first at the context and to try to work out the meaning of the unknown word from the context. If we still cannot understand the word or if we want to make sure that our 'guess' at the meaning of the word in its context is right, then we go to the dictionary. But if we have a reasonably good vocabulary, we should be able to read without too many interruptions and then our reading will be more fluent and more pleasurable.

This understanding of words in their contexts is so important that teachers of English often use 'comprehension exercises' in examinations to test whether students know the meanings of individual words as they are used in their contexts. Sometimes these questions call for the meanings directly, 'Give in your own words the meanings of the following words as they are used in the passage'. Sometimes there are little trick questions where certain words have been replaced by nonsense words and the students are asked to 'guess' from the rest of the sentences (i.e. the contexts) what the words are. The third way is the 'cloze' procedure of testing vocabulary; in this test certain words are omitted altogether, usually at regular intervals, for instance every seventh or tenth word, and students are asked to give the missing words. The cloze test is another way of testing the readability of a passage because a good writer will surround difficult words with the kinds of contexts that will explain the difficult words all the time. Examiners who ask students to explain the meanings of words used in a 'comprehension' passage should bear in mind that they should be testing understanding of words in their contexts, not knowledge of dictionary definitions; it follows from this then that the words that the students are asked to explain should have been elucidated by their contexts; if they have not been, the examiners should not ask the students to explain these words but should actually give their meanings to the students in an explanatory note. Often, however, examiners are at fault in not understanding what 'comprehension' questions really are, and they confuse dictionary knowledge with comprehension. Testing dictionary knowledge is like the game called Trivial Pursuit. There is a humorous short story in a South African setting about dictionary knowledge: it is called 'The Dictionary' by Francis Carey Slater. Once you have read this story, you will never again try to impress people with your dictionary knowledge — unless it is for the purpose of humour.

Let us now apply what we have learnt so far about reading skills. Here is a passage from the *South African Journal of Higher Education* (Vol. 2, No. 2, 1988):

> In the Republic of South Africa (RSA) no recognition has traditionally been given by universities to non-university studies. The only road to university has been the matriculation highway, the road of formal education. The side roads of diploma education have taken the student a long way past the gateway to the university, but there has been no cross-over from the side road to the main road. Although the university student and the diploma student have travelled on parallel roads, the diploma student has not been allowed to cross over into university whereas the university student has easy access to diploma studies and receives generous credits towards these. There is no recognition for professional diplomas, which are cul-de-sacs.

> Is the standard of university education so much higher than that of Technikon or Professional Institute diploma education? It is generally accepted that the qualifications of the Institute of Cost and Management Accountants (CMA) and the Institute of Chartered Secretaries and Administrators (CIS) are as good as, if not better than, the Bachelor of Commerce qualification. The standard of the CMA and CIS qualifications and the uniform curricula for all CMA and CIS students respectively throughout the Republic (and the world, almost) give the Institute examinations a reputation for consistency and acceptability. The practical nature of the curricula allows them to have the edge on the theoretical Bachelor of Commerce courses, some of which require little or no accounting.

> Is it the standard of tuition that is so much better at a university than at a college that offers professional diplomas? It is my experience that lecturers in the professional diplomas are generally as good as teachers as university lecturers in the same disciplines. Lecturers at the private business colleges are part-time lecturers engaged in full-time business careers but with a love of teaching and a dedication to their lecturing and their students. Universities in the Republic have been monopolies protected by the state, no matter how unproductive or inefficient they have been. When private educational enterprises were allowed to give tuition to University of South

Africa (Unisa) students, the private students fared consistently better than the students studying only through Unisa. At present the law prevents, through the Universities Act, private enterprise from entering the South African university arena.

Is it that the standard of university examinations is so much higher? This is a difficult question to answer. Most Professional Institutes have senior university academics as examiners. The pass rate is generally higher in institute examinations than in university examinations. Whether this tells us that the institute examinations are of a higher or lower standard is not clear. Perhaps what it does tell us is that institute students, in spite of, or because of their part-time involvement, are more dedicated or mature.

Overseas, university education is becoming increasingly open to all. Even in as conservative a country as the United Kingdom (UK), the walls of the university are being broken down, and all are allowed entrance in some way or another. In the United States (USA) a person is not only encouraged to further his education via the university, but there is also a system which allows him to gain credits for non-university education or for experiential learning. This has led to some RSA institutes advising students to follow UK or USA Master of Business Administration (MBA) courses and then to come back onto the RSA academic highroad.

In order to comprehend this passage of five paragraphs we need to read the passage a few times. Our first reading is likely to be a quick reading (i.e. skimming). We are looking for the main points or the general idea of what we are reading. What is this passage about? We may say, 'Diploma education versus university education' and we have grasped a little of what the passage is about — enough for us to go on to a second, more careful reading if we are interested in this topic. The general reader will now decide whether he wishes to go on to a closer reading or not.

Since we are using the passage as a 'comprehension exercise', we are compelled to go further whether we wish to or not. We are at the stage where we need to make notes or to draw diagrams to allow us to understand better what we are reading. One way to do this is to look at the paragraph structure of the passage: what is the writer saying in each paragraph?

Paragraph 1
RSA: no recognition by universities to non-university studies. Generous credits for university studies towards diploma studies.

Paragraph 2
Is the standard of university education higher than diploma education? Not necessarily.

Paragraph 3
Is the standard of university tuition better than diploma education? The writer thinks not.

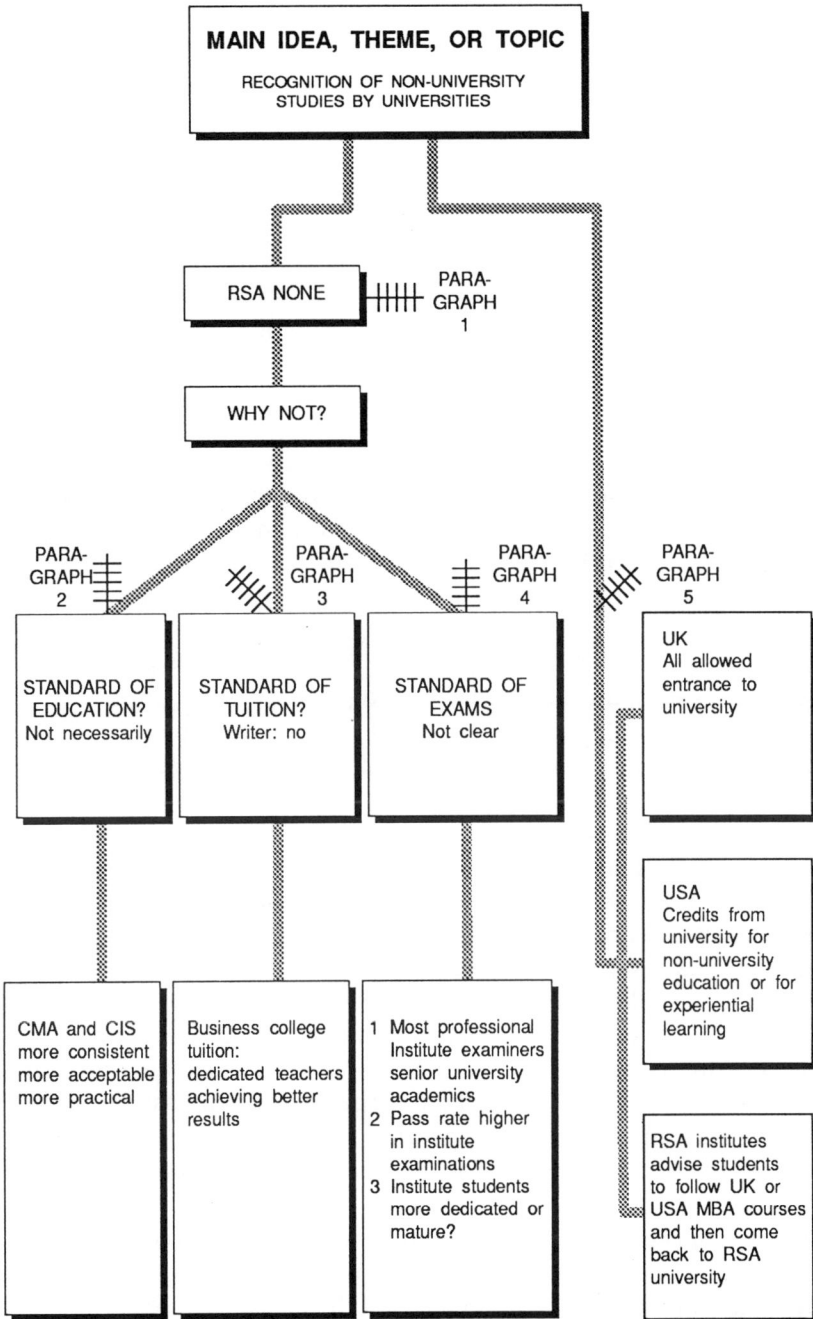

MAIN IDEA, THEME, OR TOPIC

RECOGNITION OF NON-UNIVERSITY
STUDIES BY UNIVERSITIES

RSA NONE ┼┼┼┼ PARA-
GRAPH
1

WHY NOT?

PARA-
GRAPH
2

PARA-
GRAPH
3

PARA-
GRAPH
4

PARA-
GRAPH
5

STANDARD OF
EDUCATION?
Not necessarily

STANDARD OF
TUITION?
Writer: no

STANDARD OF
EXAMS
Not clear

UK
All allowed
entrance to
university

CMA and CIS
more consistent
more acceptable
more practical

Business college
tuition:
dedicated teachers
achieving better
results

1 Most professional
  Institute examiners
  senior university
  academics
2 Pass rate higher
  in institute
  examinations
3 Institute students
  more dedicated or
  mature?

USA
Credits from
university for
non-university
education or for
experiential
learning

RSA institutes
advise students
to follow UK or
USA MBA courses
and then come
back to RSA
university

Paragraph 4

Is the standard of university education higher than diploma examinations? Not clear.

Paragraph 5

In UK and USA university education open to all. In USA credits from non-university education or for experiential learning.

By making these notes we have gained a better idea of the argument than we did from skimming. The passage is not really about 'Diploma education versus university education' but about recognition of non-university studies by universities. A second, more careful reading often changes our first response to the passage; this does not mean that our first response was unhelpful or wrong. But if we had not allowed our first impression to develop, it would have been wrong to maintain after a second reading that the passage was about 'Diploma education versus university education'. We must be prepared to change our first impression to a more informed understanding.

From our notes on each paragraph we can learn something about paragraphing. Do you see how important the beginning to each paragraph is? The first sentence often gives us the topic of the paragraph, the *topic sentence*. It is not always at the beginning of the paragraph, but it often is. Putting the topic of the paragraph in the first sentence is a rather obvious way of sign-posting the direction the paragraph will take.

We referred to diagrams as a useful way of closer reading. Let us see whether a diagram will help us to understand this passage. The 'mind-map' on the previous page helps to develop our understanding of the details of the passage and the progress of the argument through the five paragraphs.

Another useful method of comprehension is to look for **unifying images** in a passage and to see whether they help our understanding of the passage. In the passage we are studying there is the image of the *road of education.* Words that link up with this image are *road . . . highway . . . side roads . . . a long way past the gateway . . . no cross-over from the side road to the main-road . . . travelled on parallel roads . . . cross over . . . easy access . . . cul-de-sacs* in paragraph one and *to come back onto the RSA academic highroad* in paragraph five. Often an image can be expressed in a diagram. Such diagrams can be useful in a speech or a written article to focus attention. The writer of the passage used the diagrams on the following pages for this purpose.

These diagrams, which have been humorously referred to as 'lavatory-bowl' diagrams, could have been drawn by the student faced with only the written text to highlight the main ideas of the passage.

Now let us come to the study of **words in their contexts**. Suppose that you were asked the following 'comprehension question':

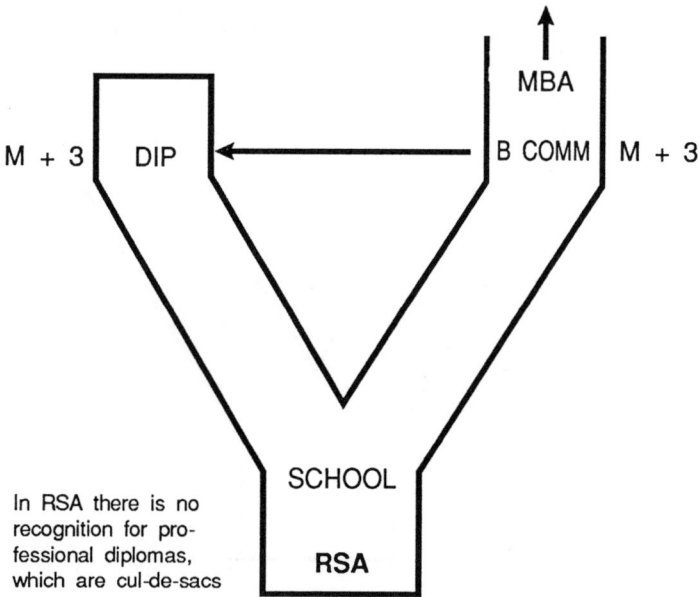

In RSA there is no recognition for professional diplomas, which are cul-de-sacs

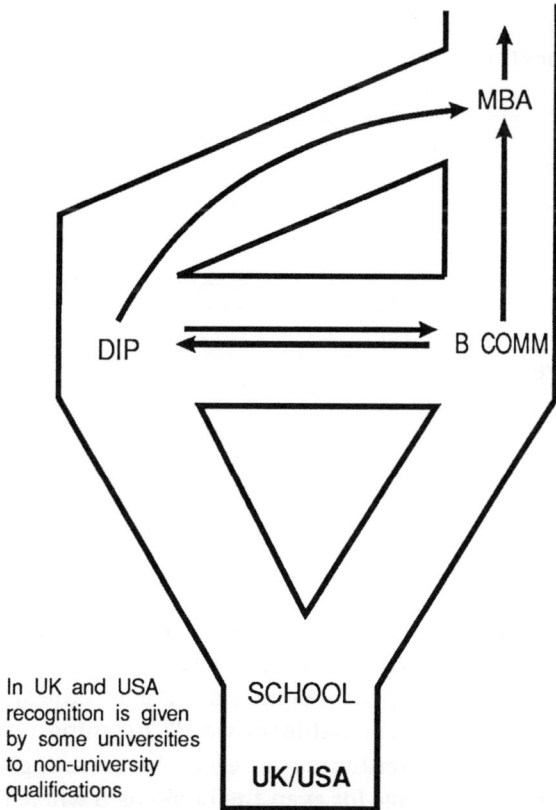

In UK and USA recognition is given by some universities to non-university qualifications

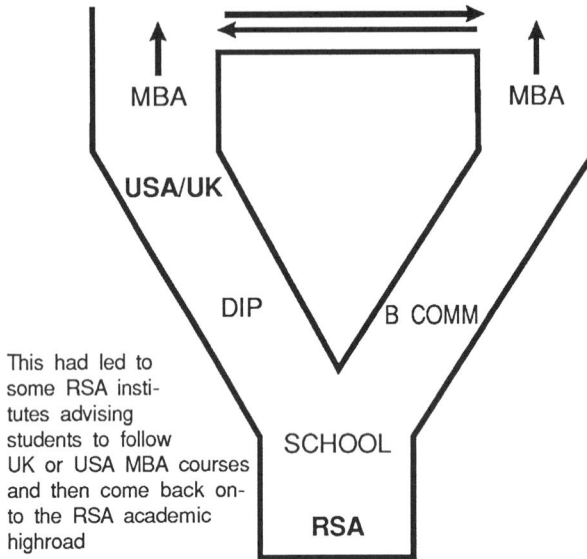

This had led to some RSA institutes advising students to follow UK or USA MBA courses and then come back onto the RSA academic highroad

Give the meaning of the following words in their contexts:

1. formal education
2. diploma education
3. credits
4. uniform
5. respectively
6. acceptability
7. have the edge on
8. disciplines
9. dedication
10. monopolies
11. unproductive
12. private enterprise
13. arena
14. academics
15. mature
16. conservative
17. experiential

In answering such a question we may have a general idea of the dictionary meanings of the words. We then look at the ways in which they are used in the sentence in which they appear. Sometimes it is not the specific sentence in which the word is used that explains the word's meaning; it may be another sentence or a number of sentences or even the meaning that the word accumulates from the passage (or even the book) as a whole that gives it its particular application. If we have never come across the word before, or have forgotten its dictionary meaning, then the context will allow us to make an informed 'guess' at its meaning. Let us try to follow this approach with each of these words:

1. *formal education*: The sentence in which the words appear is: 'The only road to university has been the matriculation highway, the road of *formal education.*' We all know the general meaning of *education* and we probably know of a few application of the word *formal*: *formal* dress, *formal* behaviour, *formal* meetings. . . . We could therefore say that *formal education* is education given according to the usual, acceptable rules of educational authorities. In the sentence quoted and in the passage as a whole, *formal education* is the system of instruction that leads from school to matriculation to undergraduate university instruction to graduation to postgraduate instruction and higher degrees. In South Africa, since the passage deals mainly with South African education, this *formal education* is controlled by the state. From this kind of exploration we can arrive at an answer as follows: the system of instruction from school to university in South Africa as laid down by and controlled by the state.

2. *diploma education*: The sentences in which these words appear are: 'The side roads of *diploma education* have taken the student a long way past the gateway to the university . . .' and 'Is the standard of university education so much higher than that of Technikon or Professional Institute *diploma education?*' From these two sentences we can deduce that *diploma education* is the system of instruction after school that is offered in South Africa by Technikons and Professional Institutes and leads to a qualification other than a university degree. But from the passage as a whole it is evident that private business colleges offer *diploma education* as well. Therefore we have to expand the meaning to include not only Technikons and Professional Institutes but private enterprise business colleges as well.

Before proceeding let us note that in explaining the meanings of words in their contexts we should not use the words themselves: our explanation of *formal education* and *diploma education* did not include the words *formal* or *education* or *diploma*. This is a rule for 'comprehension exercises' and is strictly part of examination techniques, but it is also a useful technique for any manager when trying to ensure he or someone else understands a message: if you can put the message in your own words without distorting the meaning, then you have succeeded in understanding the message and making it your own. For the first two examples we have gone through the procedure of how we arrived at the final answer.

Now let us deal with the others more briefly:

3. *credits*: acknowledgement of previous educational qualifications having been attained and of not having to repeat the same courses but being allowed to proceed to further studies.

4. *uniform:* identical, without changes from region to region or from country to country.
5. *respectively:* as applied to all CMA students or to all CIS students, i.e. the CMA curricula are uniform for all CMA students, and the CIS curricula are uniform for all CIS students; without the word 'respectively' it would mean that CIS and CMA curricula are the same for all CIS and CMA students, i.e. that CIS and CMA share curricula.
6. *acceptability:* being received with approval and belief in the high standards of the qualifications.
7. *have the edge on:* have the advantage over, be better than.
8. *disciplines:* subjects, the branches of learning that are the same, e.g. Economics, whether they are for diploma or university studies.
9. *dedication:* the state of being committed totally.
10. *monopolies:* educational institutions with rights given by the state and not allowed to others because competition from outsiders is considered dangerous and undesirable.
11. *unproductive:* without effecting results; an industrial term usually suggesting not enough of value has been manufactured; here the implication is that universities have not achieved enough of value in their education of students.
12. *private enterprise:* the undertaking of business involving risk and difficulty without aid from government; here the undertaking of educational projects without government assistance and with the objective of making profit out of those services.
13. *arena:* the word originally referred to the playing field on which competitive games or fights took place in ancient times; previously there was a certain amount of competition between universities and private enterprise in South Africa, but now private enterprise is prevented by law from taking part in competition with universities: they are no longer contestants in this area.
14. *academics:* members of a group (usually a university) that have attained high levels of scholarship and expertise in their respective fields of study.
15. *mature:* developed or adult: here the implication is that diploma students are older, more experienced, and more adult in their approach to their studies than university students and therefore they achieve a better pass rate.
16. *conservative:* holding to traditional values and not easily persuaded to change.
17. *experiential:* from doing or seeing and not from theory; practical; here the writer maintains that learning comes from practical involvement in activities and not only from academic or theoretical instruction.

From this exercise we can see how valuable it is to focus on particular key words in a passage being read and how this focus aids in giving better understanding to the argument of the passage. We have looked at the exercise from the student's point of view, but any reader is faced with key words in a passage, and if he tries to probe their meanings and implications in their contexts, he will understand better what he is reading.

Finally in this section let us give an example from the same article that will explain the **cloze** system. Remember that words are omitted at regular intervals (here every tenth word) and the test is whether we can fill in the words omitted:

> The private sector must be given the opportunity to . . . (1) and to direct tertiary education. There was a time . . . (2) the state tended to frown on private schools and . . . (3) them as a threat to government school education. Now . . . (4) state recognizes the important contribution the private schools make . . . (5) keeping the costs of government school education down and . . . (6) enabling many important reforms in educational policy to be . . . (7) outside the government school arena. There is an increasingly . . . (8) relationship between private schools and the state. The private . . . (9) college that seeks to run its school at a . . . (10) as a business venture has also been accepted and . . . (11) by the state. Private enterprise has been involved in . . . (12) education for some time and, as we saw earlier, . . . (13) been instrumental in starting the short business courses, which . . .(14) become so popular with students and business firms alike . . . (15) technikons and universities now offer such training courses. There . . . (16) no reason why the wealth and the expertise of . . . (17) private sector should not extend to other forms of . . . (18) education.

When we do this exercise, we shall see that some of the words omitted are obvious words like the definite article or prepositions or conjunctions or a simple verb or auxiliary verb. Others are words which could allow for a variety of answers. The value in the exercise is that it tests the reader's fluency with English idiom and usage and it allows a certain amount of creativity and involvement on the part of the reader. Acceptable alternatives would be allowed as long as the answers provide a coherent statement that fits in with the general argument of the paragraph. Here are the actual words from the passage:

1. finance
2. when
3. considered
4. the
5. in
6. in
7. tested
8. healthy
9. enterprise
10. profit
11. welcomed
12. tertiary
13. has
14. have

15. that
16. is
17. the
18. tertiary

CRITICAL ANALYSIS

We have studied three ways of reading: scanning, skimming and comprehension. We now come to the fourth and last — critical analysis. So far there has been little or no **evaluation** of what we have read. We have read for functional purposes of finding information or understanding. When we criticize what we are reading, we must first understand what we have read but we must then start giving our own views about what we have read; we need to analyse whether the writer's statements are based on generalizations or sound reasoning, and whether he provides a good objective statement or a biased, emotive opinion.

Let us consider the five paragraphs from the *South African Journal of Higher Education* from this angle, the angle of critical analysis. The word 'analysis' implies detailed study of the separate parts. It is what we do when we are faced with a case study; we analyse the case study sentence by sentence, trying not to miss one important point. Our first analysis of the case study in Chapter One was a critical analysis of the communication taking place.

In the first paragraph of the extract about recognition of non-university studies by universities, the writer limits his discussion to the Republic of South Africa. He uses the word 'traditionally' to refer to the past when no recognition of non-university studies has been given by universities. In the passage as a whole this word links up with the reference to the United Kingdom in the last paragraph; although it is a 'conservative' country (i.e. one governed by tradition) it has opened university education to all. The word 'traditionally' serves to prepare us for the proposal the writer has in mind — that South African universities should give recognition to non-university studies. The writer uses the image of the road: formal education is a highway; diploma education is a side road and a cul-de-sac. He does not, in these five paragraphs, deal with the different purposes of university education and diploma education and he treats them as if they are one and the same. Educationists may argue that the two should not be confused in this way.

In the second paragraph he poses the question, 'Is the standard of university education so much higher than that of Technikon or Professional Institute diploma education?' In a very brief and therefore superficial way he gives the example of CMA/CIS diploma studies in comparison with B. Comm studies. He uses words like 'generally accepted' and ' reputation for consistency and acceptability' and concludes CMA/CIS studies 'have an edge'. Such statements and the conclusion he reaches would require much more research for any valid conclusion to be drawn.

In the third paragraph there is another question, 'Is it the standard of tuition that is so much better at a university than at a college that offers professional diplomas?' He answers from his own 'experience' — an admission of subjectivity — but then uses the word 'generally' again. He shows a bias towards 'private business colleges' in his emotional language — 'a love of teaching and a dedication to their lecturing and their students' — and a bias against universities in the insinuation that universities are 'unproductive and inefficient'. Again he uses the word 'consistently' in the claim that 'private students fared consistently better than students studying only through Unisa'. He argues with subjectivity and generalizations, two unacademic weapons, and his argument is more that of a politician than a scholar. Of course, no one can expect a scholarly dissertation in a paragraph of this length, but it is important to understand the limitations of the argument. There is a challenge implied in his statements that universities and private enterprise should do battle in the same 'arena'.

The challenging, polemical tone is continued in the fourth paragraph with the third question, 'Is it that the standard of university examinations is so much higher?' Here the writer admits that it 'is a difficult question to answer' and offers a tentative statement that perhaps institute students fare better in examinations because they are 'more dedicated or mature'. Although this implies a bias in favour of 'institute students', there is a difference in the writer's attitude.

The fifth paragraph compares South African tertiary education with overseas university education. It is essentially factual and implies that South Africa has not kept up with developments in tertiary education. By using the image of the road in the first paragraph again in the fifth paragraph — 'the RSA academic highroad' — the writer reminds us of his previous objections to the closed nature of university education in the Republic.

From this analysis of the paragraphs we need, in a critical analysis, to form some sort of evaluation of the whole passage. Despite bias, the writer puts forward a challenging plea for more acceptance and could have opened the way (to continue his image) for more investigation into this controversial deficiency in South African tertiary education. The writers of this book would therefore consider that the passage (and the article from which it is taken) deserves recognition and serious consideration.

CONCLUSION

We have looked at scanning, skimming, comprehension and critical analysis. In examinations these four are frequently combined under 'comprehension' questions. Students may be asked questions that require only scanning or skimming or they may be asked questions that require comprehension or critical analysis. Usually scanning or skimming questions are awarded fewer marks while comprehension or critical analysis questions more. There is another type of question that is often asked and this is closely associated with précis or summary work. We shall deal with précis work under writing skills, but in a way skimming and comprehension involve making summaries too, as we have already seen. Even though a manager may never write an examination in communication, he needs to know how to read well and to decide which kind of reading the document before him requires. Otherwise he will waste time poring over a document not worth detailed attention, or he will scan or skim a document that requires close comprehension or critical analysis.

CONCEPTS AND TERMINOLOGY

1. SCANNING
2. SKIMMING
3. COMPREHENSION
4. CONTEXT
5. UNIFYING IMAGES
6. CRITICAL ANALYSIS
7. PARAPHRASING
8. TOPIC SENTENCE
9. CLOZE TEST

APPLICATION

Question 1

Scan the following passage and extract the information required:

1. Find the section on 'Cost effectiveness and accountability'.
2. How many references has the writer made to other works in this section?
3. If you consider that this passage was written in 1988, how up-to-date are the references to other works in the section 'Cost effectiveness and accountability'?
4. Where does the writer refer to South African universities?

THE PURPOSE OF EVALUATION
Evaluation for reward purposes

The first and most commonly recognized purpose of evaluation is the recognition of an individual's contribution to the aims and objectives of an organization (Dressel 1960). In spite of this obviously valid and legitimate reason for staff appraisal, universities have been slow in implementing modern personnel management techniques. In a survey undertaken by Gaff, Wilson and others (1970), for instance, more than 85 % of the respondents endorsed the idea that a formal programme of teacher evaluations of faculty should be 'used by the college in making decisions about such matters as salary, promotion and tenure', but also indicated that such formal mechanisms did not exist within their institutions. It has to be accepted that the application of these techniques is to a certain extent anathema to faculty members. As universities grow in size and complexity, the faculty member's reference group tends to shift from the employing university to the academic department and then to the discipline (Siegel 1978). It is therefore not surprising that large institutions, which display the greatest need for systematic organizational planning and good management, experience considerable difficulty in convincing faculty members of the validity of this need.

Cost effectiveness and accountability

Where Dressel addressed evaluation in terms of reward, a new purpose — entitled 'accountability' — has emerged in recent years. In his discussion of the upsurge of faculty development programmes, in which evaluation of instruction is an important element, Centra (1976) stated: 'Another reason for the recent emphasis on faculty development and instructional improvement is the general disenchantment — expressed by students, parents and legislators — with the quality of college instruction. Students seem less timid about expressing their dissatisfaction than they once were, and many parents are not at all sure that instruction is as effective as the high costs of a college education suggest it should be. Legislators are also pressuring public institutions to become more accountable.' Addressing the annual conference of the American Association for Higher Education, Kerr (1971) said: 'Cost-effectiveness of operations will be more carefully examined. If this is not done internally, it will be done externally by the new experts working for legislators and governors. Accountability is a basic consideration in effective management in an important area of application in faculty performance.' Gardner (1977) referred to the tremendous pressure exerted on universities by the 'accountability crisis', a sentiment also expressed by Bergquist and Phillips (1975) , Newbury (1975) and Rotem and Glasman (1977). It should be mentioned that South African universities, being state-subsidized, have not escaped the tendency towards increased regimentation and accountability imposed from outside, and that the advent of the SAPSE reporting system has heralded a new era of more intensive scrutiny by government and government-appointed agencies.

(From *The South African Journal of Higher Education* (Vol. 2, No. 2, 1988))

Question 2

Skim the passage above and in one sentence say what the general idea of the passage is.

Question 3

Now read the passage again carefully and answer the following comprehension questions:

. 1. The passage as a whole deals with the evaluation of
    (*a*) an organization
    (*b*) the personnel of an organization

    (c) teachers

    (d) universities

    (e) faculty members of universities

    Choose the correct answer out of these five.

2. What is the primary purpose and the most valid reason for staff evaluation? (Use your own words as far as possible.)

3. What other purpose is cited in the first paragraph? (Quote the actual words cited.)

4. Were the respondents to the survey undertaken by Gaff, Wilson and others in 1970 faculty members? Substantiate your answer.

5. What is meant by 'such formal mechanisms did not exist'?

6. There seems to be a contradiction in the first paragraph. What is it?

7. What is meant by someone's 'reference group'?

8. What is the reason for the slow implementation of modern personnel management techniques in universities? (You may quote as your answer the words from the passage, but the correct answer is not merely the last sentence of the last paragraph.)

9. Dressel discussed evaluation (choose the correct answer out of the seven below):

    (a) for accountability purposes

    (b) for reward purposes

    (c) for the purpose of recognizing an individual's contribution to the aims and objectives of an organization.

    (d) for both purposes (a) and (b)

    (e) for both purposes (b) and (c)

    (f) for both purposes (a) and (c)

    (g) for purposes (a), (b), and (c)

10. What is the nature of faculty development programmes?

11. What is meant by 'Cost effectiveness and accountability'?

12. Using your own words, state the reasons given for the expressions of dissatisfaction with the quality of college instruction

    (a) by students

    (b) by parents

    (c) by legislators.

13. What does Kerr (1971) mean by the distinction between 'internally' and 'externally'?

14. Give in your own words the meaning of 'the tendency towards increased regimentation and accountability imposed from outside'.

15. Here is the paragraph that follows the passage used for comprehension. Every seventh word has been omitted. Fill in the missing words: your answers must allow the passage to be read fluently and grammatically. Write down the appropriate number and word.

SELF-MOTIVATED IMPROVEMENT

It would be an injustice to (1) to conclude that external pressure has (2) the most important motivator for renewed (3) to teacher effectiveness. By and large, (4) have a proud tradition of dedication (5) scholarly excellence and an indisputable commitment (6) the renewal and improvement of their (7) function. Inner conscience will impel them (8) pursue these goals in their unique, (9) painfully slow and cautious, but characteristically (10) and thorough way, long after the (11) fad of externally imposed accountability has (12) its lustre and has been superseded (13) some other matter of national concern. (14) the point of view of management (15) or industrial psychology, formalized teacher evaluation (16) be regarded as a valuable instrument (17) policy for the determination of the (18) and fair distribution of rewards, whether (19) be in the form of salary (20), promotion, or the granting of tenure. (21), the regular and systematic appraisal of (22) performance can fulfil an important diagnostic (23) by revealing otherwise undetectable shortcomings in (24) performance, which can then be rectified (25) intensive training and goal-directed staff development (26).

(*After* you have attempted your own answers, you should refer to the words originally used: (1) universities; (2) been; (3) attention; (4) universities; (5) to; (6) to; (7) teaching; (8) to; (9) sometimes; (10) honest; (11) new; (12) lost; (13) by; (14) From; (15) science; (16) can; (17) of; (18) equitable; (19) these; (20) increments; (21) Second; (22) staff; (23) function; (24) individual; (25) by; (26) programmes.)

Question 4

Critically analyse the three paragraphs on *The purpose of evaluation*. In your answer pay attention to the following points:

1. Why is the first paragraph headed 'Evaluation for reward purposes'?
2. Is it clear that in the survey undertaken by Graff, Wilson and others (1970) the respondents were faculty members?
3. Why should faculty members endorse the idea of evaluation when its application is 'anathema' to them?
4. Does the writer make it clear what he means by 'As universities grow in size and complexity, the faculty member's reference group tends to shift from the employing university to the academic department and then to the discipline'?
5. Shouldn't the first word of the second paragraph headed *Cost effectiveness and accountability* be 'Whereas', not 'Where'?
6. Isn't the word 'his' in the second sentence of this paragraph confusing since the word to which it refers (Centra) appears so much later? Isn't it confused with 'Dressel' at first?
7. Doesn't the writer use too many quotations and not enough of his own views?
8. Is the word 'regimentation' in the last sentence of the second paragraph an appropriate word in its context?

9. What does SAPSE mean? Should the writer have used an abbreviation here?

10. Look at the linking thoughts between the first and second paragraphs and then between the second and third paragraphs.

11. Do you consider the writer substantiates his view that 'It would be an injustice to universities to conclude that external pressure had been the most important motivator for the renewed attention to teacher effectiveness'?

12. Don't the words 'By and large' in the second sentence of the third paragraph suggest reservations on the part of the writer?

13. Aren't words like 'proud tradition', 'dedication', excellence', and 'indisputable commitment' too emotively biased towards universities?

14. Similarly, in the next sentence, aren't the words 'new fad' and 'superseded by some other matter of national concern' snide cracks against the critics of the universities? Why has the passage suddenly become a battleground? Is there something hidden in this academic discussion implied by the word 'regimentation' in the last sentence of the second paragraph?

15. The last two sentences of the third paragraph return to the purpose of evaluation. The paragraph is headed 'Self-motivated improvement'. Why then do faculty members regard 'the application of these techniques' as 'anathema', as we were told in the first paragraph?

16. Conduct a FOG INDEX analysis of this passage.

13

MODES (MEDIA SYSTEMS): WRITTEN COMMUNICATION
General Business Writing Skills

GOALS OF THE CHAPTER

The goals of this chapter are to improve written skills as they affect business communication. By the end of this chapter you should know how to write or make use of the following:

❏ précis (summaries)
❏ telegrams
❏ telexes
❏ fax messages
❏ expansion of notes into an acceptable written format
❏ essays
❏ letters
❏ *curricula vitae*
❏ memoranda
❏ reports
❏ notices, invitations, agendas, and minutes of meetings

INTRODUCTION

This chapter covers the work that is usually regarded as the essence of business communication. Most questions in examinations on this subject are on the contents of this chapter. The authors have deliberately included this material in one chapter as an indication of its comparative importance in the whole range of topics that are relevant to communication in business. We do not wish to undervalue written communication but to merely restore the balance. One of the reasons that written communication has assumed so much importance in text books is that written communication is easier to test in examinations than other modes and other aspects of the subject. We consider that examination requirements should not prescribe the boundaries of a subject and that a book like this should have a wider appeal than merely to students about to write examinations. This book is aimed at aspiring and practising managers and businessmen whether they are going to write examinations or not. Adult education should not be subject-centred but problem-centred, and throughout this book we have tried to relate our discussions to the problems of communication at the work-face. Perhaps this book will serve the secondary purpose of encouraging teachers and examiners to centre their work with students on business problems rather than on the conventional 'Business English' examination requirements. In this regard we recommend the case study approach as an ideal teaching method for the more practical problem-centred parts of the syllabus, such as the communication process, communication in the business organization, group communication, cross-cultural communication, and oral communication — the very parts of the communication syllabus that most teachers and examiners regard paradoxically as 'too theoretical'. Case studies require imagination and practical experience: imagination to create imaginary case studies and practical experience to make them relevant to actual business situations. Unfortunately, as one moderator objected when moderating a 'Business English' examination paper, 'the aim is not to test the candidates' imaginative ability but only their ability to write correct English'. With such limited teaching and examining, we cannot expect anything but limited and bored students. The authors of this book encourage managers, teachers, examiners, and students to write their own case studies as a practical and objective exercise in isolating and solving business problems and to study others' case studies with the same practical objectives. Writing and reading will then become relevant tasks of business communication.

PRÉCIS (SUMMARIES)

The value of précis writing or making summaries is, for a manager, beyond doubt. Unfortunately it is one of those exercises that has been affected adversely by the abhorrence of the academic exercise of précis-writing at school or for other examination purposes. Because it is, as an academic exercise, rather uncreative and an apparently futile exercise, students tend to hate it and are intimidated by it. A manager, however, should immediately see the value of shortening what he or someone else has written. He will, in turn, appreciate abstracts of articles written for journals so that he does not waste his time wading through irrelevant material. Reviews of books serve the same purpose, as do digests and certain types of abbreviated reports of speeches and proceedings. Minutes of meetings are special kinds of summaries. In the 'busy-ness' of our businesses, summaries are necessary. Graphic representations and diagrams often serve the same purpose of giving the reader at a glance what it would take many words to explain.

Having tried then to explain the purpose of précis writing, we should now turn to what we consider the ten commandments or the ten stages of précis:

1. Skim the passage for the general idea of the passage. Express the main idea in your own words.
2. Read the passage for comprehension, giving attention to the meanings of important words in their contexts.
3. Pick out the main points as you read the passage for the third time.
4. Without looking at the passage but only the main points, write out your first draft of the précis or summary.
5. Count the number of words in your draft. Write down the number of words.
6. Add or subtract words, according to the number of words you want your summary to be. Write down the new number of words.
7. Read your summary and try to improve the style of your writing.
8. Check to see if you have used too many of the words of the original passage and make your précis your own by using your own words wherever possible.
9. Reread the passage and your précis to make sure you haven't left out any main ideas.
10. Give your summary a short title and write the number of words in your précis (excluding the title) at the end of your précis.

A few more detailed comments on some of these stages are in order. Stages 1–3 are essentially reading skills. Stage 3 may be in the form of notes or a diagram or a mind-map. Stage 4 is only a draft, not a finished work; it is what an examination candidate often calls 'rough work'. Stages 5 and 6 depend on the number of words your summary has to be. An examiner usually tells a student how many words the précis should be; if he hasn't given this information, a student should cut the passage to one-third of its original length. A writer is often told how long the finished work should be; if he hasn't been told, he has to establish for himself what the optimum length should be. Stages 7 and 8 are important because a précis can often be clumsily expressed if our main aim is to reduce it to the required number of words. Especially if we have used too many words of the original, we may not have made a coherent statement. Stage 9 guards against our having left out main ideas: often in trying to cut the précis to size or expressing ideas in our own words, we overlook a vital part of the original. The title (Stage 10) is like a précis of the précis: it encapsulates the main idea of the passage. The main idea as expressed in Stage 1 may or may not be the same as the title; usually it will have changed with greater comprehension of the passage. Examiners insist on the number of words being given; it is an invaluable check for the writer.

Let us look again at the five paragraphs about recognition of non-university studies by universities quoted in Chapter 12 and go through the various stages of précis:

Stage 1
'Diploma education versus university education.'

Stage 2
We have already studied the passage for comprehension and for the meaning of words in their contexts.

Stage 3
Main points: see our previous paragraph notes and mind-map.

Stage 4
First draft: In the Republic of South Africa no recognition is given by universities to non-university studies, whereas generous credits are given for university studies towards diploma studies. It is not that the standard of university education is necessarily higher than diploma education or that the standard of tuition is better at university than at colleges. It is not clear either whether university examinations are of a higher standard than diploma examinations. In the United Kingdom and the United States of America there is credit given for non-university education or for experiential learning.

Stage 5
101 words.

Stage 6
Let us take two different suppositions: (a) that we want the passage to be 80 words and (b) that we want the passage to be 120 words.

1. In South Africa universities do not recognize non-university studies, whereas credits are given for university studies towards diplomas. The standard of university education and tuition is not necessarily higher than diploma education and tuition, nor is it clear whether university examinations are of a higher standard. The United Kingdom and the United States have opened university education to all, and the United States universities give credit for non-university education and for experiential learning. (73 words)

2. In the Republic of South Africa no recognition has traditionally been given by universities to non-university studies, but Technikon and Professional Institutes give generous credits for university studies towards diploma studies. Why is this so? It is not that the standard of university education is necessarily higher than diploma education or that the standard of tuition is better at universities than at business colleges offering professional diplomas. It is not clear either whether university examinations are of a higher standard than diploma examinations. In the United Kingdom all are allowed entrance to university studies, and in the United States a person may receive credits from the university not only for non-university education but also for experiential learning. (117 words)

Stage 7

Stylistic improvements.

1. In South Africa, universities do not *give recognition to* non-university studies, *but university graduates obtain credits* towards diplomas. The standard of university education and tuition is not necessarily higher than *the standard of* diploma education and tuition, nor is it clear whether university examinations are of a higher standard *than institute examinations*. The United Kingdom and the United States have opened university education to all, and the United States universities give credit for non-university education and for experiential learning. (79 words)

2. In the Republic of South Africa *it is the tradition for universities to give no recognition to non-university studies, unlike* Technikons and Professional Institutes *which* give generous credits for university studies towards diploma studies. Why *don't universities give recognition? The standard of university education is not* necessarily higher than *the standard* of diploma education, *nor is the standard of tuition better* at universities than at business colleges offering professional diplomas. *Nor is it clear* whether university examinations are of a higher standard than diploma examinations. In the United Kingdom *all can enter university*, and in the United States a *university student* may receive credits not only for non-university studies but also for experiential learning. (114 words)

Stage 8

Own words. Here the meanings of key words in their contexts are helpful.

1. South African universities compel students with previous diploma qualifications to repeat courses. University graduates receive exemptions when they study diplomas. The quality of university and diploma education and tuition is not necessarily different, nor is it certain that university and institute examinations are of different standards. In Britain and America any student may go to university, while in America evidence of tertiary education, as well as practical experience, allows students to enter university at a more advanced stage than younger, unqualified students. (82 words)

2. In South Africa it is accepted practice that universities do not consider that people with diploma qualifications should enter university at a more advanced stage of their studies than younger, unqualified students. On the other hand Technikons and Professional Institutes give exemptions for university studies. Why don't universities give similar exemptions? University education is not necessarily of a higher quality than diploma education, nor is teaching necessarily better at universities. It is debatable whether examinations at university are more difficult than those for diplomas. In Britain all can enter university, while in the United States a university student with tertiary qualifications obtained outside a university or with evidence of practical experience in a relevant field may receive exemptions. (119 words)

Stage 9
Reread the précis in relation to the original passage.

Stage 10
Title: *Recognition of non-university studies by universities*
Number of words: already given.

In this exercise we should take note that précis writing is a long process, but it is not quite as long a process as we have made it seem. Much of the work through the various stages may be done by crossing out and correcting, and the various attempts need not be written out in full each time as we have done. Précis is essentially a written form of comprehension and is probably the best test of whether one understands a given passage. We should have noted that a précis does not include illustrations and examples or any ideas that elaborate on the main ideas. For instance, we did not include in the précis the references to CMA and CIS studies or the attempts by the writer to prove his contentions; in the précis we kept to his main contentions. It is an accepted principle of précis writing that a summary is written in the third person and as reported or indirect speech since the writer's ideas are being reported in the summary. A précis is usually, though not necessarily, one paragraph.

TELEGRAMS
Telegrams and summaries have much in common. A telegram is a condensed message. The difference between a telegram and a précis is that, whereas a précis uses full sentences, a telegram need not. Telegrams can and should omit all unnecessary words like articles, auxiliary verbs, even pronouns, but a telegram must not be so cryptic that the person receiving it does not understand it. Telegrams are becoming more and more expensive, and therefore the number of words used is important, but it is an even greater waste of money to send a telegram that is not understood. If there is any

doubt that the telegram will be understood, more words should be used to make it intelligible. There was a time when telegrams were sent on special occasions like birthdays, weddings, or whenever one had been forgetful. Now telegrams are used only for extreme emergencies when all other forms of communication have failed or are not available. This is, after all, the real purpose of the telegram. There are certain rules of telegram writing: the telegram should include the name and an acceptable address of the receiver, the whole telegram should be printed in capital letters, and it should be clear who the sender of the telegram is so that a reply can be sent if necessary. In a telegram the word STOP indicates a full stop and it should be written out in full whenever the sense of the telegram demands it.

The criteria for judging a good telegram are:

❏   Is it clear?
❏   Is it concisely stated?
❏   Are all the necessary facts given?
❏   Is it properly set out?

TELEXES

A telex is a combination of the telephone, the typewriter, and the telegram. The telex machine gets through to the receiver by dialling the receiver's telex number and it prints out messages for both the receiver and the sender. It is quicker than a telegram since it does not involve the delay of waiting for the post office to receive and transmit the message, and it has the advantage of providing a printed record of the message. Not every business has a telex machine because of the expense of the installation and because certain types of business would not need to use it frequently enough. Other businesses could not do without the telex machine, and find it an excellent vehicle for communication, especially since written replies can be received very quickly.

FAX MESSAGES

Closely linked to the telex machine is the fax machine. Like the telex, the fax is sent by using a subscriber's number. The special advantage of the fax machine is that it works like a photocopier as well as having all the advantages of a telephone, a typewriter, and a telex. It is particularly useful for sending copies of documents and graphics in a hurry and it has all the other advantages of the telex machine including the likelihood of speedy replies. The fax machine is probably the most popular form of speedy communication.

EXPANSION OF NOTES INTO AN ACCEPTABLE WRITTEN FORMAT

Note-taking is an important skill of reading and listening. When we study properly, we take notes. When we listen to a lecture, it helps concentration to take notes, But it is just as important to be able to expand these notes into an acceptable written format. Perhaps the notes we have received are not notes we have made ourselves but the notes handed out at a lecture or the notes given as a summary of a chapter of a book. To be able to expand notes into an essay or an acceptable letter or report or memorandum is one of the skills of written communication, and as we proceed with the various forms of written communication, we shall be able to practise this skill.

ESSAY WRITING

Preliminaries

There are two important preliminaries to essay writing:

- ❑ Your title
- ❑ Your plan (outline, scheme, diagram, mind-map).

Your title will help you to focus your attention on what the topic of your essay is and throughout your writing you will come back to the title to make sure you are not wandering off the point. If you are given a title, analyse the title carefully, picking out the key-words, and include them in your plan and in your essay. This will help you to keep to the topic. We have said all this in our discussion of planning a speech; there is little difference between planning a speech and planning an essay.

The *plan of your essay* is of the utmost importance. You need to make notes before you write. As you organize your notes into order, the scheme of the paragraphs in your essay will emerge. The outline of the structure of your essay into paragraphs is essential preparation. Without it your essay will be without logical development and will deteriorate into aimless rambling from one point to another.

We have already used notes, diagrams, and mind-maps to help us to read and to speak, and therefore it is an easy step to develop our own notes, diagrams, and mind-maps before we write. The first step is to write down any ideas that come to us as we consider the title or topic or theme. We are at this stage brainstorming: we write down any ideas that come, without any ordering or judgement of the ideas. The ideas that come should be written down as single words or groups of words (preferably not more than five words for each idea). When we have enough ideas, we need to evaluate and order them. If we use a written rather than a diagrammatic scheme, we should write down as headings PARAGRAPH 1, PARAGRAPH 2, etc. so that we realize what we are doing: we are organizing our paragraphs. If we use a diagram, again we should organize our diagram so that it is clear how our paragraphs will be separated. If you go back to our diagram on the five paragraphs on the recognition of non-university courses by universities, you will see how we can include paragraphing in a diagram.

Once we have made our scheme, it is important that we keep to the division of our essay into these paragraphs and that each paragraph will concern itself with that topic. There is no point in an outline that bears no resemblance to the essay. If, as you write, you find your ideas developing further, it will be a good idea to expand or adapt your scheme accordingly.

Components of the Essay

So much then for preparation; let us move on to the components of our essay. We have already referred to the outline as the way of arranging an essay topic into paragraph topics. An essay is divided into paragraphs, a paragraph into sentences, and a sentence into words. We could go on, of course, and say

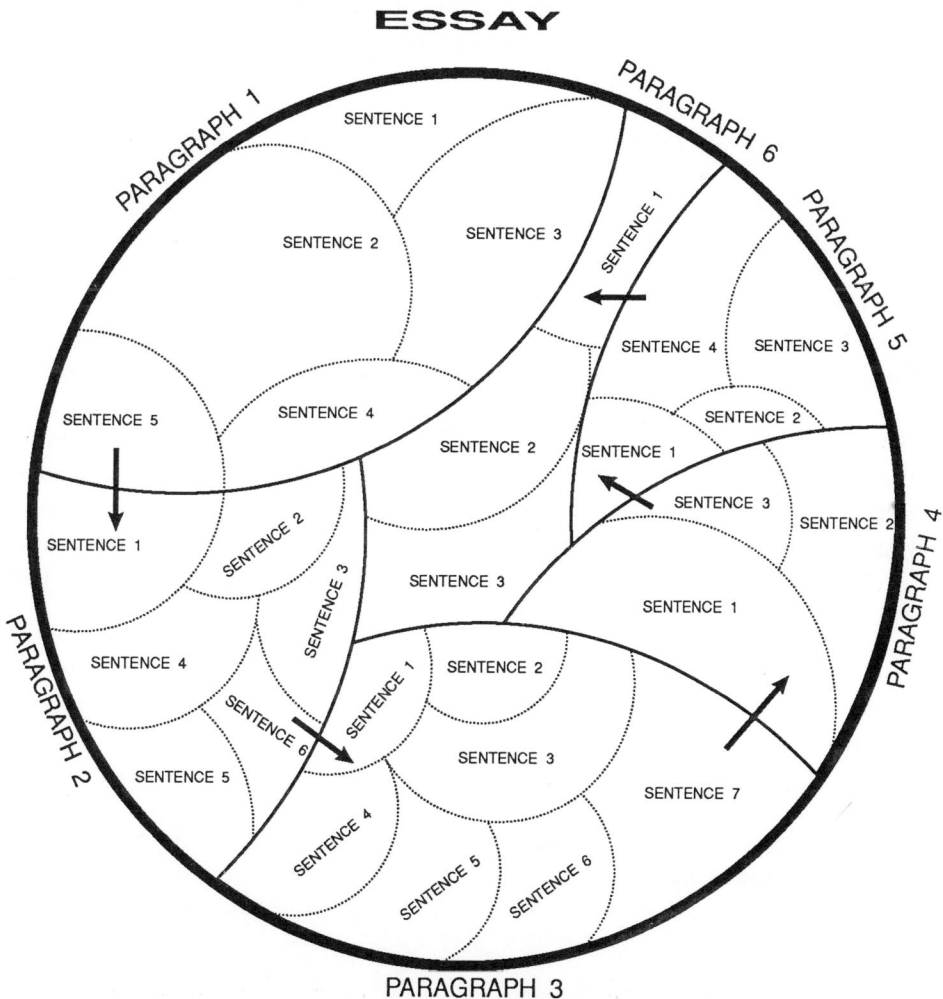

ESSAY

PARAGRAPH 3

words are divided into syllables or letters. We need not start with an essay, either: we could start with the generic term, literature or writing, and subdivide it into many different parts. But we shall be content with:

ESSAY — PARAGRAPHS — SENTENCES — WORDS.

An essay can be represented as a circle in which there are paragraphs and sentences (previous page).

An essay is a free form. We cannot insist on, say, six paragraphs, each with five sentences. A paragraph can be short or long. A sentence, too, can be short or long. Variety of sentence length and paragraph length helps to make the writing interesting, but far more important than such abstract observations is the requirement that paragraphs should be linked (the arrows in the circle) and that there should be some kind of logical order in the sentence and paragraph structure. Our diagram represents an essay with six paragraphs and twenty-eight sentences, but these numbers are chosen merely to illustrate the variety possible, not to suggest any kind of pattern for essay-writing. The last paragraph has deliberately been drawn so that it borders each of the other five paragraphs. This suggests that the last paragraph sums up the essay by referring to each of the other paragraphs. The concluding paragraph may do this, but need not necessarily do so. An opening paragraph could just as easily be the one to provide links with the other paragraphs, or perhaps a paragraph at the centre of the essay could be the one. The possibilities are infinite. All we have tried to represent is the unified structure of an essay with its paragraphs and sentences.

A sentence is a group of words that make sense when spoken or read together. Most sentences have finite verbs, that is, verbs with subjects telling us who does what. Sometimes these verbs are omitted but nevertheless understood to be part of the sentence, and it is possible to have sentences that make perfect sense but do not have finite verbs. In most business writing, however, it is a good idea to construct sentences with finite verbs. The only exceptions to this would be telegrams and advertisements, but even here the danger in not using finite verbs is that we shall compose unintelligible telegrams and advertisements. The finite verb is a requirement in a sentence that should not be lightly discarded.

There are different kinds of sentences. The **simple sentence** has only one finite verb. In its simplest form it may consist of only two parts, the subject and the verb:

❑   Power corrupts.

Here *power* is the subject and *corrupts* is the verb. We may even have a sentence of one word:

❑   Go!

Here the word *go* is a verb and the subject is understood (*you*). Sometimes a sentence may consist of one or more words in which both the subject and the verb are understood:

❑ Out!

Here the subject may be *you* or *the dog* or some subject that the context of the word *Out!* would make clear, and the verb would be *go* or *get* or some such word that would be clearly understood. Most simple sentences tend to be longer than one or two words:

❑ The beautiful woman in the green dress moved gracefully across the dance floor.

Although it is still a simple sentence since it has only one finite verb, *moved*, this sentence has a structure that shows the potential of a simple sentence :

❑ *The beautiful woman in the green dress* — SUBJECT

The	Definite Article
beautiful	Adjective
woman	Noun
in	Preposition
the	Definite Article
green	Adjective
dress	Noun

❑ *moved gracefully across the dance floor* — PREDICATE

moved	Verb
gracefully	Adverb
across	Preposition
the	Definite Article
dance	Adjective
floor	Noun

We have divided the 'simple' sentence into its two parts, subject and predicate. The subject tells us who did the action, and the predicate tells us what the action was. We then analyse the words in the subject and the predicate into the individual parts of the sentence (sometimes called, rather strangely, parts of speech) to show their relation to each other more clearly. Another way of doing this is as follows:

❑ *The beautiful woman in the green dress* — SUBJECT

woman	Subject Word
The beautiful	Enlargement of the Subject Word (1)
in the green dress	Enlargement of the Subject Word (2)

❑ *moved gracefully across the dance floor* — PREDICATE

moved	Verb
gracefully	Extension of the Verb (Manner)
across the dance floor	Extension of the Verb (Place)

This method of analysis shows clearly the relation of the words either to the Subject Word or to the Verb. We are no longer taught formal grammatical analysis at school, but some awareness of the syntax of a sentence is necessary if we are going to write effectively.

The second kind of sentence is the **complex sentence**. This type of sentence has two or more finite verbs, but one of the finite verbs forms part of the sentence that we call the Main or Principal Clause, that is, the group of words (with a finite verb) on which the other clauses depend or to which they are subordinate either in meaning or in grammatical structure. Although complex sentences can become very complex indeed, most complex sentences need not horrify us. They include common statements like:

❏   Because he is ill, he will not be at work today.
❏   The man whom we saw yesterday joined our staff today.
❏   He will report to you when he has finished that job.
❏   He wants to be better qualified so that he may be promoted.
❏   He announced that he was leaving the firm at the end of the month.

In each of these sentences there is a Main Clause and a Subordinate Clause.

MAIN CLAUSE	SUBORDINATE CLAUSE
he will not be at work today	*Because he is ill*
The man . . . joined our staff today	*whom we saw yesterday*
He will report to you	*when he has finished that job*
He wants to be better qualified	*so that he may be promoted*
He announced	*that he was leaving at the end of the mont*

To be able to separate a main clause from its subordinate clause requires a simple understanding of verbs and conjunctions: the main clause has a finite verb, whereas the subordinate clause has a conjunction and a finite verb. The conjunctions in the sentences are Because, whom (also called a relative pronoun), when, so that, and that. The conjunction, as we can see, usually introduces the subordinate clause.

Sometimes it is useful to know more about the relation of the subordinate clause to the main clause:

MAIN CLAUSE	SUBORDINATE CLAUSE AND ITS RELATION
He will not be at work today	*Because he is ill* (Subordinate Adverbial Clause of Reason modifying *will not be at work*)
The man . . . joined our staff today	*whom we saw yesterday* (Subordinate Adjectival Clause

	describing *man*)
He will report to you	*when he has finished that job* (Subordinate Adverbial Clause of Time modifying *will report*)
He wants to be better qualified	*so that he may be promoted* (Subordinate Adverbial Clause of Purpose modifying *wants to be better qualified*)
He announced	*that he was leaving the firm at the end of the month* (Subordinate Noun Clause object of *announced*)

To know about relations of subordinate clauses requires basic knowledge of functional grammar. We need to know that a noun can be subject of a verb or object of a verb or a preposition, that an adjective describes a noun, and that an adverb tells you more about (modifies) a verb. Once we know this, it is easy to transfer this knowledge to clauses: noun clauses can be subject of a verb or object of a verb (or, rarely, of a preposition); adjectival clauses describe nouns, and adverbial clauses modify verbs.

A subordinate clause can relate to another subordinate clause; it does not have to relate only to the main clause:

❑ The man who was so drunk that he could hardly stand had to be helped to his home, which was in the eastern suburbs.

MAIN CLAUSE	SUBORDINATE CLAUSES AND THEIR RELATION
The man . . . had to be helped to his home	*who was so drunk* (Subordinate Adjectival Clause describing *man*) *that he could hardly stand* (Subordinate Adverbial Clause of Result modifying *was so drunk*) *which was in the eastern suburbs* (Subordinate Adjectival Clause describing *home*)

The subordinate clause *that he could hardly stand* relates to the other subordinate clause *who was so drunk* and not to the main clause. The other two subordinate clauses relate to the main clause.

The understanding of the relationship of parts of sentences to other parts helps the writer to compose sentences that have unity and logic. The writer and the reader of the sentence know where they are going; they know what the relationship between the different ideas or clauses may be. Seeing relationships between ideas helps us to think clearly when we write or when we read.

We have now looked at the simple sentence (only one finite verb, only one idea) and the complex sentence (more than one finite verb, only one main idea, one or more subordinate ideas). There is another type of sentence that is very useful: we call it the **compound sentence**. The compound sentence has two or more finite verbs and two or more main clauses:

❑   The man called, and his child answered.

There are two clauses: (1) *The man called*; (2) *and his child answered*. They are both main clauses because neither idea is subordinate to the other; we say they are co-ordinating main clauses. Another way of describing the clauses of this compound sentence is to say they are independent clauses because they are two independent parts of the sentence with equal importance.

If, however, we were to re-arrange the sentence in this way

❑   When the man called, his child answered.

we would have a complex sentence in which the clause *When the man called* is subordinate to the clause *his child answered*. By using the conjunction *When* instead of the conjunction *and*, we have changed the relation of one clause to the other and thrown the emphasis on the idea *his child answered*. We could re-arrange the sentence differently:

❑   The man called until his child answered.

In this example we still have a complex sentence, but the relation of one clause to the other is different: the clause *The man called* is now the main clause and the clause *until his child answered* is subordinate to it. From these examples we can see the subtle variations of relationship that we can effect through changing the conjunctions. When we write, we must consider what the precise relationships are that we wish to create, and when we read, we should consider the relationships the writer wishes us (consciously or unconsciously) to understand.

There is then a difference between co-ordinating conjunctions and subordinating conjunctions. The co-ordinating conjunctions are *and, but, yet, so, then, therefore, for, either . . . or, or, neither . . . nor,* and *nor;* we could limit their number by excluding *then* and *therefore* and by saying that they are usually adverbs, but since some writers use them as co-ordinating conjunctions, we have included them with the comment that we prefer to think of them as adverbs. All other conjunctions are subordinating conjunctions: they make the clauses that they introduce subordinate to another clause. A co-ordinating conjunction can be used to co-ordinate two subordinate clauses as well so that the two subordinate clauses have the same relationship to another clause:

❑   He was annoyed when the post did not arrive and he did not receive his results.

In this sentence the clauses *when the post did not arrive* and *(when) he did not receive his results* are both subordinate to the main clause *He was annoyed*: they therefore have a co-ordinate relationship to each other brought about by the use of the co-ordinating conjunction *and.*

A compound sentence shows a close relationship between two or more clauses without implying any sense of subordination.

❏   He phoned the police, for he feared for his safety.

In this sentence there are two clauses, *He phoned the police* and *for he feared for his safety.* Neither of the clauses is subordinate: they are co-ordinating main clauses, showing close relationship but not implying that one idea has more importance than the other. If we change the conjunction from *for* to *because,* we have changed the relationship between the two ideas:

❏   He phoned the police because he feared for his safety.

The first clause *He phoned the police* becomes the main clause and the second clause *because he feared for his safety* the subordinate clause. The main idea we want to communicate is that he phoned the police. The conjunction *for* is a co-ordinating conjunction, but the conjunction *because* is a subordinating conjunction.

Most writers do not consider the relationships between clauses, but a good writer is concerned about precise meaning and will redraft sentences to sharpen relationships in order to communicate the exact shade of meaning that will serve his purpose best. Let us look at two examples from two master craftsmen of communication, Shakespeare and Milton. In *Macbeth,* Act I Scene 6, we read:

> If it were done, when 'tis done, then 'twere well
> It were done quickly: if the assassination
> Could trammel up the consequence, and catch,
> With his surcease, success; that but this blow
> Might be the be-all and the end-all here,
> But here, upon this bank and shoal of time,
> We'd jump the life to come.

In this sentence (or these sentences if we consider the colon divides it into two sentences) we have a succession of clauses that contribute to the intricate meaning of what Macbeth is saying. Let us look at their relation to each other:

CLAUSE	KIND AND RELATION
1. *If it were done,*	Subordinate Adverbial Clause of Condition, modifying *'twere well* in 3.
2. *when 'tis done,*	Subordinate Adverbial Clause of Time, modifying *were done* in 1.
3. *then 'twere well*	Main Clause.

4. *(that)It were done quickly:*	Subordinate Noun Clause in opposition to the subject *it* in 3.
5. *if the assassination* *Could trammel up the* *consequence,*	Subordinate Adverbial Clause of Condition, modifying *(would) jump* in 8
6. *and catch,* *With his surcease, success;*	Subordinate Adverbial Clause of Condition, co-ordinate with 5.
7. *(so) that but this blow* *Might be the be-all and the* *end-all here,* *But here, upon this bank and* *shoal of time,*	Subordinate Adverbial Clause of Result, modifying *could trammel* in 5 and *(could) catch* in 6.
8. *We'd jump the life to come.*	Main Clause.

Whether we regard this as a compound sentence with two main clauses or as two complex sentences (consisting of clauses 1–4 and 5–8 respectively), we should be able to see the close relationship among the clauses and the two main clauses. Unless we take the trouble to see the relations among the different ideas coursing through Macbeth's mind, we are unlikely to understand what he is saying. Such analysis of the relation of the parts to each other and to the total statement helps us to be aware of sentence structure.

The other sentence comes from Milton's poem, Sonnet XVII, often referred to as 'On His Blindness':

> When I consider how my light is spent,
> Ere half my days, in this dark world and wide,
> And that one talent which is death to hide
> Lodged with me useless, though my soul more bent

> To serve therewith my maker, and present
> My true account, lest he, returning, chide,
> 'Doth God exact day labour, light denied?'
> I fondly ask; but Patience, to prevent

> That murmur, soon replies: 'God doth not need
> Either man's work or his own gifts; who best
> Bear his mild yoke, they serve him best; his state

> Is kingly — thousands at his bidding speed
> And post o'er land and ocean without rest:
> They also serve who only stand and wait.'

Again we have a succession of clauses that build up Milton's argument and that need to be analysed into clauses and their relation to each other.

Clause

1. *When I consider*

Kind and Relation

Subordinate Adverbial Clause of Time, modifying *ask* in 9.

2. *how my light is spent,* *Ere half my days, in this* *dark world and wide,*	Subordinate Noun Clause, object of *consider* in 1.
3. *And that one talent . . . (is)* *Lodged with me useless,*	Subordinate Noun Clause, co-ordinate with 2.
4. *which is death to hide*	Subordinate Adjectival Clause, describing *talent* in 3.
5. *though my soul more bent* *To serve therewith my* *maker, and present* *My true account,*	Subordinate Adverbial Clause of Concession, modifying *is death to hide* in 4.
6. *lest he, returning, chide,*	Subordinate Adverbial Clause of Purpose, modifying *bent/To serve . . . and present* in 5.
7. *'Doth God exact day labour*	Subordinate Noun Clause, object of *ask* in 9.
8. *(when or though) light (is)* *denied?*	Subordinate Adverbial Clause of Time or Concession, modifying *exact* in 7.
9. *I fondly ask;*	Main Clause
10. *but Patience, to prevent* *That murmur, soon replies:*	Main Clause
11. *'God doth not need* *Either man's work or his own* *gifts;*	Subordinate Noun Clause, object of *replies* in 10.
12. *who best* *Bear his mild yoke,*	Subordinate Adjectival Clause, describing *they* in 13.
13. *they serve him best;*	Subordinate Noun Clause, co-ordinate with 11.
14. *his state* *Is kingly -*	Subordinate Noun Clause, co-ordinate with 11 and 13.
15. *thousands at his bidding* *speed*	Subordinate Noun Clause, co-ordinate with 11, 13 and 14.
16. *And post o'er land and ocean* *without rest:*	Subordinate Noun Clause, co-ordinate with 15 (and therefore with 11, 13 and 14).
17. *They also serve*	Subordinate Noun Clause, co-ordinate with 11, 13, 14, 15 and 16.
18. *who only stand*	Subordinate Adjectival Clause, describing *they* in 17.
19. *and wait.'*	Subordinate Adjectival Clause, co-ordinate with 18.

This analysis of Milton's sonnet into its clauses and the relationship among its clauses helps to show the intricate and confused construction of the first sentence, that is clauses 1–9, up to the semi-colon, as Milton wrestles with his ideas about his blindness: subordinate clause heaps upon subordinate clause until we reach the main clause right at the end, *I fondly ask.* The heaping of clauses like this shows his terror and his frenzy at his blindness, which he comes to realize as we detect from the word *fondly*, which has as its primary meaning 'foolishly'. After the semi-colon, the next main clause quickly appears in the usual place for the main clause — at the beginning of a sentence — and then there is a succession of short, simple co-ordinating noun clauses, in which Patience quietly soothes Milton's terror and frenzy. The use of appropriately contrasting sentence structures to convey the poet's meaning is a lesson to us all.

Managers may be asking what poetry has to do with business writing. It is our contention that a manager who has to wade through legal documents or company reports will benefit from a study of sentence structure, for the sentence structure of such documents can be as complicated, though with less justification, as Shakespeare's and Milton's writing. Managers also have to compose such documents or at least express them in their initial drafts before they are handed over to members of the legal profession or a board of directors to finalize them, and it will save time and money if the manager's drafts are composed in such a way that the intricacy of company communication can be reduced to clarity through carefully constructed sentences.

We referred earlier to the efficiency of a variety of sentence structures. Simple sentences wisely used can be very effective in expressing ideas simply and quickly. They can be useful in stating the topic sentence of a paragraph, or in the company of complex and compound sentences, they can be used to emphasize an important idea. Complex sentences are invaluable in expressing subordinate ideas and qualifying relationships of description (through adjectival clauses), expansion (often through noun clauses), and such ideas as time, manner, place, cause, purpose, condition, and concession (through adverbial clauses). Compound sentences help to show the co-ordination of ideas, to bring together associated or contrasting ideas, and to demonstrate the steps in an argument.

Without attention to sentence structure, the writer can easily produce simple sentences that irritate because they are too facile or abrupt. Similarly, complex and compound sentences can become confused and too involved when they could be clear and straightforward. There is an art in writing that comes only from constant practice and painstaking revision. As Alexander Pope says,

> True wit is Nature to advantage dress'd;
> What oft was thought, but ne'er so well express'd . . . .

a good writer pays attention to good expression, and careful sentence structure helps the writer to express himself well.

More about Paragraphing

Teachers and examiners sometimes take the sentences of an existing paragraph, jumble them up into a different order, and then set them as an exercise
for students to put the sentences together again into the logical sequence of
a paragraph. Let us take an example from our article in the *South African
Journal of Higher Education* (Vol. 2, No. 2, 1988):

1. Such programmes tend to suffer because of this kind of lack of commit-
    ment.
2. Entrance requirements to tertiary education need to be relaxed for special
    cases.
3. Mature students with experiential or non-formal learning should be
    allowed to enter at the level of tertiary education with which they can
    cope, regardless of a lack of formal qualifications.
4. Academic support programmes are offered, but often these programmes
    suffer because the staff appointed to supervise such programmes are
    temporary and are merely biding their time in the academic support
    programmes until they are able to be appointed to permanent positions
    in other departments of the university.
5. Some universities have already accepted this need for black students who
    have suffered because of political unrest and educational disadvantages.

The way to do such an exercise is to try to find the links between sentences
and the logical ordering of the ideas. The links provided are often words like
this, or *such*: We see these words in sentences 1 (*such*), 4 (*these*), and 1 and
5 (*this*). Other useful links are repeated words: *programmes* (sentences 1 and
4), *need* (sentences 2 and 5), *university/universities* (sentences 4 and 5),
suffer/suffered (sentences 1, 4, and 5), *tertiary education* (sentences 2 and
3), *students* (sentences 3 and 5), and *Entrance/enter* (sentences 2 and 3).
From this kind of investigation we see that sentences 1 and 4 are linked, and
1 seems to follow 4; sentences 2 and 5 are linked, and 5 seems to follow 2;
sentences 4 and 5 are linked, with no clear idea of order; and sentences 2
and 3 appear to be linked, also with no clear indication of order. Let us write
down the linkage in diagrammatic form:

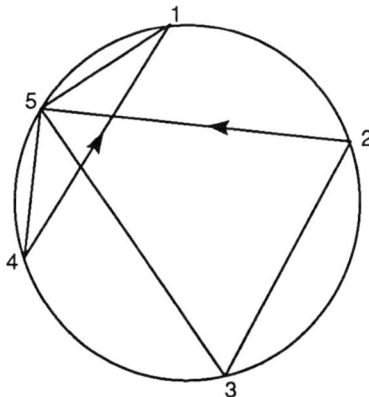

We have now established that 4 comes before 1 and 2 comes before 5. Sentence 4 does not look like a good starting point because its sense requires it to follow 5. What about 2 as a starting point? It is a short general statement that seems to be able to stand on its own. Let us start with it and show the linkages.

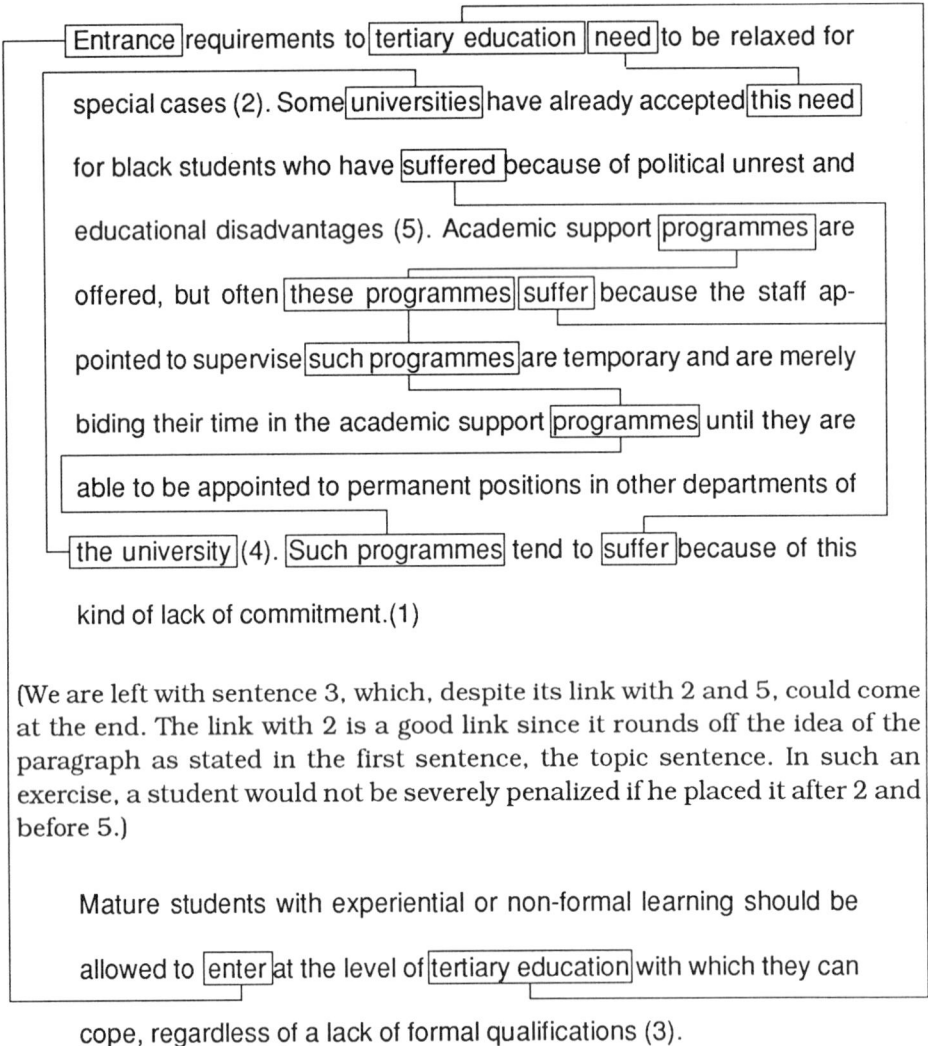

Entrance requirements to tertiary education need to be relaxed for special cases (2). Some universities have already accepted this need for black students who have suffered because of political unrest and educational disadvantages (5). Academic support programmes are offered, but often these programmes suffer because the staff appointed to supervise such programmes are temporary and are merely biding their time in the academic support programmes until they are able to be appointed to permanent positions in other departments of the university (4). Such programmes tend to suffer because of this kind of lack of commitment.(1)

(We are left with sentence 3, which, despite its link with 2 and 5, could come at the end. The link with 2 is a good link since it rounds off the idea of the paragraph as stated in the first sentence, the topic sentence. In such an exercise, a student would not be severely penalized if he placed it after 2 and before 5.)

Mature students with experiential or non-formal learning should be allowed to enter at the level of tertiary education with which they can cope, regardless of a lack of formal qualifications (3).

The position of this sentence at the end of the paragraph helps to focus on the main point of the paragraph, which is not about academic support programmes but the need to relax entrance requirements. The support programmes are an example of the acceptance of this need by the universities, even though the programmes are not altogether successful.

In looking at the structure of the paragraph, let us also look at the sentence structure:

- ❏ Sentence 2 is a simple sentence and is well suited for the topic sentence at the beginning of the paragraph.
- ❏ Sentence 5 is a complex sentence with a subordinate clause. It serves to advance the argument.
- ❏ Sentence 4 is a compound sentence with two co-ordinate main clauses and two co-ordinating subordinate clauses. The structure of this sentence serves to deal with the intricate problem of support programmes, a complicating factor in the argument.
- ❏ Sentence 1 is another simple sentence, which serves to repeat simply the problem raised in sentence 4.
- ❏ Sentence 3 is a complex sentence with one subordinate clause. It restores the unity of the paragraph, which would have been broken if sentence 3 had followed sentence 2.

It is our hope that by drawing attention to paragraphing and sentence structure we have been able to contribute to an understanding of what composition entails. Just as sentences have to be carefully constructed, so do paragraphs. There should be appropriate links between paragraphs. Sometimes we use special linking words or phrases to show the direction of our argument: when we are listing examples we may use a numbering system or use the words *first . . . second . . . third . . .* or we may use expressions such as *As a start* or *In conclusion.* If we wish to express contrasts, we can use phrases like *In contrast* or *On the other hand* or words like *nevertheless* or *however.* If we wish to express a comparison, we can use *similarly* or *in the same way.* Words like *therefore, as a result,* and *consequently* express results or effects. We should look for opportunities to give direction to our readers. We need to revise each paragraph to make sure that it does not include ideas that do not belong in that paragraph but should rather be in another paragraph. Each paragraph should be rounded off satisfactorily, but if it is not the final paragraph, there should be an opportunity for a link with the next one. Each paragraph is similar to a little essay and should have its own unity and development, while at the same time it should have its important place in the essay as a whole. A paragraph is to the essay as a chapter is to a book.

PARAGRAPH : ESSAY :: CHAPTER : BOOK

Concluding Remarks about Essay Writing

It is a necessary truism to say that an essay should, as Aristotle said, have a beginning, a middle, and an end. As we mentioned in our chapter on oral communication, the beginning will determine whether we gain the attention of the receiver, and the ending will determine whether we make an impression that will last after the communication has finished.

There are, of course, as many different kinds of essays as there are different forms of communication. Each kind of essay will require its own **register**. By register we mean the level of formality required by the target readership: register involves the level of language, the style, the sentence structure, and the tone. Let us apply this to some of the different types of essays.

A narrative essay is likely to use a less formal, more personal tone, the colloquial language of speech, shorter sentences, more humour, and a sequential order of events with some suspense till the denouement. There are, of course, different types of narrative essays — humorous, tragic, action-packed, biographical, and autobiographical. In a humorous essay, word-play and ambiguity will be common. Dialogue may be employed to make the story more actual.

A descriptive essay is likely to be more expressive of the emotions, more precise in its descriptions, more figurative, and more formal in language and tone. It will use a variety of sentence structures as the essay moves, not in a sequential pattern, but according to a carefully constructed and unified theme. Symbolic meaning that covers a wide range of imaginative implications will be quite acceptable.

An informative essay will be even more exact in its details. A great deal of attention will be paid to the factual correctness of the writing. It will be more utilitarian than entertaining. The level of language will depend even more on the level of the reader than the narrative or descriptive essay does because, if the purpose of the information is to teach Standard Five pupils, the language will be simple, while if the purpose is to address specialists in an academic discipline, the language will be very technical indeed and will assume the higher level of readership. There will be no ambiguity, and terms will be deliberately defined. The tone will tend to be directive to young readers or scholarly for advanced readers. The informative essay relies more on conclusions drawn from observations and experiments (that is, empirical conclusions) than from theories. It is likely that there will be many symbols, formulae, and numbers used in the text.

An argumentative essay will rely more on logical statement than on technical correctness (or, put differently, on theoretical rather than empirical reasoning). Since the aim is to persuade the reader to the writer's standpoint, the writer cannot afford to baffle his reader with science; he must rather argue pragmatically and according to premisses. A good argumentative essay will discuss both sides of the argument so that the writer's conclusion will not appear biased. He will use illustrations, but not generalizations that beg the question. The argumentative essay may reason inductively (that is, discovering general laws from particular facts) or deductively (that is, reaching a conclusion by reasoning from general laws to a particular case). Although deductive reasoning is more conclusive, we may use inductive reasoning justifiably in an argument as long as we accept that we are dealing with a likelihood or a probability rather than a certainty.

Example of inductive reasoning

PREMISS 1: Every election in South Africa has shown a swing to the right.
PREMISS 2: There has never been a swing to the left in a South African
             election.
CONCLUSION: It is likely that the right will win the next election.

Example of deductive reasoning

PREMISS 1: The Western Cape has a Mediterranean-type climate.
PREMISS 2: Mediterranean-type climates have rain in winter.
CONCLUSION: It will rain in winter in the Western Cape this year.

A critical essay is the written counterpart of that form of reading we called critical analysis. This is an essay in which the writer criticizes a text or a happening that he considers to be worthy of criticism. Book reviews are critical essays. Literary criticism, that is, the criticism of a work of literature, would fall under this heading. The editor's leading article in a newspaper or the editorial in a magazine or a journal is a type of critical essay. Any writing on a business topic in which the writer sets out to evaluate business trends would be classed as a critical essay for our purposes. The financial manager's analysis and interpretation of accounts could even be relevant. The basis of a critical essay is a close analysis of the text or trend or set of accounts that is being criticized. The difference between this type of essay and the others we have mentioned is that the critical essay is less creative in character since the writer is bound by the text or the trend he is criticizing. It is nevertheless one of the most valuable forms of writing because the critical essay offers comment on books or situations that might otherwise not have been brought to the reader's notice. It should go without saying that a writer of a critical essay needs to be very knowledgeable in the field where he has chosen to express his critical comments. His reader will look to him to provide informed comment, not mere opinion.

Of these different types of essays we shall see that narrative and descriptive essays will rarely play a part in business communication, although a manager who cannot write a humorous story for his in-house journal needs to sharpen these skills. Informative, argumentative, and critical essays would probably be the most relevant to the businessman who is being called upon more and more to express his views in writing.

LETTER WRITING

There are a few general rules about letter writing that we should get out of the way before we move on to the different forms of letters and the different approaches needed for them.

Layout

The layout of a letter is very important. Included in the layout is the letterhead of a business. A well-designed letterhead makes an immediately favourable impression on the reader. It is a form of advertising. In the same way a well-laid-out letter with plenty of spaces and correct paragraphing makes a good impression. Under layout we include

- ❑   ADDRESS
- ❑   DATE
- ❑   SALUTATION
- ❑   TOPIC HEADING
- ❑   PARAGRAPHING
- ❑   ENDING

Address

This includes the writer's address and, if it is a business letter, the receiver's address. If the letter is on the firm's letterhead, it is obviously not necessary to write out the address of the sender, but, for friendly letters and letters on paper without a letterhead, it is necessary to write out the address in full. The address is usually placed on the right-hand side of the page.

```
                                        TOYJOY (Pty) Ltd
                                        P.O. Box 5878
                                        JOHANNESBURG
                                        2000
```

Notice that there is no unnecessary punctuation and that it is in block form. (The days of sloping addresses are past.) The receiver's address is placed on the left-hand side of the page, also in block form, and set to the margin of the rest of the letter.

```
Mr J. G. Brown
The Manager
Browning Plastics
P.O. Box 7490
PRETORIA
0001
```

Many writers even omit the full stops after the abbreviations P.O., but we believe they should be there. This is in keeping with the rule for abbreviations: if an abbreviation ends with the final letter of the word when it is written out in full, no punctuation is needed; if an abbreviation does not end with the final letter of the word, a full stop is required. Of course, it would not be considered incorrect if the full stop is always used after an abbreviation. The abbreviation *Pty* does not require the full stop, therefore, because the full word Proprietary ends with a y, as does the abbreviation; the abbreviation

P.O. requires full stops because it stands for Post Office and the last letters of these words are not included as the last letters of the abbreviated words.

It is important that a letter should always be addressed to a person, never to a company. Even if we do not know the name of the person to whom we are writing, we should address the letter to a person such as the manager or the accountant. If the letter is an important one, it is advisable to find out the name of the person to whom the letter is directed; a phone call will always elicit this information. It makes a big difference if a person receives a letter addressed to him by name. Personalization of correspondence is an important principle of business correspondence.

In South Africa and other countries, postal codes are used. They help to speed up communication, and it is careless not to use postal codes.

Why is it important to give the full address of the person to whom the letter is addressed? Besides obeying one of the conventions of business correspondence, we are also providing our own business with important information: if we keep copies of correspondence — and in our world of too much paper this is not necessarily a good idea — we then have a record of an important address. It also serves a useful purpose of being able to check that the correct, up-to-date address was used in the unlikely event of that letter not reaching its destination.

If, instead of a box number, a street address is used, the address is given in this way:

```
346 Berg St
PIETERMARITZBURG
3201
```

Because of the influence from Afrikaans, it is important to know that in English the number of a building precedes the name of the street.

The name of the town should be in capitals throughout the word if it is typed or printed. If it is written by hand, the name of the town should start with a capital letter and continue with small letters. These are mere conventions and are not very important. What is important is that the addresses of letters should be neatly laid out on the page.

Date

There are two acceptable ways of writing the date in South Africa: either 15 June 1992 or 1992–06–15. The first is the more acceptable; the second shows the influence of the computer age and computerized forms: there are ten spaces for every date and eight digits to be inserted. The problem about the numerical date is that the United States uses a different form of numbering, and confusion could arise. Although there are different conventions about the first method with the month written out in full, at least there can be no confusion about what the date is. Abbreviations of months are not recommended. Notice again that there are no unnecessary punctuation marks.

Where does the date appear on the page? The normal place is on the right under the sender's address when the letter is not on a letterhead:

```
                                                 TOYJOY (Pty) Ltd
                                                 P.O. Box 5878
                                                 JOHANNESBURG
                                                 2000

                                                 15 June 1992
```

On a letterhead, however, it is customary to place it on the left with the same margin as the rest of the letter. This saves complicated calculations about where the date should appear on the right. There should be a blank space between the date and the next part of the letter.

Salutation

Whenever we know the name of the person to whom we are writing, we should use his name in the salutation; for example, 'Dear Mr Brown'. When we do not know the name, we should use the salutation, 'Dear Sir'. Feminists may object to this, but it is just as awkward to write 'Dear Sir/Madam' as it is to write 'he or she'. Of course, it is always preferable to use the name of the person and it is often possible to find out the name of the person to whom we are addressing the letter. As we have already said, it makes such a difference to the receiver when the letter is addressed to him by name.

The salutation begins against the left-hand margin, the same margin used for the address of the receiver. There should always be a clear space between the address of the receiver and the salutation, and between the salutation and the next part of the letter, whether it be the topic of a business letter or the first paragraph of a less formal letter. Such spacing is important because it gives the letter a pleasing impression of openness and neatness.

Topic heading

Every formal business letter should have a topic heading. It helps the receiver to know exactly what the letter is about. This in turn helps the receiver sometimes to redirect the letter to the correct department that handles such correspondence. The topic heading begins against the left-hand margin and is either in capital letters or is underlined. It should not be underlined if it is in capital letters. There should be a space before and after the topic heading.

Paragraphing

Each paragraph in a letter should begin at the left-hand margin. The days of measuring an inch from the margin for the start of each new paragraph have gone. A space is left between paragraphs. The only problem with this kind of block paragraphing is that the separation of paragraphs is not always clear when a paragraph ends close to the right-hand margin at the end of a page. Managers and type-setters should be aware of this and should avoid any possible confusion.

The first and last paragraphs of a business letter are usually short, with the other paragraphs usually longer since they contain the substance of the letter. Some writers prefer to make the first paragraph a short statement, such as 'Thank you for your letter of 16 June.' We prefer that the first paragraph should be slightly more explicit: 'Thank you for your letter of 16 June, in which you enquired about our latest range of photocopiers.' The opening sentence should be a complete sentence and should not be a phrase such as 'With reference to your letter of 16 June.' The last paragraph, as with every paragraph, should always obey the rules of sentence structure. There is an unfortunate relic from the past that persists with many letter writers: they end a letter with a present participial phrase such as, 'Hoping to hear from you at your earliest convenience'. This is not a sentence. Such endings appear because it was a convention in the past that the ending of a letter used the construction , 'I remain': the idea was that the closing participial phrase then linked with the subject of the main verb in this way:

```
Hoping to hear from you at your earliest convenience,

I remain,
Yours faithfully,
John Smith.
```

We do not use this form of ending any longer and a present participial phrase as the last paragraph is therefore wrong. It is correct to write the last paragraph as a proper sentence, for example, 'I look forward to hearing from you.' We should not, however, be so pedantic as to consider sentences such as 'Regards to Tom Jones' or 'Best wishes' as incomplete sentences. In informal letters such abbreviated sentences can be very appropriate in establishing the right tone.

Ending
A business letter usually ends with either of two conventional endings, 'Yours sincerely' or 'Yours faithfully'. Government departments often use such absurd endings as 'Your obedient servant', and American writers often turn the ending around as 'Sincerely yours' or 'Cordially yours', but in South Africa we prefer to end with 'Yours sincerely' or 'Yours faithfully'. 'Yours sincerely' is used when we have addressed the person by name and when the salutation has included the name of the person, e.g. 'Dear Mr Jones'. 'Yours faithfully' is used when we have not addressed the person by name and when the salutation has taken the form, 'Dear Sir'. It follows from what we have said previously about the desirability of addressing the receiver by name, that 'Yours sincerely' is the better ending.

After 'Yours sincerely' or 'Yours faithfully' the signature should follow and then the name of the writer of the letter should be printed or typed in capitals.

Lastly, the person's title (if any) should be written or typed. The full ending will then look like this:

```
Yours sincerely




J.G. BROWN
Manager
```

Even if the signature is readable, the name should be repeated in capitals to prevent any doubts about the correct name. A man never puts Mr after his name at the end of a letter — this is considered a bad mistake — but a woman should include (Mrs) or (Miss) after the printed or typed name in capitals — this is merely to help the person replying to the letter either in writing or by speech to know how to address the person. The 'Ms' form of address for a woman has not yet found general acceptance.

The ending of a letter should never appear on a new page on its own. The letter should be rewritten or retyped to fit the ending on the first page or re-spaced so that some of the body of the letter will appear on the second page with the ending.

Different Types of Letters

We shall now give examples of different types of letters:
- ❑ order or enquiry letters
- ❑ letters of complaint
- ❑ adjustment letters
- ❑ collection letters
- ❑ credit letters
- ❑ sales letters and persuasive writing
- ❑ official letters
- ❑ letters to the press
- ❑ letters of application for employment

Order or enquiry letters

These letters should be short and to the point and should give precise details of what is being ordered or what the enquiry is about. (For those writing examinations it is important to remember that a letter (or a report or a memorandum, for that matter) should always start on a new page. We shall obey this rule by using in this book a new page for each letter.) Here is an example of a letter of enquiry and of an order letter.

Riordan Publishers
346 Berg Street
PIETERMARITZBURG
3201

15 June 1992

The Manager
Clarens Lodge
P.O. Box 5791
CLARENS
9707

Dear Sir

ACCOMMODATION 16-22 SEPTEMBER

A party of twelve from the Riordan Publishers wishes to
spend the week 16-22 September at your hotel and to make
use of your conference facilities during this time.

We shall require three double rooms and six single rooms,
all with private bathrooms. The conference facilities required are a room similar to a boardroom and another room
with movable chairs and small tables suitable for discussions and work sessions. It is possible that we might require the conference facilities in the evenings as well.
It would be appreciated if these rooms could be sufficiently separated from the rest of the hotel so that interruptions or noise could be kept to the minimum.
Morning and afternoon refreshments would be required in
the conference rooms, but meals could be eaten in the
main dining-room as long as the party of twelve could be
placed at one table. On 19 September there will be no
afternoon work session, and I should like you to let me
know what recreational facilities or excursions would be
suitable for that afternoon. The party will arrive for
lunch on 16 September and leave after lunch on 22 September.

Please let me know whether you have accommodation and conference facilities available for these days and what your
tariff would be. I should like you also to tell me what
equipment (e.g. an overhead projector, and a video machine) is available as part of your conference facilities. As soon as I hear from you, I shall send you

the required deposit if we decide to make use of your services during this week in September.

If you wish to have any other details and to discuss them
with me on the telephone, please ring me at (0331) 942-
567.

Yours faithfully

J Riordan

. J. RIORDAN (MRS)
ADMINISTRATIVE MANAGER
Riordan Publishers

Riorden Publishers
346 Berg Street
PIETERMARITZBURG
3201
1992-06-15

Mrs S. Barnard
Sonbar & Co.
P.O. Box 5795
CLUBVIEW
0157

Dear Mrs Barnard

ORDER NO. 5874

Kindly send me the following books:

The Art of Participative Management by G. Werdna (Highlight Press, Johannesburg, 1985).

The Industrial Relations Handbook, 1992, published by the
Industrial Relations Institute, Johannesburg.

Getting It Right — The Manager's Guide to Business Communication by Adey and Andrew (Juta, Cape Town, 1990).

Please enclose your invoice and charge the cost of the
books and postage to our account (No. 374). We shall be
pleased to receive our usual trade discount of 7,5 %.

Yours sincerely

J. Riordan

J. RIORDAN (MRS)
ADMINISTRATIVE MANAGER

Letters of complaint

In business it is unfortunately necessary from time to time to have to complain about something. When this has to be done in a letter, it is important to be polite and at the same time to express the complaint firmly and clearly. Although our natural reaction to poor service may be high-handed indignation, we need to bear in mind that it is unwise to affect adversely any business relationship. Every business letter is a public relations exercise and needs to demonstrate fairness and understanding. No business can afford to set itself up as a paragon of virtue since we all know that no one is perfect and that our own business also receives complaints that are justified. The maxims of 'Judge not that ye be not judged' and 'Do unto others as you would have them do unto you' are as applicable in business as in personal life. Let us consider the following letter of complaint.

British African Corporation
P.O. Box 9124
JOHANNESBURG
2000

2 July 1992

The Registrar (Academic Fees)
Finance Division
Pietermaritzburg University
P.O. Box 537
PIETERMARITZBURG
3200

Dear Sir

Fees A.J. Marcus Student No. 80318135

Your student Andrew John Marcus is a recipient of a bursary from our corporation. On 31 March you issued a statement for Mr Marcus's fees for the balance of R1 665,00,
and we sent a cheque by registered post on 23 May for
this amount. The registered article number was 31/1734
from the Johannesburg Post Office. I trust that you have
received this amount because it was deposited in your account on 25 May and has been debited to our bank account.

Despite this we have received another statement dated 31
May indicating there is still an amount of R1 665,00 due.
We received this statement only on 30 June. A copy of
your statement is enclosed.

Your statement indicated that there is a late payment penalty levied on any unpaid balance at 30 June and that students who have not paid their accounts in full by 30 June
will be excluded from attending future lectures and de-
barred from writing examinations in the second term.

Last year we experienced the same problem, and you indicated in July to Mr Marcus that you had not received the
second term's fees and would impose the late payment
levy. I am sure that you will understand that such complications cause anxiety to Mr Marcus and affect his
studies. Although you showed consideration and did not en-

force the late penalty levy last year after we had sub-
mitted proof that our cheque was sent to you, it now appears that this continuing problem lies with your
administration, and we should like you to rectify it so
that it does not happen again.

I look forward to your reply.

Yours faithfully

P G Anderson

P.G. ANDERSON
FINANCIAL DIRECTOR

Finance Division
University of
 Pietermaritzburg
P.O. Box 537
PIETERMARITZBURG
3200
1992-07-09

Mr P.G. Anderson
The Financial Director
British African Corporation
P.O. Box 9124
JOHANNESBURG
2000

Dear Mr Anderson

Fees A.J. Marcus Student No. 80318135

Thank you for your letter of 2 July, in which you enquired about payment of Mr Marcus's fees.

I have referred to Mr Marcus's accounts for 1991 and
1992. We regret that for two years running you have been
inconvenienced by having to write to us about payment of
his fees. We accept that the cheque you sent in 1991 was
mislaid either by the Post Office or by our administration. It is for this reason that we did not impose the
late payment penalty. I understand what you say about the
effect it has on the student's studies, and I have instructed my staff that in future all queries about his account will be directed to your firm for your attention
and not to Mr Marcus.

You are quite correct that your cheque for R1 665,00 was
deposited in the university's bank account on 25 May and
therefore your statement of 31 May should have reflected
this. Please accept our apologies for this. The credit
has been shown on the statement of 30 June, which is probably on its way to you now. I cannot understand why the
statement of 31 May took so long to reach you. In case
there is a similar postal delay with the June statement,
I have enclosed a copy with this letter.

May I take this opportunity to thank you on behalf of the
university for your generous sponsorship of Mr Marcus's
studies. His Dean informs me that he is progressing well
with his work this year.

Yours sincerely

F S Wine

F.S. WINE
REGISTRAR (ACADEMIC FEES)

Finance Division
University of Pietermaritzburg
P.O. Box 537
PIETERMARITZBURG
3200
1992-07-09

Mr P.G. Anderson
The Financial Director
British African Corporation
P.O. Box 9124
JOHANNESBURG
2000

Dear Mr Anderson

FEES A.J. MARCUS STUDENT NO. 80318135

Thank you for your letter of 2 July, in which you enquired about payment of Mr Marcus's fees for the second
term of 1991 and 1992.

In 1991 the University definitely did not receive payment
by 30 June, but we allowed your firm the opportunity to
remit the fees late without imposing a late penalty. This
year we received your cheque late in May and therefore
the credit has been reflected in your June statement,
which has already been sent to you. Mr Marcus will not
suffer in any way because his fees have been paid before
the due date.

You will, I am sure, understand that we have to keep
strict control over payment of fees and it is in accordance with this policy that we have to enforce certain
regulations.

We appreciate the concern you show for Mr Marcus and we
assure you that we share this concern.

If in future you wish to ensure that no problems arise,
you may like to send payments by registered post and for
my personal attention.

Yours sincerely

F S Wine

F.S. WINE
REGISTRAR (ACADEMIC FEES)

In the first letter the tone is conciliatory and apologetic, but not too apologetic. There are two theories about apologizing in a business letter. One theory is that we should take an attitude similar to that we are advised to take by our insurance agents: never admit liability; it is considered dangerous to admit culpability in case we are sued. The other theory is to be honest and apologize freely. The writers of this book consider that there is a middle road: apologize where it does not implicate the business in a serious way but do not ever be too apologetic. The first letter takes this middle road: the writer 'regrets' that Mr Anderson has been 'inconvenienced' but does not acknowledge blame for losing the 1991 cheque; he then implies there may have been some misjudgement in referring the query to Mr Marcus instead of to the sponsor and promises a different approach in future; he openly apologizes for the indisputable error in not crediting the payment on the May statement, but does not acknowledge responsibility for the late arrival of the May statement, even though it is likely that it was the University administration that was at fault. The letter ends with a paragraph that is friendly and shows interest in both the sponsor and the student. It is unlikely that Mr Anderson could be at all offended by such a letter.

The second letter offers no apology and makes it clear that the complaint is not justified. It appeals to Mr Anderson to understand the University's policy and in its turn understands and shares Mr Anderson's concern for the student's studies. The letter ends with a positive helpful gesture to prevent any further problem. Again it is unlikely that the recipient will be offended.

Letters of adjustment
There is another kind of letter that is more of an accounting adjustment. This may be a letter to a debtor who has disputed certain debits to his account and has therefore withheld payments. The next example deals with such a letter of adjustment. The letter after this one is a letter that sets out a rather complicated adjustment arising from certain mistakes on the part of the debtor and resulting in overpayment. In each of the letters the emphasis must be on the facts, and there should be no suggestion of criticism of the debtor but rather a polite request to rectify the mistake.

ABC Trading Limited
P.O. Box 1234
JOHANNESBURG
2000
1991-10-25

Mr M.C. van Wyk
The Accountant
XYZ Retailers Ltd
P.O. Box 428
JOHANNESBURG
2000

Dear Mr van Wyk

YOUR ACCOUNT 567

Thank you for your letter of 21 September, in which you
query our June debit on the grounds that the goods were
never delivered to you.

We have in our possession a delivery note for that consignment. This delivery note has been signed by someone
who, we believe, is from XYZ Retailers. For your convenience we enclose a photocopy of this delivery note, which
we consider to be proof of delivery. We trust that you
will be able to investigate this matter and let us have
payment of this amount, as well as the subsequent debits
of R600,82 for August and R982,15 for September.

We value your custom and look forward to receiving your
cheque for R2 486,06 made up as follows:

June	52,86
August	600,82
September	982,15
October	850,23
Total Due	R2 486,06

If there are any further queries about your account,
please do not hesitate to phone me (29-2358).

Yours sincerely

P.J. Brown

P.J. BROWN
ACCOUNTANT

Encl.:
Photocopy of delivery note for June consignment.

                                        FGH Manufacturers Ltd
                                        P.O. Box 952
                                        JOHANNESBURG
                                        2000

                                        22 October 1992

The Accountant
IJK Wholesalers Ltd
P.O. Box 587
JOHANNESBURG
2000

Dear Sir

ACCOUNT NO. 586

Thank you for your recent payment of R1 026,80 together
with your remittance advice.

On comparing your remittance advice with the records in
our books, we find the following:

1. Invoice No. 57 has been overpaid by R10,00.

2. Included in your payment is an Invoice No. A278 for
    R500,00, but this invoice was not issued by FGH Manufac-
    turers Ltd. We now return this invoice to you.

3. Invoice No. 42 was for R475,00 less 10 % trade discount,
    but you have not taken this discount of R47,50.

4. Invoice No. 26 for R520,40 has not been paid although it
    was dated 15 July 1992. It appears that you have over-
    looked this payment. We have a copy of the delivery
    note for these goods duly signed on behalf of IJK Whole-
    salers and submit a photocopy for your attention.

5. According to your remittance advice you have deducted
    R78,50 for Credit Note No. 14. This credit note was ac-
    tually for R58,50 as can be seen from the copy which we
    enclose.

Because of these adjustments, we calculate that you have
a credit of R17,10 made up as follows:

	DEBIT	CREDIT
Credit from Invoice No. 58		R 10,00
Credit from Invoice No. A278		R500,00
Discount on Invoice No. 42		R 47,50
Debit from Invoice No. 26	R520,40	
Debit from Credit No. 14	R 20,00	
Balancing figure	R 17,10	
	R557,50	R557,50

Please investigate and let me know whether you agree with our findings.

Yours faithfully

N.O. BROOKS
ACCOUNTANT

Encl.:
1. Invoice No. A278.
2. Copy of delivery note with reference to Invoice No. 26.
3. Credit Note No. 14.

Collection letters

Closely associated with letters of adjustment are collection letters. These are letters that try to 'collect' outstanding debts. Debtors who receive collection letters are always sensitive about receiving them and very often complain when they receive them, even though they know that they have not paid their accounts and that there is reason for the collection letters being sent. Nobody likes to receive such a letter, and the recipient therefore looks for every excuse to object to it: perhaps he has already paid the amount, albeit late; perhaps he objects to the tone of the letter; perhaps he finds a mistake in the letter. This kind of sensitivity looks for every reason to react angrily to a collection letter.

We must therefore as managers have a clear policy about collection letters. Some firms with computerized accounts have a terse comment that is printed out automatically on the statement when the account is overdue. Other firms use standardized letters often printed on letterheads purporting to come from a debt collection bureau and containing legal jargon intended to frighten the debtor. We believe that there is a place for a series of standard letters that are sent as a matter of course when the account has been overdue for specific periods. The value of the standard letter is that, with such sensitive issues, the letter will have been approved by a senior person and it will not have been written by an inexperienced person. Standard letters save time and money, and when there are many debtors to remind, the least possible additions to the standard letter will help to get the letters out on time. There are, of course, disadvantages about standard letters: sometimes a person who should have received a different letter receives the standard letter that does not quite suit his circumstances and he is annoyed by it; if a customer's account is frequently in arrears, he will receive the same letter often and he may despise the firm for sending out standard letters. No one likes to be considered a number who is not treated as an individual.

With these reservations we do, however, consider that standard letters have a place if they are sensitively worded and sensitively used. We offer a few examples of standard paragraphs that could be used to suit various occasions.

YOUR OVERDUE ACCOUNT NO . . .

According to our records your account is three months in arrears. Since our credit policy is that accounts should be paid within thirty days of statement, we respectfully ask you to settle the overdue amount of . . .

If you have any query about your account, please telephone me so that I may help you. We value your custom and would like to be able to extend credit facilities to you in the future, but we regret that we can do this only if your account is in good standing.

URGENT REQUEST TO SETTLE YOUR ACCOUNT NO . . .

Last month I wrote to you about your overdue account. As yet we have received no reply or payment. Your account is now four months in arrears. The outstanding amount is . . .

If you are experiencing difficulties and wish to discuss the matter with me, please do not hesitate to do so. I look forward to speaking to you or receiving your payment within fourteen days.

Please regard this as urgent.

NOTICE OF DEBT COLLECTION PROCEDURE: ACCOUNT NO . . .

Despite previous reminders and offers of help we have not heard from you about your account, which is now five months in arrears. According to our records the amount of . . . is overdue.

We now reluctantly inform you that unless your account is settled within seven days of the date of this letter, it will be handed over to a debt collection agency. Such a procedure will cost you more money and will prevent you from obtaining credit facilities at a wide range of business houses.

We hope that this procedure will not be necessary and that you will send us your payment NOW.

Such standard paragraphs require the minimum of individual details to be inserted and maintain a polite but firm tone. It is important to give details of the number of months in arrears and in the second and third letters the number of days within which payment is expected. If the business adopts a policy of collection letters going out for all accounts three, four, and five months in arrears — it could , of course, be two, three, and four months — then such details can be included in the standard letters.

It is important, however, that collection letters should be personalized. Some businesses send out standard letters or notices in legal jargon without the name of the person or any personal details at all; these are inserts with the monthly statements and can be offensive to the recipient, especially if the person responsible for the mechanical insertion of the standard notices makes a mistake and sends the offensive notice to the wrong customer!

Personalization helps to avoid this, and although it may be more time-consuming, is better for customer relations.

The first and second standard letters take a more personal, helpful tone than the third letter. The reason for this is that the debtor may have serious personal problems, and the business therefore gives him the opportunity to explain these. No businessman would wish to kick a debtor when he is down, and debtors appreciate sympathy and understanding action on the part of the creditor. In South Africa where there are many social reasons for debt and family disorder, it is important not to appear hard and grasping. There will, of course, be those who will take advantage of such offers to explain their difficulties and may even make up 'hard-luck stories', but a discerning manager should be able to see through the insincere requests for help. If the firm adopts such an understanding approach, it need have no qualms about the more distant and threatening third letter and the subsequent 'handing over' to a debt collection agency. Because of the expense of tracing, debt collection, and court action, many firms do not go so far as to hand over accounts of less than three hundred rands. It is therefore all the more important that the collection letters perform their task properly.

Credit letters

We have discussed collection letters in which the creditor tries to collect the debt from a person to whom he has allowed credit; we now turn to letters asking for credit. The nature of business economics in South Africa demands the use of credit facilities, and the business that does not give credit to its customers and does not take credit facilities from its suppliers or financial institutions will not succeed in the competitive business environment of our times.

The manager should be able to compose a good letter applying for credit. This may be to a supplier or to a financial institution. His aim in writing the letter will be to provide enough information to convince the supplier of credit that he will be a trustworthy debtor and that he has sufficient commercial backing to make him a stable businessman. Although most credit applications are on standardized forms, the initial letter should make an impression of sound business principle.

A manager must also know how to reply to applications for credit. Such replies can grant or deny facilities. Both types require tact and understanding, and must also show a sound awareness of business practice.

Since there are so many different kinds of credit letters, we shall not be able to give an example of each, but let us give attention to the small businessman applying for credit to a supplier from whom he has previously been buying on a cash basis.

LMN Retailers CC No. 854762
P.O. Box 9876
JOHANNESBURG
2000
1992-07-07

Mr A.B. Seedee
The Financial Manager
IJK Wholesalers Ltd
P.O. Box 587
JOHANNESBURG
2000

Dear Mr Seedee

APPLICATION FOR CREDIT FACILITIES

My firm has been buying supplies from yours for the last
eighteen months on a cash basis. Since my business has
grown considerably during the last six months, I have
been advised by my financial advisers to apply to you for
credit facilities.

I have been buying on average R1 000 worth of supplies
per month. I envisage that, with credit facilities, I
shall be able to double this amount. I therefore request
credit facilities of R2 000 per month payable within
sixty days. If there are trade discounts applying to re-
payments within thirty days, please let me know your
terms.

To substantiate my application, I enclose my audited financial statements for the year ending 29 February 1992.
My bankers are First Azanian Bank (Bree Street Branch),
and the Manager, Mr F.G.H. Eyejay, has agreed to provide
you with any information about my financial standing that
you may require. His telephone number is 337-2358.

For an overview of my close corporation I enclose also a
copy of the founding statement of LMN Retailers CC. My
fellow members and I shall be pleased to meet with you if
you wish to discuss any details of my application. You
may ring me (337-5713 — direct line) or if I am not available, my fellow-member, Mr Kayell (337-5872).

I trust that such a credit arrangement between us will be
a mutually beneficial business venture that will be
strengthened over the years.

Yours sincerely

M.N.Opeekiew

M.N. OPEEKIEW
MANAGING DIRECTOR

Official letters

There are times when we have to write letters to people in official positions and we are expected to observe rules of protocol. The writers of this book consider that much of this protocol is affected and needs to be scrapped, but for those who wish to observe protocol the following may be helpful.

Here are some conventional forms of letter writing for the following people of rank in South Africa:

TITLE	ADDRESS	SALUTATION	ENDING
President	The Rt. Honble. the President	Your Excellency or Sir	I have the honour to be, Sir, Your most obedient servant
Prime Minister	The Rt. Honble. the Prime Minister	Your Excellency or Sir	I have the honour to be, Sir, Your most obedient servant
Cabinet Minister	The Honble. the Minister for	Sir	Yours faithfully
Administrator	The Honble. the Adminstrator of	Sir	Yours faithfully
Member of Parliament	W. Demies, Esq., MP for	Dear Sir	Yours faithfully
Mayor	The Worshipful the Mayor of	Sir	Yours faithfully
Ambassador	His Excellency the Ambassador of	Your Excellency	I have the honour to be Your Excellency's most humble and obedient servant
Chief Justice	The Honble. B.P. Jones, Chief Justice	Sir	Yours faithfully
Judge of the Supreme Court	The Honble. Mr Justice D.C. Rex	Sir	Yours faithfully
Archbishop	His Grace the Lord Archbishop of	Your Grace	Your Grace's devoted and obedient servant
Bishop	The Right Reverend the Lord Bishop of	My Lord	Your lordship's most devoted servant
Clergyman	The Rev. M.G. Drew	Sir	Yours faithfully

We have tried to pare these conventions to the minimum since we believe that it is the tone and the contents of the letter and not the conventions that are important. Again an example may serve our purpose better.

St Joseph's Orphanage
P.O. Box 3456
JOHANNESBURG
2000

12 July 1992

C. Hickson, Esq.
M.P. for Bezuidenhout
32 Rollo St
CYRILDENE
2198

Dear Sir

OPENING CEREMONY AT GARDEN PARTY IN AID OF ST JOSEPH'S OR-
PHANAGE

On behalf of the Management Committee of the St Joseph's
Orphanage I should like to invite you to perform the Opening Ceremony at the Garden Party in aid of St Joseph's Orphanage. This Garden Party will be held on 15 November at
St Joseph's Orphanage, 23 Missionary St, Observatory.

Guests will arrive at 2.30 p.m. and the Opening Ceremony
will be held at 3.10. The proposed programme is as follows:

3.00 p.m.   Welcome and Introductory Remarks
                       by the Chairman

3.05 p.m.   Introduction of the M.P. for
                       Bezuidenhout by the Rev. J.P. Marshall

3.10 p.m.   Address and Opening Ceremony by the M.P.
                       for Bezuidenhout

3.30 p.m.   Garden Party

4.15 p.m.   Tour of the Orphanage by the Guests

The purpose of the Garden Party is to raise funds for the
Orphanage and in particular for the new accommodation
block to be built in 1993. For your interest I enclose
our latest report and financial statements. The Orphanage
at present houses eighty children from the Witwatersrand
area and is interdenominational though the Orphanage was
started by the Church of the Province of South Africa. It
is now run by an interdenominational Board of Control and
is a registered Welfare Institution.

We are well aware of your interest in community affairs and social welfare and we appreciate your support in the past. Your acceptance of this invitation will contribute greatly to the success of our endeavour. In your address we would appreciate your comments on the role of social services by the private sector and the extent to which the government may be able to subsidize such efforts in the future.

We sincerely hope that you will be able to fit our function into your busy schedule of activities. Kindly let us know as soon as possible whether you will be able to accept our invitation. If you are, I shall be pleased to discuss further the details of who will meet you and your wife, the seating arrangements, and any other appropriate arrangements.

Yours faithfully

G Werdna

G. WERDNA
CHAIRMAN
MANAGEMENT COMMITTEE

Before we move on from this section on official letters, let us mention a particular barbarism that has crept into South African English usage. It is the use of the title 'Reverend Brown' or sometimes 'The Reverend'. The correct way to address a minister of religion is 'The Reverend Bill Brown' or 'The Reverend W. Brown' or 'The Rev. Mr Brown'. The word 'reverend' is an adjective and not a noun like the words 'priest', 'minister', 'pastor', 'rabbi' and 'predikant'; it should not then be used as a noun, 'The Reverend'. It is a convention of respect to the ministry that one should not write or say, 'The Reverend Brown', but one should rather use an initial, a first name, or the additional "Mr' before the surname.

Letters to the press

From time to time businessmen may consider it fitting to write letters to the press on social or topical issues. Such letters may provide publicity for the business in the same way as press, radio or television interviews do. Sometimes these letters are necessary to answer public criticism of the enterprise's social commitment; for example, criticism of pollution by a manufacturing enterprise.

The letter to the editor of a newspaper is set out differently from other letters. The address of the sender appears *after* the letter, as does the date. The reason for this is that the letter is written as if it were the printer's copy ready for publication. The letter should be concise and of general interest. Although an editor may publish a letter with a *nom de plume* (i.e. an assumed name), he will not publish a letter unless the writer's name and address are provided. Often box numbers are considered too impersonal, and physical addresses are preferred. The editor has to ensure that the letter does not contain insulting or libellous remarks, and therefore the identity of the writer is important.

Here is a letter to the press that was published in *The Star* on 24 February 1989; it was written by A.S.K. Joommal, who is a consummate writer of letters to the press and who is himself an editor. It is reproduced here with his kind permission. The letter is first shown as it would have looked when posted, and then as it appeared in *The Star*. Notice the heading or topic of the letter and the effective opening and closing sentences of the letter.

The Editor
The Star
P.O. Box 1014
JOHANNESBURG
2000

Sir

THREAT TO SALMAN RUSHDIE IS MISPLACED RELIGIOUS FERVOUR

There is no doubt that Salman Rushdie, author of 'The Satanic Verses', is *persona non grata* to the entire Muslim world and has earned its just opprobrium.

However, it is quite another thing for individuals and organizations to play judge, jury and executioner with such supercilious sanctimony. It is highly reprehensible and morally unthinkable that a spiritual leader should offer a lucrative inducement to assassins.

This action throws international standards of behaviour and the Islamic norms of justice overboard and is the first step towards creating anarchy and terrorism — something the civilized world cannot tolerate. Since when is smashing up of embassies and willful destruction of property an 'Islamic' act?

No one — not even Rushdie — can be summarily executed at the behest of one man, or any number of men, without being accorded fair trial by the country with jurisdiction to do so and being afforded the opportunity to recant and repent. The very cornerstone of Islamic Law is absolute, total, uncompromising justice.

Those who are after Rushdie's blood are violating the injunction of the Almighty, ignoring the example of Prophet Muhammed, and are taking God's law and man's law into their own hands. Religious fervour is a good thing, but when misplaced and allowed to rule reason and common sense, it will be transformed into rabid, blind fanaticism which will generate gruesome consequences.

Civilization, after all, is the triumph of persuasion over violence.

A.S.K.Joommal

A.S.K.Joommal
Editor
Al-Balaagh
JOHANNESBURG

A.S.K.Joommal
Editor
Al-Balaagh
28 Lark Street
Lenasia
1820

22 February 1989

Threat to Salman Rushdie is misplaced religious fervour

There is no doubt that Salman Rushdie, author of 'The Satanic Verses', is *persona non grata* to the entire Muslim world and has earned its just opprobrium.

However, it is quite another thing for individuals and organizations to play judge, jury and executioner with such supercilious sanctimony. It is highly reprehensible and morally unthinkable that a spiritual leader should offer a lucrative inducement to assassins.

This action throws international standards of behaviour and the Islamic norms of justice overboard and is the first step towards creating anarchy and terrorism — something the civilized world cannot tolerate. Since when is smashing up of embassies and wilful destruction of property an 'Islamic' act?

No one — not even Rushdie — can be summarily executed at the behest of one man, or any number of men, without being accorded fair trial by the country with jurisdiction to do so and being afforded the opportunity to recant and repent. The very cornerstone of Islamic Law is absolute, total, uncompromising justice.

Those who are after Rushdie's blood are violating the injunction of the Almighty, ignoring the example of Prophet Muhammed, and are taking God's law and man's law into their own hands. Religious fervour is a good thing, but when misplaced and allowed to rule reason and common sense, it will be transformed into rabid, blind fanaticism which will generate gruesome consequences.

Civilization, after all, is the triumph of persuasion over violence.

A.S.K. Joommal
Editor *Al-Balaagh*

Johannesburg

Letters of application for employment

We have already referred to interviewing in this book. Most interviewers place a great deal of importance on the letter of application if the interview is an employment interview. The letter of application is the first impression of the candidate's worth and should therefore be very carefully written. Managers receiving such letters should carefully assess the candidates by their letters of application and could save themselves time spent in interviewing unworthy candidates. Of course, the letter of application is not the only judge of a candidate's worth, but it does give a very good indication.

There are very few letters of application for employment that would not include *curricula vitae*. Most would merely be covering letters for the sub-mission of a C.V. We shall discuss the C.V. in the next section of this chapter, but let us first give an example of a letter of application.

The essential components of a letter of application are

- ❑ mention of the post applied for
- ❑ personal details
- ❑ qualifications
- ❑ work experience
- ❑ reasons for leaving
- ❑ referees
- ❑ availability for interview
- ❑ telephone number(s)
- ❑ certified copies of qualifications.

                                                    12 Lewes Street
                                                    Auckland Park
                                                    JOHANNESBURG
                                                    2092

                                                    23 December 1992

The Personnel Officer
R.S. Breweries Ltd
P.O. Box 1
JOHANNESBURG
2000

Dear Sir

POST: TRAINEE-ADMINISTRATION OFFICER OR TRAINEE-ACCOUNTANT

I should like to be considered for the post of trainee-ad-
ministrative officer or trainee-accountant as advertised
in the *Evening News* of 22 December.

I am twenty years of age, male, and unmarried. I was educated at Dalecross College, where I completed my secondary education, obtaining a matriculation exemption with
the following subjects: English First Language Higher
Grade, Afrikaans Second Language Higher Grade, Mathematics Higher Grade, Accounting Higher Grade, Economics
Higher Grade, and Business Economics Standard Grade.

I am at present studying for my Diploma in Business Administration by correspondence and have passed the first
four subjects, Economics, Management Information Systems,
Financial Accounting, and Business Law. I hold the Certificate in Business Administration from the South African
Institute of Management (SAIM) and have recently written
the next two subjects, Management 1 and Human Resources
Management 1, for which I am awaiting my results. The Diploma in Business Administration consists of a total of
twelve subjects, and I am therefore half way through the
course of study.

I have two years' experience of accountancy, working as
one of four debtors' account clerks for Wholesalers Ltd.
My present salary is R3 000 per annum and will be subject
to review in the new year.

While at school I was a school prefect and represented
the school twice in the inter-school debating contest. I
played first-team cricket and captained the school soccer
team. I now play first division soccer. My other hobbies

are reading and listening to music. I am at present the Chairman of the SAIM Students' Society.

The only reason I have for wishing to leave my present employer is that the opportunities for experience in administration and accounting are limited, and I feel I may have more to offer than my present position allows. The conditions of employment that your advertisement offers appeal to me.

Mr J.D. Brookes, M.A.,B.Sc., the principal of Dalecross College (tel. 836-2211), and the Rev. D. Fraser of St James' Church, Auckland Park (tel. 844-3214) have kindly agreed to act as referees on my behalf. I do not wish my present employees to be consulted, but Mr C.C. Morris, the Executive Director of the SAIM, is prepared to comment on my studies and my present work experience; he may be phoned at 339-6324.

If my application interests you, I shall be available for an interview at any time convenient to you. My home phone number is 844-1234 and my work number is 337-1098.

Yours faithfully

D. Smithers

D. SMITHERS

Encl.:
1. Matriculation Certificate (certified copy)
2. Certificate in Business Administration
   (certified copy).

Closely associated with letters of application for employment are testimonials, letters of resignation, and letters informing applicants of their success or failure in their applications. In all three of these types of letters it is important to be tactful and understanding of the recipient's feelings. One never knows when these letters may be used against the writer: for instance, an exaggerated testimonial may make the reader of the testimonial think badly of the writer and his organization; a letter that is too critical of a person or a firm may cause antagonism that lasts for years and may be proved totally wrong. An educator or an employer should avoid trying to be a prophet of a person's future: so often such predictions have been proved disastrously wrong. The best advice that can be offered is that these letters should be factual and sincere without judgement or flattery or recriminations.

CURRICULA VITAE

The *curriculum vitae* (or C.V. as it has come to be called) is an essential part of every manager's personal file. Whereas it is mainly used for applications for employment, it now serves a variety of purposes: if you are asked to give a talk, the organizers will ask you for a C.V.; if you submit an article for a publication, a resumé of your C.V. will be required; if you apply for a scholarship or a fellowship or if you are invited to a conference, you may have to submit a C.V. This document, for which the Latin means simply the course of your life, has become a *sine qua non* for any businessman. He must also be able to judge others' *curricula vitae*. (The plural of *curriculum vitae* is either *curricula vitae* or *curriculums vitae*.)

It is a common fallacy that a person's C.V., once written, can serve with minor updating for any purpose. This is dangerous because a C.V. should be composed with a particular purpose in mind and should be arranged for the reader's convenience. So often we receive C.V.s that are hastily photocopied and either are out of date or contain irrelevant details. Whereas it is true that certain personal details do not change, the C.V. should be carefully re-arranged for each new purpose.

Subject to these provisos, let us look at the components of a C.V. They are:

❏   HEADING: CURRICULUM VITAE
❏   PERSONAL DETAILS
❏   EDUCATION
❏   WORK EXPERIENCE
❏   REFERENCES
❏   PUBLICATIONS, RESEARCH, PUBLIC ADDRESSES, etc.
❏   PRESENT SALARY

Apart from the heading, each of these should be on a separate page or at least comprise a different section of the C.V. The advantage of this is that the C.V.

can easily be re-arranged or adapted to suit the particular purpose of submission.

Personal Details

In this section of the C.V. we include

❑ surname
❑ other names
❑ date of birth
❑ identity number
❑ marital status
❑ names of the spouse and the children (usually with their ages or dates of birth)
❑ residential address and home telephone number
❑ postal address (if different from the residential address)
❑ business address and telephone number.

Sometimes these details are also included:

❑ state of health
❑ languages spoken and the degree of fluency in speaking, writing, and reading
❑ army commitments
❑ religion.

Education

Under this heading we include:

❑ schooling with subjects included in the final examination and the name of the school attended
❑ post-school education with the name of the educational institution and the qualification(s) with details of subjects studied
❑ any other educational achievements, e.g. bursaries, scholarships, fellowships, distinctions.

Sometimes, although it does not strictly come under the heading of education, we include, either here or under a separate heading, membership of professional bodies.

Work Experience

Here we list the positions occupied during our working life. The authors of this book prefer the most recent positions to be given first because these are the most relevant to the reader. The periods of unemployment are important, and the specific duties performed should be mentioned.

References

The names and addresses of at least two referees and their telephone numbers should be given. These referees should be able to give confidential information on the personality, the academic ability, and the work performance of the person submitting the *curriculum vitae*. There was a time when testimonials were provided with a *curriculum vitae*, but these days testimonials tend to be too complimentary to be valuable, and confidential references are more highly regarded. It is important, therefore, to choose one's referees carefully to ensure that they will be able to give full and relevant details when they are approached. It is important to obtain the permission of the referees before their names and addresses and telephone numbers are provided so that they will be prepared for any possible approaches. Acting as a referee is a time-consuming task, and a person should not take such a service for granted.

Publications, Research, Public Addresses, etc.

Not every C.V. will include this information because the person may not have published, may not be or may not have been engaged in research, and may not have given any public addresses, but if one has, it is important to mention these details for certain purposes, especially for academic purposes.

Present Salary

Some consider that this is not advisable, but we consider this information to be important for certain purposes.

A *curriculum vitae* can be drawn up in such a way that each of these sections can be provided on a separate page. This allows for easy up-dating and for the selection and omission of certain sections according to their relevance to the purpose of the submission of the *curriculum vitae* .

MEMORANDA AND NOTICES

A business frequently uses memoranda for easy written communication within an organization. Usually, but not necessarily, the memorandum form is preprinted with the name of the business and the words MEMORANDUM, FROM, TO, DATE, and SUBJECT. These are the essentials for the layout of a memorandum. The body of the memorandum consists of the message in an informal but grammatically correct style. It is a good idea to keep the paragraphs of a memorandum short and to use a numbering system if there are various points to be made. Since the memorandum tends to be informal, unlike the formal report, the use of first and second person pronouns is permissible.

The word 'memorandum' is a Latin word and means 'that which must be remembered'. We frequently abbreviate it to 'memo'. The plural of 'memorandum' is 'memoranda' or 'memorandums'. The plural of 'memo' is 'memos'.

Depending on the policy within an organization, the writer will decide whether to sign the memorandum or not. If the organization uses memoranda for important communication, it would be advisable to sign the memorandum. We prefer memoranda to be used for informal communications and therefore do not think they should have to be signed. This does not, however, mean that memoranda are unimportant communications; they serve a useful purpose in placing 'that which must be remembered' in writing. One must not rely on oral messages to be remembered or interpreted correctly.

Notices are very similar to memoranda, but do not use the layout for memoranda. They are more impersonal, but use the same type of simplicity of communication and often employ a numbering system.

Since both memoranda and notices tend to communicate instructions, we should say a word about how to communicate in writing. The imperative form either in the positive or the negative, for example, 'Keep off the grass' or 'Do not litter', may be acceptable as public notices, but in business communication more polite requests are preferred, for example, 'Please keep off the grass', or 'Kindly refrain from littering'. There are many ways of giving instructions and the writer, in avoiding the blatant imperative, should vary the more polite ways of giving instructions: 'You are requested to . . . ', 'It would be appreciated if . . . ', etc.

Here is a typical memo dealing with the new arrangements within an organization about how stationery must be administered:

MEMORANDUM

TO Mr Jones

FROM Chief Clerk

DATE 1992-07-10

SUBJECT: NEW STATIONERY ARRANGEMENTS

1. Stationery will be in the central store under your control.
2. Stationery will be issued only between 9.00 and 11.00 a.m. on Mondays.
3. A formal order form will be needed, and staff must sign for stationery received.
4. At the end of each month please submit a schedule to the Manager, listing stationery issued to each staff member.

REPORTS

There are various types of reports. We may think of
- a report of a sports match or meeting
- a report of an accident to the police or an insurance company

- ❏ a report of a social function, e.g. a wedding
- ❏ a news report about an accident, a meeting, or some other noteworthy incident
- ❏ a report of a commission of enquiry
- ❏ a trade report
- ❏ a Company Report or a Company Annual Report
- ❏ an Annual Report by a Chairman or a Treasurer
- ❏ an internal report on some business-related matter following an investigation or collection of data.

Since this book deals with business communication, we shall deal mainly with the last of these types. What we shall say will be relevant to the other types in a general way, but these other reports tend to be either specific to a particular career (for example, journalism) or to the limited sphere of a government official or a chief executive. We believe that in giving practice in how to write an internal report on a business-related matter we shall prepare managers to learn the basics of report writing so that they may develop to writing more advanced and specific reports as they move up in their careers. There are books on the specific types of reports: for instance, the Southern African Institute of Chartered Secretaries and Administrators has produced a book called *How to Prepare an Annual Report* by Ben Temkin (1984).

There are a few general rules about report writing. A report should be a formal document and should be in the past tense as far as possible (that is, reported speech) and should not use the first or second person pronouns (I, we, you). There should be a simple numbering system with clear headings. A report should have these components:

- ❏ A HEADING
- ❏ TERMS OF REFERENCE
- ❏ PROCEDURE
- ❏ FINDINGS
- ❏ CONCLUSIONS
- ❏ RECOMMENDATIONS
- ❏ SIGNATURE AND DETAILS OF THE COMPILER OF THE REPORT
- ❏ THE DATE

HEADING: A report should give a comprehensive heading that states quite clearly the nature of the report.

TERMS OF REFERENCE: In this introductory section, which will use the words 'Terms of Reference' as its heading, details of the background to the report will be given: on what authority the report has been undertaken and what the specific objectives of the report are.

PROCEDURE: Again this heading will be used, and in this section the procedure of investigation or research will be stated.

FINDINGS: With this word as the heading for this section, the writer will explain the findings or objective facts arising out of the specific investigation.

CONCLUSIONS: This is the section in which the writer will interpret his findings.

RECOMMENDATIONS: Sometimes conclusions tend to become recommendations, but the writer should try to separate the interpretation of his findings (that is, his conclusions) from the proposals he puts forward for possible action (that is, recommendations).

SIGNATURE AND DETAILS OF THE COMPILER OF THE REPORT: It is important that a report should go out as the report of a particular person who is the responsible person and to whom credit or criticism should be accorded. The position that the writer holds is an important part of this report.

THE DATE: It should go without saying that it is essential that a report should include the date on which it was prepared, but unfortunately many reports overlook this simple information.

A long report usually has a synopsis (or summary), but generally speaking internal reports should be kept short. Long reports tend to be discarded or filed away without being read.

Some examples of internal reports follow.

REPORT ON STOCK CONTROL

1. TERMS OF REFERENCE

The Manager gave instructions on 25 January 1992 that an investigation should be conducted into the serious problem of stock checking at the end of each year and that a solution should be suggested.

2. PROCEDURE

2.1 The office card index system and the bin card system at the warehouse were investigated.

2.2 The Company Auditors were consulted.

3. FINDINGS

3.1 *QUANTITY*. There were about 2 500 items to be checked each year.

3.2 *OVERTIME*. A great deal of overtime was needed to take stock at the financial year-end.

3.3 *DISCREPANCIES*. Any differences between the bin cards and the card index system had to be resolved by checking the original documents for the past twelve months.

4. CONCLUSIONS

4.1 *WRONG TIME*. With year-end accounting dates to be met, there was not enough time available to check all the transactions for a whole year for each item of stock. The financial year-end is not the best time for stock-taking.

4.2 *CONTINUOUS STOCK CHECKING*. Under a system of continuous stock checking, the total stock would be checked in four months if a quarter of the stock items were checked each month. This would mean that each stock item would be checked three times a year.

4.3 *DISCREPANCIES*. Any discrepancies between bin card balances and the office card index system would involve a check of original documents dating back, at the most, four months under this continuous card index system.

4.4 *YEAR-END STOCKTAKING*. The troublesome procedure of a year-end stocktaking would not be required.

4.5 *APPROVAL OF COMPANY AUDITORS*. The Company Auditors agreed that a system of continuous stock checking would be acceptable and that, if all items were properly recorded on the card index system and the bin cards, the year-end stocktaking would not be required.

5. RECOMMENDATIONS

5.1 *CONTINUOUS STOCK CHECKING.* A system of continuous stock checking should be carried out.

5.2 *NATURE OF CONTINUOUS STOCK CHECKING.* Thirty items should be checked each working day.

5.3 *NECESSARY ACTION.* The continuous stock checking procedure should be implemented from 1 May so that each stock item would be checked twice in 1992 and three times each succeeding year.

1992-03-27

G.M. WERDNA
STORES CLERK

XYZ ENGINEERING

Report of the fire that destroyed part of the factory

A. TERMS OF REFERENCE

The directors instructed on 2 May that an investigation be carried out and a report with recommendations be written on the fire that destroyed part of the factory on 1 May 1986.

B. PROCEDURE OF INVESTIGATION

1. All staff members on duty at the time of the fire were questioned.

2. The relevant Fire Brigade and Police officers were interviewed.

3. The factory where the fire occurred was inspected on 3 May.

4. The Insurance Company officials involved were consulted.

C. FINDINGS

1. Cause of the Fire

It was established that the fire was caused by the sparks that resulted from the welding machine of the contractor who was welding and repairing the roof.

2. The Flame

These sparks landed on the bales of cotton used by the servicing team to clean up the oil from the machines. The point where roof-repairs were being effected was the landing bay where these bales were delivered by the suppliers before they were packed in the store-room.

3. Fanning of the Flame

Because of the fans that were kept running the whole night in the store-rooms, these embers became flames.

4. Extent of Damage

The store-room for bales and merchandise was destroyed. The fire spread to the room where chemicals were kept and resulted in an explosion that caused damage in the machine room. Damage of approximately 3,5 million rands was caused.

D. CONCLUSIONS

The damage was fully covered by insurance. The Fire Brigade and the Police officials agreed with this report
that no staff member would be held responsible and that
the contractor, although initially responsible, could not
be held liable, either. Certain extra precautions should
be taken, however.

E. RECOMMENDATIONS

1. The buildings that house chemicals, machinery , and
   stores should be separated.

2. Fans in the store-rooms for bales and merchandise should
   be switched off immediately after four o'clock by the
   security guard who should inspect all materials and
   cloakrooms.

3. Automatic fire extinguishing systems should be installed
   in all sections of the firm.

R.C. GUMA
ASSISTANT TO COMPANY SECRETARY   1986-05-05

<u>**REPORT ON INVOICING**</u>

1. TERMS OF REFERENCE

The Managing Director instructed on 25 April 1992 that an investigation should be conducted into the problem of the incorrect calculation of some invoices sent to customers and that measures to prevent this happening again should be suggested.

2. PROCEDURE

2.1 The company's system of invoicing was studied closely.

2.2 The accounts clerk was interviewed and his help enlisted.

3. FINDINGS

3.1 INVOICING SYSTEM

3.1.1 The sales clerk received the second copies of delivery notes for pricing.

3.1.2 The sales clerk was then supposed to pass the batches to the accounts clerk for checking.

3.1.3 The checked invoices were then sent by the sales clerk to the typist, who typed them in duplicate.

3.1.4 The top copy was sent to the customer; the second copy was used as an internal record.

3.2 CAUSE OF THE ERROR

The typist assumed that all invoices handed to her were checked, but one batch missed being checked.

4. CONCLUSIONS

4.1 The accounts clerk and the typist could not be sure that all invoices had been checked.

4.2 The accounts clerk did not have the responsibility of passing the checked invoices on to the typist.

5. RECOMMENDATIONS

A different system of checking is needed:

5.1 Invoices should be sent by the sales clerk to the accounts clerk for checking.

5.2 After checking, the invoices should be sent by the accounts clerk to the assistant accountant.

5.3 The assistant accountant should be satisfied that each invoice has been checked.

5.4 The typist should not type any invoice until it has been stamped 'CHECKED'.

5.5 The accounts clerk should check the typist's typing of the invoice before it is sent to the customer and the duplicate is filed.

G. Drew

1992-05-05   G. DREW
                                     ACCOUNTANT

REPORT ON NEW ORGANIZATIONAL STRUCTURE FOR TOYJOY

1. TERMS OF REFERENCE

The Managing Director has asked each of the Managers to propose what kind of organizational structure TOYJOY needs to meet the rapid growth in the computer games and adult games departments.

2. PROCEDURE

2.1 The existing functional line structure of TOYJOY was studied according to an analysis of strengths, weaknesses, opportunities, and threats (SWOT analysis).

2.2 A product line structure was studied according to a SWOT analysis.

2.3 A matrix structure was studied according to a SWOT analysis.

2.4 Various other organizations and their key directors were consulted, as well as TOYJOY'S management consultants.

3. FINDINGS

3.1 FUNCTIONAL LINE STRUCTURE: The SWOT analysis revealed that this structure was suitable for small business and had served TOYJOY well in its initial growth stage. There was good control since each director or manager had a specific and limited area of expertise which he could develop. There were few interpersonal problems since each director or manager was in control of his own specialized area of responsibility. There were, however, disadvantages. Functional line decision-making was slower. Too much responsibility had rested with the Managing Director to co-ordinate the different functions because each functional manager tended to be concerned only with his own area. This had created conflict and jealousy. There was little opportunity for breadth of experience for anyone except the Managing Director and consequently succession planning was limited.

3.2 PRODUCT LINE STRUCTURE: The SWOT analysis revealed that this structure was more suited to the expansion of TOYJOY. Decision-making would be speedier and more diversified: each product manager would have a wide range of experience both in his specialized area and in more general management. One of the strengths and opportunities of this structure over the functional line structure would be that each division would be responsible for its own performance and business results. A weakness would be that duplication of effort might lead to unnecessary expense. Too much emphasis on results might lead to the achievement of limited goals instead of the overall objectives of TOYJOY.

3.3 MATRIX STRUCTURE: The SWOT analysis revealed that this structure allowed for greater flexibility and involvement. Motivation would be high, and employees would be challenged to work together as a project team. There would be greater flexibility in moving experts from one project to another as the project required specific skills. This would create cost-effective employment of key personnel and would obviate duplication of effort. One of the weaknesses and threats of this structure was that there might be a feeling of being demoted when a project team disbanded and members had to regroup themselves for a different project. The feeling of let-down when the project came to an end would have to be carefully handled and would require a great maturity of inter-personal relations. There would also be the threat of too much flexibility that could lead to the collapse of a project arising from too much talk and not enough task performance. Since every person would be responsible to a line authority and a project authority, divided loyalties could result. Nevertheless, the advantages were seen to outweigh the disadvantages and the matrix structure would have few of the problems that arise from more bureaucratic structures. A major opportunity would be that top management could be freed to concentrate on strategic planning.

4. CONCLUSIONS

4.1 Appendix 1: The product line structure would be as shown.

4.2 Appendix 2: MATRIX STRUCTURE: This structure would involve the promotion of the design manager and the advertising manager to top management. It would mean the appointment of specialist product managers and advertising personnel to manage and promote the new and existing products. There would be little duplication of effort. The resulting challenges and excitement would help to motivate staff and meet the demands of the future.

5. RECOMMENDATIONS

5.1 The matrix structure be adopted to meet the needs of TOY-JOY'S growth, especially in computer games.

5.2 The Design Manager and the Advertising Manager be promoted to top management, not necessarily with increased salaries.

5.3 The existing Sales Manager be appointed as Manager (Children's Toys) and two new Managers be appointed either from existing staff or from outside to fill the posts of Manager (Computer Games) and Manager (Adult Games) respectively.

5.4 Three advertising posts be created over the next two years, each to be responsible for the advertising and promotion of a specific product group.

5.5 A Personnel Manager be appointed to take care of interpersonal relations and motivation problems and to develop in time into a new staff department.

5.6 The new structure be phased in over the next two years to allow for the new appointments and budgeting constraints.

1992-08-08

D.M. GUY
MARKETING MANAGER

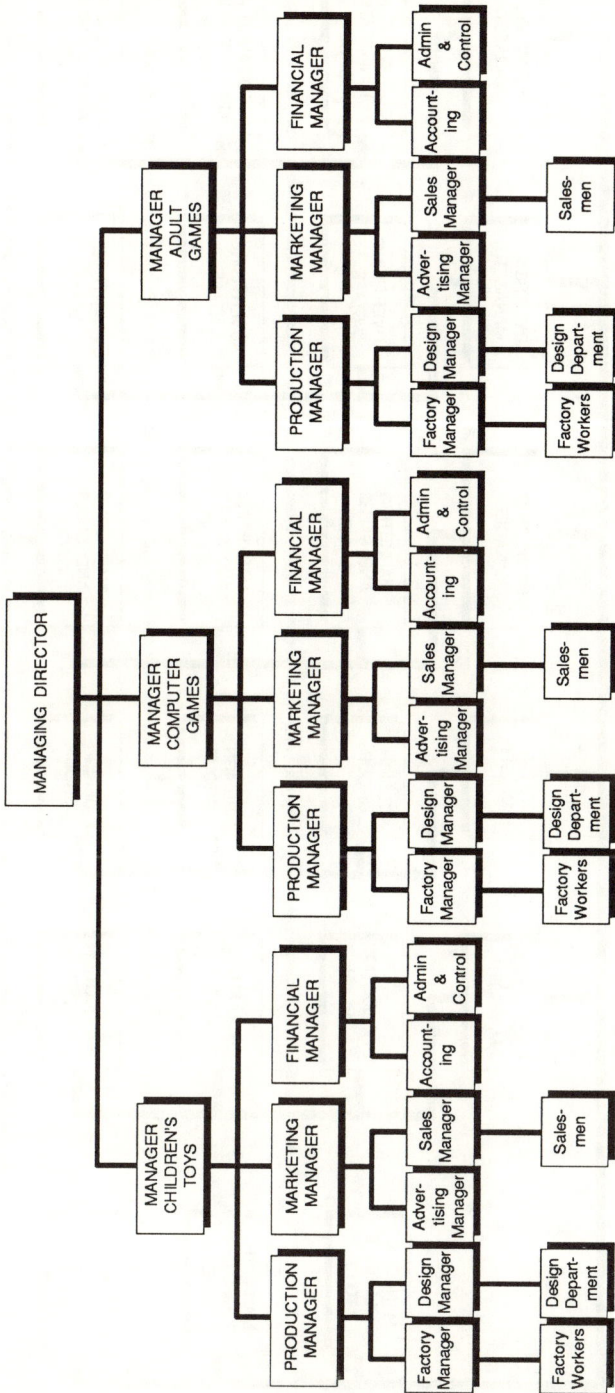

This would involve unnecessary duplication of staff and expense.

Appendix 1
PRODUCT LINE STRUCTURE

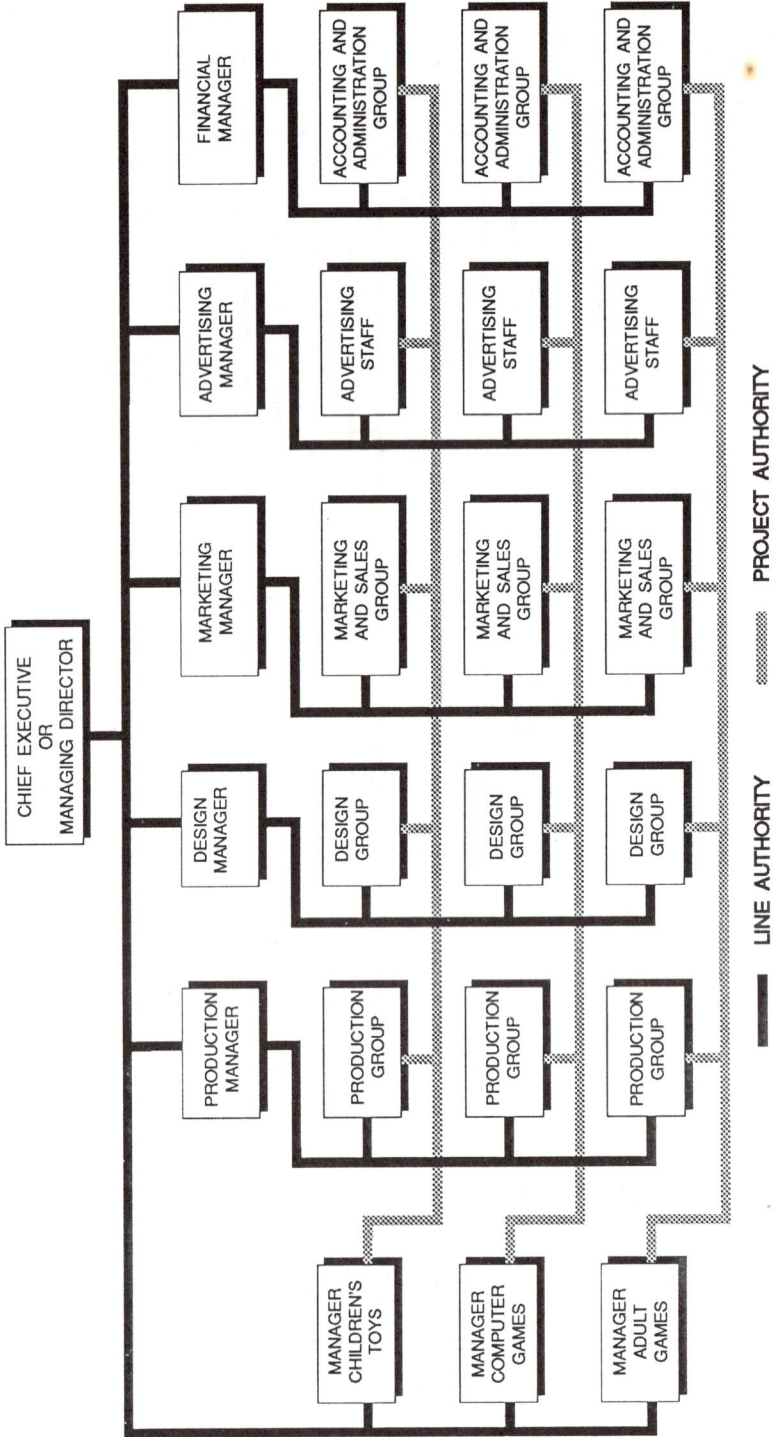

Appendix 2
MATRIX STRUCTURE

There are various types of reports as we have said. There are also combinations of a report and a letter (called a letter-report) and of a report and a memorandum (called a memorandum-report). The difference is a difference of formality: the memorandum-report would use the format of a memorandum, would use the headings of a report, would be shorter, and could use the first and second person pronouns and the present tense; a letter-report would use the format of a letter, the headings of a report, and the first and second person pronouns and the present tense, and would be longer than the memorandum-report but shorter than a formal report. The deciding factors would be the length and the level of formality.

NOTICES, INVITATIONS, AGENDAS AND MINUTES OF MEETINGS

We have already referred to the dynamics of meetings in our chapter on oral communication. We now deal with the writing of documents connected with meetings. These are notices, invitations, agendas and minutes.

Notices

These are notices calling upon members to attend a meeting. The notices can be formal or informal. Formal notices use this kind of artificial wording: 'Notice is hereby given that . . . .' Informal notices use more natural wording. As always, we prefer the more natural and less artificial style. Here is an example of a notice of a meeting:

SOUTH AFRICAN INSTITUTE OF MANAGEMENT
SOUTHERN TRANSVAAL REGION

COMMITTEE MEETING

The monthly committee meeting will be held in the National Office Boardroom, Braamfontein Centre, Johannesburg, on Tuesday 28 February 1989 at 5.30 p.m.

A. DREW (Miss)
Secretary
Telephone: 337-1210 (Business), 616-6554 (Home)
15 February 1989

The elements of a good notice are:
❑ the heading indicating the nature of the meeting
❑ the place of the meeting
❑ the date of the meeting
❑ the time of the meeting

❑ the signature and the designation of the person sending out the notice (usually the Secretary)
❑ the telephone number(s) of the person concerned
❑ the date the notice was posted.

Usually the notice gives information of the **purpose** of the meeting. In our example the words 'committee meeting' are probably sufficient, but often the agenda is given with the notice of the meeting.

Invitations

An invitation is a special kind of notice. Where there is a special function, e.g. a graduation ceremony, a dinner, or a cocktail party, invitations are usually printed on an attractive card. Formal invitations usually use the third person.

The Chairman and the Committee of the
SOUTHERN TRANSVAAL REGION
of the
SOUTH AFRICAN INSTITUTE OF MANAGEMENT

invite

_____

to the
ANNUAL DINNER

to be held in the Tudor Room of the Wanderers Club,
North Street, Melrose, Johannesburg
on 10 MAY 1989, at 7.00 (for 7.30) p.m.

GUEST SPEAKER
Mr J. Cheminais
President of the Association of Correspondence Colleges
of Southern Africa

DRESS FORMAL
TICKETS: R75 PER COUPLE

R.S.V.P. by 15 April: Miss Anne Drew, Secretary
32 Rollo Street, Cyrildene 2198
Telephone: 337-1210 (Business) 616-6554 (Home)

The name of the person to be invited is usually written in an attractive way (usually in calligraphy) on the dotted line. As can be seen, the elements are

❑ the name of the host(s)
❑ the name(s) of the person(s) to be invited
❑ the nature of the function
❑ the place where the function will be held
❑ the date of the function
❑ the time of the function
❑ the name of the speaker if this is appropriate
❑ the type of dress to be worn
❑ the cost of the tickets if this is appropriate
❑ R.S.V.P. (*Répondez s'il vous plaît* — French for 'Please reply')
❑ the date by which replies are required
❑ the name and the designation and address and telephone number(s) of the person to whom replies are to be addressed.

Invitations can be less formal: the name and the address of the person(s) to be invited are typed on the envelope and the invitation may begin

You are cordially invited to . . .

There was a time when invitations were formally accepted 'with pleasure' or declined 'with regret', but usually reply cards are enclosed or the person invited will telephone his acceptance or his inability to attend.

Agendas

As we have mentioned, the agenda is often included under the notice of the meeting:

SOUTH AFRICAN INSTITUTE OF MANAGEMENT
SOUTHERN TRANSVAAL REGION

COMMITTEE MEETING

The monthly committee meeting will be held in the National Office Board-room, Braamfontein Centre, on Tuesday 28 February 1989 at 5.30 p.m.

AGENDA

1. Welcome

2. Apologies

3. Minutes of previous meeting

4. Matters arising, not covered in the agenda

5. Regional Forums

6. Student Liaison

7. Educational Management Workshop

8. Business Game

9. General

    9.1 Vice Presidents

10. Next Meeting

A. DREW (Miss)
Secretary
Telephone: 337-1210 (Business), 616-6554 (Home)
15 February 1989

The agenda provides prior notice of what is to be dealt with at the meeting. It is a useful document to have available at the meeting to guide the chairman and the meeting about what has to be discussed and the time to be allocated to each item of business.

It is useful for the chairman to have a *Chairman's Agenda* which has more details on it than the ordinary agenda has. Usually the Secretary will provide this kind of detail for the chairman. It would include such matters as who is to be welcomed, who has sent apologies, who is responsible for particular items, references to previous minutes, and any other useful information to facilitate the orderly progress of the meeting.

Minutes

The Secretary usually takes the minutes of the meeting and then writes them out and sends them to the members as soon as possible after the meeting. The minutes provide a **summary** of what took place at the meeting and become the legal documentation for what took place. They serve as an action programme for members responsible for certain duties. At the next meeting they are formally accepted or altered and signed by the Chairman. There is a particular format for the writing of minutes, as the following example shows.

XYZ ENGINEERING

MINUTES OF THE CANTEEN COMMITTEE MEETING HELD IN THE CAN-
TEEN COMMITTEE ROOM ON THURSDAY 24 APRIL 1986 AT 5.30 P.M

PRESENT: Mr W Nkosi (in the Chair)
          Mrs X Cindi
          Mrs V Michael
          Mr P J Naidoo
          Dr W Thompson
          Miss A Mtshali (secretary)

APOLOGIES: Miss C Jones and Mr B Mkhize

MINUTES OF THE PREVIOUS MEETING: These were signed by the
Chairman as a correct record.

MATTERS ARISING:
SUPPLY OF MILK AS ALTERNATIVE TO TEA AND COFFEE: Because
the dairy supplied to schools as well, a shortage of bot-
tles might make supply erratic. The dairy would be asked
to supply milk in waxed paper containers.

CORRESPONDENCE: Mr B Mkhize has resigned from the committee because of his appointment as manager of the Bloemfon-
tein factory. The Chairman would write to Mr Mkhize,
regretting that the Committee would be losing his services.

INCREASE IN PRICE OF TEA: The price of tea has increased
by 5 cents a kilogram, the canteen would have to charge a
cent per cup more, and a profit of R5 per week would be
made. Various suggestions were made about what to do with
the profit:
(a) the extra money be shared among canteen staff as a
    gratuity;
(b) the profit be allowed to accumulate to offset future
    increases;
(c) the profit be given to the Welfare Fund.

The Secretary would write a memorandum to all employees,
mentioning the Committee's suggestions and asking for
views.

DATE AND TIME OF NEXT MEETING: 28 May at 5.30 p.m.
CLOSURE: The chairman closed the meeting.

Signed as a correct record

PJ Mullin   _28 May 1986_

Chairman   Date

The elements of a good set of minutes are:

❏ the heading providing details of the type of meeting, the name of the body conducting the meeting, the place where the meeting was held, the date, and the time
❏ the names of the people attending (sometimes at large meetings there is an attendance register and the minutes would provide details of chairman and secretary and then the words 'according to the attendance register')
❏ welcome (optional)
❏ apologies
❏ approval of the previous minutes
❏ matters arising from the previous minutes
❏ the business of the meeting, e.g. Elections, Reports
❏ general
❏ closure
❏ chairman's signature and date of signature

FINAL COMMENTS ON WRITING

It is necessary to realize that written documents are an important part of any business enterprise. We have stressed the need for correctness in any documentation emanating from an organization, but we must also consider that documents could become important evidence in litigation and therefore they should be carefully composed and retained for a certain period. There is a useful booklet published by the South African Institute of Chartered Secretaries and Administrators called *The Disposal and Retention of Documents* by Rex B. Appleton; every manager should be aware of its contents. Documentation such as board minutes, reports, personal records of staff and data bases should be carefully preserved. Off-the-record transactions are dangerous in business. Even draft documents can be important evidence in litigation to show the intention of the final documentation if there is any doubt raised about the intention of the final document.

Unskilled penmanship can be devastating in its effects. Every writer must check with meticulous accuracy. Imprecise language and discursive writing lead to extensive cross-examination in a court of law and usually to unsuccessful litigation, whereas factual documentation usually leads to successful litigation because there is no doubt about the clarity of its interpretation.

CONCEPTS AND TERMINOLOGY

1. PRÉCIS (SUMMARIES)
2. TELEGRAMS
3. TELEXES
4. FAX MESSAGES
5. EXPANSION OF NOTES

6. ESSAYS
7. NARRATIVE ESSAYS
8. DESCRIPTIVE ESSAYS
9. INFORMATIVE ESSAYS
10. ARGUMENTATIVE ESSAYS
11. PLAN (OUTLINE, SCHEME, DIAGRAM, MIND-MAP)
12. SIMPLE SENTENCES
13. COMPLEX SENTENCES
14. COMPOUND SENTENCES
15. PARAGRAPH STRUCTURE
16. INDUCTIVE REASONING
17. DEDUCTIVE REASONING
18. ORDER OR ENQUIRY LETTERS
19. LETTERS OF COMPLAINT
20. LETTERS OF ADJUSTMENT
21. CREDIT LETTERS
22. OFFICIAL LETTERS
23. LETTERS TO THE PRESS
24. LETTERS OF APPLICATION FOR EMPLOYMENT
25. *CURRICULA VITAE*
26. MEMORANDA AND NOTICES
27. REPORTS
28. NOTICES OF MEETINGS
29. INVITATIONS
30. AGENDAS
31. CHAIRMAN'S AGENDA
32. MINUTES

APPLICATION

1. Write a précis of the three paragraphs on 'The purpose of evaluation' in not more than 200 words and in one paragraph.
2. Write an abstract of the three paragraphs in not more than 60 words.
3. Your flight from London to Johannesburg has been delayed twenty-four hours. You had planned to attend an important business meeting. Send a telegram to your assistant advising him of your delay and giving him instructions to attend the meeting and what role he should play.
4. Change the following simple sentences into (*a*) complex sentences and (*b*) compound sentences:
    ❏ Migrant labour causes many problems.
    ❏ Unemployment is increasing at an alarming rate.
    ❏ There was much opposition to the appointment of the new manager.
    ❏ Performance appraisals are necessary.
    ❏ There is a need for small business development.

5. Write a plan, scheme, or outline of an essay on each of these topics:
   - ❏ CROSS-CULTURAL COMMUNICATION
   - ❏ CORPORATE CULTURE
   - ❏ ECONOMIC SYSTEMS
   - ❏ THE IMPORTANCE OF MARKETING
   - ❏ THE EVILS OF ADVERTISING.
6. Expand these notes into
   - ❏ an acceptable essay,
   - ❏ an acceptable letter to the press, and
   - ❏ an acceptable report:

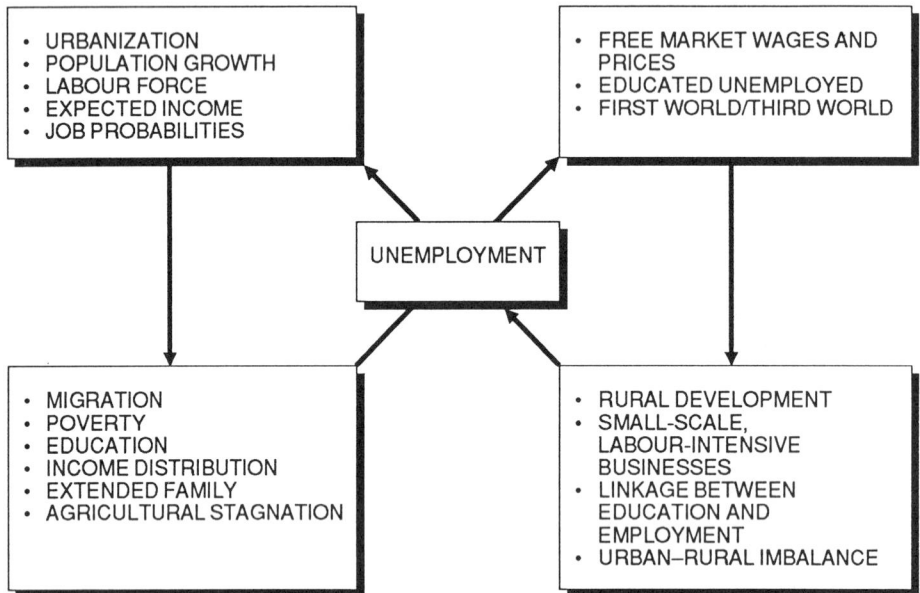

- URBANIZATION
- POPULATION GROWTH
- LABOUR FORCE
- EXPECTED INCOME
- JOB PROBABILITIES

- FREE MARKET WAGES AND PRICES
- EDUCATED UNEMPLOYED
- FIRST WORLD/THIRD WORLD

UNEMPLOYMENT

- MIGRATION
- POVERTY
- EDUCATION
- INCOME DISTRIBUTION
- EXTENDED FAMILY
- AGRICULTURAL STAGNATION

- RURAL DEVELOPMENT
- SMALL-SCALE, LABOUR-INTENSIVE BUSINESSES
- LINKAGE BETWEEN EDUCATION AND EMPLOYMENT
- URBAN–RURAL IMBALANCE

7. Arrange the following sentences into a paragraph of logically ordered thoughts:
   - (a) The field has been well charted, however, and the task of developing adequate measures is predominately of a technical nature.
   - (b) Effectiveness in the execution of teaching duties remains the central theme of faculty appraisal throughout the world.
   - (c) There is a reasonable degree of clarity as to *what* should be assessed, but unfortunately the methodologies adopted in the assessment process have lagged behind, and show a disconcerting lack of psychometric sophistication.
   - (d) Large numbers of critical incidents referring to competent behaviours across the entire spectrum of teaching at university level have been identified, and can be used for assessment purposes.

    (e) The large number of assessment instruments developed over the past decade pays ample testimony to a new awareness of and sensitivity to improved teaching and didactic renewal.

    (*After* you have attempted this question, you should test your answer against the order in which the sentences were originally arranged: (*b*), (*e*), (*c*), (*a*), (*d*).)

8. Write a narrative essay about an amusing incident at your place of work.

9. Write a descriptive essay about how a system or a machine works.

10. Write an informative essay about the free enterprise system.

11. Write an argumentative essay about which economic system suits South Africa best.

12. Give two examples of
- ❏ inductive reasoning and
- ❏ deductive reasoning.

13. Write a letter ordering or enquiring about certain commodities used in your business.

14. Write a letter of complaint about a disrespectful receptionist you encountered at a business firm.

15. Write a letter of adjustment in which you inform a creditor of a mistake in his statement of account.

16. Write three letters to a debtor about his overdue account. Each succeeding letter should refer to the account that is a further month overdue.

17. Write a letter applying for an overdraft from your bank.

18. As the bank manager reply to this letter refusing the overdraft.

19. Write a letter to your Member of Parliament in which you ask for his assistance in a particular matter.

20. Write a letter of application (without a *curriculum vitae*) for a position you wish to secure.

21. Write a memorandum to your employees about a change in working hours.

22. You have been asked to investigate which photocopier will suit your company best. Write a report to your Managing Director.

23. Write the notice and the agenda for a meeting about to be held.

24. Write an invitation to a special function soon to be held.

25. Write the minutes of a meeting.

14

MODES (MEDIA SYSTEMS): WRITTEN COMMUNICATION
Sales, Marketing, Advertising and Promotion

GOALS OF THIS CHAPTER

In business communication the ability to persuade is important. We have already defined persuasive communication as communication that intends to change the reader's behaviour and attitude in a way the sender of the communication has previously determined (Chapter Ten). By the end of this chapter you should be able to:

❏ understand the principles of persuasive communication;
❏ write and evaluate sales letters;
❏ write and evaluate elementary questionnaires and surveys;
❏ write and evaluate written advertisements;
❏ write and evaluate press releases.

INTRODUCTION

Before going on with this chapter it would be advisable to re-read the section on the persuasive use of communication in Chapter Ten. Persuasion is used mainly in sales, marketing, advertising, and promotion, which are very important parts of business. It will not be our intention to deal with these aspects of business in the detail that would be required in courses in sales management, marketing management, marketing research, advertising management, or public relations, but this chapter will be a useful, practical introduction to more advanced studies in these fields.

SALES LETTERS AND PERSUASIVE WRITING

The days of the door-to-door salesman are almost over. Much selling is conducted through correspondence or by telephone. Direct mail has become a very important tool, and with judiciously selected mailing lists, sales letters can be very effective. Many managers see sales letters as such an important part of their business that they employ professional writers or direct mail agencies in the same way as they use advertising agencies for their advertisements. Whether we use direct mail agencies or write our own sales letters, we need to know the principles of persuasive writing.

In persuasive communication the following principles are applicable:
- ❏ stressing the importance of the receiver's ego;
- ❏ appealing to the human need for love and acceptance;
- ❏ stressing the need for financial advantage and security;
- ❏ stressing the need for status and prestige;
- ❏ appealing to the need for or the status of comfort, convenience, pleasure, enjoyment and leisure;
- ❏ appealing to the need for good family relationships.

These relate directly to motivation theory, especially to Maslow's Need Hierarchy and Hertzberg's Two-Factor Theory of Motivation (see figure opposite).

We need to take into account these needs and factors when we use persuasive communication or when we read writing meant to persuade us.

The persuasive techniques are usually the following:
- ❏ references to the *famous* and *wealthy* with the purpose of persuading us to *identify* with them;
- ❏ the use of *academic* or *scientific* terms or *numerical* bias to *impress* us that a *sophisticated* or *educated* approach is being used;
- ❏ the use of *exaggerated statements or visuals* that make the product or the cause more glamorous or impressive than it really is;
- ❏ the use of the 'bandwagon' approach, that is, getting us to join the majority, the knowledgeable, or the in-group;

❏ word choice for a special purpose: emotive words to appeal to our human needs or fears; slight inaccuracies in the use of words or shifts in meaning to achieve the intended result;

❏ fact selection for a special purpose: deliberate exclusion of negative factors or facts; arrangement of facts so that by their proximity to each other a special desired effect is created; for example, the common visual effect of a beautiful woman in close proximity to a product.

When trying to persuade, the communicator has to understand what his **target audience or readership** is; for example, a University Rag letter of appeal is likely to adopt a sophisticated, up-market approach, whereas a writer of a popular magazine article is likely to adopt the approach of impressing his down-market readers with numerical or scientific facts that they are unlikely to verify but merely accept; or he may use the bandwagon approach to make his readers fear that they do not belong.

A persuasive communicator is likely to use the AIDA approach that marketers employ:

❏ get the ATTENTION of the reciever;
❏ hold his INTEREST;
❏ arouse a DESIRE to respond in the intended manner;
❏ obtain ACTION from him.

A communicator in business needs to obtain ATTENTION if the receiver is to become aware of a product or a cause or an opportunity. By holding his INTEREST the communicator has a chance to arouse a DESIRE or a liking or even a preference, and this usually results in ACTION.

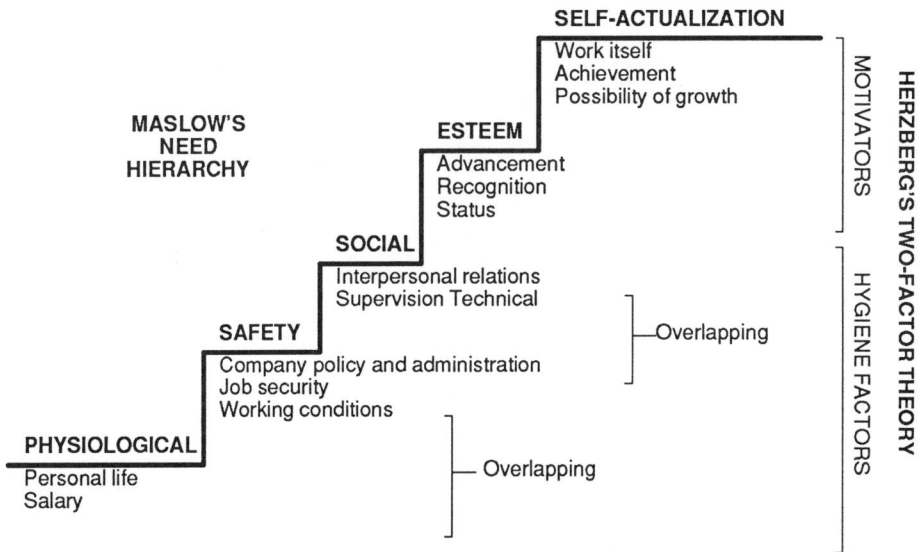

Other principles in persuasive writing are to keep the clarity index as low as possible and to bear in mind the audience at which the persuasive writing is aimed.

There are various examples of persuasive writing from brochures to advertorials to advertisements to fund-raising appeals to sales letters. If we were to define persuasion, we could say it is that form of communication that is designed to get the attention of the receiver, hold his interest, make him believe what he receives, and bring about some form of change in his behaviour in accordance with the purpose of communication to achieve the predetermined response from the receiver.

Let us look at an example of a sales letter.

TRANSPORT TASKFORCE (PTY) LTD

33 Churchill Road
P.O. Box 1336
2000 JOHANNESBURG

Telephone: 567-8910
Cables: Transtask Johannesburg
Telex: 8-67898 SA

There's only one way
to beat city traffic -
More MOBILITY ... more MAGIC

Dear Mr Peters

So traffic is getting you down. And parking is scarce and
expensive. Not to mention petrol. Or public transport:
it's overcrowded — like the streets — and so slow.

Let other people talk like this. They'll just add to the
miserable mutters on the roads.

BUT WHY YOU? You can taste the MAGIC of MOTORING. Enjoy
your ride to work or college and back again. No more traffic jams. No more late appointments. Feel the freedom of
a bike — a WONDER XL125S.

You've never ridden a bike before? You've heard it's dangerous? And what about wet weather? Mr Peters, we're
sorry: we thought you were young and informed. And adventurous. Perhaps you'd better keep to the traffic jams,
the expense, and the public transport.

But if you want MORE MOBILITY ... MORE MAGIC ... MORE EX-
CITEMENT ... MORE FREEDOM ... and LESS EXPENSE, then let
me tell you about this bike. It's for commuting AND for
scrambling, because it's on/off road. It's nippy in traffic and fun on the rough. You'll enjoy the adventure of
the outdoors — even in the city. And we stock protective
clothing to make even wet weather no problem.

JOIN THE ADVENTURE. IN the United States more young businessmen and students are buying this bike than any other.
Especially on the sunny West Coast of California — a climate similar to our own.

The WONDER XL125S is a 125 cc bike in attractive red and
black colours and weighs only 100 kg. It has excellent

suspension and is fuel friendly at 20-25 km/litre. At R6 998 with easy terms available, you cannot afford any other transport.

THE TIME FOR YOU TO ACT IS NOW. Call me today — 567-8910.

Get mobile magic — the WONDER XL125S.

Remember — we are your **TRANSPORT TASKFORCE**

UB Fearless

U.B. FEARLESS
MARKETING DIRECTOR

QUESTIONNAIRES AND SURVEYS

Most businesses will use questionnaires and surveys at some time. A good questionnaire or survey is a very useful marketing research tool and it is advisable to use a market research agency to draw up such a questionnaire or survey. Nevertheless simple questionnaires and surveys can be composed by managers and their staff without recourse to an agency.

The basic principle of drawing up a questionnaire is to make the task of the respondent as simple as possible. If we expect too much from a respondent, he will not give us the time required to complete the questionnaire, and our work will have been in vain. The principles of brevity and simplicity are therefore important. Some respondents are, however, keen to give their views in more detail, and therefore there should be an optional section on the questionnaire where a person can elaborate on a particular point if he wishes to.

We have all been to hotels, banks, or service stations where simple questionnaires are available for customers to express their views about the quality of service they have received. Or perhaps we have been visited by a researcher conducting a survey and we have been asked to fill in our answers to questions on a social, political, or business topic. Sometimes researchers ask the questions and fill in the survey form themselves. This is usually because people have a dislike of filling in forms. It is amazing how intelligent people have mental blocks about filling in forms and become resentful and untidy and stupid when they are required to fill in forms. All this teaches us that when we have to compose questionnaires, we must make the questions and answers as simple as possible.

Here are two simple examples of questionnaires designed to evaluate the quality of a service provided; the first is for a guest farm and the second for an educational service.

QUESTIONNAIRE

Please spare us five minutes of your time to complete this questionnaire. It will help us to help you and other visitors to the guest farm.

1. Name: . . . .
2. Room No: . . . .
3 Number in family: . . . .
4 Duration of stay . . . .
5. Please tick the appropriate column . . . .

	Excellent	Good	Could be improved	Poor
5.1 Cleanliness of rooms				
5.2 Dining room				
5.3 Service				
5.4 Meals				
5.5 Bathrooms, toilets				
5.6 Recreational facilities				
5.7 Meeting facilities				
5.8 Tuck shop				
5.9 Walks and hiking trails				
5.10 Overall atmosphere				
5.11 Helpfulness of staff				

6. Tariffs (please tick):
   Too high
   Reasonable
   Too low

7. What are the guest farm's strong points, if any? . . . .
   . . . .
   . . . .
   . . . .
8. What are the guest farm's weak points, if any? . . . .
   . . . .
   . . . .
   . . . .
9. Any other questions or comments: . . . .
   . . . .
   . . . .
   . . . .

Thank you

Please hand this to the manager before you leave.

EVALUATION QUESTIONNAIRE

Lecturer: . . . .

Course and subject: . . . .

Please indicate your evaluation in Section A by placing a tick (✔) in the appropriate box. Section B contains open-ended questions.

Your honest opinions will be of great value to the School in improving the quality of our service, and to your lecturer in helping him/her in reviewing his/her effectiveness.

SECTION A

How do you rate your lecturer on the following points?
E = excellent
G = good
A = Average
P = Poor
U = Unsatisfactory

	E	G	A	P	U
He shows a thorough knowledge of the subject.					
He prepares thoroughly for each lecture.					
His explanations are clear.					
He makes good use of the blackboard and/or overhead projector.					
He encourages student participation, and controls it well.					
He sets enough written assignments.					
Written work is marked and returned promptly.					
He has a good relationship with the class.					
He maintains students' interest to the end of the lecture.					
He paces his lectures according to his lecture schedule.					
He is punctual and reliable in starting his lectures, restarting after breaks, and ending on time.					
What is your overall impression of the lecturer?					

SECTION B

1. What does your lecturer do especially well? . . . .
   . . . .

2. Does the lecturer have any irritating or distracting habits? . . . . . .
   . . . .
   . . . .

3. General comments. . . . .
   . . . .
   . . . .

Questionnaires or surveys can be used as general guides to how to improve service or they can be used more scientifically to analyse strengths or problem areas. The results of the questionnaire on the educational service, for instance, are fed into a computer, and each lecturer is provided with his own results with comparative figures in the form of a printout.

No. Question	Average	Previous Average	Change	Highest all lect.
1 Thorough knowledge of subject	9.06	9.40	−3.6 %	9.89
2 Preparation	8.44	8.25	2.3 %	9.69
3 Clear explanations	7.81	8.33	−6.2 %	9.55
4 Good use of blackboard & OHP	6.72	7.50	−10.4 %	9.69
5 Stimulates student participation	8.75	8.10	8.0 %	9.69
6 Sets adequate written assignments	8.75	8.81	−0.7 %	9.89
7 Written work marked promptly	8.59	9.40	−8.6 %	10.00
8 Good relationship with class	8.75	8.45	3.6 %	9.72
9 Maintains students' interest	8.28	8.10	2.2 %	9.43
10 Paces lectures according to schedule	7.17	8.21	−12.7 %	9.77
11 Punctual in starting, restarting and ending	7.66	8.69	−11.9 %	9.81
12 Overall rating	8.44	8.25	2.3 %	9.77
Average	8.20	8.46	−3.0 %	9.51

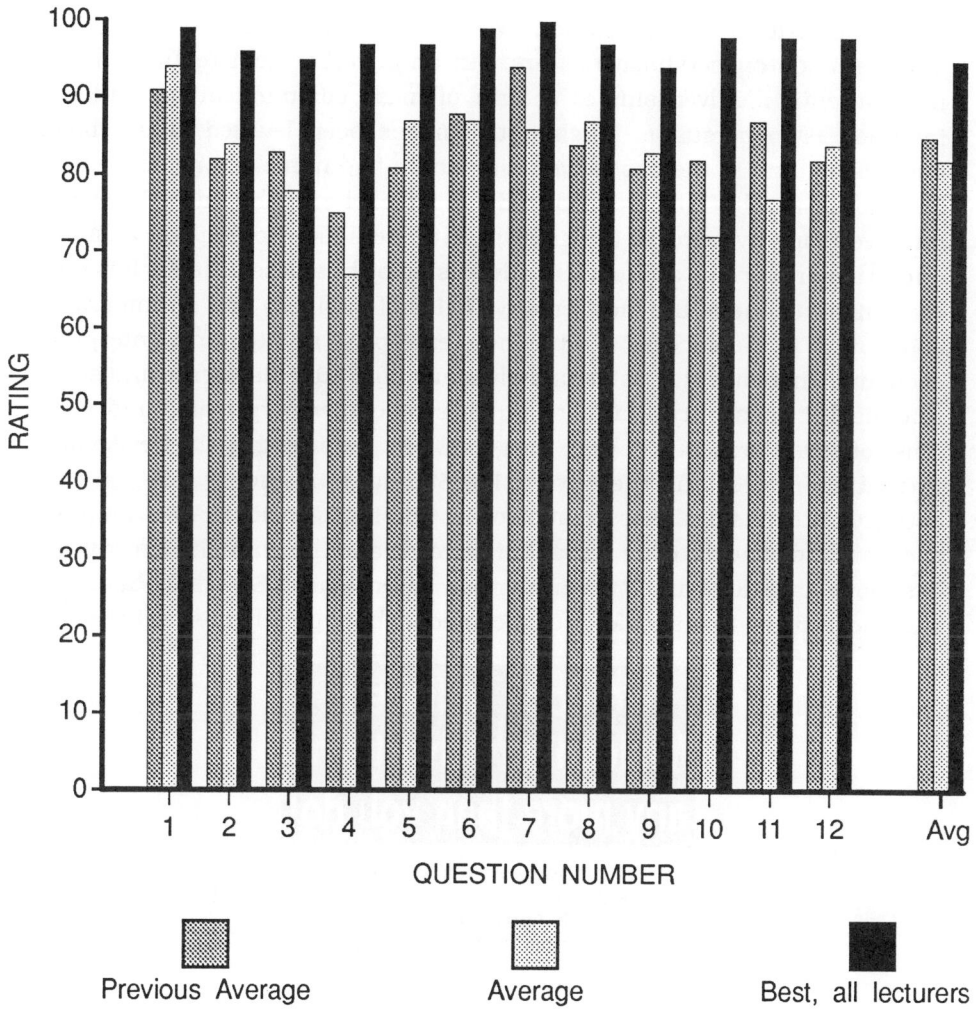

ADVERTISEMENTS

The writing of advertisements is a specialist's task, and a manager is best advised to employ a professional advertising agency to create his firm's advertisements. Nevertheless a manager should be aware of the principles of good advertising and should be able to compose an advertisement even if it is merely to give the advertising agency an idea of what he wants.

We shall restrict ourselves to the print medium because it falls under the heading of written communication. We have already introduced the subject in our section on persuasive letters, but an advertisement requires much more attention. Advertising is a form of mass communication, and the intention is to persuade. Much criticism has been levelled at unethical advertising, and in the past advertising had a bad name among academics and moralists. That this has changed can largely be attributed to the works on advertising by some of the great practitioners like Hopkins and Ogilvy, and to a more serious approach to advertising by business schools. It is now recognized as one of the most creative fields of business and an important contributor to the success of a business enterprise and to a free enterprise economy. There are still unfortunately many poor advertisements and some unethical or unsavoury attacks on public sensibilities perpetrated under the guise of advertisements, despite the good work performed by the Newspaper Press Union (NPU) and the Advertising Standards Authority (ASA) in this country. Attempts by the Association of Advertising Agencies (AAA) to improve the standard of advertising through its awards and the annual Loerie Award ceremony have done much to counter bad advertising in South Africa and to raise advertising to an art form that can contribute greatly to society.

We don't believe in Misleading Advertising any more than you do!

If you see an advertise-ment in this newspaper which is obviously untrue, or which you feel is in bad taste, write to us.

"We" are the Advertising Standards Authority. We will take action. Help us to protect *you* – because we don't believe in Misleading Advertising, any more than you do.

Advertising Standards Authority

P.O. Box 10537 Johannesburg 2000.

There are various media used for printing advertising. The word 'media' is plural for 'medium' and it is used to describe the means by which communication can be achieved. When we use the word 'media' in connection with print advertising, we refer to these ways of communication:
1. the Press
2. Outdoor Advertising
3. Direct Mail
4. Print at Point-of-Sale
5. other forms of copywriting and creative work.

1. Press
The Press may be divided into

The national press
❑ National daily newspapers (none in South Africa)
❑ National Sunday newspapers
❑ General national magazines
❑ National women's magazines
❑ National specialist consumer publications
❑ National professional, trade and technical Press

The regional press
❑ Regional morning newspapers
❑ Regional evening newspapers
❑ Regional Sunday newspapers
❑ Regional weekend newspapers
❑ Give-aways ('Knock and Drop' publications)

Specialized publications
Each of these has its own advantages and disadvantages for advertising and these need to be taken into consideration when preparing and placing advertisements. In general terms, however, one needs to consider the following characteristics of press advertising:
❑ Colour
❑ Size and format
❑ A static medium
❑ Variety of publication dates
❑ Long or short life
❑ Circulation and readership
❑ Variations in production processes and paper surfaces
❑ Space and location

Colour

When we talk about colour in press advertising, we are talking of two basic types: (a) black-and-white and (b) multi-colour. Generally we refer to the latter simply as colour. Most press advertisements are in black-and-white because the production process does not make colour available. Another reason may be the cost to the advertiser. An advertiser should always consider the possibility of colour when it is available because it makes a much greater impact than black-and-white. Various newspapers and magazines make colour advertisements not only available but, from the advertiser's point of view, almost essential. The national press usually offers colour facilities. Opportunities for colour in the regional press are more limited, but this very limitation may give the advertiser who uses a different colour a decided advantage, even if it is only one extra colour. Sometimes colour inserts are possible, but these have the disadvantage of a very short life since they are often thrown away with no more than a glance. Colour advertisements are generally far more memorable and attract more readers, but they are more expensive.

Size and format

The size and format of a newspaper or magazine affect its readership. It is easier to read a tabloid size in crowded places than it is to read the larger size newspaper. This is probably the reason for the smaller size *Sowetan* and *Citizen*; people find it much easier to read this size on a bus or a train. The advertiser has to consider various sizes and formats in deciding on his advertisement. These range from full-page to classified advertisements, and from advertisements with headlines to advertisements with single words in bold print. A second-hand stove would be advertised in the classified section, whereas a new car model might take a full page.

A static medium

The Press is essentially a static medium for an advertiser as opposed to television, cinema, or radio. Some copywriters claim to achieve movement and balance in press advertising, but essentially it is a short, simple, static medium of communication. It is important therefore to direct the reader to the main point of the advertisement, appeal to his attention, interest and desire, and persuade him to action as simply and as quickly as possible before he inevitably moves on to something else.

Variety of publication dates

The date on which an advertisement appears is important. An extreme example of the importance of a publication date was the appearance of an advertisement on 16 June 1986 for a service being offered in the centre of Johannesburg when the people to whom it was targeted were afraid of going into town for fear of unrest that day: the advertisement had a nil-response! It is well known that a 'situations-vacant' advertisement on a Friday evening has very little effect. How often have we seen an advertisement stipulating a closing date that has already passed! Careful scheduling of publication dates is very important. A media schedule is essential.

Long or short life

A magazine has a fairly long life, whereas a newspaper has a short life. Magazines have a longer life because their editorials stay relevant for a longer period. This means that people will pick up a magazine and read it long after its publication date. The advertiser can then benefit long after his advertising campaign has ended. A newspaper, on the other hand, is read and discarded almost immediately. There is limited pass-on readership and little opportunity for repeat exposure to a particular advertisement. The advertiser has, therefore, to consider whether the campaign will be a short-term or a long-term one. Of course, if a press advertisement is part of a multi-media campaign that continues on the radio, television and cinema, the detrimental effects of the short life of newspaper advertisements will be lessened.

Circulation and readership

The circulation figures and the type of readership are very important characteristics of press advertising. If a newspaper's circulation is national, then the advertisement should be a product intended for the whole community. It would be wasteful to advertise to a specialist target via the national press. Similarly it would be wasteful or confusing to advertise in the national press a product sold only regionally. On the other hand it might be wasteful to advertise certain products in a newspaper of limited circulation rather than in a newspaper with a large circulation. It is not only the *quantity* of the readership that is important; the *quality* of the readership is also important. The type of readership of the press medium is of great importance to the press advertiser and therefore the target audience of the communication must be matched with the readership of the medium on which the advertising communication will appear.

The variation in production processes and paper surfaces

The more advanced the production process and the quality of the paper, the more up-market the medium. This is a generally accepted characteristic of the press medium, and the advertiser has to take this into account since it affects the standard of his advertising copy and the ultimate acceptance of the advertisement. The more varied the production processes and paper surfaces are, the greater opportunities there will be for illustration and attractive type-faces and the better the impact on the reader will be.

Space and location

It is possible to buy a special location in press publications. It is generally accepted that the closer to the front of a newspaper or a magazine that the advertisement appears, the better its impact will be. In a magazine a cover has a particularly important impact, and the front page in a newspaper is also important. A particular section of a newspaper may be requested, for instance the financial pages or the entertainment pages or a special supplement, and this location may require a change of emphasis in an advertisement.

2. Outdoor Advertising

This covers any type of advertising through signs displayed out of doors. Included under the heading of outdoor advertising is transportation advertising. Sometimes outdoor advertising is referred to loosely as posters. Let us discuss the characteristics of posters:

❑   Size
❑   Position
❑   Colour
❑   Impact
❑   Reminder function
❑   Readability and visibility
❑   Production techniques
❑   Siting problems
❑   Problems of defacement and graffiti

Size

The size of outdoor posters can be enormous. This offers opportunities, but it also has disadvantages. Since the poster has to communicate from far away, the greater size does not really allow more space for more copy. It just allows you to use the small copy in bigger letters! A poster is probably the type of advertisement that should use the least copy. There are a variety of sizes available for outdoor advertising, from the huge sign on the freeway to the small signs on parking meters or refuse bins on the pavement. The size is determined by the purpose of the advertisement: whether it is for the car driver or the pedestrian or the person entering a supermarket to make purchases. There is therefore a creative challenge for the advertiser: how to adapt the advertising message to the variety of sizes available.

Position

Everything depends in outdoor advertising on the position of the poster. One has almost to be an expert in town planning to find the correct position for the poster; one has to be aware of changes in population, traffic patterns, and the planning of new streets. There are various factors that are important in deciding on the position of an outdoor advertisement.

The length of approach is important. There is little value in placing a poster just around a corner. It should rather be visible for a certain time before the motorist passes it. It gives time for the reader to read it and for the full impact to be made.

The speed of the traffic is relevant. The faster the traffic passes the spot where the poster is, the less impact the poster will have. Therefore the poster should rather be in a place where the traffic slows down; for example, the entrance to a town where the speed limit changes and where the driver and the passengers are often bored by the slower speed and turn their attention elsewhere.

Then there is what we may call *the poster's solitary splendour*. Ideally an outdoor advertisement should stand out. If it is near other advertisements, its impact is diminished. If a number of different advertisements are grouped together, the one closest to the road has the greatest impact. Because of the fleeting nature of the impact on the viewer, the more advertisements there are, the less clarity there will be in his mind. The outdoor advertisement will benefit from having pride of place.

Finally, *the angle of the poster* counts. The most effective posters are angled so that they are facing the oncoming traffic, that is, head-on to the driver. The least effective posters are those parallel to the traffic, the ones to which you have to turn your head in order to see them.

Using such factors advertising researchers can draw up numerical estimates of how successful the position of the poster is likely to be. Obviously an important aspect of positioning is that the advertiser needs to repeat the same advertisement, one for each direction of traffic flow, if he is going to achieve maximum response.

Colour

Outdoor advertising is another medium that depends a great deal on the proper use of colour to attract attention. There are various reasons for selecting particular colours. The natural colours of the product should obviously be used, but yellow tends to make the object appear bigger, black on a yellow background is more legible, and red attracts attention. Fluorescent colours stand out. Colour helps the viewer to interpret the product in the way the advertiser intends him to: by careful selection of colours the advertiser may create the ingredients for stimulating the desire to satisfy some need in the viewer; for instance, thirst by a colour that suggests coolness, life or spirit by combinations of colours that suggest happiness or exuberance. It is not a good idea to use red and green combinations because they have poor visibility, while blue or green together with white have medium visibility.

Visibility

A poster must have initial impact. The type of poster that becomes a talking point for travellers obviously has succeeded. In the United States an actual-size motorcar illustration projecting from a poster was used to advertise an adhesive, with the words 'It also sticks handles to teapots.' Often impact comes from flashing signs at night or from the poster being associated with television or press campaigns.

Reminder function

Because posters have a long life, the passer-by is likely to see the same poster often. This has both positive and negative effects. One can become so accustomed to a poster that remains unchanged for weeks that its effect is minimal, if not detrimental, on the viewer. The poster usually remains for a period of thirty days, and the subconscious effect of this continual reminder can be effective. The reminder function of posters is demonstrated by the frequent use of posters as part of a wider campaign. As a visual back-up to advertising in the press or on television, the poster is very effective, especially if it uses an enlarged frame of the actual TV commercial and viewers are then reminded of the longer TV advertisement. A very effective example of this reminder function some time back was the Cremora advertisement on top of a Johannesburg bus: after a successful campaign on TV during which the expression, 'It's not inside. It's on top', became a household expression, the later advertisement on top of the bus gave a new twist to the advertisement and reminded viewers of the previous campaign. This reminder function operates well outside or inside supermarkets: not only can advertisements serve as reminders of wider campaigns, they can also serve as impulse-triggers, just at the time when the consumer is about to make her purchase.

Readability and visibility

Type must be the largest possible and must be suited to readability: too many capitals can be hard to read; headlines super-imposed on illustrations do not read well; type in reverse, i.e. white on black, instead of black on white, is hard to read; and type arranged in unusual shapes or at unusual angles causes difficulty. Five or six words are ideal for an outdoor poster; eight is considered to be the maximum, excluding the trademark or logotype. Any more become confusing, and the message is lost. We have already spoken about visibility when we mentioned position, but we need to emphasize that the attention of the viewer has a span of only about five seconds, and the message must be clear and complete within this time span.

Production techniques

With outdoor advertising there are limited production techniques available. We cannot use movement (except for the limited movement of neon-lights flashing and video screening), and we cannot use sound. The production techniques are therefore almost entirely related to typography, graphic production, and colour production. The picture is what will make the initial impact and it must have a story appeal that will make the reader curious to read the headline. It has been established by advertising research that photographs have more story appeal than drawings. There is no other medium that relies more on the illustration effect than outdoor advertising does. With this medium it is a good idea to use silhouette illustration so that the illustration stands out from its background and is easily identifiable from far away. As regards typography, the headline should be in lower case, not in capitals. Most large posters are printed by the lithographic process, which allows a wide variety of work in black and white and in colour at relatively low cost. Since the life of the poster will be a long one, it is important to choose colours that will not fade.

Siting problems

As we shall see in the next paragraph, there are siting problems because posters can deface the environment. But there are also siting problems because of the competition for pride of outdoor advertising place. This has become increasingly important in South Africa, and therefore most of the arrangements for siting are made through one agency. As we have seen, town-planning aspects must be considered. There is no point in siting an outdoor advertisement in a place that will shortly be obliterated by a new building or that is on a road that is or will become a minor road. A great deal of research, usually beyond the normal advertiser's ability, has to be under- taken, and some of the data necessary are not available or reliable in the Republic. Where the advertisement is to be sited will affect the different types of advertising techniques to be used. Will the advertisement be on street level? If so, is it aimed at the passer-by in his car or the pedestrian passer-by? Should his copy be in English, Afrikaans, or an African language, or in two or more of these languages? If the advertisement is to be placed on an elevated site, should it be an electric display mainly visible at night or an all-day advertisement? If it is an interior siting (e.g. railway platforms, an airport, or a bus shelter), will the reader have more time to read a longer message?

Problems of defacement and graffiti

The advertising industry has a bad name among environmentalists. Ogilvy, in a section of his book *Ogilvy on Advertising* called 'Down with billboards', argues persuasively against outdoor advertising on the grounds that it promotes 'the forces of uglification'. If advertisers kept their advertisements up to date and did not persist in displaying meaningless faded notices that are not only out of date but also illegible, perhaps the outcry against posters would be less justified. Political posters are probably the worst culprits, and stricter controls on such advertising need to be imposed — and enforced. Then there is the problem of graffiti. Much natural humour and even art — especially in Yeoville in Johannesburg — can come from graffiti, and it is probably too puritanical to oppose it altogether. But if posters are changed regularly, no great harm can be caused by the contribution of would-be creative writers or artists in the form of graffiti. An interesting slant on this topic is an advertisement high up on a previously blank wall on the corner of two busy streets in central Johannesburg. It is a colourful, humorously romantic painting of a little cottage set in a rural environment and it is jointly sponsored by an estate agent, a paint firm, a scaffolding firm, and a sign-writing firm. If more advertisements beautified or entertained rather than uglified, there would be no such outcry against outdoor advertising.

3. Direct Mail and Sales Letters

One of the main problems with direct mail and sales letters is that unsolicited mail is disliked and therefore it is a problem to get people to open their letters. It is considered that the average businessman receives seven pieces of direct mail a day and that a good percentage of these letters will end up in the waste-paper bin. Many of these letters, if they are easily recognized as unsolicited sales letters, may end up in the bin without even being opened. This is probably unlikely, though, since it is an extremely dangerous business practice to throw away any letter that has not been opened and read.

Another problem is that a good mailing list is difficult to compile and to maintain. One of the secrets of direct mail advertising is to *choose* the recipients of the mail, and yet many sales letters are sent indiscriminately to all and sundry. This means that the rate of response will be poor and that the cost per letter will be much higher.

The last problem is that many dishonest people have tried to benefit from direct mail advertising and have 'disappeared' before they have delivered in full what they promised. This has given direct mail a bad name, and some people are still suspicious of it.

Here are some of the characteristics of direct mail:

Selectivity of audience

One of the main advantages of direct mail advertising is that it can be directed to exactly the people you want to receive the advertising. It is possible to use details of demography, of how many times a buyer has purchased, and of the amount of each purchase made, to pinpoint exactly which people ought to receive the mail. It is possible to generate one's own mailing list or to obtain mailing lists from other sources, but it is important to keep the mailing lists current, as we have already noted.

Computers are very useful to remove deadwood from mailing lists.

The most personalized form of advertising

Direct mail is the most personal and intimate of all the media. Through the use of computers it is possible to address each person by name, but, more importantly, the style of the letter can be personal and it is possible to refer to a customer's recent purchase and to offer him something that will appeal directly to him. Direct mail is intimately concerned with creating and developing customers, not merely in making sales. Through developing customer response files and identifying key customers an advertiser can develop a regular communication plan that will make a customer feel that he is wanted and that he belongs in the membership of the firm. Once a customer has opened the envelope, the advertiser has the opportunity of the full attention of the reader, unlike other forms of advertising where the competition for the customer's attention is immense.

Advantages of space and layout

There are very few restrictions on the advertiser in direct mail. The letter can be as short or as long as the advertiser decides. Letters of five to eight pages have been successful with certain prestige products. The advertiser can try out new forms of production with different materials and processes. The innovative and creative opportunities are great.

Direct mail is easily tested

This is probably the main advantage of direct mail. Good direct mail advertisers test the recipients' responses in terms of recency, frequency and monetary (RFM) principles: in other words, how recently, how frequently, and to which monetary value customers have bought. In this way key customers are identified, and the Pareto Principle that 20 % of the customer base is responsible for 80 % of sales can be applied to isolate who the 20 % are. Almost every variable in direct mail can be tested: responses to samples, prices, terms of payment, special offers, premiums, prizes and just about every form of novelty. Measurement of results leads to better results.

Greater control on direct mail

Through testing and other research, direct mail advertisers have greater control over their advertising schedules, their territorial targets, their timing, and their whole organization. Organization is of the utmost importance in direct mail campaigns: there is nothing so annoying to a customer as finding that his response is not promptly handled or that the switchboard knows nothing about the campaign.

Ease of response

These days people rarely use cheques. This is typical of the changing nature of our business transactions. We prefer credit cards or electronic fund transfers. The same applies to our buying behaviour. The easier it is for us to respond, the more likely we will respond. And direct mail usually makes it very easy to respond through coupons or reply-paid postcards or some other such device. Credit card numbers and a signature are usually quite enough to effect payment.

Special advantages

Direct mail can communicate detailed and complicated messages better than other media. It can select its audience specifically and can avoid the wastage of mass circulation. Its message can be personalized. Its timing can be very accurately organized. It can use coupons to great advantage. It is very useful to prepare for personal selling either in the show-room or through a salesman. As part of an advertising campaign, direct mail can precede or follow up on newspaper or magazine advertisements.

Writing techniques and tactics

The recipient must feel that the communication is intended for him alone, otherwise he will regard it as junk mail. This personalized approach is a specialized technique, and it must avoid flattery and other forms of insincerity. Awareness of the target readership will affect the style of language, the type of emotional appeal, and the layout of the letter. Correct, but not always formal, language should be used. In sales letters the use of headlines is advisable.

4. Print at Point-of-Sale

This type of print advertising is in the form of posters, pamphlets, cards, shelf-strips, dispensers, banners, etc. at the place of purchase. The advertising must be short and eye-catching. It is especially effective if it is linked with a press or television campaign. It includes both basic package design and in-store display material.

In advertising, brand identification is of the utmost importance and it is achieved largely through packaging. The basic package design of most products is the best way to advertise them. The bottle of Worcester sauce on the table or the container of the cereal, the drink, the washing powder, or the tissues is the surest way to get consumers to identify with a brand. We must remember that with products like soap, cigarettes, and perfume it is the package that differentiates the product from its competition and that it is largely the package that sells the product. Packaging must serve the basic purpose of protecting the product, and therefore we must not be so carried away by the advertising potential that we produce packages that are difficult to open or difficult to store. As an advertising tool, package design and display contribute to the advertising of the product through

- ❑   Impact
- ❑   Identification
- ❑   Benefits
- ❑   Overcoming competition
- ❑   Packaging inserts
- ❑   Timing and mood

Impact

Packages must have immediate eye-appeal if the buyer is to reach out and put the product into her trolley. Photographs are frequently used to identify the target-user, for example, children on a cold-drink advertisement or the dish of food in its final state when cooked and ready to eat. Sometimes the impact may come from the familiarity of the trademark or the brand name as advertised through other media. We have already stressed the importance of brevity: package advertising should be limited to the brand name, some pictorial or photographic presentation of the product, and a short statement about its characteristics and uses. The advertiser must be able to say a lot in a few words if he is to make the necessary impact on the consumer as she is passing by the package. Much research has gone into such aspects as colour, shape, and size of the packaging, and all of these play an important role in making the impact on the purchaser.

Identification

The purchaser must be able to recognize and identify with the product. That is why the link with the overall advertising campaign is important. The brand image must be clearly represented in a familiar form. The brand name must be easily identifiable. The art of choosing names with which people will identify could be a topic for a whole book. When George Eastman coined the name KODAK, he wanted a brand name that people could pronounce and spell easily and he liked the use of the K. The same device is used in the word XEROX. The continual investigation into company logos is evidence not only of an easily identifiable name but a style of using that name that will become easily identifiable. Familiarity and identity go hand in hand. Of course that does not mean that one logo must be used *ad infinitum* and that a change will not create the desired impact, but then the new logo must become something with which the buyer identifies as more modern than the old one.

Benefits

As part of the copy of the package, a benefit should be promised to the purchaser. This could be implied in the pictorial or photographic design or it could be in a stated benefit: the copy would then be in the form of a statement of the want-satisfying characteristics of the product. We must recognize that many items are bought and consumed on impulse, and therefore the benefits of buying and consuming should be clearly visible. The importance of impulse-consumption takes us further than the supermarket shelves and into the home itself: the greater the benefit of consuming the product, the more likely it is that the product will be purchased again and again, and a brand preference and a pattern of purchase will be achieved.

Part of the benefit that is stated on the package is the short and simple statement of how the product may be used: if the purchaser sees that a particular food product is easy to prepare, it is more likely that she will purchase and consume the product. The changing lifestyle of the modern housewife who is also a career woman makes this aspect of packaging design more important.

Another benefit is the consumer's convenience in using the product. The type of packaging may appeal to the convenience of using it. The easily opened can or bottle appeals to the convenience of the user: rather than having to use a bottle opener or can opener, he can easily open it and consume the contents. Sometimes the benefit is in the ability to re-use the package or container: margarine may be sold in a container that can be used as a container for other household purposes. There is then an added advantage to the advertiser: the benefit contributes to the reminder function and often does not need explicit advertising of the benefit.

Overcoming competition

We have already mentioned that the competitive nature of selling almost homogeneous products makes the basic package design of the product very important. Comparative advertising is not allowed in South Africa, but the designer of a product's package must bear in mind competitors' products. The more a product is differentiated from a competitor's, usually the better the purchaser will be able to distinguish one product from another. There is legislation that prevents too close an identification with a competitor's trade name and brand image, but there is still the danger of the consumer confusing brands. This is a danger in advertisements which causes the viewer to remember an aspect of the advertisement but to attribute it to a competitor.

In order to overcome competition the advertiser needs to take into account people's lifestyles and interests. There has been much emphasis on attitudes in behavioural studies of the consumer, but perhaps it is more important to study her activities and to try to establish a brand image that relates to her lifestyle, interests and activities. In this way a package can be developed that appeals to the consumer in a way that other products do not and the package gains a competitive edge on the other products.

Another way in which we can overcome competition is to respect the competition that exists for the shelf space on the retailer's shelves. We must be able, through packaging, that is, through its shape, its impact, and its size, to persuade the retailer to display it prominently and to persuade him that it will increase his sales. If we can come up with a package that makes it more convenient and more profitable to display the product, we have already achieved a competitive advantage.

Packaging inserts

We need to bear in mind that often packaging includes an outer package, a package insert and the packaging of the container itself. For instance, there might be a box, an insert of a folded piece of paper, and then a liquid container. In such cases there should be advertising messages that are unified: the outer container may be thrown away soon and its impact must be on the purchaser at the point of purchase; the insert should be easily unfolded, and the outer fold should arouse further interest to read what is on the other folds; and the actual container should have a continuing impact that will encourage a purchasing pattern of repeat purchases. The insert can be a valuable advertising tool and should be designed so that the consumer will be encouraged to keep it: one method may be to include recipes or ways of using the product in different combinations with other products with the same brand name. Again one could write a book on the effective use of the package insert.

Timing and mood

Special occasions are important: the start of school, Christmas, spring, summer, winter. All these provide special considerations for in-store display. Closely associated with this is the mood of the buying public. The end of the month offers more opportunities than the middle of the month, Christmas time more than January and February, times of economic well-being more than recession. The creative team must consider such moods, as well as the moods of particular target markets, such as young married couples and teenagers.

5. Other Forms of Copywriting and Creative Work

There are many other types of printed material intended to give the public information about products that can be bought. These range from leaflets and brochures to straightforward catalogues, price lists and salesmen's portfolios. Other forms are the naming of new products, the writing of editorial feature material, and the designing of specialties such as calendars, novelties and gifts. Sometimes it is necessary to prepare house magazines to advertise companies to their clients.

Normally a brochure has opportunities for design and interesting copy and may use all the creative techniques available to direct mail. The brochure usually has the same advantage of a known audience as direct mail has: we can assume that a person who reads a brochure has a particular interest in the product being advertised and therefore there is ample opportunity for good copy. In the same way a catalogue, price list, or a salesman's portfolio, (that is, the details about his product that a salesman carries about with him) contains information about products that have known attractions: prospective buyers have usually requested such a catalogue or at least the advertiser has some buying history of the customer to know the target audience of his advertisement. The use of colour is important in this kind of advertisement: colour photographs give the prospective buyer a better idea of what it is he is considering buying. Even with colour advertisements, the photograph of a product may be misleading: the size of something photographed is often nothing like what the reader thinks it is and can lead to customer disappointment and dissatisfaction: a handbag in a catalogue may not look like the actual handbag when it arrives after being ordered. We must remember some of the constraints that apply to other forms of advertising; we must also create a customer base that will buy and buy again — and again and again. To achieve this, accurate and attractive information must be given.

Some response apparatus is useful with leaflets, brochures, and catalogues. Such response mechanisms must be easy to understand, easy to complete, and easy to test. In a small coupon the instructions must be very clear, there should be the minimum effort on the part of the person responding, and the information received either through the post or via the salesman must be valuable for effecting the order and for follow-up.

6. Conclusion on Advertisement Writing

There are various elements of a print advertisement:

- ❏ Headline
- ❏ Subheading
- ❏ The body text
- ❏ The closing idea
- ❏ Signature slogan or strapline

The headline is a statement in words which attracts the attention by being witty, surprising, newsworthy, helpful, brief, specific, or topical, or by providing a promise of a benefit. It must have distinctiveness: it must stand out in some way. Often a headline is helped in achieving its purpose by an illustration, attractive typography, or by skilful advertisement design.

The subheading has as its purpose to amplify the idea in the headline and to develop the initial interest into knowledge of the product.

The body text must either promise a benefit or develop the promise of the benefit that may have been part of the headline or the subheading. It explains the features of the product and its value. It will support or prove in a believable and logical way any claims that may have been made about the product.

The closing idea supplies additional motivation for the buyer to act and it provides further information and directions, such as the price and the name and address where the product can be obtained. This would be the place for the coupon if a coupon is to be used.

The signature slogan or strapline is the slogan that helps to draw attention to the logo, for example: 'NASHUA — saving you time. Saving you money. Putting you first.'

PRESS RELEASES

The purpose of a press release is to inform the press about some noteworthy event so that it may consider whether this piece of news is sufficiently noteworthy to publish. This can be very important publicity for a business, and usually a public relations firm is employed to prepare press releases. A manager must, however, know enough about what a press release is and how it is composed either to guide the public relations firm or to prepare (even if only in draft) a good press release.

A press release should be typed on A4 paper, and copies should be available for all the media that may be prepared to use the information. Consideration should be given to where the information is most likely to be accepted: for instance, would it be best placed on the women's pages, the finance pages, or the general news? It is a good idea to inform the particular editor that such a news release will be available and to deliver it personally to the appropriate person. This requires an informed awareness of news-paper, magazine, radio and television organization.

The **heading** should be PRESS RELEASE. On the upper left of the page should appear the name and address and telephone number of the company submitting the press release, with details of the contact person. On the right hand side of the page below the **identification details** should appear an indication as to the **release date**. Most press releases would be for immediate release, but sometimes it is necessary to state that the press release must be held for release after a particular date so that no one is embarrassed by premature release of what may be regarded as confidential information until the particular release date.

It is not the task of a press release to provide headlines, but it is a good idea to leave spaces for the editor to include his own headlines where appropriate. Use double spacing and wide margins to allow for editing by the editor. A press release should be as short as possible with short sentences that are grammatically correct. It should *not* be like an advertisement and should not appear too 'pushy'. A press release should *not* be on a letterhead.

The formula for a press release is WHO? WHAT? WHEN? WHERE? WHY? HOW? Obviously these questions are not used in the press release copy, but they help to make sure that the information is detailed enough and important facts are not omitted.

As with a fax message, it is always important to specify the number of pages if the press release goes to more than one page, and to number the pages clearly with a heading to identify each page after the first. If there is more than one page, type the word 'MORE' at the bottom of each page except the last and type 'END' at the bottom of the concluding page even if it is the only page. If at all possible it is a good idea not to have a paragraph running from one page to another. All these are for the benefit of the news staff who will be more likely to consider your news release for publication if you show consideration to them. A good relationship with contact newspeople helps.

It is of the utmost importance to eliminate all errors and to be sure of your facts.

The press release will look something like that shown on the following page.

PRESS RELEASE   Number of pages: 2

South African Institute of Management
P.O. Box 31828
Braamfontein
2017

Contact Morris Cowley
Telephone 339-2364/5/6 (Business), 706-1916 (Home)

Immediate Release

A diploma in Business Administration has been launched by
the South African Institute of Management (SAIM). Following extensive research, the SAIM has identified key competencies which have strong links with high performance
in the management field. Through this new approach, organizations and, in particular, managers can develop these
performance-linked competencies.

Employers now have the means to bridge the gap between
management learning and delivery. The programme is cost
effective because managers continue to work whilst taking
part in the programme; the flexibility of the course
meets unique requirements; and the costs are much lower
than those for typical academic courses, and yet the manager can reach the heights of business academic achievements. Employers can have the assurance of a national
professional standard rated as M + 3 (the same as a degree) by the Human Sciences Research Council. Top level
directors, managers, and educationists continually assess
the standard of the qualification and award accredita-
tion. The corporate culture of the organization is important: employers may develop their managers' skills within
their corporate culture while they are studying, and in
this way their performance at the workplace will improve.
The SAIM welcomes input from employers.

Managers have the advantage of a modular programme that
aims to develop managers' abilities to perform where it
counts — at the work place. The qualification, nationally
recognized by commerce, industry, and government, will be
a significant benchmark in the manager's career. It is a
truly portable qualification which stays with the manager
as his career develops. The flexibility of the programme
enables the manager, with his employer, to select those

                                                    MORE

PAGE 2

subjects which suit his needs best. Time commitment is minimal with the programme running alongside his job. If the student-manager wishes to have a senior practising manager as a tutor and a director as an assessor, this will give him the benefit of real experience.

Each module of two subjects requires up to seventy-five hours' study — less if the student has covered the ground already. For the Certificate in Business Administration, four subjects have to be passed; for the Intermediate Diploma in Business Administration, a further four subjects; and for the Diploma in Business Administration, a further four subjects. Graduates of the SAIM Diploma in Business Administration may progress to MBA studies on successful completion of an entrance examination.

There are unique features of the SAIM approach. Managers may develop competencies in specific areas without doing unnecessary subjects. The single-subject-certificate concept allows them to choose any of the subjects and specialize in these areas only. The modular nature of the Certificate, Intermediate Diploma, and Diploma courses allows the manager to pace his studies according to his needs and to study as far as his needs dictate. He may stop after the certificate stage or progress as far as an MBA or Doctorate in Business Administration.

The wide range of options in the Diploma course (nevertheless with essential core business studies) allows the student to major in Management and Finance or in Management with sub-majors in Finance and one of the other core management subjects — Marketing or Human Resources.

Further information may be obtained from the SAIM, P.O. Box 31828, Braamfontein 2017 or by telephoning the Executive Director (011) 339-2364. A booklet on the new programme called GOING FOR PERFORMANCE is available.

END

CONCEPTS AND TERMINOLOGY

1. SALES LETTERS AND PERSUASIVE WRITING
2. THE AIDA APPROACH
3. QUESTIONNAIRES AND SURVEYS
4. ADVERTISEMENTS
5. NATIONAL PRESS
6. REGIONAL PRESS
7. OUTDOOR ADVERTISING (POSTERS)
8. DIRECT MAIL AND SALES LETTERS
9. PRINT AT POINT-OF-SALE
10. LEAFLETS
11. BROCHURES
12. CATALOGUES
13. PRICE LISTS
14. SALESMEN'S PORTFOLIOS
15. NAMING NEW PRODUCTS
16. EDITORIAL FEATURE MATERIAL
17. CALENDARS
18. NOVELTIES
19. GIFTS
20. HEADLINE
21. SUBHEADING
22. BODY TEXT
23. CLOSING IDEA
24. SIGNATURE SLOGAN OR STRAPLINE
25. PRESS RELEASES
26. WHO? WHAT? WHEN? WHERE? WHY? HOW? FORMULA

APPLICATION

1. Compose a sales letter about a new product or service your firm is about to offer to the public.
2. Compose a questionnaire about a service that is offered.
3. Find an advertisement in each of the following:
   - ❑ a newspaper
   - ❑ a magazine
   - ❑ a direct mail letter
   - ❑ a product package
   - ❑ a catalogue

   Evaluate each advertisement.
4. Compose an advertisement for each of these:
   - ❑ a vacancy in your business
   - ❑ a second-hand car you wish to sell
   - ❑ a product your business wishes to sell
   - ❑ a service your business offers
5. Write a press release about a new appointment made in your company.

15

MODES (MEDIA SYSTEMS): NON-VERBAL COMMUNICATION

GOALS OF THE CHAPTER

In this chapter we set out to understand non-verbal communication of these four types:

❏ kinesics (body and facial movements)
❏ proxemics (bodily positioning)
❏ paralinguistics (voice sounds but not verbal sounds)
❏ graphics (diagrams, pictures, charts, graphs)

INTRODUCTION

We have concentrated so far on verbal communication — oral and written. Much more could be said about verbal and intonational communication; we could go into detail about words as signs and about conventional codes of syntax and grammar that give these signs their contexts and denotations; we could analyse the different intonations that change the meanings of a sentence. But we wish merely to emphasize now that communication has various components that interact with each other: there is a verbal component, a vocal or intonational component, and a non-verbal visual component, to name just three. Other components are, as we have seen, the psychological or cultural setting and the participants in the communication. In analysing any communication we must be aware of which components are the most relevant and understand that communication is a dynamic process.

The different components may be categorized in different ways: we could call intonational communication non-verbal or we could link it with verbal communication and call it linguistic or vocal. We could group verbal, intonational, and paralinguistic communication together and call them vocal. But, for our purposes, we have decided to group together these four '-ics' as non-verbal communication:

❏ kinesics
❏ proxemics
❏ paralinguistics
❏ graphics

KINESICS

The word 'kinesics' comes from the Greek word for motion or movement. Ray Birdwhistell invented the English term to refer to such channels of communication as facial expressions, gestures, eye contact, and posture. Kinesics is commonly referred to as body language and is a very important part of communication. Often one's words are betrayed by one's body language. It has been said that, when a person touches his nose or eye or any other part of his face while he is talking, he is likely to be lying. We do not take such a rigid interpretation of kinesics as this — after all, perhaps his nose or eye *is* itching — but we do believe that body and facial movements may communicate or help to communicate.

As managers, we need to be aware of our facial movements: we need to control those that are meaningless or distracting and to practise those that are meaningful and assist the communication process. Actors spend a great deal of time practising movements till they perfect them; when they use them on the stage or on film, the intention is that the audience should perceive the movements as perfectly natural and should not think of them as studied or practised or artificial. It is only when movements are natural that they will assist in communication. When they are artificial, they distract and hinder communication.

We should not only try to perfect our own facial movements, we should also be able to interpret others' movements. Especially in an interviewing situation, an interviewer can learn more of the interviewee if body and facial movements are carefully observed. Body language can show if someone is ill at ease and needs to be relaxed, or it can show hostility that needs to be taken into account during the interview.

An important point to remember in interpreting body and facial movements is that culture is an important influence. We should not be so prejudiced as to interpret others' body and facial movements outside their cultural contexts. A black person may have been taught that it is disrespectful to look an older person or a superior person straight in the eye, whereas a white person expects to be looked at when he is speaking to someone. The white person may therefore interpret the downcast look of the black person as sullenness or disrespect, whereas it is intended to be just the opposite.

Kinesics can be divided into various categories:

❑ **Involuntary gestures** are those movements we make without meaning to do so. For instance, we may wince at pain, we may yawn when we are tired, or we may hiccough. Some involuntary gestures are meaningful even though they are involuntary: wincing and yawning, for instance; others are comparatively arbitrary, like sneezing or hiccoughing.

❑ **Voluntary gestures** are deliberately used to communicate. We bang the table to emphasize a point; we point at something; we may give a black power or *amandla* sign (this is called an emblematic movement because it is an emblem with a precise meaning that is understood generally or by a group of people — another example would be the sign of the cross made by Catholics).

   There is a fine line between voluntary and involuntary gestures: Is clenching of the fists voluntary or involuntary? Is nodding of the head a deliberate action or not?

❑ **Facial expressions** are usually used to express emotion: a smile, a grimace, a raising of the eyebrows, a frown. They can be voluntary or involuntary. To give an idea of the range of facial expressions possible, some of Birdwhistell's ways of notating facial expressions are shown on the next page.

❑ **Eye contact and movements** are meant to influence the degree of interaction with the person or persons in the communication exercise. When a speaker addresses a group, he looks from one to another to try to hold their attention. A person may look downwards to show shyness or guilt. A wink may express friendship, playfulness, or an invitation to flirt. These are all deliberate movements, but sometimes, as when eyes dilate with fear, they are involuntary.

Symbol	Description	Symbol	Description
S👁L	Slow lick of lips	—O—	Blank faced
Q👁L	Slow lick of lips	‿⌒	Single raised brow; ⌒ indicates brow raised
⬭	Moistening lips		
⬭	Lip biting	— ⌣	Lowered brow
ẘ	Whistle	\ /	Medial brow contraction
-👁-	Pursed lips	⬚	Medial brow nods
👁	Retreating lips	⌒⌒	Raised brows
-👁-!	Peck	O O	Wide eyed
-👁-!	Smack	—O	Wink
▦	Lax mouth	> <	Lateral squint
⬮	Chin protruding	✕ ✕	Full squint
⬯	'Dropped' jaw	ᵜᵜ	Shut eyes
⊢✕✕⊣	Chewing	◐◑	Sideways look
Ɛ Ɜ	Ear 'wiggle'	◖◗	Focus on auditor
⋀⋀⋀	Total scalp movement	⊗ ⊗	Stare
⬭	Out of side of mouth (left)	◎ ◎	Rolled eyes
⬭	Out of side of mouth (right)	∅ ∅	Slitted eyes
‿	Set jaw	◕ ◕	Eyes upward
‿	Smile	-◔ ◔-	Shifty eyes
⊢—⊣	Mouth in repose	⊗ ⊗	Glare
⌢	Droopy mouth	O Q	Inferior lateral orbit contraction
⟩	Tongue in cheek	△ₛ	Curled nostrils
⋀	Pout	ₛ△ₛ	Flaring nostrils
⋀	Clenched teeth	⋏	Pinched nostrils
ᴡ	Toothy smile	△	Bunny nose
▤	Square smile	▲	Nose wrinkle
◎	Open mouth	∿	Right sneer
ᴠ	Left sneer		

❏ **Body postures** tend to be less voluntary, but the way we stand or walk or lounge tells a great deal about us. Of course at times a body posture could be deliberately provocative, especially the studied posture of a woman or model trying to make an impression. Most times, however, we are communicating through body postures without realizing it.

We can understand the significance of body postures by using stick figures to represent various body postures and by discussing possible interpretations of what they may mean.

Let us look at this posture:

It suggests a shy person who feels inferior. Such a person may be sad or ashamed or just very humble. He is not a dominating person but may be subordinate or respectful. When we see such a posture, we should try to make the person feel more at ease and try to integrate the person into the business organization or the social group in a tactful, friendly way. We must understand that, whereas this stick figure representation is a symbol of an emotional state, we must not expect it to be exactly duplicated in real life; it merely indicates the kind of body posture that may suggest a self-conscious state. There may be other body postures that represent the same emotional state, but this has become the accepted notation for this state.

Here are two postures that represent opposite emotional states:
The one on the left represents a self-satisfied attitude. Perhaps it could be that the person is impatient or even angry, but then on the other hand he could be acting very casually. The important interpretation of this posture is that the person is not likely to be shy or feel inferior unless he is deliberately

hiding such an emotional state by trying to appear casual when in reality he is uncertain and in need of assurance. We must be careful not to isolate kinesic communication from its context. We are studying body posture not so that we may jump to conclusions about what it may communicate but so that we may widen our range of sensitivity to how people may communicate.

The stick-figure notation on the right may represent a superior attitude. The folded arms suggest a person closed off or aloof from others and the straddled legs suggest a dominant personality. Of course, it may be that the person is in reality surprised or suspicious or undecided about something and is also in need of assurance of some sort.

Before we give other stick-figure notations with the minimum of comment, let us look at another one merely to prevent too easy an interpretation. Most interpretations of this posture would say the person is affected or perhaps the interpretation would be less complimentary than this. We should, however, not jump to conclusions: perhaps it merely represents a person who has just thrown a dart at a dart board. The context would determine the accuracy of the interpretation.

Here then are other typical stick-figure notations of body postures with their usual interpretations suggested:

| Doubtful Indifferent Resigned | Puzzled Perplexed Thoughtful | Angry Frustrated Violent | Excited Happy Triumphant |

| Accepting
Welcoming
Loving | Hostile
Rejecting
Inflexible | Determined
Proud
Obstinate |

PROXEMICS

Proxemics deals with human proximity, that is, with how close one is to someone else. In business we may as managers choose to keep our distance from others. We may keep away from others by making it difficult for them to come into our offices, or we may separate ourselves from others by placing our desks in such positions as to make them barriers to communication. Counter space between staff and customers serves as a type of security so that staff and customers keep their distance. Again culture inculcates certain norms of distance: English people tend to be more aloof, whereas Mediterranean peoples tend to be more intimate. Blacks in South Africa do not worry much about close proximity, probably because they have had to live most of their lives in close proximity with others because of their cramped living quarters: consequently in a lift or a queue they do not mind bunching together, whereas a white person would probably like to have a clear territory reserved for himself without his space being invaded by anyone else. Of course, we can be misled into generalizations about proxemics too: the games of cricket and soccer are typically English sports, but lately we have witnessed behaviour of players in those games that is not what we would expect from the typical stiff-upper-lip, stand-offish Englishman; when a goal is scored or a wicket falls, the hugging and kissing are more like what we would expect of Mediterranean sportsmen. We should not, therefore, use proxemics to encourage generalizations.

The study of proxemics is not reserved for students of communication: the study of how space is used is part of the drama student's task and, of course, of the art student's. A journalist or advertiser needs to know how to arrange space satisfactorily. The study of proxemics could be regarded as a very important part of the study of life itself, but let us keep to business applications.

Let us divide our study of proxemics into three categories each using the term space:

☐ body space
☐ home space
☐ neutral space

Of course, we could have used the word 'territory' instead of 'space'. Konrad Lorenz has done much work in comparing attitudes of birds and animals towards territory with people's attitudes towards territory.

Body space is that area which we regard as our own and which is not to be violated. Of course, we can choose to be intimate when we allow our body space to be explored by a loved one, but it is this special intimacy that is reserved for one other person or very select people (usually our family) that creates a special personal relationship. Different people have different ideas about their body space: a more outgoing, extrovert person will allow and desire more body contact than an introvert, who jealously guards his space. A person in love or in his home territory will allow intimacy, but a person who is hostile or in a strange territory will protect his body space. Thus norms or accepted behaviour are created: at times we judge a person to be a flirt or to be promiscuous because he allows too much intimacy, or at other times we judge a person to be 'up tight' or too 'stand-offish' because he is too reserved about his body space. As businessmen and as people we have to learn to respect people's space: so often the manager thinks he has the right to dominate another person's space, whereas to the subordinate this is invasion of his or her body space and may be regarded as a form of sexual harassment. But at other times the opposite extreme of keeping apart may be regarded by subordinates as unfriendliness and being too conscious of his space. Managers need to be aware of their own and others' attitudes to body space so that they may be sensitive to the communication opportunities that body space affords. In an interviewing situation the movement towards a person in greeting can be regarded either as too informal or as too friendly, and the right degree of formality or friendliness is difficult to achieve. At the end of a conversation a too abrupt physical moving away may be seen as a slight, whereas a well-timed moving away may be accepted as a mutually acceptable close to the conversation.

Home space is that area which one has a right to regard as one's own in a home or in an office. A person's study or workshop or bedroom or office may be regarded as his home space and is not to be invaded lightly. One should respect another's home space. For example, one should knock before entering another's home space; but the other extreme of having a closed-door policy rather than an open-door policy may give offence and restrict communication.

The different attitudes that people adopt need to be dealt with sensitively. A housewife may regard her kitchen as home space not to be invaded by anyone, or she may, if she does not like to be thought of merely as a housewife, wish others to be involved in 'her' kitchen and may regard the notion of the kitchen as the woman's place as sexist; she may appreciate or expect others' involvement in 'her' kitchen.

A visitor to somebody else's home may casually help himself to a drink from the refrigerator and may offend the owner of a home who regards this as his territory, or else the owner may expect the visitor to 'feel at home' and help himself.

An employee's work station can be jealously regarded as his home space and he may lock up his cupboards each day, or he may be too casual about important documents and leave them lying about. Here there is doubt about the distinction between home space and what the business organization regards as business space, and the manager needs to provide clear communication about what is home space and therefore inviolable and what is business space and therefore to be governed by business procedures. The more the employee regards his work station as his home space, the more will he regard it as his own domain where he can decide whether it is to be kept tidy or not. If he regards it as business space, he may keep it tidy according to regulations issued but he will not regard it as his own with an accompanying sense of belonging. The sensitive manager will allow a nice balance between the two.

In one's home space what we may call orientation is important. An office or a home may promote or discourage interaction by the positioning of the furniture. If the furniture is arranged like the furniture in a waiting room, there will be little chance for communication except with the person next to you. If the furniture is arranged to allow for a cosy, friendly conversation among the people seated, then communication will be encouraged. It is therefore important for the manager when arranging his furniture to allow for informal as well as formal conversations. Orientation is not only a matter of furniture, however; it is also a matter of where one positions oneself in a conversation. The closer one is to a person without barriers such as a desk, the more likely it is that co-operation will be achieved. The more barriers and the further one is away from the other person, the more likely it is that there will be hostility or competition or differences of opinion. The diagram on the right makes this clear.

It is likely that A and B will be in a better communication position than A and C because they are closer together, but there is the possibility that A and B will be facing towards D and this will restrict their communication and this will mean that A who is facing D will find it easier to talk to D. Nevertheless they are in an orientation of competition and

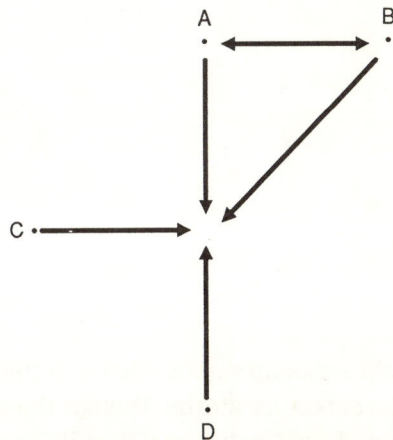

the greater the space between them, the more difficult communication will be. C is in a position that is difficult: if he turns towards A, he will be turning away from D, while even the act of turning to A suggests some kind of compromise and some difference in point of view. If we place a table in this diagram, these differences are magnified:

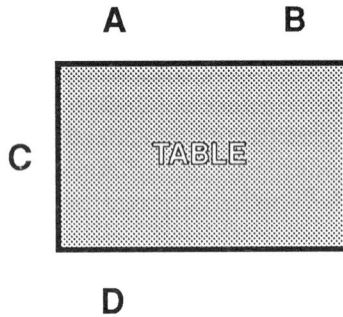

Now A and B are definitely on the same side of the table and therefore symbolically on the same side as far as communication is concerned. A and D face each other across the table and there is a natural context for competition. A and C have the table as a wedge between them and their orientation suggests disagreement. In terms of status the proxemics of this diagram could tell us much. C could be regarded as at the head of the table and therefore in charge. A and D could be next in importance but in opposition to each other, whereas B is somewhat left out in the cold and the least important member of the group, but on A's side.

This kind of orientation, which of course should not be over emphasized or taken out of context, is merely one of the considerations of communication, and leads to many businessmen favouring a round-table policy.

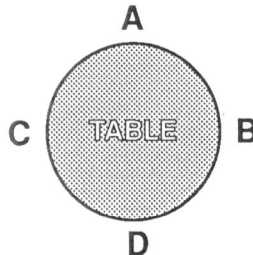

With a small round table and the four people seated round it there is less of a context for status, though the orientation may suggest conflict between A and D and between C and B.

Of course if the table is large and there are only four people, the space may cause other complications:

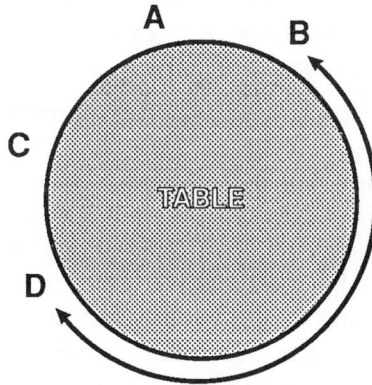

We are back to the closeness between A and B and the natural context for co-operation or intimacy; C and D now have the same kind of relationship as they are ranged together on the left 'side' of the round table. The communication between B and D may be difficult because of the space between them or because of the barrier of the table between them. A and D might also suffer from this kind of disadvantage, but the very great distance of empty space round the table from D to B or B to D emphasizes the void between them. A round table with a small group may not be a help but rather a hindrance.

Many businessmen therefore arrange their offices to allow easy movement of chairs and to make the kind or arrangements of space to suit the occasion. The fewer pieces of furniture acting as barriers, the better for the communication process.

Neutral space does not belong to anybody in particular. Of course the dynamics of proxemics allows neutral space to change quickly to home space: a lecture room is neutral space until the lecturer arrives and occupies his home space as the lecturer in control; a cinema is neutral space until a rowdy group takes over and dominates the space, to the discomfort of the other cinema-goers.

Normally, however, neutral space has the effect of inhibiting communication and emphasizing strangeness or differences. A lift is an example of neutral space: when strangers are in a lift together, they look up or down and very seldom look at each other because this would be considered an invasion of privacy.

Neutral space can, however, be an opportunity for communication and interaction. A lecture room or even an elevator can provide such opportunities, but one has to be sensitive to others' needs and wishes. The person in an audience who wishes to turn a lecture into a discussion group may not have assessed the occasion wisely. The man in a lift who strikes up a conversation with a woman who is a stranger to him may be regarded as a threat to her. A person in a lecture room often feels shy to express an opinion in public and is inhibited by the vast ground of neutral space: the larger the room and the larger the audience, the less likelihood that there will be participation. The lift, on the other hand, is a relatively small space and often people are crowded together. The dynamics of elevator communication would make an interesting study; here we have various factors of communication at work:

1. *Sex:* The communication or lack of it may be different if there are only men, if there are only women, or if there is a mixed group.

2. *Posture and Positioning:* this is an interesting case because usually all the occupants would be standing, but some may be facing each other (making communication easier) while others may be standing back-to-back or at least not facing each other (making communication more difficult). Do the occupants lean against the wall or stand stiffly or with arms folded?

3. *Distance:* Sometimes the elevator will be crowded and each person is in close contact with at least two or three people. It is often amusing to see white people trying to shrink into their own body space and trying to avoid touching the person or persons next to them. At other times the elevator may be occupied by only one or two people. What do we do if we are alone in a lift? Comb or re-arrange our hair, look at ourselves in the mirror? Anxiously watch the light indicating which floor we are on? Look at the papers we have in our hand? Or stand patiently and peacefully? It is quite a psychological study, isn't it? If there are only two people in the lift, they usually greet each other, whereas if there are more, they are less likely to. The initial greeting is like a feeler: Does the person want to talk or not? Is it neutral territory, body territory, or home territory? If the two people are strangers to the building, it is neutral territory. If one is employed in the building, the elevator is more like home territory and he will be more proprietary. If the two people are in love they may hold hands or use the opportunity to kiss each other or hug each other. If they are business associates, they may start a business discussion or ask after each other's families.

4. *Visual Behaviour:* Do the occupants look at each other or at the floor or at the light or at the roof? Do they make eye contact or deliberately avoid it?

5. *Temperature and Smell:* Is it hot? Are people perspiring? Are body temperatures and body odours obvious? How do people respond to these?

6. *Loudness of Voice:* Is there any talking? If not, the silence can be quite oppressive. If there is talking, do people talk softly, almost inaudibly? Or do they allow others to hear their conversation? Is the conversation intimate or general? Or is the speech loud and brash?

7. *Mood:* Is the mood of the people restrained or happy or depressed?

This fleeting analysis of the short period people are together in an elevator gives an insight into how communication works at its various levels.

PARALINGUISTICS

When we analyse non-verbal communication, we should take into account the sounds we make that are not actual words. These are often means of communication, nevertheless, and we call them *paralanguage* and the study of these sounds *paralinguistics*.

A public speaker often intersperses his speech with 'ums' and 'ahs' and 'ers'. He may clear his throat, he may laugh audibly, he may even use sounds like 'ugh' or expletives, which though they are words in themselves, do not have any precise verbal meaning. These characteristics of communication are often involuntary but they can tell us a great deal about the speaker, whether he is well-prepared, whether he is nervous, tense, or relaxed.

Paralinguistics concerns itself also with a person's tone of voice and the rate at which he speaks and the pitch of his voice. For instance, does a speaker pause often or does he speak very fast? Does he use silence as a communication aid or is he afraid of silence? Does he shout or does he whisper? Does he vary his tone of voice or does he speak in a monotone?

Emotion often causes us to use paralanguage. If we are sad, we may cry or groan or moan. If we are happy, we may laugh or giggle. If we are discontented, we may whine. If we are angry, we may shout. The good communicator tries to use emotion to good purpose. The poor communicator is controlled by the emotion, and although he communicates, he may not do so to his own advantage. But the person who controls emotion by repressing it is seldom a good communicator and is likely to become a frustrated person. There are involuntary sounds we make, like yawning or belching. Cultural influence will determine whether we belch loudly to express approval of the meal we have enjoyed or whether we suppress such natural sounds. One will yawn loudly in the privacy of one's home, whereas one would hesitate to do this audibly on neutral territory and would suppress it politely behind one's hand or with as little observable indication as possible.

Paralinguistic analysis allows us to observe our own and others' non-verbal communication so that we may understand what is happening behind the words. We often hear that we must 'read between the lines'; in the same way we must 'hear beyond the words'.

In a multicultural country like South Africa, where people are often not able to express themselves adequately in English, it is important not only to hear the words people say but to read or listen to the whole character of the person speaking to us. Sometimes the words that are used contradict the real message, which is given non-verbally. A manager must be sensitive to non-verbal messages and through sympathetic communication should be able to integrate the spoken and the non-spoken messages.

It is the ideal, of course, for the speaker of English as a first language to create harmony between the spoken and the non-spoken messages. Disharmony leads to uncertainty and distrust, which can destroy a business. It is the manager's task to integrate his own verbal and non-verbal communication and, without being patronizing, to become an expert in interpreting (or decoding) others' communication, where the verbal and the non-verbal may be at variance.

GRAPHICS

Introduction

The three types of non-verbal communication we have discussed so far in this chapter — kinesics, proxemics and paralinguistics — are complements to oral communication. The last — graphics — complements written communication as well as oral communication.

Visual media in communication are today a necessity. Our society has become so used to television and the cinema that any speaker or writer who does not use visual media runs the risk of not being heard or read. A speaker will find it very difficult to represent statistical information without graphic representation. A writer will find that graphic representation can say in half a page what would require pages to express in words and that the graphic communication may be more effective than the verbal.

A manager need only turn to his newspaper or to a magazine like *Time* or *Newsweek* or to the *Harvard Business Review* to see how important it is for him to understand graphic communication. Every issue contains a graphic representation of some business or economic statement. Any business student will be faced with graphs, pictorial illustrations, or diagrams to explain the verbal statements in his text books. Unfortunately, both for managers and students, the visual medium often turns out to be not an aid but a hindrance because they do not understand how to read graphic communication. This part of this last chapter is intended to assist managers and students to understand graphic communication and to assist them to compose their own visual media.

In an article in *Business Day* (October 5, 1989) Neil Jardine, a prominent South African headmaster, wrote:

> The 21st century will need a new model of student who is literate to the level of reasonably sophisticated comprehension, numerate in both the statistical and arithmetical sense, and comfortable with graphicacy — the interpretation of modes of communication involving shapes, diagrams, graphs, three-dimensional drawings and the like.

Although we do not like the term 'graphicacy', we approve of the emphasis Jardine gives to the importance of being able to interpret 'shapes, diagrams, graphs, three-dimensional drawings and the like'.

Shapes, Pictures, Symbols, Photographs

Let us begin with shapes, pictures, symbols and photographs. These communicate in different ways: a road sign with a message; an outline merely intended to give a fleeting suggestion of meaning or a feeling or a mood; a shape or ink blot intended to test a person's ability to project attitudes and personality problems onto the shape as in the well-known Rorschach ink-blot test; or a photograph that might be on the one hand a highly skilled work of art with many different interpretations or on the other hand a child's unsubtle attempt to capture a moment on his instamatic camera. All these shapes, pictures, symbols and photographs communicate usually without words or sounds and can become the objects of detailed study in psychology, advertising, or communication. For instance, is it better to use a photograph than a drawing in an advertisement? Which communicates to the prospective buyer better? Such questions could involve a market research agency in hours of surveys and analyses, and no general answer to such a question could be given since each photograph or picture would have to be treated on its own merits and not according to some general pontification.

In order that we may go a little deeper into the analysis of such shapes, pictures, symbols and photographs, let us briefly refer to three levels of meaning that we should try to see in any visual representation of this type. These three levels are based on Roland Barthes's essay, 'The Third Meaning — Research Notes on Some Eisenstein Stills'. Barthes calls them:

1. the informational meaning,
2. the symbolic or obvious meaning, and
3. the obtuse meaning.

The **informational meaning** tells the message; the **symbolic meaning** does not deal only with the message but with what the symbols signify according to the creator's intention and according to the common store of symbols which we all share; the **obtuse meaning** is that meaning which is greater than the informational and the symbolic in the same way that an obtuse angle is an angle greater than 90°. The obtuse meaning transcends information or reason, and whereas the symbolic meaning is a fixed emphasis, the obtuse meaning is not clear: it may cause ambiguity, irony, uncertainty, but it enriches the interpretation with a disguised, emotional, or thematic accent that is in the visual representation.

Not every visual representation has all three meanings. A traffic sign intends only one meaning, though our sense of humour may give even a traffic sign a symbolic meaning: a road sign reading 'Right turners must yield' might suggest a political message as well. A serious work of art usually has the first two meanings, the informational and the symbolic, though abstract art may work only on the second level. Barthes calls the third level the 'filmic' — 'that in the film which cannot be described, the representation which cannot be represented'. We do not consider that the third meaning is restricted to the film; it can be in any form of visual representation. Barthes uses the 'still'

from a film to substantiate his thesis. Why not use the still life of art, whether it be a painting, a sketch, or a photograph?

To illustrate the three levels of meaning, let us look at 'The Tightrope Walker' by David Andrew. This black and white charcoal drawing communicates on the informational level as a drawing of a circus scene. The black and white contrasts give the effect of the light in the circus tent focused on the arena where the tightrope walker performs, while the rest of the circus tent is in comparative darkness. The second level is the symbolic meaning the artist signifies. Why are the artists at the top of the tent — the trapeze artists — in darkness? Why are there animals in the audience? What is the role of the most dominant spectator perched almost as precariously as a tightrope walker and looking at the trapeze artists and not at the tightrope walker? What does the artist symbolize by these figures? We must remember that the symbolic meaning is meant to accentuate the informational meaning, not to distract from it. The symbols we have mentioned reinforce the circus theme: the trapeze artists are like actors behind the scenes preparing to make their entrance; the animals are seen not only as performers but as spectators, as human beings; the dominant spectator is crouching like an animal and is as involved in the circus performance as the performers themselves, He 'sees' into the darkness of the circus, the dark side as well as the light side of what makes the circus. As such, he is the artist himself, the self-portrait as part of the larger canvas. Then there is the structure on which the tightrope walker is walking: it is not a tightrope at all. It is more like an organic structure growing in the centre of the circus arena; it is more from the recesses of the jungle than from the structures of steel and rope such as are usually found in a circus. And the tightrope walker is, as we have seen, not a tightrope walker at all, but an absurd clown with a hat and a shabby suit, performing perhaps rather poorly to a nondescript audience of heads unaware of the darker side of the circus.

What then is the obtuse level of meaning in this drawing? The obtuse meaning, we will remember, is that accent which may run counter to the informational and need not be more than a hint. It may subvert the narrative but it will not destroy it. In this drawing the third meaning is that feeling of unease and uncertainty about what is at first seen as familiar. The darkness assumes a potential of danger which is associated with the heights of the circus tent, but there is also a danger to the tightrope walker clown: the structure on which he stands has suggestions of rotating blades threatening to knock him off and of a heavy roof-like structure above him that may fall on top of him. The dominant spectator as he looks up appears to be about to swing on the rope that he holds and to join the dangerous circus action. The small audience in the foreground (including the bears) appears to be more aware and intelligent than the audience of heads in the background that mingle more with the incongruous music of the band; they are insensitive to the real drama of danger and darkness. The obtuse level of meaning hints at the dark side of art and the different ways of seeing and participating.

What, you may ask, has this to do with the manager and business communication? First, the proper appreciation of art is an asset for any businessman. Art has become a major investment opportunity in the world today. Second, whether we realize it or not, this third level of meaning, the vague unarticulated feeling about a photograph or an illustration in an advertisement or a book, plays a part in our everyday life. Market researchers rely a great deal on these qualitative responses to products and advertisements. There is a meaning beyond the obvious, beyond the literal and the analytical, beyond the symbolic, and it is similar to the 'gut feel' we have for things. Managers would do well to be aware of the existence of this third meaning and to become sensitive to it.

Examples and Illustrations

In any presentation, whether it is oral or written, examples and illustrations will heighten the level of response from the receiver of the communication. Since we are now discussing graphic communication, we shall give attention to graphic examples and illustrations, but we should not ignore the value of verbal examples and illustrations as well.

From childhood we have wanted illustrations to make our reading more pleasurable. The comic strip has become an important mode of communication. It gives a 'slice of life' that is used as an example to illustrate a particular point. The cartoonist has a value in modern society that has probably been unequalled previously. We are becoming more and more visual in our understanding probably because of the influence of the cinema and television. Though some may regret the loss of verbal skills, the businessman will make the most of graphic opportunities to attract and interest.

Most graphic examples or illustrations will consist of three elements:

1. the linguistic,
2. the denoted iconic, and
3. the connoted iconic.

The **linguistic message** will come from the words that usually form part of the example or illustration, even if they are only a title. They help to elucidate the visual or iconic message by directing the receiver's response or anchoring it to a particular denoted meaning. Sometimes the linguistic message may complement the visual; sometimes the linguistic is more important than the iconic, as in some comic strips; and at other times, as in a film, perhaps the visual will be more important than the script. In this sense, the linguistic message does not anchor or direct but tends to relay the connoted message with the help of the visual.

The **iconic elements** are visual elements. Historically, an icon was a painting or mosaic of a sacred person, and the icon itself usually assumed sacred significance. Nowadays the word icon is used for the special visual significance of an image. The **denoted** iconic element is the literal image, whereas the **connoted** iconic element is the symbolic image. In the same way as we say a word denotes its obvious meaning or meanings, its dictionary meanings, so we may say that an image denotes what is obvious when we first look at it. It is the informational meaning that we spoke about in the previous section of this chapter. It is the perceptual, fundamental meaning: it identifies what it is that is represented. Barthes claims that the photograph is the perfect example of denotation because the photograph constitutes 'a message without a code': it does not 'intervene *within* the object' as a drawing does ('there is no drawing without style'). The connoted iconic element is, on the other hand, the symbolic suggestion *in addition to* the fundamental meaning. With a photograph, it would depend on the way in which the photographer arranged her material, the particular slant or emphasis she may have created by lighting and distance, the way in which she framed the photograph or reduced it, or the colours used — whether in black or white or in natural colours or heightened colours. The connoted iconic element depends on symbols which have personal, cultural, and aesthetic associations for the creator of the example or illustration and for the viewer as well. Far from being the obvious, fundamental meaning, the connoted iconic element provides surprising interpretations and implications that may tend to be fleeting and unrelated to the linguistic and denoted iconic element.

The success of an example or illustration can be judged by the way in which these three elements have been unified: does the linguistic message anchor or direct the denoted iconic meaning or does it relay the connoted iconic meaning? Does the denoted iconic meaning support the connoted iconic meaning? Does the connoted iconic meaning allow an excitement and development of meaning stretching beyond the obvious?

Figures, Charts and Diagrams

Throughout this book we have tried to break up the verbal communication with figures, charts, and diagrams. For example, we have used diagrams for our communication model, we have used figures to represent different perceptions, and we have used organizational charts in our section on business communication. There have been many other such figures, charts, and diagrams. The purpose of these is to present information in a variety of ways. Although we communicate mainly with the spoken or the written word, we need to use every opportunity to present information effectively. We have spoken of the advantage of space and time in presenting information graphically. There are also advantages of quickening interest by the use of visual or statistical material.

Before we move on to the use of graphics in statistics and economics, let us look at some of the uses of figures, charts, and diagrams in a non-statistical way. Often by using circles, boxes, symbols, and arrows we can create an interesting visual effect with the minimum of words or figures.

With judicious choice of colours, the following diagram could be even more effective.

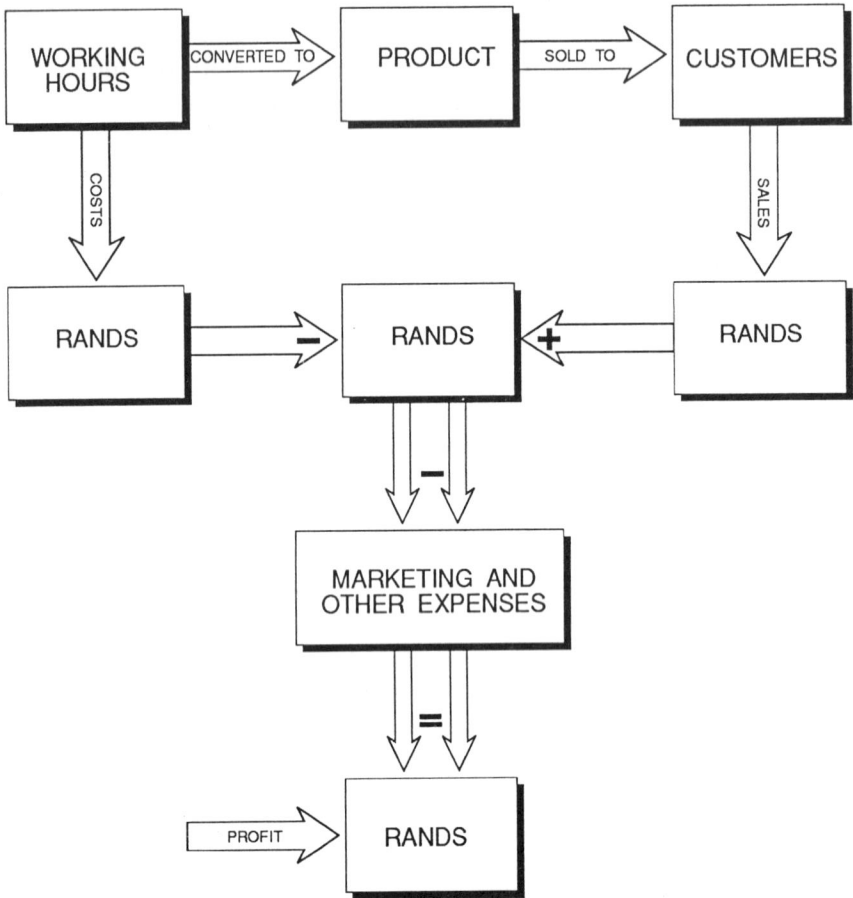

Organization charts, flow charts, decision tables, algorithms, and network diagrams are examples of non-statistical graphics. Managers and students will come across such graphics more and more frequently as they progress. **Network analysis** is an important part of planning, and various names are given to it, such as Critical Path Analysis (CPA), Critical Path Methods (CPM), and Programme Evaluation Review Technique (PERT). Here is a simple **network diagram**:

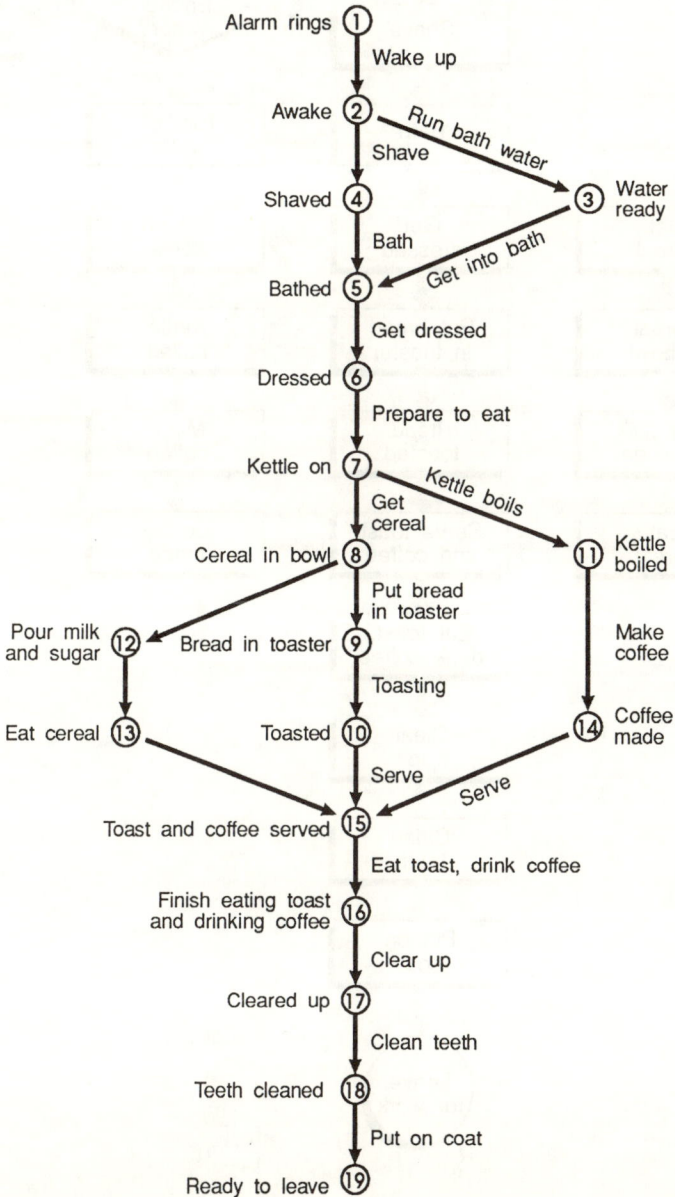

Alarm rings ①
    Wake up

Awake ②
    Run bath water
    Shave

Shaved ④   ③ Water ready
    Bath
    Get into bath

Bathed ⑤
    Get dressed

Dressed ⑥
    Prepare to eat

Kettle on ⑦   *Kettle boils*
    Get cereal

Cereal in bowl ⑧   ⑪ Kettle boiled
    Put bread in toaster

Pour milk and sugar ⑫ Bread in toaster ⑨   Make coffee
    Toasting

Eat cereal ⑬   Toasted ⑩   ⑭ Coffee made
    Serve   *Serve*

Toast and coffee served ⑮
    Eat toast, drink coffee

Finish eating toast and drinking coffee ⑯
    Clear up

Cleared up ⑰
    Clean teeth

Teeth cleaned ⑱
    Put on coat

Ready to leave ⑲

The same information could be put into a **flow chart**, using the following symbols:

○ For starting or ending   ☐ For activities   ◇ for decisions

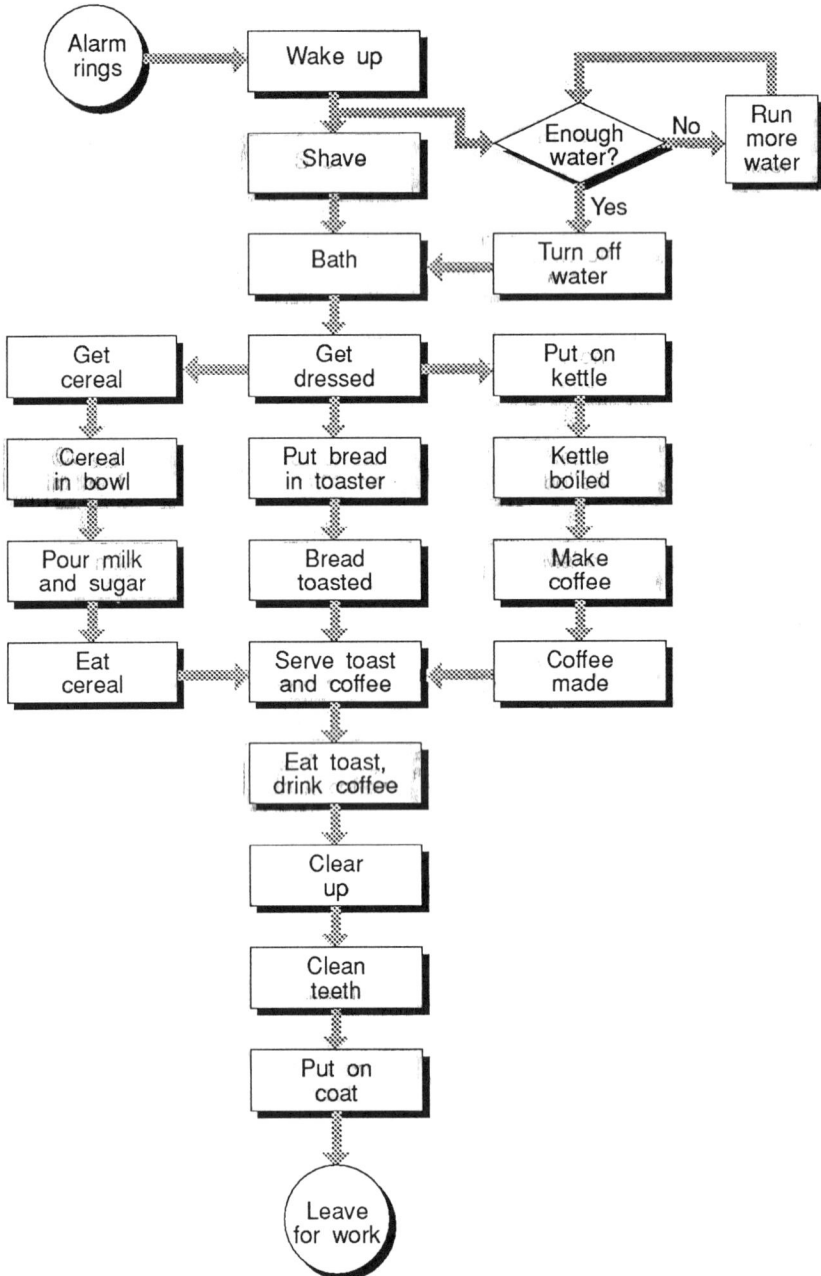

Alarm rings → Wake up

Shave → Enough water? — No → Run more water

Yes

Turn off water → Bath

Get cereal ← Get dressed → Put on kettle

Cereal in bowl   Put bread in toaster   Kettle boiled

Pour milk and sugar   Bread toasted   Make coffee

Eat cereal → Serve toast and coffee ← Coffee made

Eat toast, drink coffee

Clear up

Clean teeth

Put on coat

Leave for work

Here is an example of a **decision table** that could be used for admission of a student to a professional diploma course:

DECISION TABLE

ADMISSION PROCEDURE	ACTION				
1. Does the student have a Standard Ten?	YES	NO↓			
2. Does the student have an equivalent or higher qualification?		YES ↘NO			
3. Is the student over 23 years of age?			YES ↘NO		
4. Has the student been employed for three years?				YES ↘NO	
ACCEPT REGISTRATION	✓	✓	✓	✓	
REJECT REGISTRATION					✗

If the answer to question 1 is yes, the student would immediately be accepted. If the answer to question 1 is no, and the answer to question 2 is yes, she would be accepted. If the answer to questions 1 and 2 is no but the answer to question 3 is yes, she would be accepted. If the answer to questions 1, 2, and 3 is no but the answer to question 4 is yes, she would still be accepted. If the answer to questions 1, 2, 3, and 4 is no, she would be rejected.

Such decision tables can be very useful for repeated routine decisions. The same applies to flow charts and algorithms. An **algorithm** is similar to a decision table, but the flow is represented by a diagram rather than a table (see next page).

The Use of Graphics in Statistics and Economics

Statistical and economic information is frequently represented graphically. Yet students and businessmen often do not understand these **graphic representations**. A few words of explanation of basic statistics and economics are therefore necessary.

The advantages of graphic presentations of economic and statistical information over verbal presentations have been clearly established for some time. Fairly recently mathematical presentations have also been introduced. Although the well-known economist, John Maynard Keynes, hardly used any mathematics in his economic theories, mathematics to represent linear equations in graphic representations, especially in macro-economic theory, has become a necessity. The use of mathematical presentations in conjunction with graphic presentations has always been an important part of statistics.

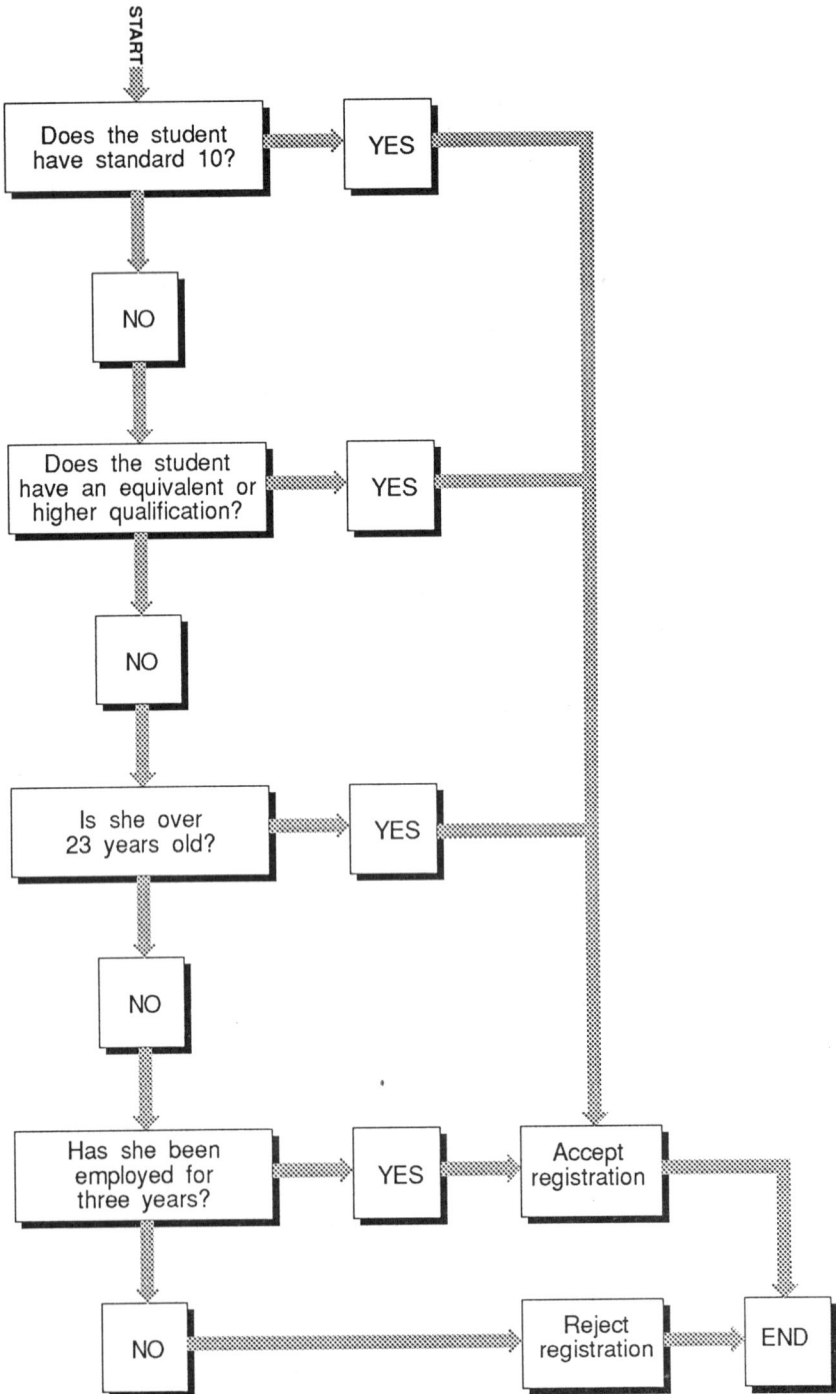

START

```
┌─────────────────────┐         ┌─────────┐
│ Does the student    │────────▶│  YES    │───────────────┐
│ have standard 10?   │         └─────────┘               │
└─────────────────────┘                                   │
         │                                                │
         ▼                                                │
    ┌─────────┐                                           │
    │  NO     │                                           │
    └─────────┘                                           │
         │                                                │
         ▼                                                │
┌─────────────────────┐         ┌─────────┐               │
│ Does the student    │────────▶│  YES    │──────────┐    │
│ have an equivalent  │         └─────────┘          │    │
│ or higher           │                              │    │
│ qualification?      │                              │    │
└─────────────────────┘                              │    │
         │                                           │    │
         ▼                                           │    │
    ┌─────────┐                                      │    │
    │  NO     │                                      │    │
    └─────────┘                                      │    │
         │                                           │    │
         ▼                                           │    │
┌─────────────────────┐         ┌─────────┐          │    │
│ Is she over         │────────▶│  YES    │──────────┤    │
│ 23 years old?       │         └─────────┘          │    │
└─────────────────────┘                              │    │
         │                                           │    │
         ▼                                           │    │
    ┌─────────┐                                      │    │
    │  NO     │                                      │    │
    └─────────┘                                      ▼    ▼
         │                              ┌───────────────────┐
         ▼                              │ Accept            │
┌─────────────────────┐   ┌─────────┐   │ registration      │──┐
│ Has she been        │──▶│  YES    │──▶│                   │  │
│ employed for        │   └─────────┘   └───────────────────┘  │
│ three years?        │                                        │
└─────────────────────┘                                        │
         │                                                      │
         ▼                                                      ▼
    ┌─────────┐          ┌───────────────────┐       ┌─────────┐
    │  NO     │─────────▶│ Reject            │       │  END    │
    └─────────┘          │ registration      │       └─────────┘
                         └───────────────────┘
```

Let us start with graphs. A simple line graph has two axes, the vertical axis and the horizontal axis:

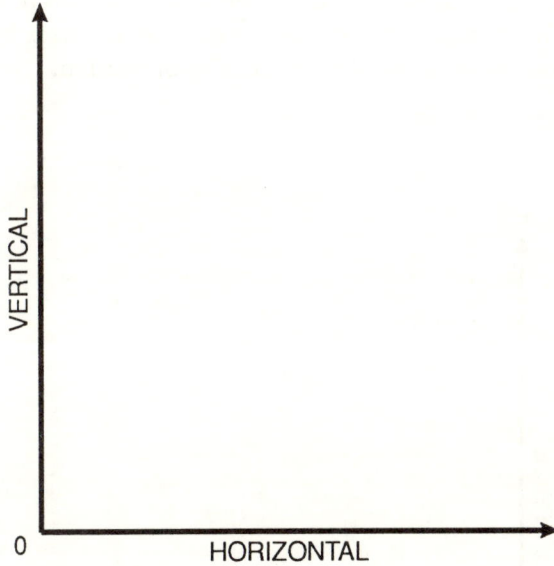

A graph shows visually and quickly the relations between different quantities in mathematical, statistical, and economic problems. This is described in a system of linear equations by the notation

$y = f(x)$ or
$x = f(y)$

This means that y is related to or dependent on x in some way and that x is related to or dependent on y in some way. (Please note that it does *not* mean that y is equal to f multiplied by x or that x is equal to f multiplied by y.) We read these mathematical statements in this way: y is a function of x, or x is a function of y. In graphic form we would represent this relation in this way:

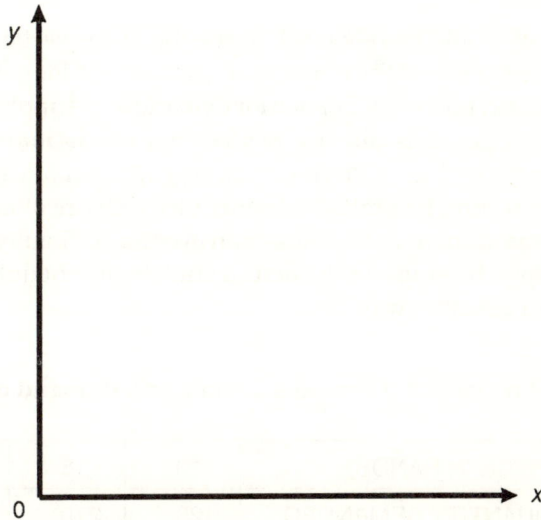

By marking the vertical axis as the *y* axis and the horizontal axis as the *x* we are stating the same relation: for any value of *y* along the vertical axis, *y* is related to or dependent on a corresponding value of *x;* in other words *y* is a function of *x* and *vice versa*. It is a convention in algebra to call the vertical axis *y* and the horizontal *x*. Of course, we can call the axes by other names, either written out or by some other form of abbreviation.

For instance we could use

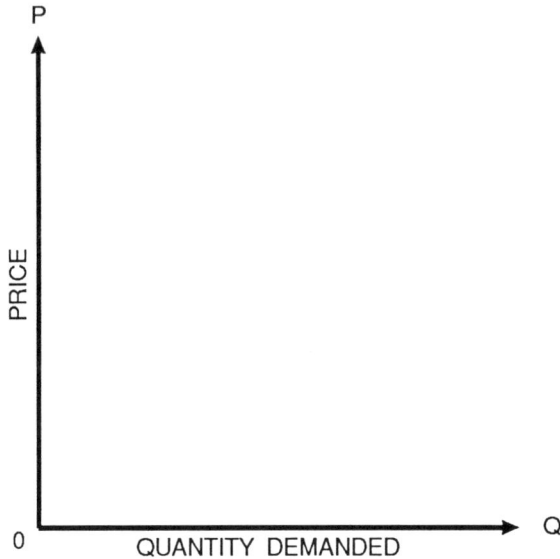

or we could merely use P at the top of the vertical axis to stand for price and Q at the end of the horizontal axis to stand for quantity. This is the convention used in micro-economics for demand and supply graphs, as we shall see later.

A graph is directly related to a **statistical table** or **schedule**. Whether that schedule is given or not, a graph can always be understood as graphic shorthand for statistical schedules that are often clumsy and boring to read. If the student or businessman ever has difficulty with a graph, he can always apply the graph to the actual statistical schedule which the graph interprets in a succinct way.

Let us look at a typical schedule and **demand curve**:

PRICE IN RANDS	10	15	20	25	30
QUANTITY DEMANDED	425	270	160	95	50

Similarly we could look at a typical supply schedule and **supply curve**:

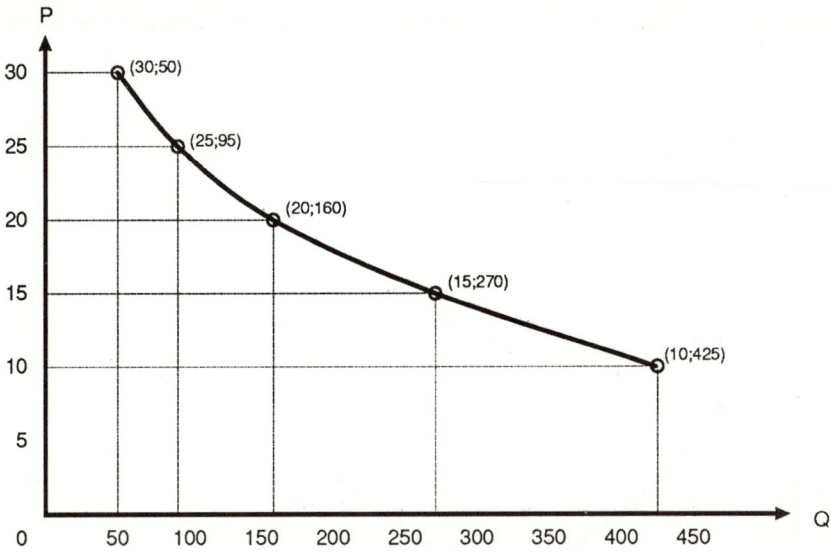

PRICE IN RANDS	10	15	20	25	30
QUANTITY SUPPLIED	45	155	250	320	350

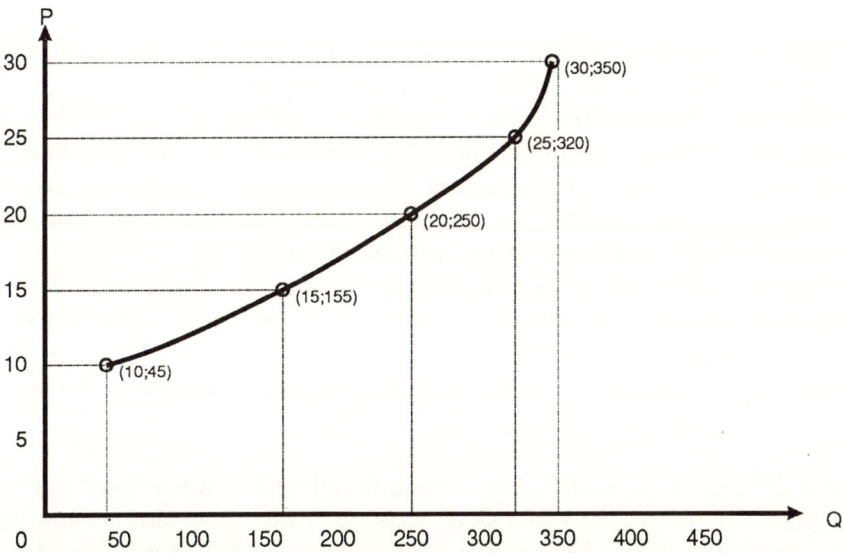

And we could combine these into demand and supply schedules and into demand and supply curves showing the market equilibrium at the point of intersection:

PRICE IN RANDS	10	15	20	25	30
QUANTITY DEMANDED	425	270	160	95	50
QUANTITY SUPPLIED	45	155	250	320	350

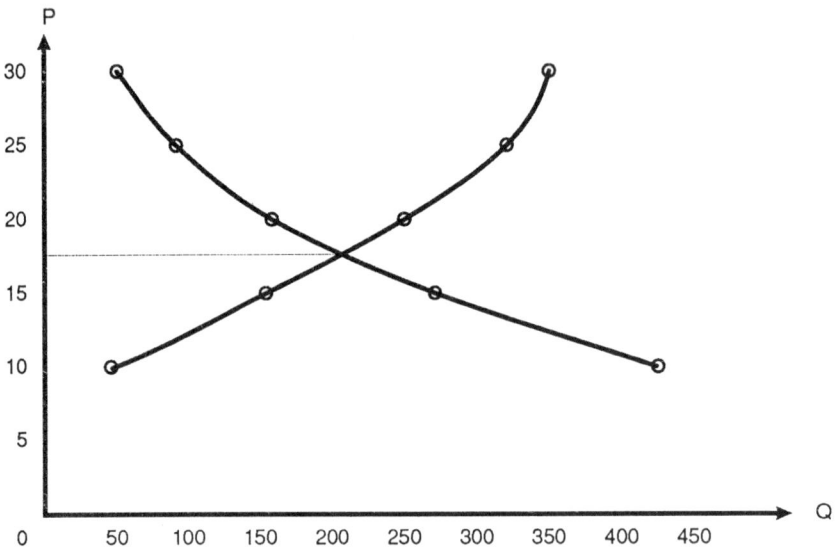

At the price of R17,50 we have the market price that is determined by the point at which the supply and demand curves intersect.

We have demonstrated rather laboriously the connection between the schedules and the graphs by showing the co-ordinates for each point and by the dotted lines across to the vertical and horizontal axes. Of course, the more familiar we are with graphs, the less we do this. Most economic graphs do not use schedules or figures on the axes at all.

Graphical or geometric representations work in two dimensions: in other words with two variables. But economic analysis uses **mathematical symbols** and **equations** as well as graphs and geometry to show the relation between more than two variables. By using a **linear equation** such as

$y = a + bx$ (Where $a > 0$ and $b > 0$)

we can go further than saying that y is a function of x: we can say that y is an *increasing* function of x. If x were equal to 0, then y would be equal to a and as x increases by one then y would increase by an amount equal to b. Let us put this in a schedule:

x	0	1	2	3	4
y	a	$a + b$	$a + 2b$	$a + 3b$	$a + 4b$

Now let us represent this in a graph:

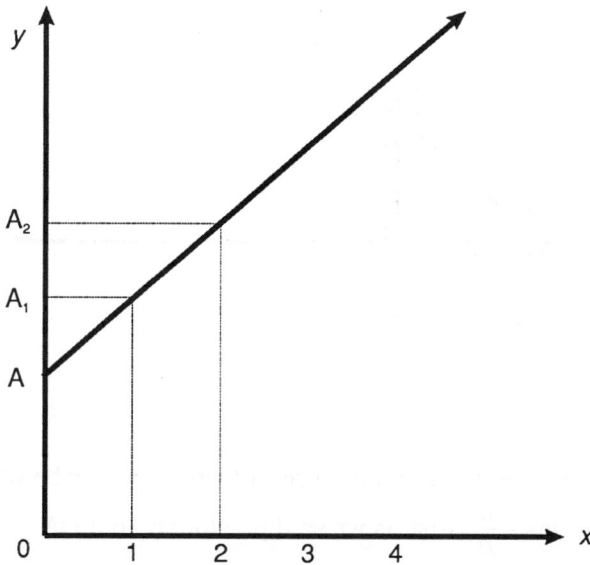

When $x = 0$, then y must have the value OA, which would be a (OA on the y axis). When $x = 1$, then y must have the value OA$_1$, which would be $a + b$ (OA$_1$ on the y axis). When $x = 2$, then y must have the value OA$_2$, which would be equal to $a + 2b$ (OA$_2$ on the y axis), and so on. The term b is called the **slope** or **gradient** of the function (y is a function of x): since b is positive (b has a + sign), y is an increasing or a positive function of x and the straight line graph will slope upwards from the left to right.

From the equation we can work out the value of x:

If $y = a + bx$

then $bx = y - a$

$\therefore \quad x = \dfrac{y - a}{b}$

When $y = 0$, then $x = - \dfrac{a}{b}$.

This can be represented on the graph by extending it (see following page).

Our graph now shows possibilities of negative values for x (to the left of 0) and from y (below 0 on the y axis).

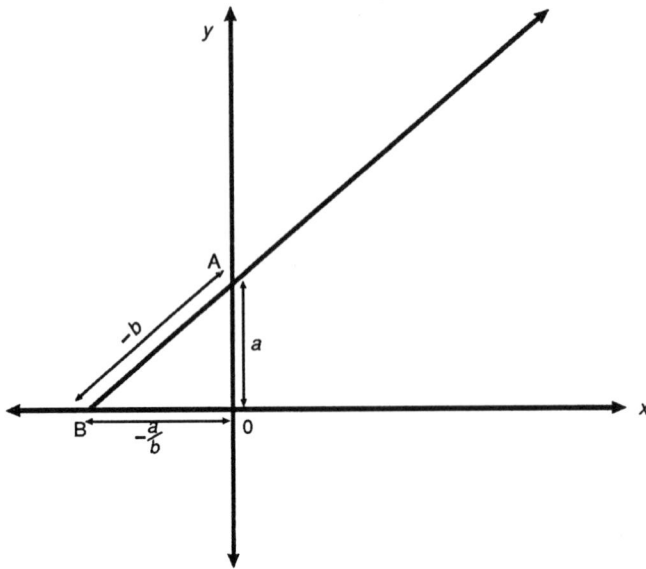

The negative value OB for x would represent what x would be when $y = 0$. We said this value was $-\frac{a}{b}$. Just as we said previously that OA = a, now we say that OB = $-\frac{a}{b}$. If we divide OA by OB $(\frac{OA}{OB})$ we get:

$$\frac{OA}{OB} = \frac{a}{-a/b}$$

$$= \frac{a}{1} \times \left(-\frac{b}{a}\right)$$

$$= -b$$

We have already said that b is the slope or the gradient of the function (y is a function of x) and now we see it graphically: b is the slope of the straight line $\overrightarrow{BA}$ or $\overrightarrow{AB}$ and can be found by dividing OA by OB. We can ignore the negative sign (–) before b because obviously the gradient is the same on the positive part of the graph as on the negative part.

We can see y as a negative or decreasing function of x as well:

$y = c - dx$ (where $c > 0$ and $d > 0$).

This means that when $x = 0$, y will be equal to c and as x increases in value to one, so y will decrease by an amount equal to d.

x	0	1	2	3
y	c	$c-d$	$c-2d$	$c-3d$

We represent this graphically in this way:

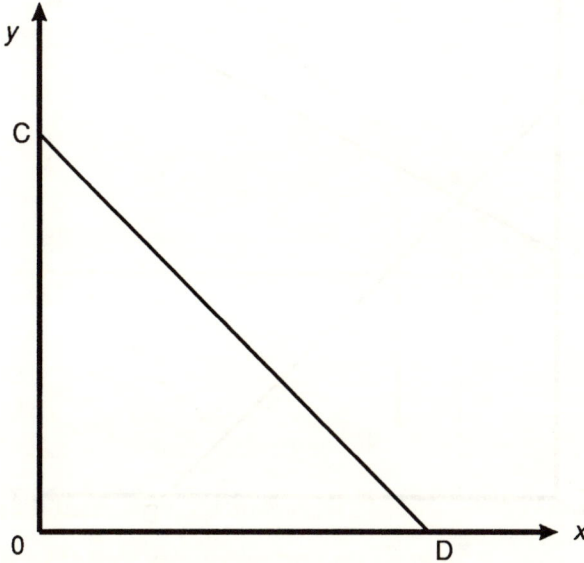

When the value of x is 0, then the value of y is OC = c. When the value of y is 0, then the value of x is OD. Mathematically,

if $y = c - dx$

then $dx = c - y$

$$\therefore \quad x = \frac{c - y}{d}$$

If y is 0, then $x = \frac{c}{d}$

$$\therefore \qquad OD = \frac{c}{d}$$

In the same way as we did with the equation $y = a + bx$, we can now find the gradient CD:

$$\frac{OC}{OD} = \frac{c}{c/d}$$

$$= \frac{c}{1} \times \frac{d}{c}$$

$$= d$$

The two equations

$y = a + bx$ and

$y = c - dx$

can now be represented on the same graph.

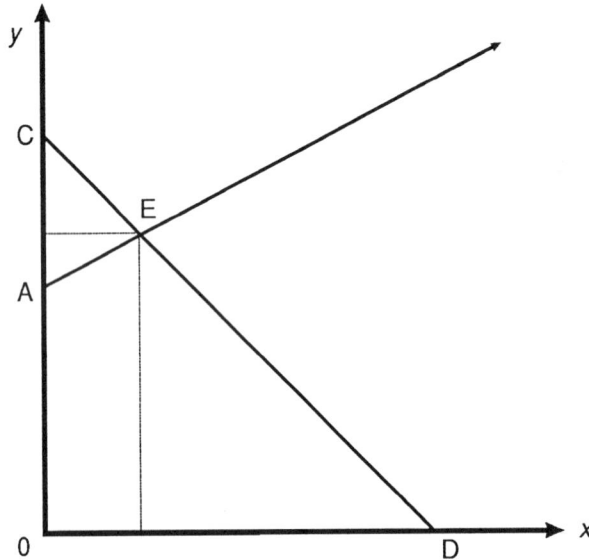

The point of intersection is E and could be measured on the x and y axes. What is important is that what we have done graphically by finding the point of intersection is the same as finding the algebraic solution of the two linear equations. We shall discuss this later.

Now it does not take a very perceptive reader to notice that what we have here is easily applied to demand and supply curves. In fact it can be adapted to many economic applications. If we change the two equations slightly we have the demand equation

$Q = c - dP$

and the supply equation

$Q = a + bP.$

Let us then apply the economic model for demand and supply to a practical example with a demand schedule and a supply schedule and see how the model works.

Price		0	300	600	900	1 200	1 500	1 800
Quantity Demanded	1 200	1 000		800	600	400	200	0

Price		0	400	800	1 200	1 600
Quantity Supplied		300	600	900	1 200	1 500

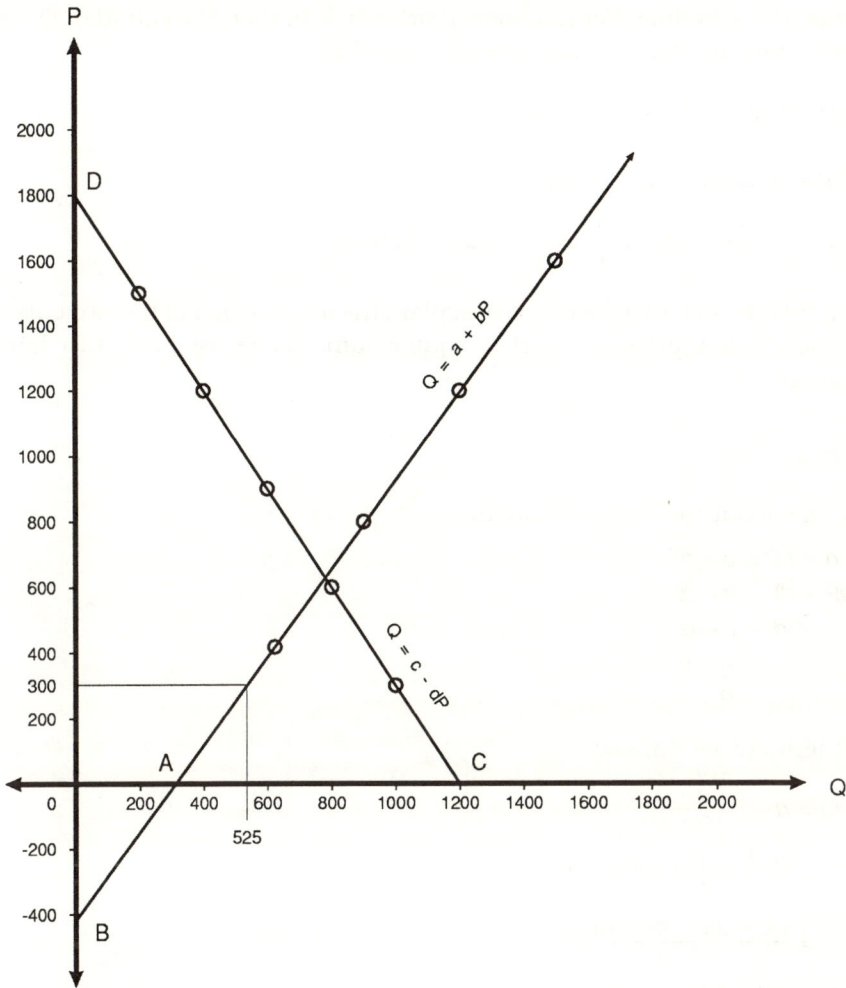

This shows that the demand equation $Q = c - dP$ may be specified as $Q = 1\ 200 - \frac{2}{3}P$, for when P is 0, then c is 1 200 and the gradient $d = \frac{OC}{OD} = \frac{1\ 200}{1\ 800} = \frac{2}{3}$. Similarly the supply equation $Q = a + bP$ may be specified as $Q = 300 + \frac{3}{4}P$, for when P is 0, then a is 300 and the gradient $b = \frac{OA}{OB} = \frac{300}{-400} = -\frac{3}{4}$. As we said previously the negative sign (–) is of no special significance.

Returning to the demand schedule we can check each point on the graph against the schedule. For instance, if price is 300, then the equation $Q = c - dP$ will show us that the quantity demanded is:

$$Q = 1\ 200 - \frac{2}{3}\ (300) = 1\ 000$$

and the quantity supplied is:

$$Q = a + bP = 300 + \frac{3}{4}\ (300) = 300 + 225 = 525$$

But a further step may be taken to explain the intersection of the two curves, i.e. the market price or market equilibrium. Since we have two linear equations

$$Q = a + bP \quad \text{and}$$
$$Q = c - dP,$$

we can substitute for Q and say that

$$a + bP = c - dP$$
$$\therefore\ bP + dP = c - a$$
$$\therefore\ P\ (b + d) = c - a$$
$$\therefore\ P = \frac{c - a}{b + d}$$

Furthermore we can say

$$Q = a + b\left(\frac{c - a}{b + d}\right)$$
$$= \frac{a\ (b + d) + b\ (c - a)}{b + d}$$
$$= \frac{ab + ad + bc - ab}{b + d}$$
$$= \frac{ad + bc}{b + d}$$

What we have done is that we have solved these two equations by expressing P and Q in terms of a, b, c, and d. Now if we substitute our knowns for a, b, c, and d as we have specified them for these particular line graphs, i.e.

$$a = 300$$
$$b = \frac{3}{4}$$
$$c = 1\ 200$$
$$d = \frac{2}{3}$$

we can calculate:

$$P = \frac{c - a}{b + d}$$

$$= \frac{1\ 200 - 300}{\frac{3}{4} + \frac{2}{3}}$$

$$= \frac{900}{\frac{9+8}{12}}$$

$$= \frac{900}{1} \times \frac{12}{17}$$

$$= \frac{10\ 800}{17}$$

$$= 635,3$$

and

$$Q = \frac{ad - bc}{b + d}$$

$$= \frac{200 + 900}{\frac{3}{4} + \frac{2}{3}}$$

$$= \frac{1\ 100}{1} \times \frac{12}{17}$$

$$= \frac{13\ 200}{17}$$

$$= 776,5$$

If we compare the graphic solution with the algebraic solution we shall see that the solutions are the same. What may at first have appeared to be a graphic solution of P = 600 and Q as 800 is shown to be slightly more than 600 and slightly less than 800.

We have spent some time on linear equations and their solutions both graphically and algebraically because this type of communication causes difficulty to many students of economics. Let us now turn to basic statistics and graphical representations of basic statistical concepts.

Graphical Representation

There are three statistical terms that need explanation (they are usually called measures of central tendency): the arithmetic mean (or average), the median, and the mode. Most of us know that the average is obtained by finding the total of all the scores and then dividing the number of scores: the **arithmetic mean** (or **average**) usually uses the symbol $\overline{X}$, and the formula for finding the arithmetic mean is:

$$\overline{X} = \frac{X}{N}$$

where X = the total of the scores and N = the number of scores. If we were to find the arithmetic mean of the scores

0, 12, 58, 64, 3, 17, 18, 102, 5, 72

we would add them together (351) and divide by 10 and the average would be 35,1. The arithmetic mean is greatly influenced by very high or very low scores: for instance, if we were to omit the first score 0, the average would rise significantly to 39 or if we were to omit the score of 102, it would drop significantly to 27,7.

The **median** helps to keep us on our guard against any distorted average because of very high or very low scores. It is a good idea therefore to find the median and compare it with the average. To find the median, we arrange the scores sequentially in order of magnitude and find the middle score in this arrangement:

    0, 3, 5, 12, 17, 18, 58, 64, 72, 102 (ascending order of magnitude)
    102, 72, 64, 58, 18, 17, 12, 5, 3, 0 (descending order of magnitude)

The median of the figures when arranged in an ascending order of magnitude is between 17 and 18, and the median of the figures when arranged in a descending order is between 18 and 17. (There are 10 scores and the median is between the 5th and 6th score. If there were 9 scores the median would be the 5th score.)

When we compare the median with the arithmetic mean in our example of ten scores, we see that the arithmetic mean has been distorted by the four comparatively high scores 58, 84, 72 and 102. Although it is useful as a check, the median does not give an accurate statistical statement on its own because it does not take into account extremes of very high and very low scores.

The **mode** is a term used in statistics to refer to scores that occur frequently. It is useful in dealing with frequency distribution, skewed distribution, and standard deviation. Suppose we were to group our ten scores of 0, 3, 5, 12, 17, 18, 58, 64, 72, 102 into groups of: 0–10, 11–20, 21–30, 31–40, 41–50, 51–60, 61–70, 71–80, 81–90, 91–100, 101–110, we would have:

0–10	I I I
11–20	I I I
21–30	–
31–40	–
41–50	–
51–60	I
61–70	I
71–80	I
81–90	–
91–100	–
101–110	I

This shows a very erratic tendency to either very low scores or significantly higher scores. The mode is 0–20 in this example, because it is where the frequently occurring scores are grouped. It would become even clearer if we were to group the scores in groups of: 0–20, 21–40, 41–60, 61–80, 81–100, 101–120:

0–20	⁺⁺⁺⁺ ⁣ I
21–40	–
41–60	I
61–80	I I
81–100	–
101–120	I

(The batching of five scores in a group is referred to as ⁺⁺⁺⁺).

Besides knowing the mean, the medium, and the mode, it is also useful to know how an individual score deviates from the mean and to find the **standard deviation**, which will tell us how individual scores are distributed in relation to the mean. Let us look at these scores:

96, 94, 86, 82, 82, 80, 76, 72, 68, 64

The arithmetic mean for these scores is $\dfrac{800}{10}$ = 80. To find the standard deviation we find out how each score deviates from the mean, then we square each of these deviations, add up the squares of the deviations, divide by the number of scores, and then find the square root. This is expressed by the formula:

$$\sigma = \sqrt{\frac{\sum x^2}{N}}$$

Where:

    σ = standard deviation

    $\sqrt{\ }$ = square root

    $\sum$ = the sum of

    x = the deviation of each score

    N = the number of scores in the distribution

Individual scores	Deviations from the mean	Deviations squared
96	16	256
94	14	196
86	6	36
82	2	4
82	2	4
80	0	0
76	−4	16
72	−8	64
68	−12	144
64	−16	256
800		$\sum x^2$ =976

$$\text{Mean} = \frac{800}{10}$$
$$= 80$$

From these figures we can calculate the standard deviation to be:

$$\sigma = \sqrt{\frac{976}{10}} = \sqrt{97,6} = \pm 9,9$$

(The reason we square the deviations is to remove the negative signs.)

Now that we have established what the arithmetic mean, the median, the mode and the standard deviation are, we can return to graphical representations as used in statistics. A **frequency distribution curve** is often used to make statistical analysis more simple to understand. There are three types of distribution curves:

1.   the normal (Gaussian) distribution curve,
2.   the positively skewed distribution curve, and
3.   the negatively skewed distribution curve.

The normal distribution curve is a bell-shaped curve that looks like this:

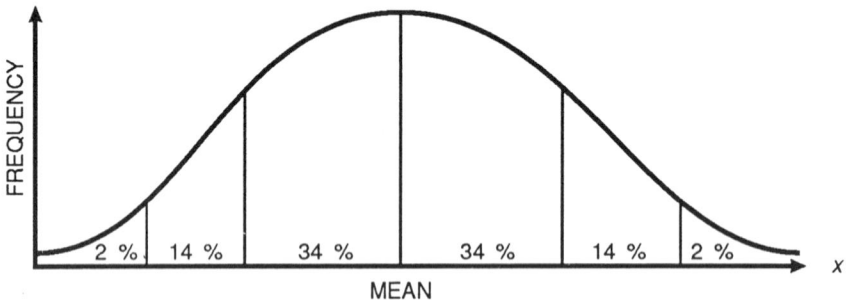

This graph would mean that 2 % of scores would be in the lower ranges (to the left) or in the higher ranges (to the right); 14 % of the scores would be to the right of the lower ranges and 14 % of the scores would be to the left of the higher ranges; and 34 % of the scores would be grouped either on the left or the right of the mean. The normal distribution curve divides scores into these standard deviation units and provides a good guide to examiners, for instance, to ensure that their marking has not been too severe or too lenient. Although the normal distribution curve is often given in this way without numerical pointers, it may help us to understand it better if we keep to our examination analogy:

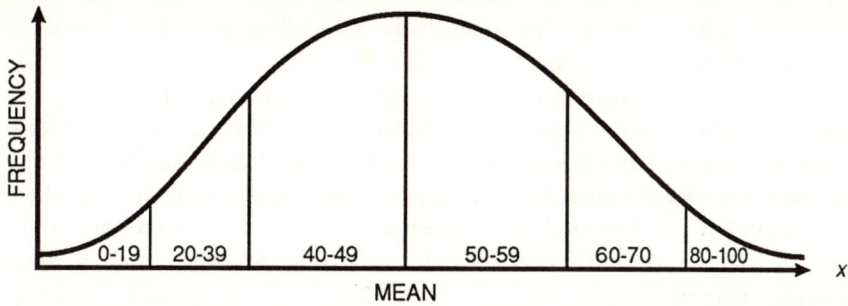

This would mean that 2 % of candidates scored between 0 and 19; 14 % between 20 and 39; 34 % between 40 and 49; 34 % between 50 and 59; 14 % between 60 and 79; and 2 % between 87 and 100. It would also tell us that the mean was 50, that the mode was 40–59, and that the average would be likely to be close to 50. A normal distribution curve is always symmetrical; in other words the right half is the mirror image of the left.

If the distribution curve is not normal, then we refer to it as a skewed distribution curve. It can be positively or negatively skewed. The positively skewed distribution curve looks like this:

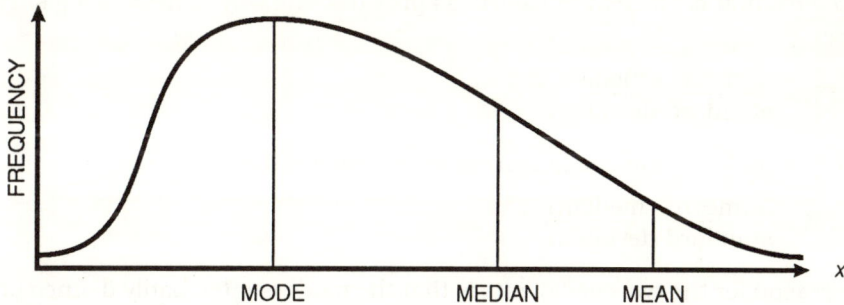

The negatively skewed distribution curve looks like this:

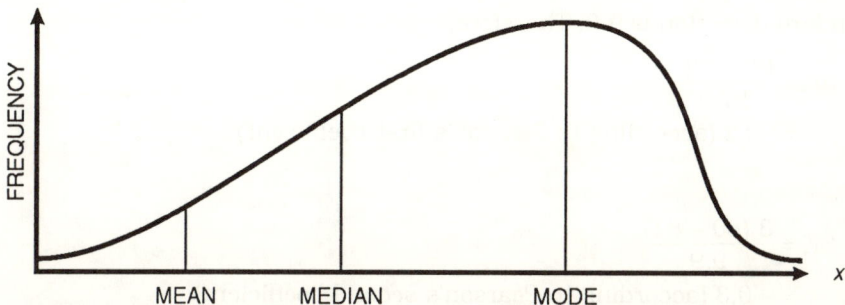

The positively skewed distribution curve is not symmetrical and has a longer tail to the right, whereas the negatively skewed distribution curve (also non-symmetrical) has a longer tail to the left.

In a normal distribution curve, the mean, the median, and the mode are all the same value. For a positively skewed distribution curve, the mean has the highest value, whereas for a negatively skewed distribution curve, the mean has the lowest value. In both the positively and the negatively skewed distribution curves, the median is between the mean and the mode, and it is closer to the mean than to the mode. Put in another form in a normal distribution curve,

Mean = Median = Mode

in a positively skewed distribution curve,

Mean > Median > Mode

in a negatively skewed distribution curve,

Mean < Median < Mode

These differences among the mean, median and mode can be used to calculate arithmetic measures of skewness: if the mean = median = mode, then the skewness = 0; if the mean > median > mode, then the skewness > 0 but < –3; if the mean < median < mode, then the skewness < 0 but > –3.

Pearson's first coefficient of skewness provides one way of measuring skewness:

$$SK = \frac{mean - mode}{standard\ deviation}$$

and Pearson's second coefficient for skewness another:

$$SK = \frac{3\ (mean - median)}{standard\ deviation}$$

The reason for the two coefficients is that the mode is often badly defined and not particularly accurate. In the example we used when referring to the median where the scores were:

96, 94, 86, 82, 82, 80, 76, 68, 64

the mean = 80, the median = 81, and the mode is 82. We worked out the standard deviation is 9,9. Therefore:

$$SK = \frac{80 - 82}{9,9}$$

= –0,2 (according to Pearson's first coefficient)

or

$$SK = \frac{3\ (80 - 81)}{9,9}$$

= – 0,3 (according to Pearson's second coefficient)

There is therefore a slightly negatively skewed distribution.

We have now come to the end of our section on the use of graphics in statistics and economics. In our next section we look at some of the typical graphs used to present data.

Graphic Presentation of Data

As we have already seen, data may be represented in the form of tables or schedules. These can then be presented in turn in graphic form.

Suppose we had fifty employees whose weights ranged from 50 kg to 99 kg. We could draw up a table or schedule to represent the frequency distribution for the weights of the fifty employees:

Grouped Frequency Distribution of Body Mass for 50 Employees

Mass (kg)	Tally marks	Number of employees (frequency)
50–59	‖‖	4
60–69	‖‖‖ ‖‖‖	10
70–79	‖‖‖ ‖‖‖ ‖‖‖ ‖‖‖ ‖	21
80–89	‖‖‖ ‖‖‖ ‖‖	12
90–99	‖‖‖	3
		50

This can be represented in a **histogram** as follows:

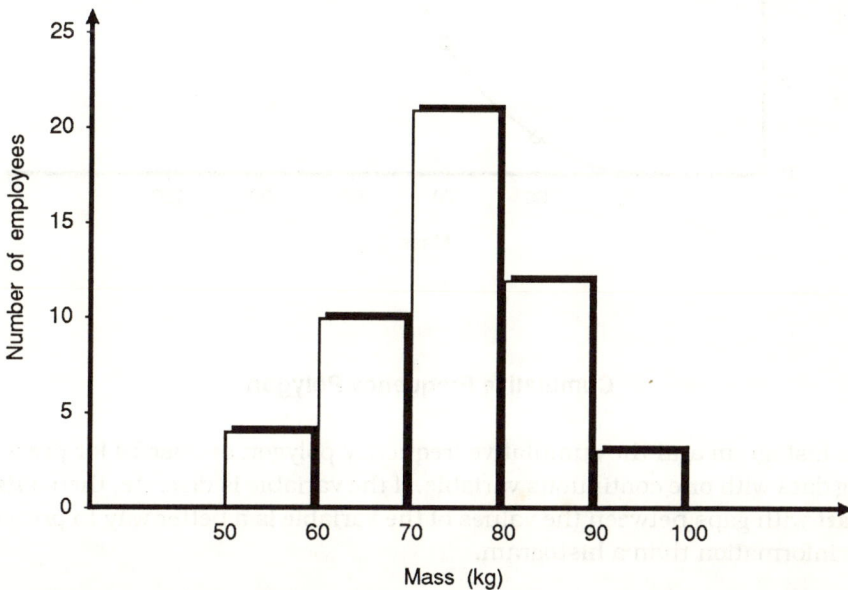

Histogram

We can represent the same information in a cumulative frequency distribution table and in a **cumulative frequency polygon**:

Cumulative Frequence Distribution of Body Mass for 50 Employees

Mass (kg)	Cumulative No. of Employees (cumulative frequency)
Less than 50	0
Less than 60	4
Less than 70	14
Less than 80	35
Less than 90	47
Less than 100	50

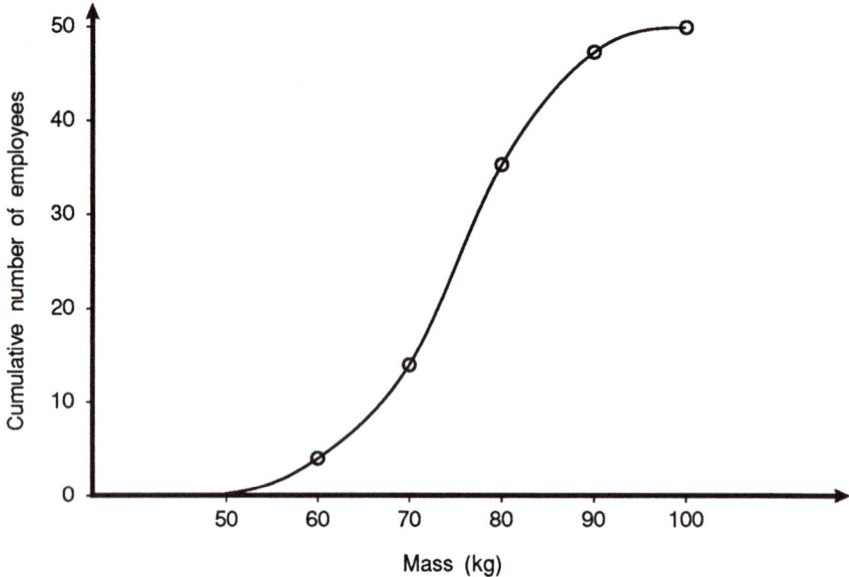

Cumulative Frequency Polygon

The histogram and the cumulative frequency polygon are useful for presenting data with one continuous variable. If the variable is discrete, then a **line chart** with gaps between the values of the variable is a better way to present the information than a histogram.

**Grouped Frequency Distribution Table for Children
of 50 Employees**

Number of children	Number of Employees
0	3
1	22
2	9
3	4
4	2

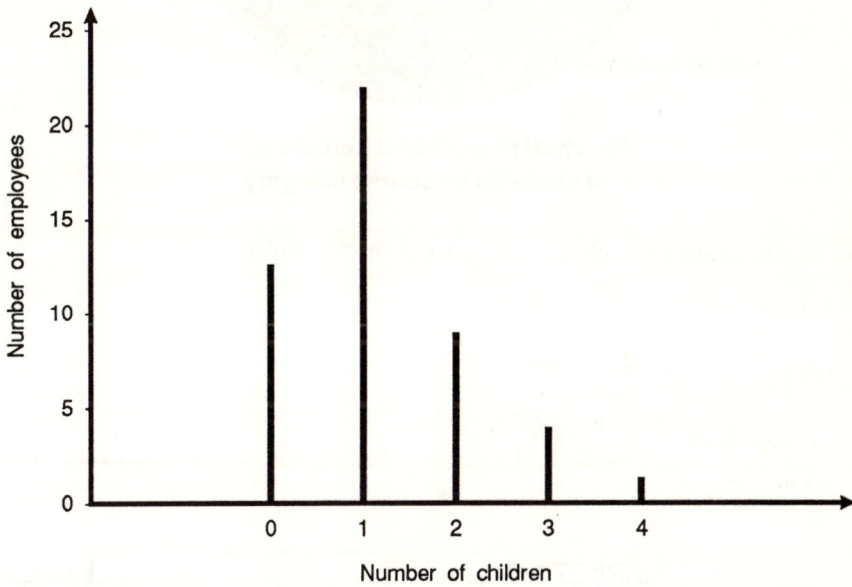

Line Chart

What we mean by a discrete variable is that the variable has only a distinct value: for instance, a person cannot have 1½ children, so there must be distinct gaps between 0 and 1 on the graph. With the histogram and with the continuous variable the bars do not have distinct gaps but join up with each other.

A **pie chart** or a **bar chart** is used to represent data that refers to a ranked or categorical variable:

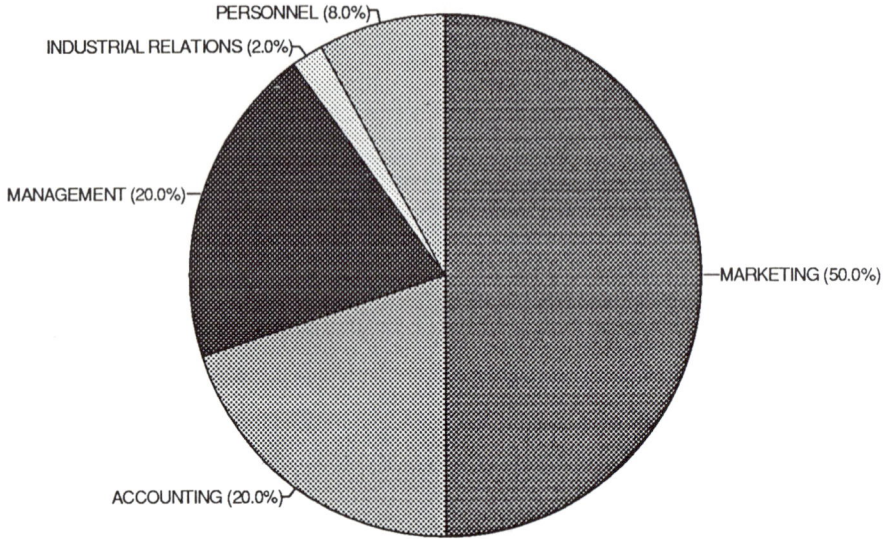

**Pie chart to represent percentages
of students by course category**

The way to draw a pie chart is to get the angles right:

$$50\ \% = 180° \text{ (i.e. } \frac{50}{100} \times \frac{360}{1})$$

$$20\ \% = 72° \text{ (i.e. } \frac{20}{100} \times \frac{360}{1})$$

$$8\ \% = 28{,}8° \text{ (i.e. } \frac{8}{100} \times \frac{360}{1})$$

$$2\ \% = 7{,}2°$$

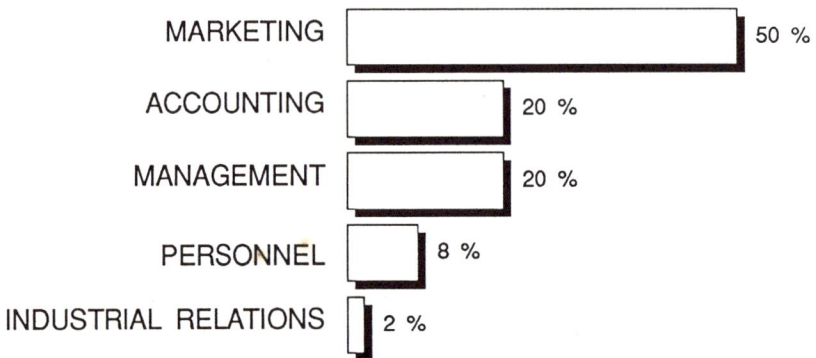

**Bar chart to represent percentages
of students by course category**

A pie chart should not have too many segments, otherwise some of the 'slices' will be too thin and not easily noticed. A pie chart is useful because it presents the information simply and is easy and attractive to look at.

When we are presenting data with two variables, we generally use pictograms, scatter diagrams, cross diagrams, or time-series graphs.

A **pictogram**, like the pie chart, expresses information simply and can be understood easily. It cannot, however, give detailed statistical information but merely indicates general comparisons or tendencies. As we have seen in our section on kinesics, you don't have to be an artist to use a pictogram: stick figures will suffice:

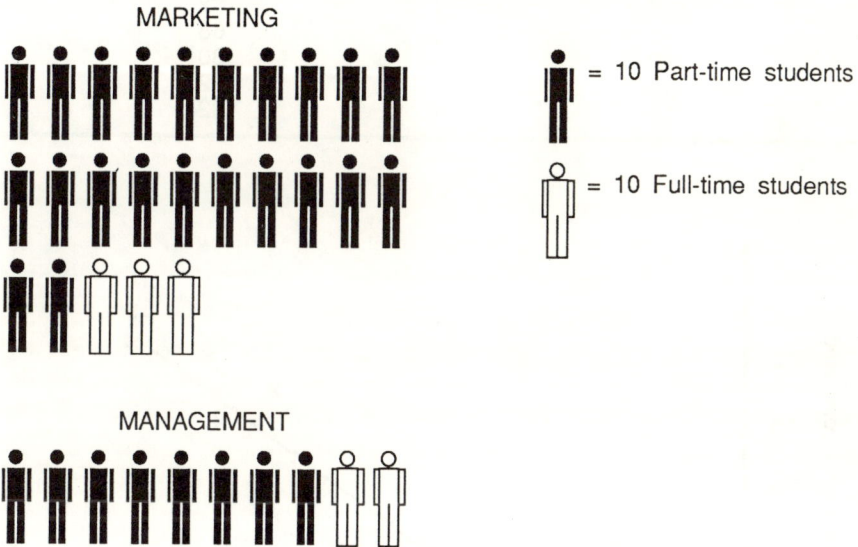

MARKETING

= 10 Part-time students

= 10 Full-time students

MANAGEMENT

Pictogram indicating number of students studying marketing and management part-time or full-time

At a glance this should show us that there are many more part-time students studying marketing than management, but not so many more full-time students studying marketing than management. It also shows that part-time study is more popular than full-time study. Looking more carefully you could work out that there are 220 students studying marketing part-time and 30 full-time in comparison with 80 students studying management part-time and 20 full-time.

A **scatter diagram** shows the relation between the two variables in such a way that any correlation will be shown. There does not necessarily have to be a correlation; the scatter diagram may merely be the first indication that there may be a correlation.

Let us look at this example:

NUMBER OF ASSIGNMENTS COMPLETED BY 10 STUDENTS, AND PERCENTAGES OBTAINED IN THE FINAL EXAMINATION

Number of assignments completed out of possible 12	Percentage in final examination
0	15
2	24
4	32
6	42
7	54
8	42
9	68
10	80
11	72
12	82

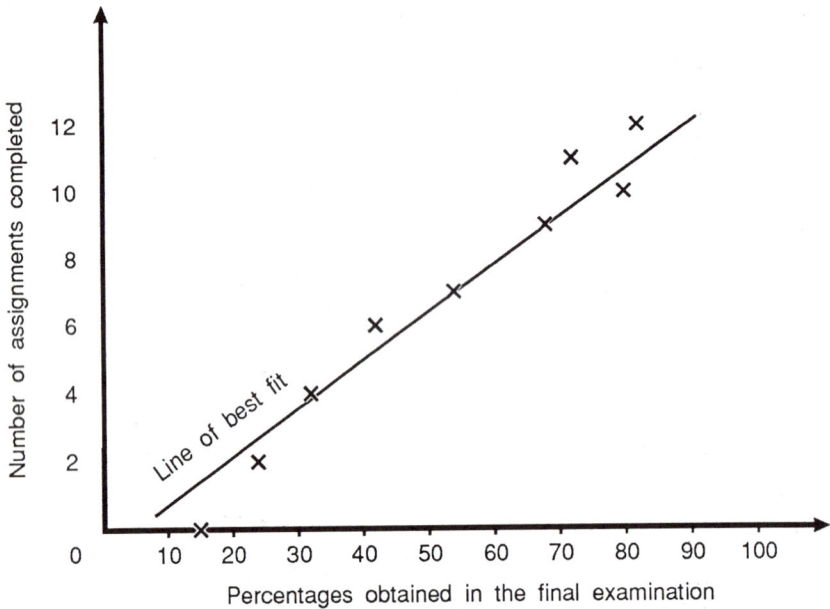

Scatter Diagram

This scatter diagram indicates a positive correlation between the number of assignments completed and the percentages obtained in the examination. It cannot provide statistical 'proof' but it does indicate a tendency. The 'line of best fit' indicates this pattern best: it has the same number of crosses on each side of it.

A **cross diagram** is useful for a discrete variable and for a categorical variable with a comparatively small number of cases.

EXAMINATION MARKS AND TYPE OF STUDY OF 12 STUDENTS

Type of study	Percentages
By correspondence	24 42 51 75 54 21
By attending classes	30 50 58 61 45 70

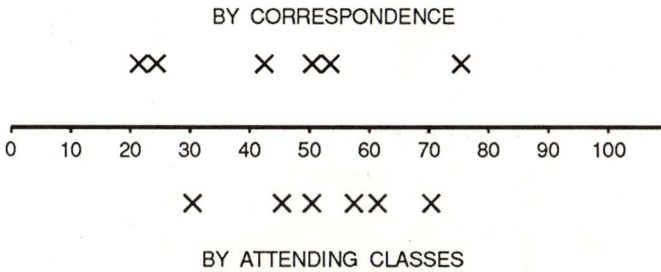

BY CORRESPONDENCE

XX   X XX   X

0   10   20   30   40   50   60   70   80   90   100

X   X X XX   X

BY ATTENDING CLASSES

**Cross diagram for examination marks
and type of study of 12 students**

This type of diagram gives a quick visual check of any significant relationships: in this example there are more passes of students attending classes even though the top student is a correspondence student.

In a **time-series graph** the time is usually on the horizontal axis and the other variable on the vertical:

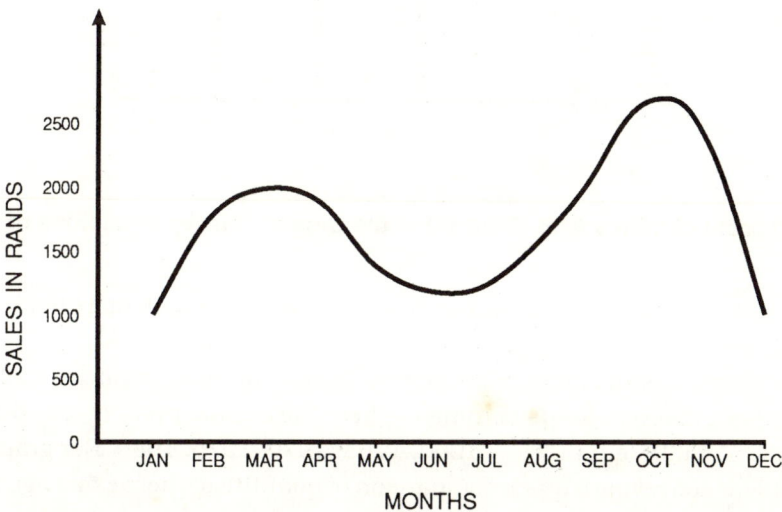

MONTHS

This time-series graph shows that January and December are the slowest months but that sales pick up in February and March and then from June to mid-September, with a trough from April to June and declining sales after mid-September.

We have discussed the basic graphic ways of presenting statistical data. Let us now look at some special applications in business.

Special Graphic Representations of Statistical Data

In this section let us look critically at ways of presenting the same or similar data. In doing so, we shall consider the particular uses and values of different kinds of graphic presentations.

A simple bar chart represents fairly straightforward facts:

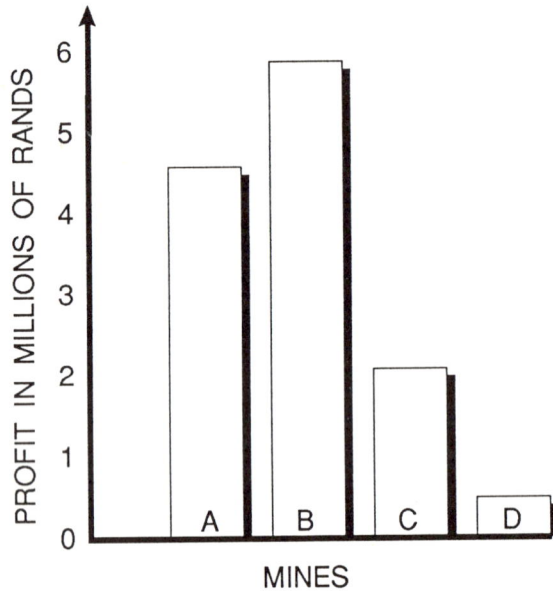

VERTICAL BAR GRAPH
1980 profit of mines A, B, C, and D of the Diggers' Group in millions of rands

Now let us look at the multiple bar graph and see how much more information it can provide.

A bar graph has the merit of conveying discrete or non-continuous information about different kinds of things — here the annual profit of four different mines — at different times — 1960, 1965, 1970, 1975, 1980. Bar graphs are useful for conveying a quick comparison of quantities where exact figures are not particularly important. Vertical charts are used to represent chronological data and quantitative data. Each bar is kept separate from its neighbour

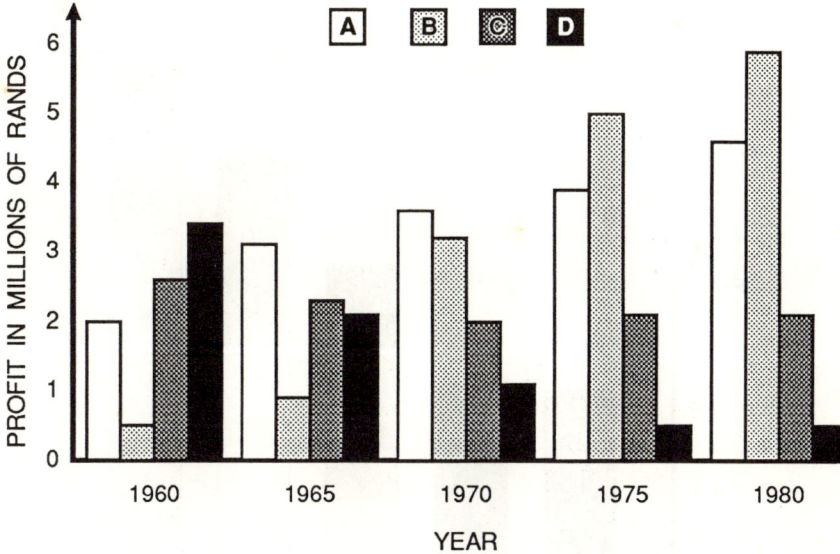

MULTIPLE BAR GRAPH
Annual profit of mines A, B, C, and D of the Diggers' Group
in millions of rands

to emphasize that the information is discrete, not continuous as in a histogram. No attempt is made to join the tops of the bars to form a curve. The problem with this bar graph or chart is that we cannot easily distinguish the increased or decreased profitability over the years for each mine: we have to look very carefully to see in our example that the profitability of mine A increased over the years and the profitability of mine B increased greatly, while mines C and D decreased their profitability.

If we look at the graph on the next page — the component or divided graph — we see that each bar is divided into a number of parts to compare the components as well as the total value. We see that the total profitability of the group increased steadily from R8,2 million to R12,7 million. Each part of the vertical bar may be labelled or shaded or coloured differently and an explanatory key may be provided.

The disadvantage with this type of bar graph is that it is again difficult to compare at a glance the comparative profitability of the different mines, except for mine A. Without the inclusion of figures in the bars it would not immediately be seen that B's profitability increases dramatically and D's decreases dramatically.

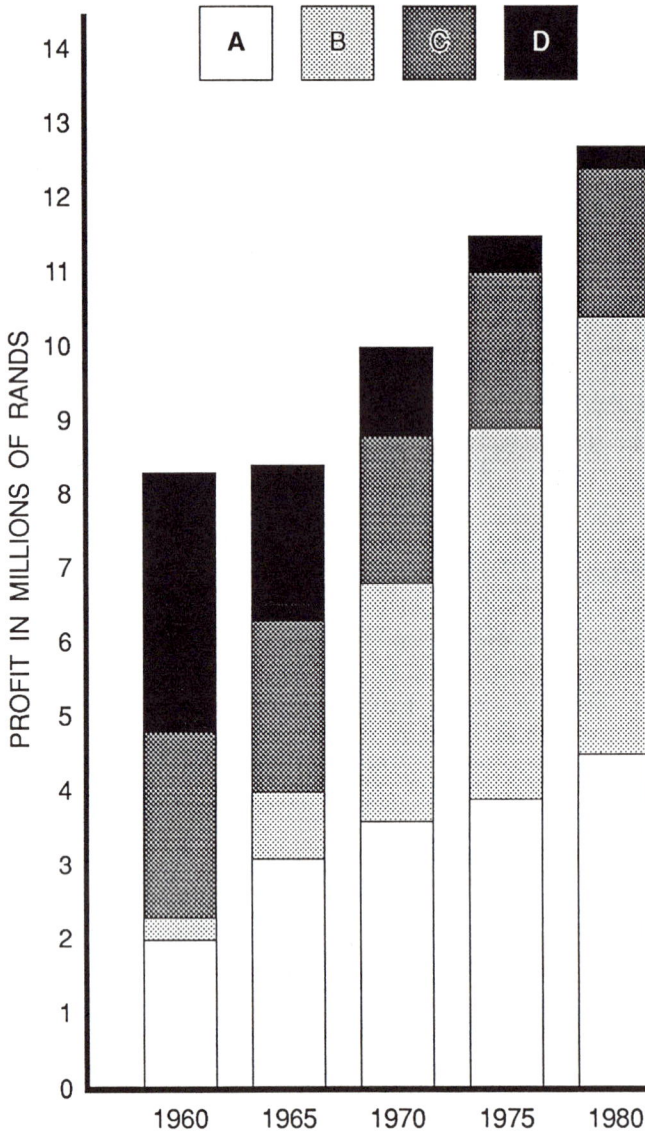

DIVIDED BAR GRAPH
Annual profit of mines A, B, C, and D of the Diggers' Group
in millions of rands

We have already seen that a line graph provides a simple way to show increases and decreases. Since in our example of the annual profit of the mines we are dealing with just these increases and decreases, let us see whether a line graph will serve our purpose. Since we need to show trends of more than one mine and compare them, we shall use a **multiple line graph**.

This is possible by the use of solid, dotted, and other distinctive lines since confusion would arise if we used ordinary straight lines.

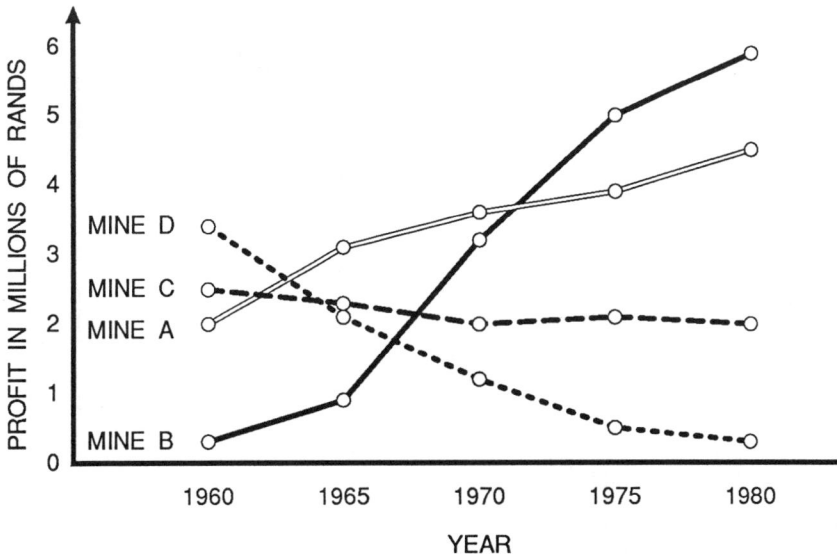

MULTIPLE LINE GRAPH
Annual profit of mines A, B, C, and D of the Diggers' Group
in millions of rands

We immediately see the main trends of each mine's profitability and we have a good basis for comparison. It does not, however, show us the combined profit of all the mines for each year as effectively as our divided bar graph did.

This should show us that the different kinds of graphic representation have different purposes. Some graphs that have special reference to business and are frequently used are:

1. The ABC/Pareto curve,
2. Breakeven charts, and
3. Z charts.

The ABC/Pareto curve is used to demonstrate what is often called the 80/20 law. This law suggests that only 20 % of a product range provided 80 % of sales and that only 20 % of the work force will effect 80 % of the work in the enterprise. In inventory control the curve expands this law into an ABC distribution:

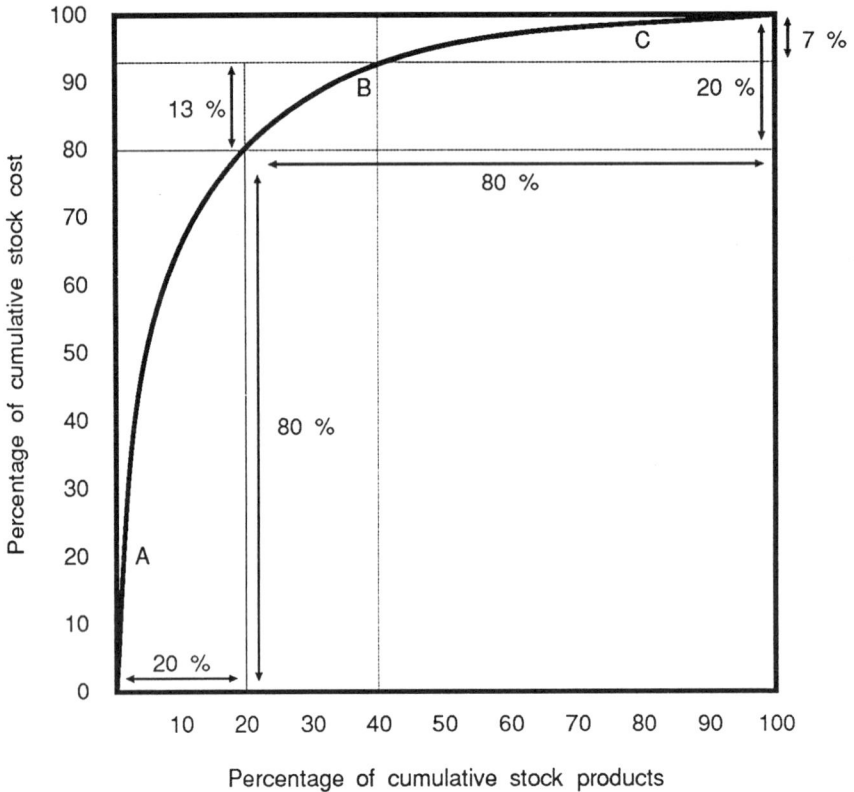

ABC/PARETO CURVE
Demonstrating 80/20 law as applied to inventory control

The 20 % of stock which costs 80 % of the total cost comprises usually the stock that moves rapidly out of and into the stockroom. These are the 80/20 items of the Group A items. The Group B items are items that are of medium cost and move not too fast and not too slow; they account for 13 % of the cost. Finally there are the slow-moving items of low cost that account for only 7 % of the cost. This law tells us therefore that we have to give most attention to the 20 % of the stock items that cost so much and move so fast in and out of the stockroom.

Breakeven charts are useful when planning a new venture.

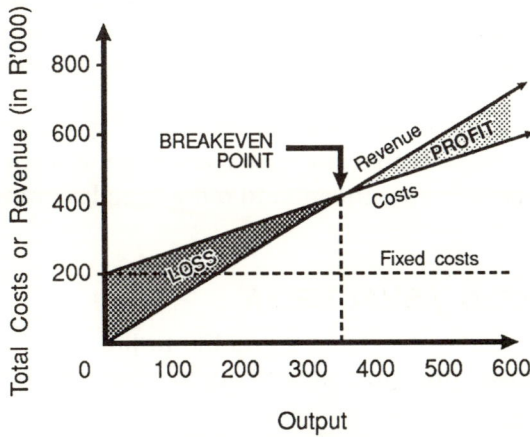

BREAKEVEN CHART

This breakeven chart tells us that 350 units of the new product will have to be sold before any profit can be made. The shaded area between the two line graphs represents the profit.

A **Z chart** is given this name because of the three line graphs which look like the letter Z:

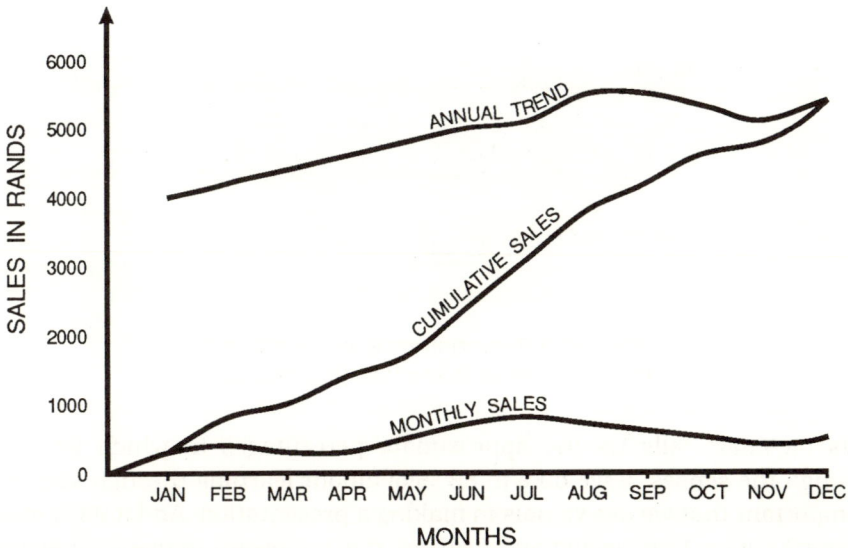

Z CHART

The line representing monthly sales should be clear: it offers a comparison of the sales for each month and whether the trend is favourable or not. The cumulative sales line shows the January + February sales for February, and January + February + March sales for March, and so on. The annual trend is the total of the sales for that month plus the sales for the previous eleven months. With these three trends the manager can monitor his sales very accurately.

We can never hope to deal with every kind of graphic that is used in business, but our hope is that the manager or the student will be able to build on this introduction to understand more complex graphics.

THE USE OF AUDIO-VISUAL MEDIA

Let us start this section by using a graphic to link up with the previous sections and to stress the importance of audio-visual media:

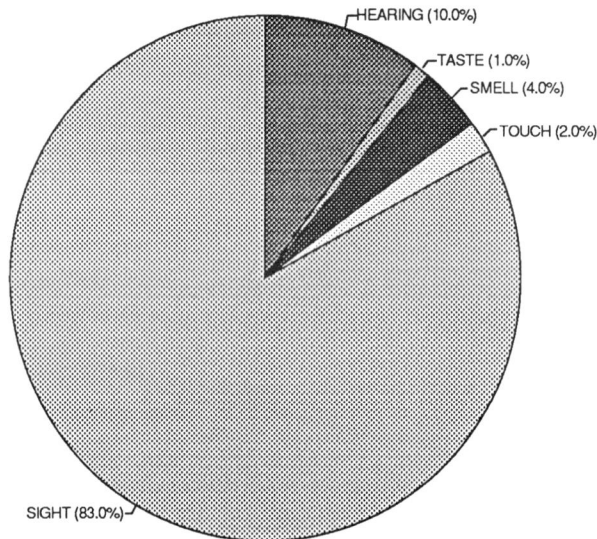

HEARING (10.0%)
TASTE (1.0%)
SMELL (4.0%)
TOUCH (2.0%)
SIGHT (83.0%)

**Pie Chart demonstrating percentages
for each sense in the learning process**

This pie-chart tells us the approximate percentages in which we learn through the senses. If we take in 83 % of all our learning through seeing, it is important that we use visuals in making a presentation. And if 93 % of our learning comes from seeing and hearing, it is important to use audio-visual media in our presentations.

The most common media (visual, audio-visual, or audio) are:

- ❏ the film
- ❏ the video
- ❏ the tape recorder
- ❏ the slide projector
- ❏ the overhead projector
- ❏ boards
- ❏ the episcope
- ❏ the epidiascope
- ❏ the microphone.

The **video** has virtually taken over from the **film**. Both are audio-visual media that can be effective but can also be very ineffective in the learning process. We are accustomed to being entertained by the film or the video and therefore it is often difficult to prepare the right environment for learning to take place while a film or video is being shown. The good teacher will make the film relevant to what she is talking about and will prepare a series of discussion topics or assignments to reinforce the point of the audio-visual. Stopping and starting a film or video is often disruptive and therefore the film tends to dominate the presentation. Unless the film or video has been specially prepared for that particular presentation — and this is rare because of the high cost — it is seldom a successful audio-visual medium.

The same applies to the **tape recorder**: there is not much to be gained from sound alone. It would be better to allow the audience to see the speaker. Nevertheless the tape recorder can be useful it the tape has been carefully prepared. It has a very great advantage over the film or the video: the tape can easily be made and at low cost. The tape recorder is also easily handled and allows quick turning on and off. With the right kind of amplification it can be used for large audiences. It can be helpful in a talk on music, language, or literature.

The **slide projector** is a much more useful aid to a speaker. The slides are especially prepared for the talk at a comparatively low cost, and the projector can be easily operated by the speaker or his assistant with the minimum disruption. A slide show can be a very professional aid to an impressive presentation, and taped sound can be synchronized with the slides, if necessary. A word of warning, though: we have all been bored to sleep by amateurish presentations of badly taken slides.

The **overhead projector** is a useful aid to a teacher, but it has limitations as far as presentations are concerned. The South African Market Research Association (SAMRA) does not allow overhead projectors to be used at its annual congress. The reasons are probably that presenters rely too heavily on them and the transparencies or foils are often shabbily prepared. It is advisable to have transparencies professionally prepared. The secret of overhead projection is that there should be a minimum of reading on each transparency and that any wording should be crucially important. Pictures to attract the attention and to help focus on the point are an important part of the well-prepared foil. Research has shown that we remember 30 % of what we see, 20 % of what we hear, but only 10% of what we read. We should therefore try to speak to a visual, not to a whole lot of words. The biggest problem about overhead transparencies is that they become a substitute for teaching or presenting and they are not used as media. An inexperienced teacher or presenter uses them as props, and inexperienced students often try to take down every word that is projected. They become hindrances to learning, not media. Nevertheless well-prepared transparencies with interesting overlays and the right pens can be very effective. The overhead projector has become popular because the presenter faces his audience as he works with his transparencies and projects them in a magnified form onto a screen. Despite magnification, typed transparencies are not effective unless the typing has been enlarged a few times before the transparency is made. When using transparencies, a presenter should have them properly ordered or numbered so that they will not be out of sequence: there is nothing worse than a presenter fumbling to find the transparency he wants to use.

Boards such as chalk boards, white boards, flip charts, flannel boards, and magnetic boards have the advantage of allowing spontaneous, creative skills to be exercised during the presentation. Although the overhead projector can be used for this too, the board is usually preferred. A presenter must realize that, like an actor on stage, he must raise his voice when his back is turned to his audience. A great deal of criticism has been levelled at teachers for too much 'talk and chalk', but a good teacher is a skilled chalk board or white board practitioner. Good handwriting and a sense of effective layout are important assets. Because of its negative association with school, the chalk board could effectively be replaced by a white board with a variety of coloured felt-tip pens.

Flip charts have the same purpose as chalk or white boards with the added advantage of being able to retain each sheet and to display it on the wall as a summary of the presentation or discussion. Flip charts are generally used for small presentations or group discussions.

Flannel boards and **magnetic boards** allow for material that has been carefully planned and prepared so that the presenter may build up an impressive display as he goes along. They have the advantage of being easily assembled, dismantled, and adapted; as such they are popular at exhibitions and as poster-type displays publicizing an event or conference. These boards are often used in offices as planning and control devices.

The **episcope** and the **epidiascope** were very useful visual media. It is amazing that they are no longer generally available. The reason is probably that there are not enough continuing benefits to the makers in the form of transparencies and software that need to be bought by the users. The episcope and the epidiascope project direct from books and sheets of paper and do not need transparencies to be made. The epidiascope can project transparencies as well, whereas the episcope does not. The room needs to be darkened, and this is a disadvantage, but for sheer convenience these machines cannot be bettered. It is our hope that they will come back onto the market again, for they are invaluable to teachers.

Finally, although it is not a visual aid and is not generally considered to be an audio aid either, the **microphone** is an important part of presentations to large audiences. Speakers should be familiar with the correct use of the microphone and not speak too far from it or too close to it. A faulty microphone or the incorrect use of the microphone is a great distraction to the audience and turns a potential aid into a hindrance.

With all these machines, the correct functioning of the equipment is crucial. Any presenter who has not checked his equipment before the presentation deserves to fail. A working knowledge of the machines helps, but if the presenter does not have this knowledge, it is important to prepare for a breakdown and have a contingency plan. The anticlimax of a machine breaking down and a presentation being called off is unnecessary: if the presenter has prepared for this and overcomes such a difficulty in a professional way, he will be acclaimed by the audience. A manager, like an actor, must allow the show to go on, no matter what may happen.

Concluding Remarks about Preparing Effective Visuals

Graphic presentation should be prepared with certain objectives in mind:
- to be simple
- to be clear
- to be attractive
- to be well ordered or displayed or laid out
- to be accurate
- to be brief, with only the essential information.

There are various rules or conventions that should be followed.

Tables or schedules should always have titles that give the reader a clear and informative idea of what data the tables provide. There should be clear and informative subheadings, and columns should be drawn. The data (usually in the form of figures) should be correctly aligned. There is often an acknowledgement of the source of the data.

Graphs are drawn to scale and should usually be in multiples of 5, 10, 100, 1000 . . . . The vertical axis is usually the y axis and this usually represents the independent variable. The captions for the vertical axis should be on the left of the axis, and the captions for the horizontal axis should be below the axis. The title can be either above or below the graph grid, but there must always be a clear and informative title. Any acknowledgement of the source is usually given below the grid. If more than one curve is used, the curves should be clearly distinguishable. Shading can be very useful to highlight a particular area.

Colours will also make the visual more attractive, but the presenter should consider colours carefully: yellow makes an object seem larger, black on a yellow background improves legibility, and red attracts attention; a combination of red and green gives poor visibility, and blue or green and white combinations have medium visibility. When a graphic is used in print, it must always follow the text that refers to it and never be placed before it.

The presenter must always be wary of bias in a graphic representation. Although an advertiser may use the technique of emphasizing the positive and omitting the negative, a graphic representation of statistical data must be accurate and without bias. In a graph, perspective should not be used in a deceptive way to distort size.

TERMINOLOGY AND CONCEPTS

1. KINESICS
2. PROXEMICS
3. BODY SPACE
4. HOME SPACE
5. NEUTRAL SPACE
6. PARALINGUISTICS
7. GRAPHICS
8. INFORMATIONAL MEANING
9. SYMBOLIC OR OBVIOUS MEANING
10. OBTUSE MEANING
11. LINGUISTIC MESSAGE
12. ICONIC ELEMENTS (DENOTED AND CONNOTED)
13. NETWORK ANALYSIS
14. NETWORK DIAGRAM
15. FLOW CHART
16. DECISION TABLE
17. ALGORITHM
18. GRAPHIC REPRESENTATION
19. VERTICAL AND HORIZONTAL AXES
20. STATISTICAL TABLE OR SCHEDULE
21. DEMAND AND SUPPLY CURVES AND EQUATIONS
22. LINEAR EQUATIONS
23. SLOPE OR GRADIENT
24. ARITHMETIC MEAN OR AVERAGE
25. MEDIAN
26. MODE
27. STANDARD DEVIATION
28. FREQUENCY DISTRIBUTION CURVE (NORMAL AND SKEWED)
29. HISTOGRAM
30. CUMULATIVE FREQUENCY POLYGON

31. LINE CHART
32. PIE OR BAR CHART
33. CONTINUOUS OR DISCRETE VARIABLE
34. PICTOGRAM
35. SCATTER DIAGRAM
36. CROSS DIAGRAM
37. TIME-SERIES GRAPH
38. VERTICAL BAR GRAPH
39. MULTIPLE BAR GRAPH
40. DIVIDED BAR GRAPH
41. MULTIPLE LINE GRAPH
42. ABC/PARETO CURVE
43. 80/20 LAW
44. BREAKDOWN CHART
45. Z CHART
46. AUDIO-VISUAL MEDIA

APPLICATION

1. Write an essay about how body language (kinesics and proxemics) affects communication.
2. Show how paralanguage fits into the communication process.
3. Choose any drawing or painting and apply Roland Barthes's three levels of meaning to it as you analyse the drawing or painting.
4. Choose a comic strip about a business or a human relations experience and analyse it in terms of
    (a) the linguistic element,
    (b) the denoted iconic element, and
    (c) the connoted iconic element.
5. Choose a business system and illustrate how it works with
    (a) a network diagram and
    (b) a flow chart.
6. Prepare a decision table or an algorithm to simplify a typical routine decision procedure.
7. Suppose that demand and supply curves have an equilibrium price of R600 and an equilibrium quantity of 800 units. (The demand equation may be taken as $Q = c - dP$ and the supply equation as $Q = a + bP$.) If the gradient of the demand curve is ½ and of the supply curve is ⅔, calculate c and a respectively and then draw the demand and supply graph.
8. A class of ten students produced the following results in an examination: 28, 33, 40, 44, 50, 54, 54, 55, 60, 62.
    Calculate:
    (a) the arithmetic mean,
    (b) the median,
    (c) the mode, and

(d) the standard deviation.

Then work out whether the distribution curve would be normal, positively skewed, of negatively skewed. Then draw a curve to represent
each of these three frequency distributions.

9. Suppose there were sixty employees with heights ranging from 1,4 metres
    to 2 metres. From this table representing the frequency distribution for
    these sixty employees, draw:

    (a) a histogram,

    (b) a cumulative frequency distribution table, and

    (c) a cumulative frequency polygon.

GROUPED FREQUENCY DISTRIBUTION
OF THE HEIGHTS OF 50 EMPLOYEES

Height (metres)	Tally marks	Number of employees (frequency)
1,4–1,49	|	1
1,5–1,59	ℍℍ |||	8
1,6–1,69	ℍℍ ℍℍ ℍℍ ℍℍ ℍℍ |||	28
1,7–1,79	ℍℍ ℍℍ ℍℍ ||	17
1,8–1,89	|||	3
1,9–1,99	||	2
2,0–2,09	|	1
		TOTAL: 60

10. Draw a line chart to present the following information:

GROUPED FREQUENCY DISTRIBUTION TABLE
FOR NUMBER OF BROTHERS AND SISTERS FOR 40 PUPILS

Number of brothers or sisters	Number of pupils (frequency)
0	10
1	15
2	8
3	4
4	2
5	1
	TOTAL: 40

11. Present the following information in:
   (a) a pie chart
   (b) a horizontal bar chart
   (c) a vertical bar chart

	(R'000 000)
Total Sales	580
Production Costs	290
Marketing Costs	145
Customs Duties	116
Depreciation	11,6
Profit	17,4

12. Compare the uses of the following graphic methods:
   (a) a histogram,
   (b) a line chart,
   (c) a pie chart, and
   (d) a pictogram.
13. Draw a scatter diagram to represent graphically the following information
    and then draw a 'line of best fit':

**SALES REVENUE AND ADVERTISING EXPENDITURE
FOR XYZ (PTY) LTD FOR THE YEARS 1992–1997**

Sales (R'000)	Advertising (R'000)
1 700	570
1 750	640
1 760	700
1 780	760
1 830	710
1 850	820

14. Draw a cross diagram to represent the following information:

EXAMINATION MARKS AND SEX OF 10 STUDENTS

Boys	94	68	41	28	38
Girls	88	75	45	56	61

What, if any, conclusion can you draw from this cross diagram?

15. Draw a time-series graph to represent the following information (remember to round off numbers to thousands):

INCOME PER MONTH (IN RANDS)
OF THE ABC BUSINESS SCHOOL FOR THE YEAR 1990

January	370 749	July	530 712
February	483 722	August	182 432
March	16 584	September	4 975
April	6 633	October	3 316
May	8 292	November	11 609
June	33 169	December	14 926

16. With the information in 15 above and the table below, draw a Z chart showing the income per month (the same as your graph in 15 but on a different scale), the cumulative income per month, and the annual trend:

INCOME PER MONTH (IN RANDS)
OF THE ABC BUSINESS SCHOOL FOR THE YEAR 1989

January	384 888	July	198 592
February	256 081	August	242 424
March	8 344	September	5 835
April	3 398	October	9 062
May	6 535	November	15 194
June	22 092	December	10 678

17. Look at the vertical bar chart, the multiple bar graph, the divided bar graph and the multiple line graph showing the annual profit of mines A, B, C and D of the Digger's Group in the chapter.
    (a) Write out the table or schedule to reflect the graphs.
    (b) Compare the different graphic methods used and comment on the specific value of each type of graph.
    (c) Compose a written report on what these figures and graphs indicate about the profitability of the group and of the individual mines.

18. Draw a breakeven graph to illustrate the breakeven point from the following figures:

REVENUE AND EXPENDITURE PER SEMINAR
FOR MANAGEMENT SEMINARS (PTY) LTD FOR 1988

Revenue for one seminar	R150 per person
Expenditure per seminar	
Premises	R300
Lecturer	R1 000
Refreshments	R50 per person

19. Write an essay on the use of audio-visual media in oral communication.
20. Write an essay on the use of visual media in written communication.
21. What are the important rules to remember in preparing graphic visuals?

REFERENCES

Chapter 1

Bell, Shirley; Marais, Tracy; Stewart, Graham (1985), *Communication for Managers and Secretaries*, Johannesburg, Southern, Chapters 2–3.

Fourie, H.P. (1982), *Communication by Objectives*, Johannesburg, McGraw-Hill.

Hodgetts, Richard M. (1979), *Management: Theory, Process and Practice*, Philadelphia, W.B. Saunders Company: Chapter 11.

Katz, M.; Rome, K.; Stodel, C. (1982), *Business Communication Assignments*, Johannesburg, McGraw-hill.

Van Schalkwyk, Helena (1988), *Language Communication — English*, Johannesburg, Lexicon Publishers, Introduction.

Van Schoor, Marthinus (1982), *What Is Communication?* Pretoria, Van Schaik.

Chapter 2

Hodgetts, Richard M. (1979), *Management: Theory, Process and Practice*, Philadelphia, W.B. Saunders Company: Chapter 11.

Chapter 3

Hodgetts, Richard M. (1979), *Management: Theory, Process and Practice*, Philadelphia, W.B. Saunders Company: Chapter 11.

Chapter 4

Schiffman, L.G. and Kanuk, L.L. (1983), *Consumer Behavior*, Englewood Cliffs, New Jersey, Prentice-Hall, Chapter 14.

Tajfel, Henri, and Fraser, Colin, eds. (1987), *Introducing Social Psychology*, Penguin: Chapter 3.

The Black Market Report provides useful local information on cross-cultural communication. It is published twice a month by the Damelin Education Group, Johannesburg.

Williams, Keith C. (1981), *Behavioural Aspects of Marketing*, Oxford, Heineman Professional Publishing, Chapter 5.

Chapter 5

Blake, R.R. and Mouton, J.S. (1964), *The Managerial Grid*, Houston, Texas, Gulf Publishing Co. (The Leadership Grid Mirror used in our Chapter 5 is adapted from that of Blake and Mouton on page 10 of their book.)

Hodgetts, Richard M. (1979) *Management: Theory, Process and Practice*, Philadelphia, W.B. Saunders Company, Chapter 13.

Tajfel, Henri, and Fraser, Colin, eds. (1987), *Introducing Social Psychology*, Penguin, Chapter 7.

Chapter 6

Hodgetts, Richard M. (1979), *Management: Theory, Process and Practice*, Philadelphia, W.B. Saunders Company: Chapter 17.

Tajfel, Henri, and Fraser, Colin, eds. (1987), *Introducing Social Psychology*, Penguin: Chapter 7.

Torrington, Derek, and Hall, Laura (1987), *Personnel Management: A New Approach*, London, Prentice-Hall, Chapter 4.

Chapter 7

Allen, W. Stannard (1960), *Living English Structure*, London, Longmans, Sections 21–31.

Chapter 8

Allen, W. Stannard (1960), *Living English Structure*, London, Longmans, Section 1.

Greig, J.Y.T. (1950), *Structure and Meaning, Part II*, Johannesburg, Witwatersrand University Press, Chapter 7.

Chapter 9

Adey, David; Orr, Margaret; Swemmer, Derek (1989), *Word Power*, Johannesburg, A.D. Donker.

Davis, Edward (1958), *Introduction to Modern English Usage*, Cape Town, Oxford University Press.

Fowler, H.W. (1952), *Modern English Usage*, London, Oxford University Press.

Greig, J.Y.T. (1950), *Structure and Meaning*, Part II, Johannesburg, Witwatersrand University Press.

Partridge, Eric (1982), *Usage and Abusage*, Penguin.

Strunk, William Jr., and White, E.B. (1979), *The Elements of Style*, New York, Macmillan.

Treble, H.A., and Vallins, G.H. (1950), *An A.B.C. of English Usage*, London, Oxford University Press.

Vallins, G.H. (1954), *Perfect Your English*, London, Ward, Lock & Co. Ltd.

Chapter 10

Ansell, Gwen, and McMenemy, Marilyn (1985), *English in Business*, London, Pan, Chapter 3.

Bell, Shirley; Marais, Tracy; Stewart, Graham (1985), *Communication for Managerrs and Secretaries*, Johannesburg, Southern.

Du Toit, Andrew P., and Orr, Margaret (1987), *Achiever's Handbook*, Johannesburg, Southern Book Publishers, Study Units 7 and 20–25.

Harris, Thomas (1969), *I'm OK—You 're OK*, New York, Harper and Row.

Ogilvy, David (1983), *Ogilvy on Advertising*, London, Pan.

Sandage, C.H., and Fryburger, Vernon (1977), *Advertising Theory and Practice*, Homewood, Illinois, Richard D. Irwin, Inc., Chapter 9.

Schiffman, L.G., and Kanuk, L.L. (1983), *Consumer Behavior*, Englewood Cliffs, New Jersey, Prentice-Hall, Chapter 2.

Williams, Keith C. (1981), *Behavioural Aspects of Marketing*, Oxford, Heinemann Professional Publishing, Chapters 5 and 7.

Chapter 11

Lyons, T.P. (1978), *The Personnel Function in a Changing Environment*, Johannesburg, Pitman, Chapter 6.

Mahony, D.P., *CIS Guide to Meetings*, Johannesburg, The South African Institute of Chartered Secretaries and Administrators.

Torrington, Derek, and Hall, Laura (1987), *Personnel Management: A New Approach*, London, Prentice-Hall, Chapters 9, 16, 24, and 26.

Woolcott, L.A., and Unwin, W.R.(1983), *Mastering Business Communication*, United Kingdom, Macmillan, Chapter 7.

Chapter 12

Du Toit, Andrew P., and Orr, Margaret (1987), *Achiever's Handbook*, Johannesburg, Southern Book Publishers, Study Units 1–4.

South African Journal of Higher Education, Vol. 2 No. 2 (1988), Pretoria, Committee of University Principals of South Africa.

Van Schalkwyk, Helena (1988), *Language Communication—English*, Johannesburg, Lexicon, Chapters 13–17.

Chapter 13

Appleton, Rex B. (1985), *The Disposal and Retention of Documents*, Johannesburg, Southern African Institute of Chartered Secretaries.

Bell, Shirley; Marais, Tracy; Stewart, Graham (1985), *Communication for Managers and Secretaries*, Johannesburg, Southern, Chapters 12, 15, 16, 17, and 18.

Du Toit, Andrew P., and Orr, Margaret (1987), *Achiever's Handibook*, Johannesburg, Southern Book Publishers, Study Unit 18.

Fletcher, E., *Manual of Modern English*, Maskew Miller, Cape Town, Eighth Impression, pp. 160–162.

Milton, J. *Sonnet XVII*

Shakespeare, W., *Macbeth.*

South African Journal of Higher Education, Vol. 2 No. 2 (1988), Pretoria, Committee of University Principals of South Africa.

The Star (February 24, 1989), Johannesburg.

Van Schalkwyk, Helena (1988), *Language Communication—English*, Johannesburg, Lexicon Publishers, Chapters 18–22 and 24–25.

Woolcott, L.A., and Unwin, W.R. (1983), *Mastering Business Communication*, United Kingdom, Macmillan, Chapters 1, 2, and 6.

Chapter 14

Part of this chapter is an adaptation of work from a Damelin study booklet on Copy and Design written by one of the writers of this book. It is adapted with the kind permission of the Damelin Education Group.

Herzberg, Frederick (1966), *Work and the Nature of Man*, New York, World Publishing.

Hopkins, Claude C. (1986), *My Life in Advertising and Scientific Advertising*, Lincolnwood, Illinois, U.S.A., NTC Business Books.

Jefkins, Frank (1985), *Advertising*, Estover, Plymouth, U.K., Macdonald and Evans.

Maslow, A.H. (1970), *Motivation and Personality*, New York, Harper and Row, 2nd ed., pp. 35–38.

McGregor, Eric (1973), *Advertising*, London, St Paul's.

Moelwyn-Hughes, Tim and Beard, Paul (1986), *Assessment of Lecturer Performance*, Johannesburg, Academic Staff Development Centre, University of Witwatersrand, Occasional Bulletin No. 1, 4th ed.

Ogilvy, David (1983), *Ogilvy on Advertising*, London, Pan.

Sandage, C.H., and Fryburger, Vernon (1975), *Advertising Theory and Practice*, Homewood, Illinois, U.S.A, Irwin, 9th ed.

Skinner, J.C., and Von Essen, L.M. (1987), *South African Handbook of Public Relations*, Johannesburg, Macmillan, 4th ed.

Van Schalkwyk, Helena (1988), *Language Communication—English*, Johannesburg, Lexicon Publishers, Chapter 21.

Wright, J.S.; Warner, D.S.; Winter, W.L.; Ziegler, S.K. (1977): *Advertising*, New York, McGraw-Hill, 4th ed.

Chapter 15

Barthes, Roland (1989), *Barthes: Selected Writings*, Fontana Press.

Barthes, Roland (1979), *Image, Music, Text*, Glasgow, Collins.

Birdwhistell, R. (1970), *Kinesics and Context*, University of Pennsylvania Press.

Business Day (October 5, 1989), Johannesburg.

Eyre, E.C. (1987), *Business Communication*, London, Heinemann, Chapters 11 and 23.

Ferguson, George A. (1987), *Statistical Analysis in Psychology and Education*, Singapore, McGraw-Hill, 5th ed.

Kazmier, Leonard (1979), *Basic Statistics for Business and Economics*, Tokyo, Japan, McGraw-Hill.

Lord, G.A. (1978), *Know What I Mean?*, London, McGraw-Hill, Unit 8 Section A.

Rees, D.G. (1985), *Essential Statistics*, London, Chapman and Hall.

Roelofse, J.J. (1982), *Signs and Significance*, Johannesburg, McGraw-Hill.

Tajfel, Henri, and Fraser, Colin, eds. (1987), *Introducing Social Psychology*, Penguin, Chapter 5.

Thirkettle, G.L. (1985), *Wheldon's Business Statistics*, Estover, Plymouth, U.K., Macdonald and Evans.

Van den Bogaerde, F. (1978), *Elements of Macro-Economics*, Pretoria, Van Schaik, Chapter 3.

Van den Bogaerde, F. (1978), *Elements of Price Theory*, Pretoria, Van Schaik, Chapter 1.

Willemse, Isabel (1990), *Statistical Methods and Financial Calcultions*, Cape Town, Juta.

Woolcott, L.A., and Unwin, W.R. (1989), *Mastering Business Communication*, London, Macmillan, Chapters 13 and 14.

THE FREEMARKET SERIES FROM JUTA

SOUTH AFRICA'S WAR AGAINST CAPITALISM   WALTER WILLIAMS

Williams analyses the negative economic impact made by apartheid and he illustrates how discriminatory legislation (of any kind) militates against the development of a free market economy. He shows how costly this legislation has proved itself to be and why it was deemed necessary in the first place. He also warns that its perpetuation in a changing society is not only possible, but probable. A vital work for students of labour relations, policy makers, industrial relations practitioners and the informed layman.

LIBERTY AND PROSPERITY — Essays in Limiting Government and Freeing Enterprise in South Africa   VORHIES & GRANT

This collection of essays advocates a market-based economy and a decentralized, non-racial and democratic system of government for South Africa. Issues addressed include: sanctions; monopolies; privatization; the distribution of wealth; conscription; education; the role of a free press, etc. These essays show how liberal reforms and institutions can be used to the benefit of our society. This book will prove invaluable to anybody, inside or outside of government, connected in any way to the emerging process of negotiated change.

CONSUMER POWER IN A FREE MARKET

South African consumers have long been accused of being among the most apathetic in the world. The message that emerges from these essays is that economic freedom and the threat of competition give consumers — not government or big business — the ability to decide the goods, the services and the prices in an economy. This book provides the South African consumer with a clear and comprehensive introduction to consumer issues in South Africa and the importance of a market economy to protect consumer interests.

COMPREHENDING KARL MARX   VORHIES

The ideas of Karl Marx are introduced from a non-Marxist, individualistic perspective in this concise and non-technical book. It presents his theories in an objective and balanced fashion and, because this is the case, the serious flaws in Marx's approach to social development begin to become apparent to the reader. It is crucial that educators, industrial relations practitioners, negotiators and the informed public in favour of a free market have a source which provides them with a clear and straightforward introduction to Marxism.
Publication: End 1990

SOUTH AFRICA — THE NEW REVOLUTION   DON CALDWELL

'Essential reading for all South Africans yearning to exhume themselves from beneath the dead myths and the dying ideologies of both left and right. It is a revelatory and uplifting vision of a South Africa that could easily be.'   RIAN MALAN

'An extraordinary book . . . It blasts fresh air through the South African debate.'
FRANCES KENDALL & LEON LOUW

SOUTH AFRICA AND GLOBAL LIBERALISATION   VORHIES & DEAN

Although comparisons are odious and have, more often than not, been used to promote the very policies that have brought this country's economy to the verge of collapse, they can be used constructively. Lessons learnt elsewhere in the world can be incorporated into models for the economic future of South Africa. This wide-ranging collection of papers draws on global experience and, by applying those experiences to the uniquely South African situation, offers positive and practical answers to the very dangerous and complex economic and social problems which bedevil our society.
Publication: Early 1991

PRIVATISATION AND ECONOMIC JUSTICE   VORHIES

The nationalisation/privatisation debate, although far from being conclusively settled, has enjoyed a very high profile on the agendas of people who have the economic wellbeing of South Africa at heart. This book, which cuts through all the rhetoric which invariably clouds the issue, argues convincingly for privatization as being the only means of ensuring economic justice in a future South Africa.

MANAGEMENT TITLES FROM JUTA

GETTING IT RIGHT — The Manager's Guide to Business Communication

ADEY & ANDREW

This work is more an introduction to business practice than a book about theoretical communication. Management, marketing, advertising, and industrial relations are approached from the perspective of business communication. Each chapter has a summary of concepts and terms, as well as case studies that test the understanding of these concepts. The syllabi of the diplomas of various professional institutes, including that of the Communication Course of the Diploma in Business Administration as examined by the SA Institute of Management, are covered.

COMMUNICATING FOR CHANGE — A Guide to Managing the Future of South African Organisations

A D MANNING

Communicating for Change is based upon this simple idea: 'Business has a serious responsibility to remain viable, create wealth, and generate jobs and opportunities for personal growth; to sensitise people to the need for change; and to help them learn new behaviours and thus bring about change.' This book not only shows the reader how to increase profits, but it also addresses the all-important changes in our South African society and shows how a climate for change can be created in every workplace.

WORLD CLASS! — Strategies for Winning with Your Customer

A D MANNING

Tony Manning, one of South Africa's leading management consultants and an expert in customer care, believes that obsessive attention to your customer is the surest way to boost business profits. But, he says, training 'front line' people is not enough. Continuous improvement of everything is vital for success. This book helps managers to create an holistic attack strategy and the market-focused culture that it needs. It is the first total blueprint for success in the competitive business arena—a practical, step-by-step approach to reinventing the organisation; complete with charts, questionnaires, workshop agenda and planning guides.

MARKETING MANAGEMENT

MARX & VAN DER WALT

Written to suit South African conditions, the style of this text is easy, while figures and tables are used liberally to explain complicated concepts. While characterised by a practical approach, the content is scientifically founded. The twenty chapters are divided into four parts. The first is a general introduction providing a broad perspective; the second deals with the marketing environment; the third with marketing decisions and the fourth part, including topics such as the product life cycle, marketing warfare, strategic marketing, product portfolio etc, deals with the integrated marketing strategy. This work is also available in Afrikaans.

ASSESSING MANAGERIAL COMPETENCE

HERMANN SPANGENBERG

This book is based upon research results and years of experience which show that the tasks and roles of managers at various organisational levels differ substantially, calling for different success criteria and, consequently, differences in the required competencies. Competencies in themselves are complex, differing in type and level, and this work should prove to be indispensable in the assessment of the potential of managers and supervisors.

THE PROFIT FROM . . . SERIES

PROFIT FROM DYNAMIC PEOPLE MANAGEMENT   BRIAN ANGUS

Business organisations depend wholly on the ability of their employees to produce more value than they consume in costs—to add value during the process which will enable the organisation to operate at a profit. This book is aimed at those managers and supervisors who want to learn, not only how to apply routine people management techniques but also, more importantly, how to implement dynamic as opposed to static human resources management to the ultimate benefit of their employees, their organisation and themselves.

PROFIT FROM PRODUCTIVITY   JOHN HUMPHREY & FIONA HALSE

This book lays bare the opportunities for productivity improvement in any organisation. It is written in a style that is simple, thorough and practical, and managers, trainers and supervisors will have no trouble in implementing and maintaining the strategies contained in this important work.

PROFIT FROM PERSONAL PRODUCTIVITY
JOHN HUMPHREY & FIONA HALSE

Most of us think of productivity as something that goes on in factories and businesses, and it's therefore of little general interest. Productivity is in fact something which greatly affects all of us in both our business and our personal lives. Knowing how to measure and improve your personal productivity is to be able to take charge of your life and start to direct it in the way that you wish it to go. The insights offered by this book will enable anyone to realise their full potential.

PROFIT FROM EFFECTIVE COMMUNICATION   NEAL DuBREY

Professional and business people know that personal communication skills determine the success or failure of any venture. But very few do anything to address their own shortcomings in this area. This book is a goldmine of practical, helpful advice that will enable the reader to develop his or her personal communication skills—to listen effectively—to formulate thoughts into words—to write clearly and to benefit from the use of sound argument and persuasion.

PROFIT FROM QUALITY SUPERVISION   JOHN HUMPHREY

Change is in the air. We have the Green Revolution, the Technological Revolution, the Productivity Revolution, and now, the Quality Revolution. Imported from the USA and Japan this, like other revolutions, causes customers to be dissatisfied with things as they are. In this case, our traditional standards of performance. This book addresses the concept of Quality in full—its definition, implementation, and its maintenance. A dedication to Quality is the key to improving productivity, resource utilization, and efficiency, and its pay-off benefits the company, the supervisor, and the worker.

PROFIT FROM EFFECTIVE SELLING   BILL HENDERSON

Selling is a process. It is the 'creation of a sale' between two people and can lead to a long, lasting relationship of mutual trust between the sales person and the customer. This book is a practical guide to step-by-step selling which will benefit anybody engaged in selling in the retail or the wholesale trade, company buyers, or the sole agent. It is divided into eight modules, each prefaced by specific learning objectives. It has been written expressly to assist in the study of the selling process and in the practical techniques of selling.

INDUSTRIAL RELATIONS TITLES FROM JUTA

INDUSTRIAL RELATIONS HANDBOOK — Policies, Procedures and Practices for South African Managers ANDREW PONS

This loose-leaf publication assists the management team to promote successful relationships with employees in order to continue to develop in the medium to long term. It has been designed to take congnisance of developments both in labour law and the current practice of industrial relations in South Africa. Practical guidelines are set out in detail ensuring the value of this book as a "hands-on" text suitable for all levels of management.

INDUSTRIAL RELATIONS IN SOUTH AFRICA SONIA BENDIX

In some 600 concise and informative pages, frequently punctuated by tables, figures and charts, Sonia Bendix skillfully analyses international industrial relations principles and specifically gives in-depth insight into our own. It includes the 1988 Amendments to the Labour Relations Act and a chapter is devoted solely to dispute settlement machinery in South Africa, dealing with the question of fairness, unfair labour practice and the industrial Court.

PERSONNEL MANAGEMENT — The Business Owner's Handbook for Small and Medium Sized Companies JULIA HOLDEN

Written specifically for any business that is operating without in-house personnel management staff, this easy-to-read, subscription publication provides a working system that is quick to implement and provides the procedural 'knowledge' required to deal with employees. It is the only publication available that provides vital working documents that the subscriber is free to copy and to use. The only entrepreneur who can afford to be without this handbook is the specialist who consults and works alone.

WORKER PARTICIPATION — South African Options and Experiences

MARK ANSTEY (Editor)

A future South Africa will demand industrial relations that operate beyond the adversarialism of strikes and stayaways, dismissals and litigation. This text comprises a unique collection of papers by South African and international industrial relations practitioners and academics—all experts in their field. The book contains not only theoretical insights, but practical guidelines for implementing various approaches, and helpful South African initiatives.

NEGOTIATION — Theory, Strategies and Skills

PROFESSORS M SPOELSTRA & W PIENAAR

Although various approaches and theories of negotiation are acknowledged, the authors of this text clearly view negotiation as a process wherein the development of alternatives is strongly emphasised. Verbal and non-verbal strategies and skills in negotiation receive detailed attention. The book explains how power can be deployed during negotiation and how attitudes and behaviours can be changed through the use of a few step-by-step recipes.

CONFLICT MANAGEMENT PROFESSOR D DE VILLIERS

This is a pathbreaking text on one of the most important aspects of industrial relations written by one of South Africa's leading academics from the School of Business Leadership at UNISA. It is of value to anyone affected in any way by employer–employee relationships and, indeed, interpersonal relationships in every sphere of their lives.

COACHING AND THE BLACK MANAGER   J A E CHAROUX

Dr Charoux provides an easy to read book which also turns out to be easy to use and easy to keep using. It is a manual for managers who strive for the best results from, and the best results for, their subordinates.

    The context is South African. Current changes and stresses are taken into account and this book might well prove to be a valuable building block for a new South Africa.

INTEGRATION OF BLACK MANAGERS INTO SOUTH AFRICAN ORGANISATIONS   J A E CHAROUX

This book addresses commerce and industry, the academic and the black manager himself, providing a practical, reliable method of advancing and integrating the black manager into the higher levels of South African organisations. It is based on wide-ranging case histories and discusses the latest research in this area of industrial relations.

BLACK MANAGERS IN SOUTH AFRICAN ORGANIZATIONS
L HUMAN & K HOFMEYR

This work will enable readers to formulate a strategy for black advancement within their company and it will help in the selection of potential managers. It will assist in motivating and training employees and enable employers to relate more meaningfully to the aspirations of the members of their new management teams, thereby harnessing the considerable economic resources of a vast talent pool.